# PRAISE FOR *THE HIGHEST LAW IN THE LAND*

"As this nation seeks to make sense of the alarming rise of far-right extremism as well as the excessive power and everyday abuses of law enforcement, Pishko's study of American sheriffs is a startling must-read. As she makes clear, these threats to our democracy are inexorably connected—sharing not just insidious ideologies and ugly practices, but also extraordinary power and popularity. That local sheriffs drive this recent and most pressing danger is something that we overlook at our peril."

—Heather Ann Thompson, Pulitzer Prize–winning author of
*Blood in the Water: The Attica Prison Uprising of 1971 and Its Legacy*

"Blending superb reportage and indispensable history, Jessica Pishko's book could not be more timely. *The Highest Law in the Land* is essential reading for anyone concerned about the unbridled power of law enforcement in twenty-first-century America. An absolutely fascinating and harrowing read."

—Gilbert King, Pulitzer Prize–winning author of *Devil in the Grove:
Thurgood Marshall, the Groveland Boys, and the Dawn of a New America*

"Deeply researched, wide-ranging, and explosive, *The Highest Law in the Land* lays bare the troubling history of the fringe movements whose self-proclaimed authority and unorthodox interpretations of the Constitution are threatening to enter mainstream American political life. Jessica Pishko has delivered a most timely read for our troubled times."

—Scott Ellsworth, author of *The Ground Breaking:
The Tulsa Race Massacre and An American City's Search for Justice*

"In *The Highest Law in the Land*, Jessica Pishko shines a much-needed spotlight on the right-wing extremism brewing in sheriffs' offices across the country and asks the tough question about whether we still need this inherently problematic institution."

—Alex S. Vitale, author of *The End of Policing*

"Deep reporting and even deeper intelligence mark this invaluable contribution to the chronicle of our decaying democracy. Jessica Pishko is brave, indeed, taking on the metastasizing movement of little big men who call themselves 'constitutional sheriffs,' and use their legal delusions to promote white supremacism across the country. But *The Highest Law in the Land* reaches beyond the current crisis to reveal how the very idea of the sheriff, like the 'sheriff's president,' Donald Trump, wages war against the hope of democracy. Read this essential book to preserve that hope, and to stay safe on county roads."

—Jeff Sharlet, *New York Times* bestselling author of *The Undertow: Scenes from a Slow Civil War*

"Sheriffs are the most powerful, terrifying, and fascinating elected officials in America today—and no one knows more about them than Jessica Pishko. Pishko is a remarkable storyteller and a brilliant journalist who has spent years trying to untangle the growing extremism in law enforcement. Whether you care about the criminal justice system or just love a good story, I absolutely guarantee you will love this book."

—Josie Duffy Rice, host of *Unreformed: The Story of the Alabama Industrial School for Negro Children*

"Thanks in large part to Hollywood, the American sheriff has often been regarded as either a bumbling figure of comic ineptitude or a towering protector of virtue and justice. Jessica Pishko tunnels deep into the myth and emerges with a harrowing exposé that not only dispenses with those stereotypes but reveals a disturbing and dangerous state of affairs. With Pishko's impeccable research, *The Highest Law in the Land* sounds a dire warning that every American should heed."

—Doug J. Swanson, author of *Cult of Glory: The Bold and Brutal History of the Texas Rangers*

"Intensely reported and beautifully written. A scathing examination of how sheriffs' departments became the scandal-plagued agencies they are today, and what to do about it. If you don't care about elected sheriffs, this book will make you want to."

—Keri Blakinger, author of *Corrections in Ink: A Memoir*

"It might be painful to confront how the American myth of the sheriff, that righteous figure in a cowboy hat, has curdled into partisanship and white supremacy. But Jessica Pishko is here with eye-popping scenes and deep-dive history to show us that sheriffs have long been local power brokers, often above the law even as they claim to enforce it. She shows how and why they're becoming the Trumps of their own communities. Anyone concerned about the future of policing and justice in America should read this book."

—Maurice Chammah, author of *Let the Lord Sort Them: The Rise and Fall of the Death Penalty*

# THE HIGHEST LAW IN THE LAND

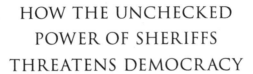

HOW THE UNCHECKED
POWER OF SHERIFFS
THREATENS DEMOCRACY

## JESSICA PISHKO

DUTTON

**DUTTON**

An imprint of Penguin Random House LLC
penguinrandomhouse.com

LIBRARY OF CONGRESS CATALOGING-IN-PUBLICATION DATA
Names: Pishko, Jessica, author.
Title: The highest law in the land: how the unchecked power of
sheriffs threatens democracy / Jessica Pishko.
Description: [New York] : Dutton, [2024] | Includes bibliographical references and index.
Identifiers: LCCN 2024018715 (print) | LCCN 2024018716 (ebook) |
ISBN 9780593471319 (hardcover) | ISBN 9780593471333 (ebook)
Subjects: LCSH: Sheriffs—United States. |
Sheriffs—Political activity—United States. |
Law enforcement—Corrupt practices—United States. |
Abuse of administrative power—United States. |
Discrimination in criminal justice administration—United States.
Classification: LCC HV7979 .P47 2024 (print) | LCC HV7979 (ebook) |
DDC 363.28/20973—dc23/eng/20240709
LC record available at https://lccn.loc.gov/2024018715
LC ebook record available at https://lccn.loc.gov/2024018716

Printed in the United States of America

1st Printing

BOOK DESIGN BY PATRICE SHERIDAN

*To my daughter, the future*

# CONTENTS

# THE HIGHEST LAW IN THE LAND

# INTRODUCTION

ON A TUESDAY NIGHT IN MARCH OF 2021, I JOINED ABOUT fifty people, all unmasked, in the sanctuary of Ponderosa Bible Church, located a ninety-minute drive north of Phoenix in Payson, Arizona. On each chair, someone had carefully arranged a small pocket Constitution and a pen tucked inside a donation card for the church.

The event was sponsored by the Payson Tea Party, a group of self-described "constitutional conservatives" who agreed on "fiscal conservatism and reducing the size of the executive branch of government of the United States." Its president was Shirley Dye, a petite seventy-something woman with a gray bob who wore a purple Patagonia vest over a purple sweater. She energetically worked the crowd.

"We are a loose affiliation of people that get together, and the only thing that ties us together is I send out a Friday mail list," Dye said, explaining that the group was not formally tied to other right-wing organizations but focused on the U.S. Constitution as seen through a Christian lens. The association runs with ten key principles, the first of which is "America is guided by morality, having an origin in God. Human rights are not granted by the government but by our Creator."

While some attendees wore business-casual gear, as if they came straight from work, a handful sported red Make America Great Again hats. One man boasted a T-shirt that said "Impeach 46!"—referring to the current president, Joe Biden—across the back in a Gothic font. A baby, cradled in the corner, cried off and on faintly. Two young women in their twenties sat up front, one wearing a "Back the Blue" hat, ponytails bouncing as they nodded in agreement with the speakers.

I had come that evening because the guest speaker was Pinal County sheriff Mark Lamb, who represented the latest reincarnation of a far-right ideology often called the "constitutional sheriff" movement. The movement is composed of sheriffs and their supporters, who believe that the county sheriff is the highest law in the land, with the ability to determine which laws are constitutional. Sheriffs, according to this movement, can—in fact, must—block all other government branches and officials, including the president, the governor, and other law enforcement agencies like the Federal Bureau of Investigation (FBI) from enforcing laws and regulations within their county that might conflict with their specific, originalist interpretation of the Constitution.

On my drive there, I was struck by the immense desolation of the desert, the way the scrub brush gave way to colorful peaks, punctuated with a few casinos along the way. The small town's vibe catered to both nature lovers and survivalists. Along the main road, stores advertised CBD and camping gear as well as firearms, knives, and swords. In this place, like many other places I visited in the course of reporting this book, state and federal lawmakers felt physically and spiritually distant. Part of understanding the appeal of the county sheriff and the far-right movement the office inspires requires understanding these parts of the country, places where the U.S. Constitution remains revered, but the people making the laws feel far away.

After Shirley introduced Lamb, he strode to the front of the room, commanding attention in a relaxed way. He began by talking about the office of the sheriff. "We're not politicians. You know, it's funny because you'll hear me talk about the government and I'm not so fond of it. And people will say, 'That's funny, Sheriff, because you *are* the government.' No, I'm not. I'm your county sheriff. My job is to protect the people from the bad guys and from government overreach."

Lamb says in his self-published memoir—piles of which sat on a table near the door for sale—that he is six foot three and 240 pounds. That night, he wore a chambray shirt tucked into Wranglers, well-worn cowboy boots, a prominently displayed sidearm, a shiny badge, and his signature white cowboy hat. He was welcoming, with an affable smile, and made self-deprecating jokes, taking in stride the rancorously righteous outbursts of his audience.

His talk was wide-ranging, covering recent news that some libraries had removed especially racist Dr. Seuss books, "cancel culture," immigration, and the dangers of sex traffickers and pedophiles. When Lamb raised the topic of criminal justice reform, the people around me hissed, "Soros," referring to George Soros, the progressive Jewish philanthropist, and, for a moment, I felt afraid I would be spotted as an intruder.

He wrapped up by exhorting everyone to stay calm for the fight ahead and trust their county sheriff: "Sheriffs are the last line of defense in this country. We don't work for anybody but you. People ask me, 'Well, who's your boss?' Well, I don't have a boss. 'Who do you report to? The governor?' No. Not the governor. 'Who do you report to?' I report to the people. I represent the people of this community. There is power in that. We talked about that at the beginning of this. There's power in the people. And the sheriff represents you, the people."

This meeting was a far cry from the crowd armed with bear spray, flagpoles, knives, and other makeshift weapons who broke into the Capitol building almost three months earlier, on January 6, wreaking havoc and sending members of Congress and their staff into safe rooms to huddle in fearful silence. But Lamb was expressing the same distrust in the election results, the same worry that the federal government no longer represented the "real America." Everyone here was nodding, occasionally murmuring, "Uh-huh" or "That's right," just as I imagined they might in church on Sunday. These were members of the new patriot movement, the far-right ideology that disdains Black Lives Matter, MSNBC, immigrants, and Joe Biden in equal measure. Their leaders were the sheriffs, represented that evening by Lamb and the sheriff of Gila County (where Payson is located), Adam Shepherd.

Perhaps the most chilling moment in the evening came when Shepherd talked about militias in his county. "If you don't think we have [a militia], come with a busload of people into town," he said as people cheered. He was referring to recent, unfounded rumors on far-right media that armed antifascist protesters were penetrating rural America.

"They"—meaning the people of Payson, his people—"will come out armed."

He paused. "If people come out here and are gonna go into some of your businesses, what happens?"

In unison everyone cheered, "Not on our watch!"

Lamb added, "That's the beautiful thing about the power of the sheriff."

————

If you live in a city, as most Americans do, you probably know very little about your county sheriff. Nevertheless, sheriffs are a vital part of the mass incarceration and policing apparatus. America's roughly three thousand sheriffs exist in every state except Alaska, Connecticut, Hawaii, and Rhode Island, and they are almost all democratically elected by county. Unlike police chiefs, sheriffs do not report to city councils, mayors, or governors. They see themselves as independent of oversight. While they must work with other parts of county government—sheriff budgets, for example, are generally set by elected county leadership—they are not required to compromise when setting policies and priorities.

While they receive so much less media attention than police, sheriffs employ 25 percent of sworn law enforcement officers, which means one in four people in uniform report to a sheriff. They are an important part of the carceral apparatus as well. In addition to running county jails, sheriffs and their deputies make approximately 20 percent of all arrests in the nation, which translates to around 2 million arrests every year. Sheriffs' departments are the largest law enforcement agency in roughly one-third of U.S. counties, which equates to about 56 million people whose primary law enforcement are sheriffs' offices. While sheriffs primarily police rural counties and unincorporated areas, some departments, like the Los Angeles County Sheriff's Department, have concurrent jurisdiction with city police departments as well as sole policing authority over dozens of smaller cities via contractual arrangements. Often called "contract cities," these municipalities pay sheriffs' offices for policing services, ordering from a menu of options. This is common throughout the country. About 65 percent of municipalities in America are contract cities that pay the countywide agencies, usually the sheriff, for law enforcement. Sheriffs' departments may also be more deadly—one calculation found that 30 percent of all law enforcement killings were committed by officers working for a sheriff.

Today, sheriffs have many of the same functions as police. They patrol the streets, make traffic stops, execute arrest warrants, and investigate crimes. But their jobs are also so much more varied than those of police. Many sheriffs issue and track concealed carry permits for firearms. They run county jails, which admit 10 million people every year, some of them for the federal Marshals Service or U.S. Immigration and Customs Enforcement. They oversee evictions, sometimes using military-grade equipment to break down doors and remove tenants at gunpoint. They enforce and serve protective orders in cases of domestic violence. And in rural areas they are often medics, marriage counselors, and coroners. They are the people who get called when a wildfire threatens to destroy a town or when someone's cattle has broken through a fence. They are first responders at traffic accidents, shootings, and overdoses. They book people into the jail and transport them to court or the hospital.

Despite all of this, or perhaps because of it, sheriffs pride themselves on being in touch with the community. One sheriff bragged to me that residents call him, not the city police, when someone is manufacturing meth next door. Sheriffs are more likely to need to cooperate with state troopers and federal law enforcement because they are positioned to cover larger expanses of land. Like Mark Lamb, they are also more likely to speak with community groups as a way to rustle up votes, always looking ahead to the next election cycle.

Highly localized and disparate in job description, office size, and departmental policies, sheriffs are unsurprisingly best known for their likelihood of committing misconduct that often borders on criminal. In South Carolina, sheriffs in nearly a quarter of the state's counties were accused of breaking the law between 2009 and 2019. There are places throughout the country where no one clearly has the power to arrest or remove a sheriff, even if he is accused of plotting a murder (North Carolina) or using money intended to feed jail inmates to purchase a beach house (Alabama). Even when sheriffs are ousted for official misconduct, voters can restore them to office, as in the case of a Texas sheriff who was removed and criminally charged for attempted arson in 1981.

---

This book is different from books about the increasing threat and history of far-right violence, political power, and terror. Most books about the far right do not engage with the history of law enforcement and its complicity in far-right violence. Instead, law enforcement officers are the heroes of these stories, the protagonists of thrilling manhunt scenes. These stories set white supremacists and other far-right domestic terrorists on the opposite side of the officers tasked with tracking and arresting them.

While I have no desire to slight the law enforcement agencies who do track and arrest domestic terrorists, these popular narratives ignore how often the police and the white supremacists are one and the same—or at least have some of the same aims and goals.

Many writers, scholars, and activists have pointed out that the history of law enforcement in America is inextricable from white supremacy. As Michelle Alexander explained in her book *The New Jim Crow*, there is a direct line back in time from the modern-day police agency to the Jim Crow South to the slave patrols of antebellum America. Even further, the modern-day system of mass incarceration—sometimes called the "prison industrial complex"—is a form of racial subordination, a form of Jim Crow, as the book's title implies. And while other legal scholars disagree with parts of Alexander's book, I return to it time and again because of its central moral truth. It is impossible to look at the disproportionate number of Black Americans who are shot, choked, chased, harassed, arrested, fined, and murdered by the police and not see an obvious incarnation of white supremacy, the original sin of America.

And yet, we have come to rely on law enforcement so completely that it is now impossible for some people to imagine a world without it, despite witnessing in real time the victims of police violence. We have no other mechanism in place to hold white supremacists accountable other than an institution that is, itself, a product of white supremacy.

Sheriffs, I have found, provide a useful inflection point, especially in the current moment when one of the major political parties appears willing to endorse white supremacy. I could not talk about white supremacy without talking about sheriffs. (Around 90 percent of sheriffs are white men, not coincidentally.) At the same time, I could not discuss far-right movements without illustrating how sheriffs enable and legitimize the far right's ideas, tactics, and political goals.

I hope that this book helps readers to understand that the increasing public awareness of far-right movements must be considered in light of law enforcement, not in contrast to them. After January 6, some pundits were confused: How could a group of people who claimed to "Back the Blue" also kill and maim law enforcement officers?

The office of sheriff helps to explain this seeming paradox. Sheriffs are politicians as well as enforcers of the law. They are independent while also deeply reliant on local, state, and federal governments for funding. They claim deep roots in American history—deeper than the invention of America even—while also utilizing the most up-to-date technology available to surveil, police, and jail people. They decide who is part of the community and who is not. They are indeed the highest law of the land.

## HOW THIS BOOK WAS REPORTED

This book combines on-the-ground reporting with historical and legal research. In some instances, events are described using a combination of my own impression and observations, video or other social media postings about the event, interviews of people at the event, and available public records. In situations where I was not physically present—this book was written in part during COVID—I have culled video, social media, blogs, radio talk shows, and public records to reflect what happened to the best of my ability.

An important aspect of reporting on far-right movements is the distance between what leaders say is the truth and what evidence suggests. Because listening to what the far right actually says is an important part of the book, I have often reported their own words so readers can understand their import and why they resonate with listeners. At the same time, I have, where appropriate, pointed out places where available evidence does not match what sheriffs and their followers say.

Finally, a note on reporting on far-right events and personal safety. In some situations where events were open to the public, I attended and only identified myself as a journalist when asked. Because such events often target journalists and turn them into part of the spectacle—using them as an example or playing to their desire for shocking quotes—I preferred not to be used as part of their message. This also enabled me to watch the audience and understand their reactions.

Partway through reporting this book, many of the sheriffs I was writing about knew my name and face and thus identified me readily, which may have impacted their words and actions. Any and all interviews with sheriffs were done as a journalist with their full knowledge that they were on the record.

## A NOTE ON TERMINOLOGY

Throughout this book, I use the term "far right" to describe sheriffs, activists, affinity groups, community organizations, and politicians who adhere to an ideology or constellation of ideologies that are associated with the more extreme factions of the GOP.

There is a plethora of research material that categorizes far-right activities and behavior. The historian Kathleen Belew uses the term "white power" to describe movements that, while not explicitly calling for a white ethnostate or white supremacy, utilize the same referents, tactics, and key texts. Two popular designations with political scientists are "right-wing extremism" and "anti-government extremism." Other historians and scholars prefer the term "domestic terrorism" to contrast with terrorism from "abroad."

While many of these terms overlap with the ideologies of some of the sheriffs in this book, I have opted to avoid categorization where possible. For one thing, my intent is to describe the specific, rather than categorize general phenomena. For another, the frames of "extremism" and "terrorism," in particular, have been and still are weaponized against religious minorities, immigrants, and people of color to justify surveillance and additional policing.

The FBI, for example, categorizes many far-right groups like the Oath Keepers as "violent extremists," which they place alongside groups like "antifa" or "Black Identity Extremists." Members of Black Lives Matter were subject to police scrutiny and violence, justified by their perceived association with left-wing extremists. Such terms are constructed by law enforcement, not innately descriptive of movements.

This book presents a unique combination of ideas that defy easy categorization. Sheriffs are elected officials who operate within the government. While many actively oppose the federal government—by arguing that the FBI is being weaponized or by asserting that the Bureau of Alcohol, Tobacco, Firearms and Explosives (ATF) has no authority to create gun regulations—many of the same sheriffs are willing to cooperate with the Department of Homeland Security to deport immigrants and take money from various federal entities. Are they anti-government?

Some sheriffs and their supporters do believe that violence is necessary to overthrow the government and return the country to some imagined state; others appear to desire even something more revolutionary. Some see sheriffs as the "peaceful solution." Others focus on anti-immigrant animus or extremely broad interpretations of the Second Amendment. With laws in flux, it is hard to categorize all of these ideas.

I use the term "far right" in general as a catchall to mean sheriffs and their supporters whose ideas and political beliefs span from GOP standard-issue ideas (outlawing abortion) to those on the fringes of the GOP and beyond (ending income tax). Even this is in constant flux. Where other terms are appropriate, I use them. What "far-right" groups have in common includes an ideology that seeks to return to an imagined state that values Christianity, traditional gender roles, American nativism, and a "color-blind" form of white supremacy that fails to acknowledge the harms of the past and inequities of the present. These adherents also generally believe in libertarian principles: free market capitalism, deregulation, private property, and individual liberty without regard to collective good.

The intent of this book is not to disaggregate all of the complexities of far-right movements—I do not think I could if I tried—which is why I have opted for the simplest terminology. Most important to me is the acknowledgment that these sheriffs and their supporters are plainly opposed to the left and progressives.

At the same time, there have always been grassroots organizers who have sought to reduce the imprint of law enforcement, including the county sheriff. Communities of color have long sought to transform the office of sheriff into a position that will protect civil rights to the benefit of the community. Many such advocates are motivated because of recent far-right events, like January 6, that were endorsed by sitting sheriffs. In some cases, such advocates have been successful after dedicated and persistent efforts and have elected sheriffs who promised to minimize the use of jail for those accused of nonviolent crimes and who seek to protect immigrant communities.

All too frequently, media outlets and pundits attempt to cast the effort of reform-minded sheriffs as utilizing their discretion in the same way far-right sheriffs do, only for progressive goals. This is, as I will explain in the book, misguided and unhelpful. There are a number of sheriffs who are sincerely committed to their communities and put genuine effort into reforming the system despite great resistance. Their use of limited discretion in no way mirrors what sheriffs on the far right claim as their right. I do not want to both-sides the issue. The threat is coming from the right.

ONE

# THE SHERIFF RESURRECTION

## *The Rebirth of Constitutional Sheriffs*

ON MAY 15, 2021, A CROWD GATHERED IN A SMALL PARK BE-
hind the only high school in Battle Mountain, Nevada, for a "Patriotic Social
Gathering."

The town's name is misleading, because Battle Mountain is not a mountain but rather a valley nestled among three mountain ranges at the juncture
of two rivers where the Union Pacific Railroad still stops to pick up loads of
gold and copper. The *Washington Post* once called it the "armpit of America"
because of the "lack of character and charm, [a] pathetic assemblage of
ghastly buildings and nasty people." Its most famous event is a yearly World
Human Powered Speed Challenge, in which people race small pods on the
"straightest, smoothest and most ideal road surfaces in the world."

Lander County, which contains the city of four thousand, had recently
decided to become a "constitutional county." The county board of commissioners, which governs the region, agreed to pay $2,500 for this dubious
designation in order to, as one commissioner put it, "do something about the
restrictions on freedoms," referring to state COVID health regulations that
for the past year had limited the size of church services, closed many businesses, and required schoolchildren to wear face masks.

The event resembled a lot of gatherings happening throughout America since the country had been thrown into chaos because of a confluence of events: a worldwide pandemic that closed schools and businesses; a massive series of protests for racial justice provoked by the May 25, 2020, murder of George Floyd by a police officer who knelt on Floyd's neck for nine minutes and twenty-nine seconds; and the events leading up to and including January 6, 2021, in which then president Donald Trump encouraged thousands of people to riot and break into the Capitol building because he did not want to cede power after losing the presidential election. "If you don't fight like hell, you're not going to have a country anymore," he told his supporters that day, urging them to hunt down members of Congress and the then vice president Mike Pence.

Now the board of commissioners thought that the people of Lander County needed an opportunity to gather and express their united opposition to the federal and state government, particularly in the wake of the recent inauguration of President Joe Biden and the swirling conspiracy theories seeded by the far right, which included rumors about rampant pedophiles, election machines changing votes, and the Great Replacement theory. It was both a protest against the state of the nation and a way to lift the spirits of residents, who, according to their leaders, were fighting a war, if not physically, then spiritually.

"It's about protecting our freedom, our liberty, our lives," one commissioner summarized.

That spring morning, I watched vendors set up for the event—people sold hamburgers (featuring the "All American" burger with, yes, American cheese), expensive coffee drinks topped with whipped cream, and empanadas. Beribboned booths advertised RE/MAX Realtors and the West Coast Patriots, a subdivision of the Three Percent (III%), a militia movement linked to January 6, whose name represents the apocryphal "3 percent" of Americans who fought the British in 1776. A stage was erected up front with a large screen that broadcast the face of the speaker from multiple angles, and the day was spitting rain. The cars in the parking lot—which quickly filled to overtake muddy patches of field—were mostly pickup trucks proudly displaying Gadsden and pro-Trump flags alongside various hand-painted anti-Biden signs: "Joe Biden is NOT my president." "America was RAPED. 11-3-20." The white blocky letters startled me.

Security came in the form of a militia whose members wore military-style fatigues in shades of Desert Storm and tactical vests decorated with the Punisher logo—a skull with dripping fangs representing justice outside the law—and Thin Blue Line patches, a pro–law enforcement symbol adopted as a direct response to the Black Lives Matter movement. Most carried a sidearm and a long gun. They patrolled the picnic tables, the porta-potties, the food booths. Unlike other attendees, some wore balaclavas to cover their faces and shield their identities. When it rained, they huddled underneath canopies. Children ran up to examine their weapons and received friendly fist bumps.

Behind the playground were parked two blue ARISE USA! ("The Resurrection Tour: 84 Stops. 50 States. 1 Chance for Change.") tour buses, whose exteriors served as backdrops for selfies. The buses were emblazoned across their sides with landscapes, the etched faces of the speakers, and a sheriff badge floating in midair as if in the firmament, alongside inexplicable drawings of Native Americans wearing feathered headdresses. Their ghostly presence as anonymously sketched faces above a depiction of Mount Rushmore, which is built on stolen Sioux land, seemed to indicate a ceremonial blessing over the entire occasion or, perhaps, wishful thinking that everyone here was somehow representative of an American destiny that had become both color-blind and distinctively white.

Similar to the imaginary American history on the sides of the buses, Battle Mountain was also built on a lie. The first history of Battle Mountain was written by the town's founder and prospector, George Tannehill, who imagined—and then wrote as "history"—an 1857 battle fought by two dozen settlers against "marauding Indians" to give the town a more glorious origin. According to Tannehill, Indigenous warriors advanced over the mountains to descend into the valley that is Battle Mountain. Obviously, the white settlers won, in Tannehill's version. But there was never a battle at all. He made the whole thing up.

The idea of an imagined America was important for the attendees of this event. Not only were there universal truths everyone could agree on—that COVID was not a serious health threat, that the 2020 election results were fraudulent, that the deep state was intentionally thwarting the people's best interests—there was also the universal truth of place. Battle Mountain was, in a word, ugly. It was far from the odd commercial appeal of Las Vegas or the multicultural landscape of Los Angeles or the liberal haven of San Francisco. It was quite literally in the middle of nowhere, and the people who assembled prided themselves on being the real Americans, a concept with lineage from Thomas Jefferson's yeoman farmers to Richard Nixon's silent majority to the "deplorables" praised by Donald Trump in 2016.

While it might be easy to attribute this all to race—many, but not all, of the people there were white—I think about a phrase the historian Anthea Butler coined, the "promise of whiteness." About one-fourth of Battle Mountain is Latino. Belonging meant adhering to a set of values, an agreed-upon story. The people of Battle Mountain had fought a battle and won in the past; they were in the middle of another fight.

During the planning sessions for the event, the county executives worried about the potential for armed conflict. The clashes between protesters and counterprotesters in places like Portland and Kenosha, Wisconsin, were burned into their minds. Bert Ramos, the Lander County manager who was responsible for the logistics of the day, claimed the militia was necessary to protect the town from protesters. "Anyone worried about BLM or anybody else," Ramos said, referring to Black Lives Matter, "I'm not going anywhere."

Despite these fears, the rally had the air of a family picnic. Wives pushed strollers as older siblings swung and slid on playground equipment. Adults sprawled on blankets and in lawn chairs in front of the stage. I was reminded of what the ex-sheriff of Gwinnett County, Georgia, Butch Conway said about Donald Trump's January 6 Ellipse rally before the attack on the Capitol: "I would describe it as a cross between tailgating at a football game and a NASCAR race—families, dogs, children. Everyone being nice. I mean, it was like a family reunion without some of the hatefulness you can find at family reunions. It was a very good crowd." (In the same interview, Conway denounced the attack and added that those who committed crimes should go to jail.)

A woman with a blond blowout designed to withstand the rain handed me a brown baseball cap with "#UNRIG" on the front, which was part of the tour's provocation: that the 2020 presidential election had been somehow subverted, despite what every judge agreed was an utter lack of evidence. When a speaker yelled, mid-monologue, "We've been fucked!" everyone applauded and cheered.

What made this rally interesting to me were the uniformed sheriffs not just protecting the public but also making a political statement. There were six currently serving Nevada sheriffs there, about one-third of the sheriffs in the state, men elected to enforce all federal, state, and local laws, even though at this moment they were endorsing the breaking of those laws. They were, in other words, perfectly fine with moving what appeared at first glance to be a culture war between red and blue America into political revolution.

---

Sheriffs are elected in every state except Alaska, Connecticut, Hawaii, and Rhode Island. Over three thousand of them must campaign for office every four years, in most cases. This means that sheriffs, unlike police chiefs, are in many ways equal to other elected local officials, with the power to set departmental policies, hire and fire staff based on political support (or lack thereof), and express controversial opinions to curry political favor. To a sheriff, city police are mere "code enforcers," and many sheriffs believe they outrank police chiefs and other appointed officials, who don't have to make their case to the public at large.

Most sheriffs are established in state—but not the federal—constitutions, and their duties are governed by complicated sets of laws. Their role, however, is extremely broad, contributing to the notion that sheriffs are particularly unique. Their jobs include policing, especially in more rural regions, investigating and solving major crimes, managing all aspects of the county jail, collaborating with federal immigration agencies, registering firearms, enforcing protection orders in cases of domestic violence, serving eviction notices, and, as framed in many state constitutions, "keeping the peace," "quell[ing] riots, routs, affrays and unlawful assemblages," and preventing "lynchings and mob violence."

They are also the whitest, most masculine, and longest-tenured. As of 2020, only 4 percent of sheriffs were Black, and less than 2 percent were women. In 2020, one Texas county elected its first Black sheriff since Reconstruction. Even though sheriffs must run for office, they often win reelection over and over. Tenures of forty or fifty years are not uncommon. Over half of all sheriff elections are not contested, and 90 percent of the time the incumbent wins reelection. As a result, sheriffs are the least diverse of any democratically elected officials.

Some states do not require sheriffs to have law enforcement experience or a college degree, and one study found that sheriffs have overall less education than police chiefs. This is not to say that experience doesn't matter in elections, but some sheriffs argue that the office should be open to anyone who wants to run. To some extent, this is because sheriffs predate the invention of professional police. The National Sheriffs' Association, which supports the need to "preserve the office of sheriff" through elections, calls sheriffs "consistent with our nation's democratic history, traditions and historical practices." Sheriffs believe they directly represent the people, their constituents, or at least the ones who can vote. Despite or because of this, sheriffs see themselves as the highest law in the land, independent and operating on equal footing with other important officials like the county supervisors, the governors, even the Supreme Court of the United States.

A sheriff in Louisiana who held office for nearly three decades put it this way in an interview with NPR:

> The sheriff . . . is the closest thing there is to being a king in the U.S. I have no unions, I don't have civil service, I hire and fire at will. I don't have to go to council and propose a budget. I approve the budget. I'm the head of the law-enforcement district, and the law-enforcement district only has one vote, which is me.

The headline speaker of the Patriotic Social Gathering was "Sheriff" Richard Mack, who has spent the past three decades organizing sheriffs to be key interpreters of the U.S. Constitution, able to use their king-like powers to advocate for far-right causes, including the centering of Christianity in public institutions, a loosening of firearms regulations, and a reduced role for federal law enforcement agencies. In 2011, three years after the election of the first Black president of the United States, Mack founded a group called the Constitutional Sheriffs and Peace Officers Association (CSPOA), the largest organization in the so-called constitutional sheriff movement, which is a political, cultural, and religious movement that claims sheriffs have expansive, unique, and often superstitious powers. Since 2020, the constitutional sheriff movement has gained mainstream popularity in response to COVID and the 2020 racial justice uprisings, largely through the efforts of Mack and events like the one in Battle Mountain.

As befitting his role as the godfather of the far-right sheriff movement, Mack was the center of attention, posing with attendees for photographs and beaming with pride. Mack, now in his late sixties, wears professorial eye-glasses and his unnaturally dark hair slicked back with what is rumored to be black shoe polish and a healthy dose of Aqua Net. He sported a black polo shirt tucked into jeans with a leather belt slung below his belly along with cowboy boots and an affable smile. Incredibly tan, he reminded me of a pro-fessional golf player.

"I used to have a term for his type," someone who knew Mack told me, "and I just call them tucked-in. The shirt's tucked in. They don't gain too much weight. They pay their bills on time."

Mack loves being a sheriff, even though he hasn't been one since 1996. The CSPOA, which at one point filed for nonprofit status but was dissolved in 2021 by the State of Arizona for failure to file annual reports, is his life. His Dodge Charger has a "CSPOA" vanity license plate. A decal of the CSPOA logo—which includes a bald eagle and a sheriff's star—covers the entirety of the car's hood. Despite not being tax-exempt, the group solicits "donations" and, as of 2022, has an advisory board, but it's clear that the group is driven by Richard Mack.

According to Mack and the CSPOA, sheriffs are not just law enforce-ment; they are special stewards of the U.S. Constitution—which is not just a regular legal document but a religious text to be interpreted literally—and can refuse to enforce federal, state, or local laws that they believe violate par-ticular tenets of the "original Constitution," which includes the Bill of Rights (amendments one through ten). Per the CSPOA's website: "The law enforce-ment powers held by the sheriff supersede those of any agent, officer, elected official or employee from any level of government."

While the ideas behind the CSPOA have recently come to the forefront of politics, the constitutional sheriff movement has deep roots in American history. The ideology echoes the same themes that sheriffs of both political parties use to resist reform and preserve their political power: the carefully built myth that sheriffs are uniquely accountable to voters and, as a result, do not require additional oversight. The constitutional sheriff movement has also benefited from the problematic rightward lurch of all members of law enforcement, who are leaping to anti-progressivism and, in many cases, far-right extremism as a way to resist community demands to reform, defund, and reduce the role of police and jails in America.

CSPOA membership and the influences of its ideas have spread widely since 2020, although the numbers are hard to quantify. In 2022, Political Research Associates, a nonprofit that tracks extremist groups, estimated the number of CSPOA-aligned sheriffs to be around 400. Mack told me that he thought it was now closer to 800, which seems like a gross overestimation to me. Two political scientists surveyed 500 sheriffs and found that around a quarter of them expressed positive attitudes about the CSPOA. And it's certain that around 50 sheriffs out of 254 in Texas attended CSPOA training sessions, which in the Lone Star State once counted as continuing education.

These numbers are difficult to verify, and many sheriffs who express the same views as the CSPOA will say (falsely or not) that they have never heard of the organization. Many others have told me that just because they are members does not mean that they agree with everything the CSPOA claims to represent. Mack himself has emphasized repeatedly in his public statements—and to me personally—that he does not care about membership in the CSPOA, and there is no list, leaked or otherwise. "Pls understand," he wrote to me, "our goal is not memberships, it is the restoration of Liberty."

Instead, Mack presents his project as an ideological one. Like a pastor, he is spreading the word. The result is a medicine show selling a variety of traditions culled from the Old West, white supremacy, rural resentment, and the current anti-government movement as propagated under Donald Trump and his associates. The CSPOA packages these ideas, many of which verge on conspiracy theories, as something appealing for county sheriffs who are seeking a guiding light that both exalts their chosen profession and provides a convenient political platform for gaining the national spotlight.

To be clear, the National Sheriffs' Association (NSA)—the principal nationwide organization that plays a critical role in connecting county sheriffs to national legislators, basically amounting to more money allocated to the issues sheriffs present as important—has disavowed Mack's claims, explaining in 2012 that sheriffs do not have "extraordinary powers." To them, Mack is an unwelcome distraction who snags headlines and casts aspersions on the office. Mack has complained that the NSA will not allow him to purchase a booth at their annual conference. When I mention Mack to the public information officer of the NSA, Patrick Royal, he sighs heavily. Yet, sighs notwithstanding, multiple members of the NSA leadership team have appeared with Mack at various events, and one NSA board member was at the Capitol on January 6. The NSA has never censured or removed any of them, and it has not made an official statement about the constitutional sheriff movement in over a decade. In fact, the NSA echoes many of the same ideas behind the CSPOA, writing in 2014 that the sheriff "is not . . . subject to the direct authority/control on a day-to-day basis by a county board of supervisors or executives."

Even if CSPOA membership itself is far from the majority of sheriffs in the United States, Mack has been successful in mainstreaming many of the ideas behind the constitutional sheriff movement, especially the portions that pertain to the importance of local law enforcement and their exalted place in society, which eliminates the need for oversight. This movement has only increased since 2020 as a result of COVID, a renewed push for police accountability and racial justice, and Trump's presidential loss, all of which reinspired many of the same fears that caused Mack to form the CSPOA after the election of Barack Obama.

———

When the Nevada sheriffs took the stage, Mack spoke first. He had nodded along enthusiastically with all of the prior speakers like a genteel patriarch, stooping gently to listen when fans came to chat him up. Throughout the event, Mack stayed close to the CSPOA tent, which hawked a variety of T-shirts, books, and pamphlets. Now the center of attention, Mack allowed his gaze to wander softly, almost in wonder, as if he beheld a miracle.

"Wow," Mack began, looking upon the crowd in genuine awe, his eyes wide, his face pleased like a child. "What a beautiful day!" He has done variations of this speech hundreds of times for over a decade. Perhaps his background as a youth in musical theater gave him this ability of projecting both expertise and wonder.

He first mentioned an NBC reporter who was planning a "hit piece"— all press is good press—and said he wanted to be clear on the purpose of the CSPOA. "The CSPOA," he said, "is about one thing. The notion that all men and women are created equal." Everyone cheered. "And that all of us answer equally to the law. . . .

"Freedom and liberty are for all God's children, and I've been saying that for four decades," he said, chopping his arm in the air. The woman in front of me had on a red hat that said "Trumpism." Another attendee, male, wore a baseball hat with a bald eagle and an American flag.

Mack also has his own imaginary history, one in which sheriffs in the American South were not there to profit from convict leasing and sheriffs in the West were not responsible for the jailing, forced labor, and genocide of Native people. In his mind, sheriffs are the noble embodiment of a chivalrous code. To emphasize this, Mack recites a made-up tale about Rosa Parks, who, in his imagined version, would have been helped by a sheriff who refused to arrest her when she did not move to the back of the bus. The story both insulates him from charges of racism and allows the audience to imagine their outrage over COVID vaccines and gun control as part of the heroic history of the civil rights movement.

"In December of 1955, Rosa Parks was arrested for not giving her seat to a white man. Would you have arrested her, Officer? Sheriff?" he said, addressing the audience. "No, our job would have been to protect her from the government that was doing evil." The sheriff, Mack implied, was on the side of Rosa Parks, whose enemy was the government, not racist white people.

At some gatherings, Mack even casts himself as the valiant sheriff and Parks as a woman in need of rescue, a courtly romance of sorts. "She [Rosa Parks] looked up at me with her beautiful eyes and kind of a scared look and said, 'Why can't we just be left alone?'" he has elaborated, providing a bowdlerized version of the story that presents Parks as a victim of government overreach. In 2009, he said, "What does the constitutional officer do today? He protects Rosa Parks the gun owner. He protects Rosa Parks the victim of the IRS. He protects Rosa Parks the tax protester. He protects and defends Rosa Parks the medical marijuana person. And he protects people who simply want to be left alone." The story often brings Mack to the verge of tears.

At the Battle Mountain rally, Mack took pains to denounce racism, pointing out that Southern Democrats were the party of chattel slavery and Jim Crow, a common Republican talking point.

"We do not want any Senator Robert Byrd in the CSPOA! By the way, he was Joe Biden's best friend," he exclaimed, referring to the West Virginia senator who led a chapter of the Ku Klux Klan. At Byrd's funeral in 2010, Biden had praised the man's career, even though Byrd had filibustered the 1964 Civil Rights Act.

Just as he creates a fantastical and ever-shifting version of Rosa Parks's story, Richard Mack is always crafting and polishing his own origin story. Mack's father was an FBI agent, and Mack, who was both athlete of the year and drama student of the year at Safford High School in 1971, originally planned to follow in his footsteps. However, he failed the entrance exam, so he joined the Provo Police Department in Utah instead, which set him on his path.

In his books, Mack describes himself as a beat cop in Provo and a devout member of the Church of Jesus Christ of Latter-day Saints. While working undercover busting "druggies"—he grew his hair long and his beard bushy—Mack became disillusioned with what he saw as a focus on "numbers" in policing. He held particular ire for the "war on drugs," writing once:

> Why did so many people have to go to jail because of marijuana, especially when it was less harmful than alcohol? Is law enforcement really about public service or public harassment? . . . After years of research, I am now totally convinced that the "Drug War" is a farce. It provides no benefit to the public and actually makes the drug problem worse.

In the early 1980s, Mack went to a two-day seminar held by onetime Brigham Young University professor and far-right conspiracy theorist Willard Cleon Skousen where, Mack says, he was transformed. At the 2022 FreedomFest—a multiday libertarian conference in Las Vegas that features far-right luminaries and financial advisers who tout the gold standard—Mack walked onstage to the soundtrack of "Return of the Mack" and explained how Skousen "changed [his] life back in 1983, when, as a rookie cop, I attended one of his seminars called Constitutional Studies for Peace Officers." He added that Skousen "converted [him] to the U.S. Constitution."

According to Mack, 240 people attended that seminar.

"I don't know what happened to the other 239 of them, but this one was converted," Mack told a Tucson newspaper reporter.

———

Skousen was an FBI agent, police chief, and anti-communist with connections to the John Birch Society and high-profile members in the Church of Jesus Christ of Latter-day Saints. His ideas deeply influenced Mack as well as other far-right and anti-government leaders. Mack's constitutional sheriff movement hinges on a belief that the entire country faces an existential threat, generally framed as coming from communists, socialists, liberals, the media, and, he told me as I wrote this book, me. Because the stakes—the future of the country—are so high, recruiting sheriffs to become constitutional sheriffs is tantamount to fighting the eternal war between good and evil.

To understand the influence of Skousen, you first have to understand the "White Horse Prophecy," a series of disputed teachings by LDS founder Joseph Smith and leader Brigham Young. The prophecy predicts that the "nation will be on the verge of crumbling to pieces and tumbling to the ground." It goes on: "You will see the Constitution of the United States almost destroyed; it will hang like a thread," an oft-repeated portion reads. When this happens, "this people will be the Staff up[on] which the Nation shall lean and they shall bear the Constitution away from the [very] verge of destruction."

Skousen, whom conservative writer David Frum once called one of the "legendary cranks of the conservative world," relied on this prophecy in his work, which reiterates the need for followers to be vigilant about dangers from the left. While Skousen's name may not resonate with a lot of people, his ideas have been influential on the right, even to this day. He wrote over twenty books, which he self-published and distributed widely among LDS leadership.

One of his most popular books, *The Making of America*, was recommended by the far-right group Moms for Liberty as recently as 2023 as well as by Mack, who described it as "the longest book I've read, except for the Bible." Prominent GOP politicians, including Utah senator Mitt Romney and former Texas governor Rick Perry, both presidential candidates, have recommended Skousen's books and discussed his work with familiarity. As part of the Tea Party movement, Glenn Beck revived Skousen's oeuvre, launching them into the Amazon top ten list for 2009.

Skousen, like Mack, grossly embellished his own background and expertise in anti-communist crusading. He spent most of his career rather unremarkably as a low-level FBI employee doing administrative work. Although he would later boast about being the "assistant to J. Edgar Hoover," ample evidence suggests that this is not true. Instead, he was just one of many foot soldiers in Hoover's bustling agency.

According to records, Skousen was the ideal FBI agent. A 1946 review described him as having "a splendid personal appearance; he dresses in a neat and conservative manner. . . . He is cooperative, industrious and possessed of considerable initiative." He was praised for his dedication to the FBI and its mission. In 1948, a reviewer wrote, "He is exceptionally interested in the Bureau's work and religiously loyal to the organization. He performs a large amount of overtime and does not request compensatory leave." Another agent described Skousen as having "more promise than any new man he had seen coming from the Bureau's Training School in a long time," capable of handling "almost any type of assignment . . . with the assurance that it would be vigorously, conscientiously, and discreetly handled."

After sixteen years of service in the FBI, Skousen was tasked by the president of Brigham Young University, Ernest Wilkinson, to root out left-wing activists among the student body. Skousen did the same for the Provo Police Department, training officers to ferret out communists. "No longer are communists considered part of the free world," he told a group of police officers in 1955. The next year, Skousen ascended to his dream job, the police chief of Salt Lake City. His fight against "vice" resulted in draconian measures against common pastimes like alcohol consumption, pinball machines, and bingo.

Finally, in 1960, the mayor of Salt Lake City, J. Bracken Lee, fired Skousen. Their rupture filled the local newspaper with flying accusations: Lee called Skousen "insubordinate" and accused him of exploiting his position as a platform for self-promotion, largely because Skousen appears to have spent more time talking about communism than policing the city. "[Skousen] operated the Salt Lake City Police Department in exactly the same manner as the Communists in Russia operate their own government," Lee wrote. Skousen scoffed that Lee was just corrupt.

Skousen transformed himself into a roving political reactionary, joining other Bircher types on countrywide tours to lecture on the evils of communism, including a 1961 event at the Hollywood Bowl in front of twenty-five thousand people alongside far-right luminaries like Fred Schwarz (founder of the Christian Anti-Communism Crusade), Ronald Reagan, and John Wayne. His advocacy became more strident. Skousen said that the country should withhold food from the Soviets and Chinese as punishment for communism. He accused federal law enforcement agencies, Dwight Eisenhower, and John F. Kennedy of being secret communists. FBI leadership distanced themselves from Skousen, calling him an "unprincipled racketeer in anticommunism" and "money mad." "It does appear Skousen has gone off the deep end to some extent," one agent wrote.

Mormon leadership, however, was not deterred by Skousen's increasing radicalization. Wilkinson made him a religious instructor at BYU, where Skousen taught that the Constitution was divinely inspired and under attack from communists and liberals. He framed the fight against communism in apocalyptic terms: "Either the people would humble themselves and say to God, 'Our heavenly Father, give us strength to endure. We will obey your commandments. We will be morally clean, we will worship you, we will be honest, and we will fight for truth and righteousness.' Or it says, 'We will abhor God and we will turn away from Him and we will become a degenerate people, and if that happens, we will be wiped clean off the land.'"

To continue to teach his ideology to local law enforcement, Skousen created the Freeman Institute, which, like the CSPOA later, trained police "to fight communism and big government." Skousen's teachings reflect what the historian Richard Hofstadter called the "paranoid style" of American politics: opposition to the IRS and the "welfare state," a fear of "activist judges" and the United Nations, and disdain of Martin Luther King Jr.'s advocacy and civil rights in general.

By the 1980s, Skousen was railing against "evil elements creeping into our schools" and the need for a "revival of the founding fathers' original concepts." At this point, he was somewhat of a fringe figure, appearing at far-right events, stooped and bald, his features craggy. Mormon church leaders, especially the more liberal professors at BYU, became increasingly critical of Skousen, calling his work "B.S.," and the violence of later Skousen-inspired movements eventually persuaded the Church to abandon their support of him.

After his death in 2006, Skousen's family took over his organization, now called the National Center for Constitutional Studies. The NCCS sells a variety of videos based on Skousen's *The Making of America*, as well as "pocket Constitutions," which periodically top the Amazon bestsellers list. They are notable because they have a portrait of George Washington on the front, holding a quill (although Washington did not write the Constitution), and are, according to the website, "proofed word for word against the originals housed in the Archives in Washington, D.C. They are identical in spelling, capitalization, and punctuation." Mack often carries a copy, as do many other far-right organizers.

———————

In 1988, Mack finally won "the best job in the world," sheriff of Graham County, Arizona. The region is incredibly rural, and its main feature is Mount Graham, which became a source of environmental activism when the University of Arizona proposed construction of a large telescope there. A substantial portion of Mack's tenure as sheriff was dealing with Earth First!, an environmental advocacy group that protested the Mount Graham construction by occupying the land, even going so far as to tie members to trees. In one press photo, a slim Richard Mack is shifting logs placed by protesters to block the road. In another, Mack carries a protester who sprained her ankle. It's clear that Mack did not think well of the protesters, whom he calls "hippies" and "druggies," but he does deploy this part of his career as a way to emphasize his cross-political appeal. "I did not like them," he has said about Earth First! But, he insisted, he treated them with respect.

Mack was reelected in 1992 as a conservative Democrat, which is when his interest turned to far-right politics. During his second term, Mack became one of a handful of sheriffs recruited by the National Rifle Association (NRA) to challenge the Brady Handgun Violence Prevention Act, a 1993 bill signed by then president Bill Clinton that instituted mandatory waiting periods and background checks for handgun purchases. The cases made their way to the U.S. Supreme Court as *Printz v. United States*, and the court ruled 5–4 in favor of the main plaintiff, a Montana sheriff named Jay Printz. The majority opinion was written by Justice Antonin Scalia. Justice Clarence Thomas wrote a concurrence in which he set forth the template that would become modern Second Amendment jurisprudence, which provides for an individual right to own firearms. This case made Mack a far-right hero; in 1994, he was the NRA's officer of the year.

The court case, however, made Mack less popular as a sheriff. There were two failed attempts to recall him. The first one was based on Mack's alleged mishandling of the 1993 death of Stephanie Proffitt, who disappeared and was found dead two months later. (Mack says this was not his fault and blamed the family.) According to a 1995 article in the *Phoenix New Times*, Mack back-burnered the case because he was working on the Brady Bill lawsuit; no one was ever arrested for Proffitt's death. The second recall attempt was in 1995, started by a resident named Debbie Campbell, who rankled at Mack's far-right political statements. Calling her recall attempt the "Mack Attack," she filed multiple police reports because, she alleged, Mack's father and another supporter in full militia gear were harassing her, which led her ultimately to drop the recall effort. (Mack said the harassment did not happen.) In a contemporaneous news report, she described Mack as "charismatic" and compared him to notorious cult leaders and dictators like David Koresh, Jim Jones, Adolf Hitler, and Charles Manson. Eventually the efforts against Mack paid off. He lost his third campaign for sheriff in a landslide; his opponent received 70 percent of the vote. Mack moved back to Provo, Utah, in 1997.

From the mid-1990s on, Mack made multiple runs at public office, running in the GOP primary for Utah County sheriff in 1998, during which he argued that incarcerated people were being "coddled" and promising to feed them "cold bologna sandwiches and cereal." His opponent defeated him handily. (Mack argued he lost because of a federal raid that he said was retaliation for his lawsuit. The raid was related to a securities fraud investigation against other individuals; Mack was not charged.) Then Mack tried for Provo city councilor in 1999 (lost) and governor of Utah in 2003 (ran as a Libertarian on a platform opposing water fluoridation). After dropping his gubernatorial campaign, he ran a pretend campaign as part of a short-lived 2004 Showtime reality show called *American Candidate*, in which contestants competed to become "president." Mack was the fourth one to leave the show.

During his fake campaign he vowed to abolish taxes, legalize marijuana, and legalize polygamy. A reporter from the *Deseret News* visited his home office in Provo and described it as "decorated with a large sword, a bald eagle statue that glows when plugged in, and a photo of Mack standing in a barn with a group of men dressed like cowboys and holding rifles." Not accepting defeat, in 2006 Mack campaigned as a Libertarian to be one of Arizona's senators. His platform included abolishing the IRS and income taxes. "I am running to restore personal liberty before it is too late," his website read.

In between these failed attempts, he went on a speaking circuit, talking to far-right groups, gun enthusiasts, and anyone protesting government regulation. His talks focused on the need to resist the feds, especially when it came to guns. Mack told reporters he was being followed by the FBI, probably a fiction to amplify his profile. As a devout LDS man steeped in anticommunist and conspiratorial rhetoric, Mack captured an apocalyptic worldview combined with religious fervor and devotion. He began to appear at Tea Party events. In need of money to support himself, he sold cars and tried to recruit more people to his movement.

In 2009, Mack met Stewart Rhodes, the founder of the Oath Keepers militia group, and published his foundational text, *The County Sheriff: America's Last Hope*, which was endorsed by Arizona sheriff Joe Arpaio. Mack became a board member of the Oath Keepers, which, like the constitutional sheriff movement, centers fidelity to a particular interpretation of the Bill of Rights and the Constitution, reminiscent of an imagined history of the American founding. "The Oath Keepers and I were a marriage that was made in heaven," he said at the time.

Tasha Adams, Rhodes's ex-wife, told me her memories of Mack are as someone who reminded her of a pastor but had very little visibility. "Stewart really started promoting him and I really blame him for Mack's ability to do this for a living. . . . He just kept promoting him and it kind of became this thing," she said. (Mack still supplements his income by teaching high school–level American history at the Heritage Academy, an Arizona charter school that uses Skousen's books.)

After Rhodes formed the Oath Keepers, he went on a nationwide tour and brought Mack along as a speaker. "Like rock stars," Adams said. When Rhodes announced the formation of the Oath Keepers in April 2009 at the Lexington Green in Lexington, Massachusetts, Mack was there alongside Mike Vanderboegh, the founder of the Three Percenters. At Lexington Green, Mack said that his goal aligned perfectly with Rhodes's and added what became his most famous tagline: "Well, the sheriff is the most powerful law enforcement officer in the country and has the ultimate say in his county. No one supersedes his jurisdiction. And I want this made very clear. The president of the United States cannot tell your sheriff what to do."

In talking to Adams, I could see how both Rhodes and Mack operated as if in tandem, relying on themselves as charismatic leaders (as well as the primary financial beneficiaries). Adams told me that Rhodes was fond of mentalists like Derren Brown, a British performer who believes he can influence his large audiences through a series of small suggestions. I could see the same influence in Mack, a performer through and through—less a religious scholar like Skousen, more Pecos Bill with an apocalyptic flair.

Both men also structured their organizations similarly with websites that have the patina of nonprofits, including board members and an option for anyone to donate money; Mack also accepts donations in "silver and gold." The CSPOA, like the Oath Keepers, currently charges a monthly fee of $11—or a onetime "lifetime" fee of $5,000—for access to extra information, including training content and additional videos. The $5,000 level also includes a "Personal Web Meeting with Sheriff Mack 30 minutes." (In the course of reporting, I have paid the monthly fee to access videos and material from the CSPOA.) The appearance of a nonprofit, however, does not make for reality. Donations are not tax-deductible, and it is unclear where any money earned by either group goes. (Mack has publicly said that he accepts only a small salary, but he has never filed financial statements for the organization.)

As he gained more visibility thanks to Rhodes, Mack moved to Fredericksburg, Texas, around 2011 at the urging of the Patriots of Gillespie County, a Tea Party group, who wrote on their website that Mack would "bring government back to its proper role in these United States." In 2012, Mack stumped for Ron Paul's presidential campaign and ran as an extremely far-right, libertarian Republican candidate for Congress from District 21, which includes parts of the San Antonio and Austin suburbs. He lost in a landslide to the incumbent, receiving only 15 percent of the vote.

Mack has publicly said he left the Oath Keepers around 2014, a date that is difficult to verify. (Mack told me in an interview that he left in 2016.) It does seem to be true that Mack distanced himself from Rhodes's organization, which was becoming more militarized, around that time, even as he continued to associate with him for the publicity. Adams said that Mack would call their house demanding that Rhodes remove his name from the website. (Mack minimizes any disagreement with Rhodes and says they simply split ways.) "Sheriff Mack was getting really mad," she told me.

Adams, who testified against her ex-husband in his criminal trial for seditious conspiracy, also believes that Mack knew about Rhodes's abusive behavior toward her and her children, which she made public in the course of her divorce and court hearings. "But I know he won't say a bad thing about Stewart even now," Adams told me. "Mack will not talk shit about Stewart." She said that, like many others, Mack would justify his silence by saying that Adams was making allegations because of the divorce. Mack has said he refused television interviews because he refused to talk about Rhodes.

But the men, and their ideologies, feed off each other. About a month after the 2021 Battle Mountain rally, Rhodes held his own training session in Wichita Falls. "The best thing would be if your sheriff started a posse," he told his audience, who listened to him talk for hours into the night.

———

The Battle Mountain celebration began with a car parade at "high noon." I could see a line of cars coming from the west, crawling along I-80 accompanied by a stream of motorcycles. The highway sweeps into Battle Mountain, which is marked at the entrance by a Super 8 motel, from around a range of hills that tumble down from the vast sands of the Nevada wilderness. Just outside Battle Mountain, the caravan would have passed through the singing sands, which moan when the wind causes the unusually shaped grains to rub together.

The militia security crew shooed spectators to the side for the caravan. One car was all pink with "Women for Trump" banners. Passengers waved their firearms out the windows and people clapped and cheered. I stood next to a Three Percenter with a large beard and serious demeanor. He was working.

The program began with a group of local elementary school–age children who uncertainly sang "The Star-Spangled Banner." They all wore red, white, and blue. One wore a black cowboy hat; one a red MAGA baseball cap; and one a flag headband Rambo-style. Their bewildered faces were projected behind them onto a large screen.

Ramos, the county manager, wore his black hair and goatee tightly trimmed, shiny with product, shirt tucked in. He served as the emcee for the day. He stood onstage uncomfortably.

"I should have written something down," he began, clearing his throat. "What brings us here today is that Lander County joined the Constitutional Sheriffs and Peace Officers Association." He encouraged the audience to "work from the ground up" by "electing good people." "That's what gets down to the magic of Lander County. We the people," he concluded, with an effort at a flourish.

There was a full slate of far-right speakers, among them Sacha Stone, a New Age musician and influencer who peddles in anti-vax conspiracy theories and Holocaust denial, and Leigh Dundas, a California attorney who dedicated herself to promoting anti-vax theories. Each speaker had their face magnified multifold by the screen behind them.

Another was Robert David Steele, who was also the main organizer for the ARISE USA! tour and a rabid anti-Semite and QAnon adherent. Steele, who claimed to be an expert in "Satanic pedophilia," helped publish a fifty-four-volume book called *Pedophilia and Empire: Satan, Sodomy, and the Deep State*, with dozens of five-star reviews on Amazon that explain how theories like QAnon start. "WAKE UP AND SEE THE TRUTH," Lorenzo Garcia wrote in 2021. "Sad but true. I double checked the notes and have NOT found anything untrue. Excellent work. Easy to read," wrote Claire, who was concerned about "the children."

Among other things, Steele was a major proponent and spreader of the PizzaGate conspiracy, an internet-fueled rumor that a Washington, D.C., pizza parlor loosely connected to the Clintons was sex trafficking children. In 2016, a twenty-eight-year-old man was so disturbed, he drove to the capital and opened fire inside the restaurant at lunchtime.

In an online discussion with Mack, Steele outlined the goals of their partnership:

> Sheriff Mack inspired in me a burning fire to take his message and mine on the road. I'm the top-dog on three topics: election fraud and reform, Wall Street treason and crime, and Satanic pedophilia with child trafficking. But those topics are not going to be understood by the American people unless they see the solutions that Sheriff Mack represents. Sheriff Mack represents

elected Sheriffs deputizing armed engaged citizens to push back against the abuse of power. And together we represent faith, family, and freedom, which is the covenant.

In Battle Mountain, Steele wore a wide-brimmed brown hat and chomped on an unlit cigar, which he wielded as a prop. His speech lagged and dragged with uninspiring conspiracy theories involving Hillary Clinton and, yes, pedophilia. He claimed to have invented a "new intelligence agency," describing himself as a "former spy." He seemed disheveled and spoke for nearly an hour in an incomprehensible ramble.

"The system is rigged," he said as he tried to rally the crowd, describing most election reforms as a "fundraising gimmick" while also calling Sidney Powell, who has pled guilty to criminal charges related to January 6, "Joan of Arc 2.0." When he called "President Trump" the "legally elected president," the crowd erupted in cheers.

Although Steele disdains politicians, he praised constitutional sheriffs and Richard Mack—the "second most important person in America"—as safeguards against tyranny. "Every sheriff can deputize every one of you," he said, calling the crowd a "militia"—"The real militia is YOU!"

Joey Gilbert came to the stage with a burst of applause and hoots of approval. The ex-boxer and lawyer had at the time just announced he was running for governor of Nevada. Gilbert's Reno firm built a business suing election officials over the 2020 election and opposing mask and vaccine mandates as well as partnering with the Proud Boys and other far-right groups. He was in D.C. on January 6. Billboards across the state featured Gilbert thrusting his knuckles at the viewer with his catchphrase, "Fighting for Nevada."

Obscure before 2020, Gilbert became famous when he represented a rural church just east of Reno in a lawsuit against the state for COVID restrictions on attendance size. The Ninth Circuit, relying on a July 2020 decision by the U.S. Supreme Court holding that a Catholic church could not be forced to comply with attendance caps, ruled for the church. (The governor dropped the attendance caps before the decision went into effect.) Gilbert had won. He was a fighter. In 2022, Gilbert lost his campaign for governor and filed a lawsuit so lacking in merit that he was forced to pay around $250,000 in sanctions.

"It's these rural county sheriffs . . . that stood up for y'all, and adhere to their oath to protect their communities from all enemies foreign and domestic!" Gilbert hollered. As he spoke, he seamlessly blended concern about the 2020 election results with mask mandates, adding praise for "unmasked faces." "This can never happen again. Never again!" he concluded. He was referring specifically to COVID-related business closures and health mandates, but he was also tapping into something else, some more fundamental distrust about everyday life, whose closest representatives were elite government officials on the East Coast, which was a full three days' drive away.

Steele died of COVID in August of 2021. His final blog post, on August 17, said, "I will not take the vaccination, though I did test positive for whatever they're calling 'COVID' today."

———

Toward the end of the rally, a thirty-something sheriff named Jesse Watts took the stage. Watts was elected the sheriff-coroner of Eureka County, Nevada, in 2018 with a promise to bring transparency to the department. Despite this promise, a group of his constituents tried to recall him from office in 2020, led by the wife of the county attorney. While Watts is much shorter than some of the other sheriffs, with glasses, big ears, and a prickly beard that makes him look much younger than he is, he has a charisma when he steps onto a stage. His voice is loud and cuts through the chatter.

"All I got to say is we are here because of you. We don't answer to the president. We don't answer to the Senate. We don't answer to Congress. We don't answer to the governor. Each and every one of them can go piss up a rope!" In a flourish, he rolled up his sleeve after fidgeting only for a moment with the buttons. His forearm from elbow to wrist is tattooed with the American flag, a bald eagle, and the phrase "We the People," in Founding Father script.

"We the People made the government! The government doesn't make us. God bless you. God bless America!"

The moment would, according to Watts, go "viral on TikTok and Facebook." He would also repeat the same move at other ARISE USA! rallies throughout Nevada. When I asked him about the tattoo, he said he got it when he won his first sheriff election in 2018, but, he said, it wasn't about winning an election; it was "about the Constitution," as if that were an obvious response and not a document under limitless debate in all three branches of government.

The thing you have to understand about Richard Mack is that he sees "the sheriff" and his life's work as a divine and necessary part of a coming apocalypse in America. His vision can feel welcome in the far-right politics of violence. Far-right groups like the Oath Keepers and other militias believe in an impending civil war. Rhodes specifically believed that on January 6 he was serving as part of Trump's avenging army. People died for Trump's lost cause.

In contrast, Mack's message offers something like hope.

"The sheriffs will be the peaceful solution," Mack said, arguing that when the chips are down and militias reach for their guns, the sheriffs will mediate and prevent widespread civil war. Mack's call to sheriffs is one of peace but also assumes violence: "There is still hope to keep this revolution a peaceful one. There is a man who can stop the abuse, end the tyranny, and restore the Constitution, once again, as the supreme law of the land. Yes, it is you, SHERIFF! You can do it. You have the power, the authority, and the responsibility. You are the supreme keeper of the peace, you are the people's protector, you are the last line in the sand."

At the time I went to Battle Mountain, January 6 had come and gone. I had naively thought that "Stop the Steal" had ended. Mobs streamed into the Capitol building, sure, but the firmament of democracy held steadfast.

What I saw in Battle Mountain, however, were the people who had not forgotten. Their war was not over. They genuinely believed in the righteousness of their cause. Trump might not be in the White House, but he would be again. Biden's inauguration represented the justness of their cause, not the foolishness. Their loss, their perceived victimization, represented their strength of conviction. It was one thing to support the winner of a fight. It was quite another to believe that the fight would continue until both sides were annihilated.

---

The rain began to fall in earnest. People picked up their lawn chairs and took off.

After the events ended in Battle Mountain, I watched the West Coast militia members gather in a circle where the coffee cart had been. The leader gave a pep talk, telling everyone they had done a great job that day. "Drive home safe," he exhorted.

I went into the HideAway steak house, which was the only restaurant around and a short walk from the park. I sat next to two women in their sixties at the bar and asked if they had come from the rally. They had. "We love our sheriff," the one farthest from me said, referring to Jesse Watts of the forearm tattoo. She had short, light curly hair, styled like a halo around her face. She told me that she preferred Watts to the previous sheriff. Watts stood for something, she explained. He cared about the people of the county.

I asked the woman next to me what attracted her to Trump. She had worked in mining and as a bartender and security guard. She had strong shoulders, brown hair down to her waist under a baseball cap, and skin that wrinkled pleasantly from time in the sun. Once, when a patron bothered her while she was bartending, she threw him out the door, literally, she told me. Her complaints ran the gamut, from the "new math" in schools, to "cancel culture," to the perceived excesses of Black Lives Matter.

"But does the way Trump talk bother you?" I asked, referring to his sexism, his rudeness, his racial epithets.

She called me a snowflake.

I objected and made an argument I thought would appeal to someone who seemed independent: Why should women be forced to endure the groping and foul language of Trump?

"He's no worse than anyone else," she said.

Then we talked about hiking. I had driven through the singing sands to get to Battle Mountain.

---

The ARISE USA! tour continued throughout the summer of 2021 and made stops in other Americana places in Nevada, South Dakota, and Tennessee. The stop in Keystone, South Dakota, was billed as "the beginning of the second American Revolution," and, for $1,000, attendees could tour Deadwood and take photos with Richard Mack at Mount Rushmore. But the bus never made it as far as promised. According to a CSPOA 2021 annual report, the tour made thirty-five stops, not fifty. Members of the tour's crew allege that Steele's profligate style drained the funds and stiffed workers on their final paychecks in July of 2021.

A part of me could understand how, in this place, far from the city, at the end of a highway that was most famous as the "Loneliest Road in America," the rally was simply a community gathering of like-minded people. Everyone was jolly, talking about motorcycles and ranching. There were no counterprotesters as there were in Portland. The presence of openly carried long guns did not strike me as alarming, maybe because everyone was on the same side. The sheriffs were not a threat; they were allies. They worked with the militias to direct traffic and ensure attendees did not have their beliefs questioned. They chatted and ate together and avoided the bad weather under the same tarps. Black Lives Matter did not arrive as anticipated and feared.

Battle Mountain was one place, but it represented many places across America whose personality was now the aggressive opposite of everything the left had come to value. Restaurants demanded that patrons take off their masks or be removed. "Trump 2024" signs were abundant all around. I had a painful sense that I might be discovered at any time even as I knew my whiteness protected me from scrutiny.

At the same time, I knew that this peaceful event came at great societal cost. Across the country, Proud Boys clashed violently with antifa as law enforcement watched. Police kettled protesters demanding racial justice. Sheriffs ran jails where people died often in pretrial detention. COVID deniers refused vaccines, encouraged by events just like this one to follow their rage even if it killed them.

While the Southern Poverty Law Center and other experts in extremism point to the CSPOA as an example of anti-federalism and extremist ideology—ideas that are outside of the proper democratic process—Mack and his ideas continue to appeal to sheriffs. Unlike online conspiracy theorists or militia members, sheriffs are elected officers. They do have a lot of unchecked power. And a lot of it has been used to maintain white supremacy.

As I contemplated what shape this book would take, I felt it was vital to emphasize how the constitutional sheriff movement uses the same historical justification that many sheriffs use to explain their own powers. Most mainstream sheriffs distance themselves from Mack and constitutional sheriffs. But all sheriffs in this country benefit from the mythos of the American sheriff, which—like the history depicted on the side of the ARISE USA! bus where a cowboy, a Native American, and white settlers coexist in eternal harmony—is one where the history spoken aloud obscures the history seen in the streets, usually at the end of a gun.

In 2018, then attorney general Jeff Sessions, appointed by then president Donald Trump, gave a speech at the National Sheriffs' Association's annual meeting, where he received a small bronze sheriff statue for his work advancing sheriffs' interests. He said, "Since our founding, the independently elected Sheriff has been seen as the people's protector who keeps law enforcement close to and amenable to the people. The Sheriff is a critical part of the Anglo-American heritage of law enforcement." Many civil rights organizations objected to Sessions's speech, even as some acknowledged the truth of it. Sessions's comment, however, wasn't just about historical fact; it was about how sheriffs see themselves as part of a grand tradition based on a nostalgia that elides the history of violence toward Native people, immigrants, Black communities, and people of color.

Certainly many sheriffs, especially those who run as progressive or liberal, view themselves as distinct from Mack and his followers both in policy and in action. While they continue to see the role of sheriff as rooted in American history and deeply important to the fabric of daily life, these sheriffs are more likely to align with the consensus on the left that is pushing for community policing and diversity in hiring. During the Trump era, some sheriffs went so far as to designate their counties as "sanctuary counties," meaning they would refuse to cooperate with federal immigration authorities as part of an ongoing progressive rebellion against Trump's immigration policies.

Mack and the CSPOA are not philosophically distant from Jeff Sessions's "Anglo-American" heritage comment. The question is, are constitutional sheriffs trying to change the role into something it is not, or are they simply reflecting the truth about violence, power, and race in America? What if constitutional sheriffs are just a symptom of the sheriff persisting as an institution?

# TWO

# POSSE COMITATUS

## The History of Sheriffs

TO UNDERSTAND WHY THE PEOPLE AT BATTLE MOUNTAIN felt so devoted to their county sheriff, we need to take a quick trip through history.

Most historians credit the birth of what became the constitutional sheriff movement to a man named William Potter Gale, whose life is detailed in Daniel Levitas's book *The Terrorist Next Door*.

Born in 1916 to a Jewish immigrant father, Gale had a peripatetic career. After serving in the U.S. military during World War II, he moved to Southern California, where he met Wesley Swift, a far-right political figure who tried to revive the Ku Klux Klan in Southern California during the 1940s. In 1956, Swift ordained Gale as a minister in the Christian Identity movement, which was born of the far-right anti-communist hysteria fueled by the KKK, Christian nationalism, and McCarthy-era conspiracy theories, the same soup from which W. Cleon Skousen emerged. While Skousen was deeply influenced by LDS theology and politics, Gale plunged into militant white supremacy through a relatively new movement that blossomed in parts of Southern California: the aforementioned Christian Identity.

Gale ran for governor of California in 1957 on the "Constitution Party" ticket. His platform consisted of "states' rights," opposition to the income tax, the impeachment of President Dwight D. Eisenhower, and a return to the use of gold coins in lieu of paper money. After losing the election in a landslide, Gale became disillusioned with electoral politics. He drifted away from his family and further dedicated himself to a racist and anti-Semitic form of grassroots militia organizing.

Christian Identity was not really a religion, but it did take on the trappings of Christianity. Members believed that white people of Germanic heritage were the true chosen people of the Bible, not the Jews. Decades after Gale joined the movement, Christian Identity adherents formed an Aryan Nations white separatist compound in Idaho during the 1980s and '90s, which became a gathering place for assorted neo-Nazis, Klan members, and other white supremacy groups. Gale's ideas were deeply influenced by the white supremacist commitment to states' rights, virulent anti-Semitism, and the military vibe of groups like the Minutemen, an anti-communist militia that focused on the Second Amendment right to bear arms.

From this extremely racist and anti-Semitic mix—"If a Jew comes near you, run a sword through him," Gale once said—the Posse Comitatus movement was born.

The term "posse comitatus" predates Gale's Posse Comitatus movement by hundreds of years. The term is Latin for "the power of the county." Originating in medieval England, the posse comitatus was a group of "able-bodied" men over fifteen years old, summoned by the county sheriff to quell insurrections or deal with unsavory characters.

Traditionally, the sheriff summoned the posse through the "hue and cry." Riding through the town, the sheriff called for local residents to pick up their arms and join him in a manhunt. Some historians posit that sheriffs were originally the leaders of local militias, much like small armies entrusted with defending the local community from highway robbers or ensuring new-comers didn't get too drunk and disorderly.

The image of the posse has long held immense mythical appeal in America. According to the 1941 *Treatise on the Law of Sheriffs, Coroners, and Constables, with Forms*, written by an Idaho attorney, "[The sheriff] is also to defend his country against any of its enemies, when they come into the land; and for this purpose, as well as for keeping the peace or pursuing felony, he may command all of the people of his county to attend him; which is called the posse comitatus or the power of the county."

Most states retain a posse comitatus law on the books—some states require that citizens serve if they are summoned or else face criminal charges—and in many places, the ability to call a posse is still considered a "core, essential power of the county sheriff." In 1968, Sheriff Joseph Woods of Cook County, Illinois, interviewed hundreds of men under age forty-five to create a volunteer posse that, he said, would be used to prevent disorder at the Democratic National Convention, which roiled with antiwar protesters. "We are going to have psychological tests to help filter out sadists and kooks," the sheriff explained.

———

The idea of "posse comitatus" as an organizing principle appealed to Gale because it was militaristic, intensely local, and medieval-sounding. Law enforcement everywhere was militarizing—the first SWAT teams were created in the 1960s—and state and federal governments were becoming more involved with the funding and regulation of law enforcement. Gale, like many on the right, sought refuge in local governments, which, as the political scientist Michael Barkun explained, represented a romantic vision of a "pre-industrial past of free Aryan yeoman farmers, governing themselves under a common law." Who else could someone like Gale trust but the county sheriff?

Beginning in the 1960s, Gale organized rural white citizen groups to oppose federal authority, naming his movement Posse Comitatus, with a goal "to repudiate the unlawful acts . . . of the federal government." He recommended that communities form posse groups to serve as quasi-vigilantes, primarily for the purpose of preventing school desegregation, but also to rout out communism, which he linked to a Jewish influence on business and international politics. (Gale also opposed income taxes and was convicted of tax evasion in 1987.)

As part of this movement, Gale argued that the sheriff should be the seat of all policing and executive power in the county. In 1971, Gale defined the role of the sheriff for his adherents in his newsletter, *Identity*, which he wrote under the pseudonym Colonel Ben Cameron, the leading character in the 1915 film *The Birth of a Nation*, which infamously spread racist fears and spurred the second reincarnation of the Ku Klux Klan. There, he wrote, "The county Sheriff is the ONLY LEGAL LAW ENFORCEMENT OFFICER IN THE UNITED STATES OF AMERICA!"

The writing style, with its haphazard capitalization and arcane sentence structure, was intended to sound like legalese, giving the ideas legitimacy and a pseudo-magical quality. And, as Levitas points out, Gale's ideas were also presented in an "elaborate, American-sounding ideology that married uncompromising anti-Semitism, anticommunism, and white supremacy with the appealing notion of the extreme sovereignty of the people." Gale, much like W. Cleon Skousen would for the Mormons, interpreted the U.S. Constitution and the Bill of Rights as holy documents, subject to the same kind of literalism with which many born-again Christians treated the Bible.

Gale spread his ideas throughout the country using taped sermons and the aforementioned newsletter *Identity*. Across the Midwest, listeners were urged to "arise and fight."

One man who took the call seriously was Henry Lamont "Mike" Beach, a Portlander who would spread the constitutional sheriff ideology throughout the Pacific Northwest. Beach, like Gale, had long been attracted to far-right movements. During the 1930s, he was a member of the Silver Shirts, a pro-fascist, pro-Nazi organization. In 1973, Beach formed the Citizens Law Enforcement Research Committee (CLERC), a paramilitary organization that appealed to those who found the John Birch Society—an extremely far-right organization—too staid. In the 1970s, Beach began to encourage the formation of "Sheriff's Posse Comitatus," groups of "every able-bodied patriotic male of good character, who is interested in the preservation of law and order." He charged $21 to issue organizational charters— posses had to be at least "seven Christian men" to qualify—and $6.50 for each individual badge.

Each posse was governed by the rules set out in *Sheriff's Posse Comitatus*, nicknamed "the Blue Book," a sixteen-page pamphlet with a sheriff's star on the front cover. (Posse members pinned the same star to their jackets—big, bright stars decorated with a hangman's noose, a Bible, and a sword.) The Blue Book set forth an alternative system of governance in which the sheriff was "the only legal law enforcement officer in the United States of America. He is elected by the people and is directly responsible for law enforcement in his County. It is his responsibility to protect the people of his County from unlawful acts on the part of anyone, including officials of government." Beach's posses believed that they could ignore or violate state and federal laws, especially laws that regulated taxation, which was governed by the Sixteenth Amendment and, therefore, not originally part of the U.S. Constitution. The movement included a rejection of legal expertise, arguing that everyday citizens, not lawyers, were best positioned to interpret the law. "The Constitution is a simple document," the Blue Book said. "It says what it means and it means what it says."

Posse Comitatus groups were relatively obscure until the mid-1970s, at which point they had spread throughout the Midwest and Pacific Northwest. Their numbers were hard to estimate but probably stayed small. The group had a habit of grossly exaggerating their popularity; at one point they claimed four hundred thousand members when the number was, at best, closer to ten thousand at its peak.

Throughout the 1970s, adherents to the Sheriff's Posse Comitatus refused to pay taxes and threatened public officials with "treason trials," removal from office, and even violence. They also served as self-styled vigilantes responding to incidents when the official police were not available or willing to intervene. The FBI began to warn of these groups "setting up training facilities on farms and in rural areas" all over the country, including Louisiana, Wisconsin, California, Idaho, and, most of all, Washington State and Oregon, where Beach was based. The 1980s farm crisis, in which farm banks failed and farmers lost their land through foreclosure, created a fertile atmosphere for rural resentment to turn on the federal government. Nearly one thousand farmers across five Midwestern states committed suicide.

Local posses donned the mantle of righteousness, reacting in part to right-wing arguments that the U.S. Supreme Court under Justice Earl Warren, who was the chief justice from 1953 to 1969, cared more for the due process rights of defendants than the potential harms to "law-abiding Americans." Posse leaders claimed that they were there to fight crime and prevent a "communist takeover" of law enforcement, even though in some cases, sheriffs were not sure that they wanted their help. They echoed a lot of other far-right movements in terms of virulent opposition to the left, which represented a broad category including people of color, Jews, and their enablers. One organizer in Kansas told a reporter that people were "tired of this radical (liberal) crap. They're tired of seeing our country just given away and thrown away."

This far-right movement spread, emphasizing the county sheriff as the local law enforcement official most likely to support the Posse Comitatus's vigilante style and, as a result, to act free of federal interference. "We, in Ector County, have organized the 'Sheriff's Posse Comitatus' in order to restore constitutional government to all levels of government," wrote one leader in the local paper in 1974. While some of these groups downplayed overt white supremacy, it was implicit that "restoring the Constitution" meant returning to the Bill of Rights and voiding the post-Reconstruction amendments, the ones that freed Black Americans from enslavement, granted them the right to vote, and assured equal protection under the law.

These groups eventually got the attention of local reporters, who clamored to cover what appeared to be renegade militias. "The group believes in God, guns, and its interpretation of the U.S. Constitution," an Arizona reporter wrote in 1975. At the time, most law enforcement officials opposed the group and saw them as a threat to their safety due to Posse members' willingness to use firearms. A Northern California sheriff said he viewed them with "complete disregard and disdain."

Posse Comitatus adherents became infamous for their embrace of violence, leading to a series of dangerous encounters with law enforcement that made the news and would contribute to the movement's downfall. In the San Joaquin Valley, growers summoned members of the local Sheriff's Posse Comitatus to chase away unionizers attempting to organize agricultural workers. Actual sheriff's deputies arrived to pursue the vigilantes through tomato fields as both sides fired shotguns. One law enforcement officer was hospitalized with a concussion; police arrested three men as well as a fourteen-year-old boy, who was armed with an "AR-15 military style weapon."

In Wisconsin, a heavily armed contingent of Posse Comitatus adherents confronted an IRS agent named Fred M. Chicken, arguing that the tax assessor was enforcing "unconstitutional" laws. There were showdowns with sheriffs. In rural Oregon, posse members occupied potato sheds to "repossess" a farm purchased by a Japanese American family from a farmer who faced foreclosure. Others stockpiled firearms and conducted vigilante trials in which they would prosecute and convict government agents who failed to obey their interpretation of the Constitution.

Despite their reverence for the sheriff as an ideal, Posse Comitatus adherents were willing to implement the same violence against their favorite local official if he was unresponsive to their demands. "We like to work with the sheriff departments," one member said, "but if the sheriff department isn't upholding the law . . . we can go over their heads with grand juries." Gale wrote that citizens were entitled to form a posse and, vigilante-style, arrest, try, and execute "at high noon" government officials who violated "Natural Law" or the Constitution.

By the 1980s the Posse Comitatus movement was beginning to fade, mostly because of some high-profile shootouts. In 1983, a Posse Comitatus adherent named Gordon Kahl got into a firefight with law enforcement officials; he killed two federal marshals and hid in a fortified bunker. When law enforcement came to flush him out, the county sheriff was shot and killed. The entire building went up in flames, and Kahl's body was burned beyond recognition.

As evidence of the importance of the sheriff in these movements, in 1985 a group of "sovereign citizens"—people who believe that they are not subject to the laws of the United States—reissued the 1941 sheriff treatise with a new introduction. The authors framed the Posse Comitatus movement as a "restoration movement" to return to a government that is a "negative force." "There is already an existing method and it is just waiting for us to pick it up and put it into action. That method is to utilize the only legitimate law enforcement officer, and his support force, in America. That is, the Sheriff and Posse Comitatus," it read.

Beach, disillusioned, retired to Oregon and died in 1989. The movement largely flamed out. But its ideas planted the seed for other groups, like the militia movement, tax protesters, neo-Nazis, and sovereign citizens. In common with Posse Comitatus, these groups based their particular beliefs and actions on a strict interpretation of the Constitution, with an emphasis on Second Amendment rights, and rejected taxes and federal laws, especially those regulating the environment, landownership, and firearms. Just as the Posse Comitatus movement recruited farmers who were being dispossessed of their land, the remnants also recruited mostly white, rural people who felt as though shadowy forces—Jewish bankers, the global elite, or African Americans—were taking away what was properly theirs to own. All of these groups also had one thing in common: a reverence for the county sheriff as the only legitimate law enforcement official.

It's not a coincidence that adherents to Posse Comitatus adopted the sheriff as their ideal mode of law enforcement. While sheriffs are government actors, with responsibilities and limits defined by state law, their elected status sets them apart from other forms of law enforcement like police chiefs or state troopers. Sheriffs also have a brand image, a mystique, that is uniquely American and rooted in a medieval fantasy of Anglo-Saxon law.

As a result, the area of sheriff history is full of exaggerations, unsupported summaries, and just plain lies. Many histories of sheriffs' offices are written by sheriffs or historians with strong sheriff sympathies who have a vested interest in perpetuating the institution as one that is incorruptible and necessary. These tales tend to focus on individual sheriffs and their mighty feats, creating a family tree that emphasizes a heroic history with roots that in some cases predate the printing press.

To learn more about how constitutional sheriffs understand the history of the office generally, I called Sheriff Dar Leaf of Barry County, Michigan, who is on the board of directors for the CSPOA and works closely with Richard Mack. (More on him to come.) Even though I was a reporter working for an admittedly left-leaning publication, as soon as I mentioned that I was working on a longer book project, he sent me documents explaining the history of sheriffs. One is a PowerPoint presentation called "The American Sheriff: At the Common Law," which he described as "useful background" for my work.

The document begins with a lithograph from King Alfred the Great, who ruled the Anglo-Saxons in ninth-century England after successfully fending off Viking invaders, that touts the following virtues: "Wisdom, humility, caution, moderation, justice, mercy, discretion, constancy, benevolence, chastity and temperance." "King Alfred Effect," another slide reads, showing Barry County, Michigan, and the United States, and comparing the divisions to those of shires, or counties, in King Alfred's time. "The Office of Sheriff has existed at least as long as civilizations were ruled by a sovereign." Another slide explains, "The elected Sheriff gets powers directly from the people."

Leaf has also taught classes on the history of the sheriff, emphasizing these medieval roots and relying heavily on a Christian nationalist interpretation of U.S. law, one that, like the Posse Comitatus groups, also upholds the sheriff as the sole law enforcement capable of enforcing God's law. In this, he relies on the work of sovereign citizen groups as well as Christian dominionists—people who believe that Christians should take control of all aspects of politics and society—like Matthew Trewhella, whose book, *The Doctrine of Lesser Magistrates*, argues similarly that the sheriff "has both the God-given right and duty to refuse obedience to that superior authority; and if necessary, actively resist the superior authority." (Leaf told me he was familiar with *The Doctrine of Lesser Magistrates* but did not specifically remember the book or Trewhella.) Trewhella's group had a booth at the 2023 National Sheriffs' Association conference, and he a gave a twenty-five-minute sermon on the importance of "defying tyrants," by which he meant Democratic governors. (The NSA said he was invited, but they were not aware of the content of his sermon beforehand.)

Like the documents Leaf sent me, the websites of sheriffs' offices are rife with histories verging on the fantastical. There's a general story that most official sheriffs tell, one that situates their job as part of a distinguished lineage, predating and surpassing other forms of law enforcement. Some argue that the sheriff is "the only law enforcement mentioned in the Bible." Others point to the office's Anglo-Saxon heritage and roots in English common law to explain why sheriffs can operate with autonomy and, often, impunity. From that 1941 treatise: "A sheriff is an officer of great antiquity, dignity, trust and authority."

Sheriffs lay claim to many famous European historical documents as evidence of their antiquity, like the Magna Carta, which describes sheriffs as agents of the crown, or, as one book states, that sheriffs "virtually exercised the powers of a viceroy within the limits of his county. He received and interpreted the king's mandate not only in matters concerning the peace, but in military, fiscal, and judicial affairs as well." Some historians, like the ones Leaf cites, believe the origins of the office go back to the first millennium.

Most histories agree that the word "sheriff" is a compression of the words "shire" (county) and "reeve" (local official). These "shire reeves" operated in England and Scotland, where they acted as the local enforcement for the monarchy, mostly by collecting taxes. They were the Sheriff of Nottingham, in other words, quasi-administrative posts tasked with the unpleasant job of taking other people's money. As a 1933 treatise on rural law enforcement explains, "The power—even grandeur—of the early English sheriff is gradually worn away" as a result of industrialization and the petty corruption of power. The same document describes the decline of the sheriff as one of "demolition and the leisurely process of decay."

When Anglo settlers came to the American colonies, they imported this position and had largely appointed sheriffs, or as the 1933 treatise explains, "The American sheriff acquires new vigor and importance." Over time, the sheriff became an elected position, largely because of an American tradition of local control, and, at the same time, the colonies introduced term limits to prevent sheriffs from becoming too powerful and prone to corruption, especially because the sheriff was tasked with managing elections and collecting taxes, two jobs prone to misuse. A chronicle of North Carolina sheriffs noted, "No single officer in the county exercised such plenary executive and administrative powers as did the colonial sheriff. Nor did any other officer make for misrule and retard the colonial government quite so much as the sheriff."

Many sheriffs, including Leaf, use a quote from Thomas Jefferson as evidence of the importance of sheriffs: "The office of Sheriff is the most important of all the Executive offices of the county." While Jefferson did pen this line, it comes from a letter in which he is actually complaining about the abuse of office by local judges. The sheriff is incidental, and the quote is out of context. So far as I can tell, there is little evidence that the Founding Fathers thought much about sheriffs at all, and, certainly, law enforcement offices did not have the powers and funding that they do in the present day.

William Murfree, who wrote an early treatise on American sheriffs in 1884, also described the position as relating to King Alfred and coming from a distinguished lineage: "It has already been said that the office of sheriff is of venerable antiquity. . . . For a thousand years the sheriff has been the principal conservator of the peace in his county, with full power to command, whenever necessary, the power of the county; and it has been during all that time his function to execute the mandates of courts, and to keep securely in confinement, all such prisoners as may be committed to his charge by civil or criminal process emanating from courts of adequate jurisdiction."

In the past few years, more scholars have examined the history of police as descendants of slave patrols in the South. Sheriffs, in contrast, come from a slightly different strain. In America, the position of sheriff became more complex, powerful, and authoritative as the colonies transformed from mercantile outposts to locally run states, many remote and covering vast territory, to the country we know today. When the United States claimed additional territories on the continent through expansion and colonization, new political leaders—white men who had moved from the East seeking career advancement—wrote state constitutions hastily, often copying those of other states in order to establish governments and begin to conduct business, including the forcible relocation of non-white inhabitants.

The sheriff's job transformed as well, from tax collector to jailer to lawman. It also became an elected position, alongside other local officials, one of the ways the new American government showed the superiority of its democracy (limited to white men as it was). And there was some indication that sheriffs, as elected representatives, were considered superior—or at least different—from appointed police. The 1941 treatise explains, "In the exercise of executive and administrative functions, in conserving the public peace, in vindicating the law, and in presenting the rights of the government he (the sheriff) represents the sovereignty of the State and he has no superior in the county."

Two important developments contributed to the rise of sheriffs as a distinct style of policing. One was the role of the sheriff as "principal conservator of the peace." Unlike slave patrols, which hunted down enslaved people seeking freedom, or night watchmen, which was the typical law enforcement in cities, sheriffs saw their role as serving the residents—the white, Anglo ones—against all sorts of threats. During the westward expansion, those threats included Native Americans, Mexicans, and so-called cattle rustlers and train thieves. The Western United States was vast, so the job of the sheriff became attached to the land itself; hence, the connection to the county, rather than to settlements or cities. This still holds immense allure for the right, which lionizes the imagined frontier and demonizes urban landscapes, both appealing to the mythology of the American settler as a white man who seeks (and finds) freedom and an imagined empty landscape of the West.

A second influence on the upward trajectory of the sheriffs was the rise of Jacksonian Democracy during the 1800s as the nation defined itself as a country, expanded westward through genocidal warfare, crafted a history, and sought to legitimize chattel slavery before the inevitable war. Americans saw themselves as standard-bearers for democracy. Sheriffs became part of this reimagining. As one treatise explains, "The widespread enthusiasm for local popular election which came to be applied throughout the list of county officers gradually wore away the ancient tradition [of appointment]."

President Andrew Jackson, while not a sheriff, reflected the rise of the American masculine ideal, a farmer, soldier, and general who worked the land and upheld the values of self-sufficiency and independence. Those who worked the land were the "chosen people" who were self-governing and had rights; they were also only white men. The frontier was available for exploitation, and the people who policed it were the sheriffs.

Murfree described the elected position in terms that mirrored Jacksonian ideals of representative democracy, with common law powers emerging directly from white male voters. "The sheriff is, in each of the United States, a constitutional officer recognized as part of the machinery of the state government," he explained. "And therefore, although it is competent for legislatures to add to his powers or exact from him the performance of additional duties, it is, upon well-established legal principles, beyond their power to circumscribe his common law functions or to transfer them to other officers."

This idea of the sheriff remained consistent through time even as other types of law enforcement agencies formed. Fifty years after Murfree, legal experts would write that the sheriff "is the chief law enforcement officer in the county today even as he was at common law. His jurisdiction is coextensive within the county including all municipalities and townships."

Elected sheriffs also reflected how the West and South would come to be defined as both democratic and racist, withholding civil rights from Native Americans, Mexicans, Chinese immigrants, and Black Americans while claiming fairness through the enfranchisement of white men. Local democracy, the ability of counties and states to decide for themselves how to govern, legitimized chattel slavery as a "choice" made by the real Americans. Both the 1830 Indian Removal Act and the formation of the Republic of Texas in 1836 reflected the ways in which the American West adopted many of the white supremacist ideas of the slaveholding South.

Sheriffs—white-hatted and often on a horse—elided with other popular Western figures, the cowboy and the outlaw, and became fixtures in the American mythology of masculine independence. The historian Frederick Jackson Turner famously argued that the West and its ever-expanding frontier (in his eyes) produced the principles of America, the same ideas of pioneer-style self-sufficiency that Gale would draw from for his Posse Comitatus.

———

Richard Mack entered the far-right milieu just as the Posse Comitatus movement was fading. As Mack's infamous lawsuit over the Brady Bill worked its way through the courts during the 1990s, the federal government, newly attuned to the threat posed by far-right groups, engaged in multiple violent encounters with the rising tide of extremists. These incidents, which further radicalized the far right and turned them against federal law enforcement, contributed to Mack's radicalization and gave legitimacy to his nascent constitutional sheriff movement.

In 1992, U.S. Marshals engaged in an eleven-day standoff with Randy Weaver and his family, white separatists living in Idaho, because Weaver had failed to appear in court on a charge of selling illegal firearms. The tragic incident, which came to be known as Ruby Ridge, ended in the deaths of Weaver's son and wife, who was holding her infant daughter when a sniper shot her. A federal agent was also killed in the confrontation.

Ruby Ridge catalyzed the far right; it was also an inspirational event for Richard Mack, who would write the preface for one of Weaver's books about the standoff and defended Weaver's beliefs, using his influence to paint over Weaver's white supremacy, even going so far as to compare Weaver to Rosa Parks. He once told a reporter, "All [Randy Weaver] wanted was to live with his family and be left alone. He has nothing against any race." Mack then put the reporter on the phone with Weaver, who called himself a "racist" and began to rail against then president Barack Obama for being a "bigot." Mack clamored to take the phone back and distance himself from Weaver, setting up a pattern that would repeat to the present day: "My views are not his views, and I don't want to accept responsibility for his views."

In 1993, federal agencies botched a fifty-one-day siege of the Branch Davidian compound in Waco, Texas, which ended in a fire that killed more than seventy Branch Davidians, including roughly two dozen children. The Branch Davidians were a cult led by the charismatic David Koresh, who was allegedly sexually abusing children and stockpiling illegal weapons. The ATF, tipped off by a UPS worker who found a box containing grenades, had hoped to arrest Koresh and seize the illegal weapons to prevent violence. It was the local sheriff who negotiated the ceasefire. Mack claimed that, had the sheriff handled the situation from start to finish, no one would have died: "If the sheriffs had remained in charge in both of those locations, we never would have heard of David Koresh or Randy Weaver, and the law still would have been enforced and obeyed."

In a devastating culmination of far-right radicalization, in 1995, a military veteran named Timothy McVeigh, enraged by Ruby Ridge and the Waco siege, bombed a federal building in Oklahoma City, Oklahoma, killing at least 168 people, including 19 children. While McVeigh was not in a militia, he was familiar with many of the same ideas as William Potter Gale, political talking points he mostly absorbed by attending gun shows across the country, which trafficked in many anti-government ideas, and by listening to Rush Limbaugh's caustic radio show, which mainstreamed much of the same.

After the Oklahoma City bombing, the Senate Judiciary Subcommittee on Terrorism held a hearing to discuss militias as a terrorism threat. While the successful prosecution was narrowly focused on McVeigh and his co-conspirators, the bombing was serious enough that far-right groups began to shy away from violence. Militias scattered, and few were willing to be associated with such an act of terror. Federal, state, and local law enforcement focused on far-right groups as a threat until 9/11 moved all resources to focus on terrorism from abroad.

Richard Mack and the CSPOA's beliefs flowed directly from this history of the far right in America. These groups, which all believed that the county sheriff was the only legitimate law enforcement, caused massive numbers of fatalities and were often in conflict with law enforcement on the federal, state, and local levels. The encounters with federal law enforcement at events like Waco and Ruby Ridge only proved to these adherents that the government could not be trusted.

———

Another legacy of William Potter Gale and the Posse Comitatus movement that Mack would adopt for his own constitutional sheriff ideology were the two theories of nullification and interposition. Both ideas justify resistance to the federal government, historically as a means to preserve chattel slavery and segregation. In essence, these legalistic theories are based on a reading of the Constitution and select writings by the Founding Fathers that argue states are entitled to resist or nullify laws that contradict the Constitution. As opposed to a court order declaring a law unconstitutional, nullification and interposition refer to the act of refusing to follow the law in question.

While backers of nullification argue the Founding Fathers intended states to have this right, there is little support for the doctrine enduring as actual law. Thomas Jefferson did talk about nullification in a 1798 draft, writing that states could determine that a federal law was "unauthoritative, void, and of no force," but no state adopted it as law. In 1809, the U.S. Supreme Court delivered the deathblow to nullification in a case called *United States v. Peters*. Chief Justice John Marshall wrote for the majority, "If the legislatures of the several States may, at will, annul the judgments of the courts of the United States, and destroy the rights acquired under those judgments, the Constitution itself becomes a solemn mockery, and the nation is deprived of the means of enforcing its laws by the instrumentality of its own tribunals." Despite what seems like clear authority to the contrary, proslavery politicians continued to argue nullification was a viable legal doctrine.

Nullification's main backer was former senator and vice president South Carolinian John C. Calhoun, who dedicated his life to justifying the enslavement of Black Americans—calling it a "positive good"—through nullification. As two political scientists wrote: "All subsequent advocates of nullification, however fond of quoting Jefferson, depend on Calhoun whether they recognize it or not." Under Calhoun's vision of democracy, allowing the majority of people to determine the future of slavery was undemocratic because it suppressed the will of a powerful minority—slave owners. He argued in front of the U.S. Senate that states should adopt nullification to protect the interests of slavers.

While Calhoun's method did not carry the day, it did force the federal government to compromise, which he considered enough encouragement to continue to press the idea of nullification as a form of "concurrent government" to protect the "different interests, orders, classes, or portions, into which the community may be divided." In other words, nullification remained a way for Southern planters to retain control when faced with a federal government that sought to limit slavery as an institution. This was immensely appealing to the Confederacy, which would lose the fight to retain slavery if democracy ruled the day. Nullification supporters borrowed the word "liberty," but it was plainly never used to support the liberty of Black Americans. "This is not mere hypocrisy," two political scientists explain, "but connected with the very nature of nullification."

Far-right groups continued to borrow the language of nullification when faced with the reality of a pluralistic democracy. Nullification had the benefit of being color-blind on its face, but it clearly came from and bolstered a system in which some races did not have the same rights as others. William F. Buckley, the famous thought-leader of the right and founder of the *National Review*, wrote, "It is more important for any community, anywhere in the world, to affirm and live by civilized standards, than to bow to the demands of the numerical majority." Nullification came back in 2013 as a theory to defeat the Affordable Care Act, and the Cato Institute even supported limited, but not total, nullification authority by the states.

The idea persists as a far-right fairy tale, promising a way for local officials when faced with changing demographics and a popular will that runs contrary to their own views to subjugate residents to a vision of the U.S. Constitution rooted in white supremacy and Christianity. When the government passes laws contrary to the plain text of the Constitution—a process not unlike the "textualism" of modern legal scholars—or the law appears to violate Christian morality—such as laws that legalize abortion or protect the rights of LGBTQ+ Americans—local government, especially sheriffs, can refuse to enforce such laws because, Mack argues, they answer to the greater good or higher law.

At its core, nullification is undemocratic, as the CSPOA's website states, "The law enforcement powers held by the sheriff supersede those of any agent, officer, elected official or employee from any level of government when in the jurisdiction of the county." While constitutional sheriffs would argue that this power is inherent in the elected nature of the sheriff, it ignores the checks and balances system of government, especially the legislative branch. In fact, nullification is particularly hostile to lawyers and anyone claiming expertise in the law. Mack has frequently dismissed the views of lawyers when they contradict his views. Dar Leaf sent me a booklet by the National Liberty Alliance—which advocates for constitutional sheriffs—called the *County Sheriff's Handbook*, which says, "If a Sheriff must depend upon a lawyer to determine the Law, it's no different than giving up their responsibility and breaking their oath."

While he does not emphasize this often, Mack dismisses lawsuits as ineffectual, even though he filed one himself. He argues, somewhat paradoxically, that the decision in the *Printz* case supports nullification and interposition, although he also argues that courts do not have the sole authority to interpret law. He has even asserted that law enforcement can use their power to arrest as a way to physically stop government actors: "And even if a court tells me I can't stand in their way . . . I'll stand in their way. . . . And you know what? Maybe I'll give him a tour of the Mack hotel [meaning the county jail] and let him see what that's like."

To support his position, Mack frequently turns to Martin Luther King Jr.'s "Letter from Birmingham Jail," in which the civil rights leader writes, "I would be the first to advocate obeying just laws. One has not only a legal but a moral responsibility to obey just laws. Conversely, one has a moral responsibility to disobey unjust laws." But King is quite clear he does not mean nullification, which he specifically cites as a tactic used by those who resist desegregation. Instead, King is referring to the act of civil disobedience, which he clearly distinguishes as an individual objection to a law on moral grounds: "In no sense do I advocate evading or defying the law, as would the rabid segregationist. That would lead to anarchy. One who breaks an unjust law must do so openly, lovingly, and with a willingness to accept the penalty."

Alongside nullification, the constitutional sheriffs have also argued that the county sheriff can stand between county residents and the federal or state government, called "interposition." Interposition is closely related to nullification, and they are sometimes used interchangeably. Interposition supporters point to James Madison's 1798 Virginia Resolutions that "called on states to 'interpose for arresting the progress of the evil,'" but political scientists counter with the fact that Madison later repudiated nullification and interposition.

Interposition, like nullification, appeared after the ruling in *Brown v. Board of Education* that required school desegregation and was epitomized by the "massive resistance" movement as local officials across the South refused to comply with court orders to desegregate schools and other public places. Mack appears fond of the term because it calls to mind a group of citizens— a posse—physically interposing between residents and federal law enforcement. Take a comment he made to the Marshall Project in 2022: "If we had officers who interposed, George Floyd would still be alive." He seems to imply that interposition means something more like "intervention," but he is eliding the meaning of the word in order to minimize its racist origins.

In fact, interposition was a talking point for Southern political leaders— nearly every Southern congressperson signed the 1956 Southern Manifesto opposing school desegregation—and multiple states passed resolutions calling the historic *Brown* court ruling "null and void." The segregationist editor of the *Richmond News Leader*, James Kilpatrick, wrote the most lasting justification for interposition in the 1950s, encouraging Southern leaders to resist the Supreme Court under the rhetoric of states' rights. In 1955 he laid out the "right of interposition," mustering historical evidence to justify Virginia's resistance to desegregation, which, through interposition, would "[elevate] this controversy from the region field of segregation to the transcendent national field of State sovereignty." (He also called Black people an "inferior race.") In 1956, the Virginia legislature passed, by a near-unanimous vote, a resolution "interposing the sovereignty of Virginia against encroachment upon the reserved powers of this State." A report in 1957 argued that interposition made sense because there was "good reason" to have segregated schools for white and Black children.

Interposition remains core to the constitutional sheriff movement, and Richard Mack has been clear that—even though he tones down Calhoun's overt racism—he means states' rights and local control. In his book *Are You a David?*, which casts county sheriffs as the brave biblical David facing down almighty federal government authority, he wrote, "We must have the courage to interpose, intervene, and interfere!" In Mack's version, these are the solemn duties of the sheriff: "We must erect the barriers and keep those at bay who would confiscate bank accounts, guns, land, property, and children. Sheriff, you are the people's sworn protector."

As Mack wrote, the sheriff must "interpose between the people and the government," especially when the FBI, IRS, or "any other alphabet soup bureaucracy" comes calling. He means it literally. In one oft-used example, he praises an Indiana sheriff named Brad Rogers who "interposed" between a dairy farmer and the FDA, which had fined the farmer for illegally selling unpasteurized milk. In another example, a Texas sheriff bragged that he "interposed" between the Secret Service and a resident investigated for threats against President Joe Biden.

There is also a veiled threat of violence implicit in nullification and interposition; as Mack says, "I guarantee you the federal government . . . they do not want to fight with the sheriffs." Law professor Jared Goldstein points out in his work that nullification justifies all sorts of anti-government violence: "Insurrection thus is simply nullification performed at the most local level of all: the individual citizen." As this book will discuss in chapters 7 and 8, Mack's nullification theory, especially when applied to gun laws and militias, justifies vigilante violence against both government actors and some private citizens.

Contrary to the assertions of Mack and other constitutional sheriffs, there is no argument that interposition or nullification are not antidemocratic and anti-equality. While some of the sheriffs, including Mack, use interposition to justify resistance to gun laws, not desegregation, he is wrong to say that the doctrine has ever been anything but deeply racist. Despite some writers and scholars who might claim that left-wing resistance, like the nonenforcement of marijuana laws, which mostly rely on noncooperation, constitutes something like interposition, there is just no evidence this is so. It's important to bear this in mind throughout the book because the false claims that interposition and nullification are grounded in history and are race-neutral—like the office of sheriff itself—are a main reason why the constitutional sheriff movement has been so successful. Constitutional sheriffs argue that they are resisting tyranny and restoring the original purpose of the Constitution when they interpose; they do not see what they do as rebellion. To the contrary, they see their purpose as respectable and within the bounds of ordinary governance.

In a 1981 interview with a political scientist, GOP strategist Lee Atwater explained what became known as the Republican "southern strategy." "You start out in 1954 by saying, 'n——, n——, n——,'" he said. "By 1968 you can't say 'n——'—that hurts you, backfires. So you say stuff like, uh, forced busing, states' rights, and all that stuff, and you're getting so abstract."

After Oklahoma City, far-right movements took the Atwater strategy seriously and tried to minimize the overt racism of groups like Gale's Christian Identity flock. This included uplifting Black members of far-right movements and casting anti-government attitudes as consistent with civil rights. In 1995, the Senate Judiciary Subcommittee on Terrorism held hearings on the militia movement, which included famous white militia leaders like John Trochmann and Norman Olson as well as James Johnson, a Black militia leader from Ohio who described the movement as "the civil rights movement of the 1990s." According to Michael German, who was once an undercover FBI agent who infiltrated far-right groups and now works for the Brennan Center for Justice, the new militias laundered their old far-right ideology through ostensibly "color-blind" issues like immigration, federal land use, and the Second Amendment.

In forming the constitutional sheriff movement, Mack adopted the same method, concealing white supremacy as "color-blindness" and distaste for equal rights as opposition to federal intervention. The results, however, have been consistent with far-right goals. Mack has rejected LGBTQ+ rights, arguing they are being "shoved down" people's throats. He has complained about the IRS—the "American Gestapo"—the FBI, regulatory agencies like the FDA, and the Securities and Exchange Commission.

Unlike many other far-right movements—Johnson, the militia leader, said, "People are tired of being terrorized by law enforcement"—Mack specifically targeted active sheriffs and other like-minded police professionals. He was united in this cause with an ex-cop from Arizona named Jack McLamb, who formed the Police Against the New World Order in the 1990s, an organization that believed communists had infiltrated law enforcement around the country. "God is gone from government," McLamb said, "the scum of law enforcement has risen to the top."

In 1992, McLamb published his most popular work, *Operation Vampire Killer 2000: American Police Action Plan for Stopping World Government Rule.* The seventy-five-page booklet regurgitates anti-Semitic conspiracy theories, accusing federal officials of "treason" and linking the Clintons to "globalists" in a plot to take over the United States and install an anti-Christian regime. He writes, "The main goal of this special police publication will be to promote an active program that will defend America from those at work forming an oligarchy of Imperialism against this nation of free people. The here-in described plan to halt this unAmerican activity can succeed only with the combined efforts of the People's Protectors (the Police, Guardsmen and Military) and their countrymen in the private sector."

Mack and McLamb often appeared together, since they were both avid supporters of unfettered gun access and ran in the same survivalist circuit, which picked up steam in the 1990s as Y2K approached. By 1999, McLamb had helped found a utopian, all-white community in Idaho called Doves of the Valley. Mack at that point had decided to go a different route, one in which he skirted associations with direct violence and overt white supremacy and focused instead on the sheriff as a mediating figure. While McLamb stood alongside Randy Weaver at Ruby Ridge, Mack only appeared after the fact when it was clear that federal law enforcement had blundered in shooting Weaver's wife and son. In this way, Mack was able to present his ideas as more palatable to the mainstream right. As an example, I once asked Mack about Timothy McVeigh's views, and he responded, "I have heard you say horrible things before, but this one goes way too extreme. Comparing . . . Randy Weaver to McVeigh is beyond absurd."

It's worth pointing out that Mack didn't find it that absurd in the months right after Oklahoma City. Then still a sheriff, he went on CNN and, while he condemned the loss of innocent life, he argued that the biggest threat was the federal government, who would use the bombing as a pretext to go after militias. He then claimed that he received a fax (Mack told me it was a phone call) saying that McVeigh "would only talk to Mack." This conversation did not materialize.

—————

As Mack was developing and refining his ideas, always changing them to fit the current political moment, other states also were experimenting with versions of localism that echoed the Posse Comitatus movement. One was the "county movement," sometimes called the "county supreme" movement, which was a loosely organized far-right movement that "promotes increased power for county government and decreased federal authority." These groups, mostly in the West, turned their focus to returning federal lands to county control. They also encouraged the passage of resolutions that gave county officials the right to block the federal government from collecting taxes or enforcing other laws, namely gun laws.

Like the preceding far-right movements, county supreme hailed the sheriff as the only law enforcement official capable of making righteous decisions. This usually included supporting ranchers and opposing environmental groups as well as backing anti-federal sentiment. The Montana state legislature even proposed a "sheriff empowerment" bill that would require federal law enforcement to register with the local sheriff before entering their jurisdiction. The governor killed it. In 1995, Representative Helen Chenoweth of Idaho floated a federal law that would require all federal agents "to get written permission from county sheriffs before taking action." Chuck Schumer, then a House representative from New York, called it "loony."

These county movements were rather fringe, but they did coincide with the mainstream revival of states' rights as a threat to federalism. The National Conference of State Legislatures even published a report in 1995 in which they warned that such local movements could succeed "because so many state officials are angry."

Unlike the more violent far-right movements, the county movement was diffuse enough that it remained in the political atmosphere, where it became a component of the populist, far-right Tea Party movement in 2009. The Tea Party took on many of the nationalist white power ideas from Posse Comitatus, combined them with localism, and, aided by large financial backers, sought to transform the Republican Party. One of the first Tea Party candidates was Ron Paul, a key figure for both Stewart Rhodes and Richard Mack. The election of Barack Obama as the first Black president, as well as his use of federal power to expand health care access, allowed the Tea Party to grow from grassroots to the mainstream GOP.

That year, Mack began speaking at local Tea Party groups about the threat of the federal government, even going so far as to argue on InfoWars that sheriffs needed citizen-backed militias. He argued that sheriffs were key to resisting Obama's federal government. Standing with Rhodes, Mack told an audience of believers, "This is a battle for our country, our Constitution, our nation. The fate of our country does not lie with Barack Obama. It lies with us. It lies with you, the boss of your sheriff, who has the authority, the duty, the jurisdictional responsibility to protect you from all enemies both foreign and domestic."

In a 2010 video, Mack stands in Arizona with scenes of rugged mountains and a soaring eagle, talking about the United Nations and gun control. "How do we stop the tyranny of Washington, D.C.?" he asks his imagined audience. "I totally believe in jury nullification, sheriff nullification, and state nullification," he says, announcing the "sheriff convention" to make them "constitutional sheriffs" and teach about the Tenth Amendment, the "states' rights" amendment that the Confederacy used to justify the Civil War.

In 2011, Mack formally created the Constitutional Sheriffs and Peace Officers Association as a vessel to recruit law enforcement to the far right by appealing to the long-standing history of the sheriff as a common law institution. In the founding documents, he points to sheriffs as the "solution" to the problem of an increasingly diverse—and less Christian—America. "We will take America back, Sheriff by Sheriff, County by County, State by State," reads a CSPOA pamphlet. And just a year later, Mack held the first CSPOA conference in Las Vegas. He claimed he already had five hundred sheriff followers.

In *The County Sheriff: America's Last Hope*, Mack outlines the main ideas of the constitutional sheriff movement. He writes, "The COUNTY SHERIFF is our nation's LAST LINE OF DEFENSE, for the preservation and return to fundamental and individual liberty. Sheriff, you are the people's last hope. When you connect with this astounding truth, your people in your county or parish reconnect with freedom. This principle is what makes the position of sheriff such a high and noble office."

---

Mack's 2021 ARISE USA! tour was a call to sheriffs as well as a call to the people. While much has been written about how the far right recruits using social media, Mack and his allies use an old-fashioned method, something more akin to a tent revival. For the people of Battle Mountain, like in many rural places, it meant something for Mack to come to town with his ostentatious blue buses.

That year was actually not the first time Mack had tried to implement the constitutional county strategy. In late 2014, when it looked like Hillary Clinton would become president in 2016, Mack proposed the "Constitutional County Project," which the (now defunct) website described as "Restoring American Liberty . . . one county at a time." His first target, intended to serve as a "blueprint," was Navajo County, Arizona, which is mostly tribal land, something Mack does not address. "I am moving there to run for sheriff," he told a small crowd in Washington State, who applauded this announcement. This was new information for the actual sheriff, a Democrat who, after his retirement in 2019, would campaign against far-right candidates running for office in Arizona.

Mack continued, calling the project a movement toward "state sovereignty": "We're going to give this one more try. The election is in 2016. I'm going to be moving there in spring of 2015 so I can start getting ready for this." The project never got off the ground.

His method, in-person pleas that resemble medicine shows, is not incidental to the ideology. Mack's appeal rests on nostalgia—nostalgia for a time before modernity, even before civil rights. It's nostalgia for the Revolutionary War era, a time when kings were tyrants and the only person you could trust was the county sheriff. The wistful longing is not for peace, however; it is a longing for the blood of tyrants, for a cause that the people can get behind. Hence all of the military symbolism, the militias, the guns, the flags, the protests. The appeal was both the American tradition of rebellion and violence and deep patriotism for the country and what it could be. Embedded in that nostalgia is a deep denial over how the country of America came to be through genocidal violence and land theft.

For the people who attended the ARISE USA! tour, the idea of a constitutional county was a logical extension of the Posse Comitatus movement, adapted to the modern time and imbued with a sense of urgency. Like other, similar rural movements—the patriot movement, tax-resister movement, and sovereign citizen movement—constitutional sheriffs and their supporters argued that government should be centered at the county level. In essence, county commissioners were more powerful than the United States Congress or the state legislature. And above everyone else was the county sheriff, something like a cross between a knight and a king. According to Mack's 2009 book, *The County Sheriff*, "The federal government, the White House, or Congress do not hire us, they cannot fire us, and they cannot tell us what to do."

# THREE

# "THERE'S [NOT OFTEN]
# A NEW SHERIFF IN TOWN"

## *Sheriffs as Politicians*

ON A HUMID SEPTEMBER MORNING IN WASHINGTON, D.C., Trump stood for a planned media event, backed by almost four dozen sheriffs, who had come to the White House at his invitation, jittery with excitement to meet the president of the United States in person.

The then sheriff Thomas Hodgson of Massachusetts, who has a bristle-comb mustache and wears a bedazzled dress uniform with military flair, presented Trump with a plaque and praised him for his "strength of purpose" and "commitment to his convictions," specifically referring to the Trump administration's extremely punitive policy toward immigrants, including the campaign promise to build a wall between the U.S. and Mexico, limits on asylum seekers, and the president's inflammatory, racist rhetoric.

The sheriff added that the National Sheriffs' Association "has done a crowdfunding page . . . to build [the border] wall." The website, SheriffsWall .org, which no longer exists, took in around $25,000 in tax-deductible donations that never made its way to the federal government. During Trump's presidency, Hodgson sent a series of unctuous emails to immigration czar Stephen Miller, reporting his own church for distributing pamphlets in Spanish that, he said, gave advice to undocumented people on how to avoid

ICE detention. He even offered a "chain gang" of detainees to help Trump "build the wall."

The then president accepted the plaque from Hodgson as a token of appreciation from sheriffs nationwide for Trump's "strong leadership."

The inscription: "There's a new sheriff in town."

"We've got your back, Mr. President," Hodgson concluded as the rows of sheriffs puffed their chests and stood for a photo op behind the president and Vice President Mike Pence.

Holding the plaque, Trump did not praise law enforcement heroics or spout bromides about funding better local police. Instead, he complained about the "dishonest press," backed by a cadre of smiling, star-adorned sheriffs nodding vigorously in approval.

————

The press conference was winding down when a reporter in the audience asked about an anonymous *New York Times* op-ed. The piece, titled "I Am Part of the Resistance Inside the Trump Administration," was written by a staffer (later revealed to be Miles Taylor, chief of staff in the Department of Homeland Security) to explain why he and others were staying to work for the federal government despite the erratic behavior of the commander in chief.

Trump paused, pleased to have a captive audience. "Sheriffs, can you imagine this," he said. "We have someone from what I like to call the failing *New York Times* that's talking about he's part of the resistance in the Trump administration." He pulled wrinkled paper from his pocket and read from a highlighted portion that touted his successes in ending budget gridlock, creating jobs, and lowering unemployment. The sheriffs clapped and whistled and hooted. This was the Trump they were hoping to see.

"You poke the bear, the bear pokes back," one sheriff later told the *Washington Post* in praise of Trump's unscripted attacks.

Trump had more meetings at the White House with sheriffs than any other president in American history. During his four years in office, he held over a dozen televised roundtables to talk to sheriffs about immigration and border security as well as topics like housing insecurity, fentanyl importation and use, and mental health in county jails. Such meetings do not even include the many times Trump appeared with sheriffs onstage at rallies or other campaign events.

In terms of dollar amounts, the Trump administration actually defunded law enforcement, giving less money to local law enforcement through federal programs than the later Biden administration. On his way out the door, Trump proposed cutting an additional $244 million from a program that distributed money to local law enforcement, including sheriffs. During the 2020 campaign, Biden argued that Trump cut around half a billion dollars from federal programs that go to local law enforcement agencies.

But politically Trump emboldened sheriffs. There were his words—suggesting that law enforcement should not "be too nice" to criminal suspects and calling police "great people." Trump also tried to connect his Democratic opponent to progressives who sought to reduce police funding, even though Biden never said he wanted to defund the police in any way. In this task, Trump got a lot of help from sheriffs and other law enforcement who were eager to ensure that Democrats did not come into power and threaten their claims to righteousness.

Trump's administration reversed many of the Obama-era police reforms and eliminated or did not use federal accountability mechanisms, allowing sheriffs to operate without consequences. The Department of Justice under Trump ceased implementing consent decrees, a mechanism the Obama administration used to force law enforcement departments to reform. The Trump administration restarted the 1033 program, allowing law enforcement departments to purchase military-grade weapons on the cheap.

Further, Trump relaxed Obama-era rules governing jail standards, and he expanded the use of civil asset forfeiture, which involves taking property or money without a criminal conviction. The then president even said he would use some of the funds to build that border wall. When a Texas sheriff told Trump that a particular state legislator was trying to limit asset forfeiture, Trump offered to "destroy his career." The sheriffs in attendance laughed.

Most important—and more lastingly—Trump gave sheriffs the spiritual boost they needed and promoted many of the ideals of constitutional sheriffs within the federal government. Much as Richard Mack took the ideas behind Posse Comitatus and applied them to law enforcement, Trump's tough-guy, xenophobic, and conspiracy-minded persona gave sheriffs a new model in the White House. He mainstreamed the diminishment of federal agencies. The GOP under Trump lurched dramatically to the right, part of a decades-long political project that has shifted the Overton window such that all the Republican politicians seeking the presidency agreed on limiting federal power as a matter of party principle. Some even suggested eliminating federal agencies and expanding local power.

Trump accelerated constitutional sheriff discourse, which is now a part of day-to-day conversation in a way William Potter Gale could not have imagined. Under Trump, constitutional sheriffs had a friend and protector at the highest level of government. Even when Trump lost the 2020 election, his brand was so strong that sheriffs continued to run for office based on their support for the ex-president. The consequences of this are still unfolding.

---

While 1964 presidential candidate Arizonan Barry Goldwater represented the rise of the West in modern politics—there was even a campaign sheriff's star reading "Goldwater in '64"—it was Ronald Reagan who was one of the first modern presidents to talk to sheriffs directly. In 1984, Reagan addressed the National Sheriffs' Association and gave a speech in which he recalled the romance of Hollywood Westerns: "You know, in America's frontier days the sheriff's badge was the symbol of our nation's quest for law and justice. And today that badge still stands for commitment to the law and dedication to justice." There was even a button with a sheriff badge that read "Reagan's Posse '84."

Recalling his acting career, Reagan joked about how he once played a television sheriff "who thought he could do the job without a gun." Such a sheriff was a fantasy, he continued. The 1980s "crime wave" required a more violent kind of policing, one that sheriffs were uniquely able to handle.

During the same speech, Reagan blamed "a liberal social philosophy" for creating a "hardened criminal class." He praised sheriffs for "carrying out a new mandate from the American people . . . that utterly rejects the counsels of leniency toward criminals and the liberal philosophy that fostered it." And he praised sheriffs for grassroots anti-crime programs like the Neighborhood Watch program, which is still run by the National Sheriffs' Association.

Sheriffs historically were not involved in national politics; their elections instead relied on local affiliations and name recognition, not party platform. While the vast majority of states have partisan sheriff elections—meaning sheriffs run as Democrats or Republicans—sheriff elections (or reelections in most cases) rely on incumbency more than any other factor. Over half of all sheriff elections are not contested, and 90 percent of the time the incumbent wins.

There is not a lot of data on how people choose their sheriff, but one study that looked at local news found that, at least before Trump, sheriffs ran based on experience. Most sheriffs, in fact, not only have previous experience working in the office they run, they often went to high school in the same county where they work, which means they tend to have deep roots in the community. This ends up being a complicating factor in electing sheriffs who reflect the changing politics of a community because of, say, immigration

trends or urban workers moving to suburban counties. In these places, sheriffs often remain white and conservative even as their constituents become
more diverse and progressive.

As the GOP shifted to embrace the Southern strategy in the 1960s, appealing to pro-segregationists and anti–federal government types, and the
Democratic Party became the party of civil rights, Southern Democrat sheriffs remained in office (and remained Democrats) precisely due to this incumbency advantage. According to political science researcher Michael Zoorob,
this "delayed realignment" with national politics meant that the party of a
county's sheriff was generally unrelated to presidential voting patterns. For
example, in Loudoun County, Virginia, a fast-growing suburb of Washington, D.C., the sheriff Mike Chapman won reelection as an incumbent Republican even though the county voted overwhelmingly Democrat in national
and local elections.

This changed in 2016 with the election of Donald Trump. There was a
distinct difference. Many political observers noted that Trump had brought
together disparate factions of the right, but he also embraced a populist ethos
that happened to mesh very well with the mythos of the sheriff as larger-
than-life and above the law. Every constitutional sheriff rally I attended included large numbers of pro-Trump flags, including slogans like "Trump
2024," "Make America Great," and "God Guns and Trump." Sheriffs repeatedly praised Trump for his dedication to law enforcement, good governance,
and tough-guy personality.

This support was backed up by numbers. During both his 2016 and
2020 campaigns, members of law enforcement, particularly sheriffs, supported the Republican candidate in unprecedented numbers. There was also
a simple geographic explanation for sheriffs' support of Trump. Eighty percent of all counties voted for Trump. Even though those counties did not
represent a majority of the population, it did mean that 80 percent of all

sheriffs held office in Trump country. This created disproportionate representation when Trump stood with dozens of sheriffs because it created a picture of more support than the one-term president actually had.

According to one study, Trump garnered the most law enforcement support ,than any American presidential candidate ever. He even obtained the endorsement of the three-hundred-thousand-member-strong Fraternal Order of Police—which had declined to endorse Mitt Romney—alongside the union for New York City police. (All this despite the fact that Trump and the GOP have never supported public-sector unions.) While the National Sheriffs' Association does not endorse presidential candidates, many state sheriff organizations did, as did individual sheriffs, including notably public (and often polarizing) sheriffs like infamous Arizona sheriff Joe Arpaio, Milwaukee sheriff David Clarke, and Massachusetts sheriff Thomas Hodgson.

Sheriffs have long seen their office as populist. They view themselves as the original "community policing" because sheriffs are indeed required to make a name for themselves locally, which generally includes many meetings with constituents. As Sheriff Brad Rogers of Indiana—now no longer a sheriff but still a member of the CSPOA advisory board—once said, "I'm answerable to the people. I have a face and name. Try asking the federal government for a face and a name." The National Sheriffs' Association has echoed the same point, writing that sheriff elections are "consistent with our Nation's democratic traditions and historical political practices."

The general lack of requirements to run for office means that sheriffs can be, well, anyone. As mentioned above, the main requirement everywhere is that sheriffs must live in the county where they seek election. Some states forbid people running for sheriff if they have felony convictions. Others disqualify sheriffs who have committed crimes of "moral turpitude" or require "good moral character," both of which are difficult to define. But some do not.

Only a handful of states require any law enforcement experience or training for sheriff candidates. California is among the states that require the most experience, at least one to five years of hands-on work, combined with educational requirements. While most sheriffs must obtain some sort of basic certification in order to be qualified to carry a firearm and make arrests, in many states, sheriffs can fulfill this requirement after an election. Even in states where sheriffs hold other jobs, like that of coroner, there are no additional training or educational requirements. At the same time, it's not clear that more experience or education makes for a better sheriff. In California, for example, advocates argued that the state should eliminate the law enforcement experience requirement so that more diverse individuals could run.

Ironically, in every state, deputies hired by the sheriff are generally required to meet standards for law enforcement certification for that state. So, it might occasionally happen that an elected sheriff has less experience or certification than the deputies he commands. Such training does not guarantee that deputies have not been accused of misconduct in other agencies, and it is not uncommon for some sheriffs to hire deputies who have been credibly accused of misconduct, including violence. One rural sheriff's office was described as a "second-chance oasis for cops," and sometimes sheriffs will hire officers without completing their background checks, a situation exacerbated by the fact that sheriffs have no requirement to be transparent about their hiring practices.

The fact that sheriffs are elected has been one of the major talking points sheriff supporters use in their favor. Police chiefs are interviewed and recruited from across the country, more like CEOs. Unlike police chiefs, who are appointed by city councils or mayors and are, as a result, generally more sensitive about avoiding national political issues for fear of running afoul of their primary job, sheriffs are elected at the county level and are given wide leeway to wade into politics. The National Sheriffs' Association does not have guidelines on how sheriffs should approach the political nature of their job. For most sheriffs, aligning with the national GOP only helps their election chances. Further, sheriffs have a unique position as representatives of the popular will and as members of the elite law enforcement system. They are, as shown through their involvement in issues like gun ownership, militia formation, and immigration, the law enforcement official most able to relate to those who are willing to overthrow the federal government, even if by force. This was a position they had fostered throughout the history of the office by positioning militias and civilian firearm ownership as markers of good citizenship, by uplifting an interpretation of the Constitution and Bill of Rights that supported a libertarian and Christian view of the government that excluded large swaths of the nation, and by legitimizing violence as a viable tactic for political change.

While members of Congress make laws far from their communities and their actions seem like just political speech, sheriffs are in the communities every day, making decisions that impact everyone. With their vast budgets earmarked for policing and jails, sheriffs are diverting money from public safety in order to follow vacuous ideas touted by right-wing politicians who will probably never see the consequences of their actions. With their military-grade equipment and license to use lethal violence, sheriffs can threaten community members, many of whom are already disproportionately impacted by mass incarceration, discouraging people from voting and making communities *less* safe.

Trump presented a new and appealing style of politics for sheriffs, who have long reveled in their autonomy. Not only did Trump embrace his power as the chief executive of the country, he was willing to use it to benefit his friends and hurt his adversaries, a form of lawless law and order. The election of Trump gave sheriffs a unique opportunity to hitch their political futures to a man who treated the law with disdain when it suited him while wielding it as a weapon against those he hated.

Trump's first foray into "law and order" was a 1989 full-page ad he paid to place in the *New York Times* calling for the execution of the so-called Central Park Five, five teens of color falsely accused and wrongfully convicted of attacking a female jogger in Central Park. Police used brutal interrogation procedures to get some to confess; all were under eighteen. "Bring back the Death Penalty. Bring Back Our Police!" read the headline. During his presidency, long after it was clear that the teens had been unjustly prosecuted, Trump refused to admit that he was wrong, insisting there were "people on both sides" of the story.

As president, Trump exhibited a gross disregard for the lives and rights of criminal defendants. During his inauguration speech, he presented a society where he claimed that "the crime, and the gangs, and the drugs . . . have stolen too many lives and robbed our country of so much unrealized potential." The solution, he said, would be "America first." "This American carnage stops right here and stops right now," he proclaimed.

He doubled down on this rhetoric in his many meetings with sheriffs, promising to enact stricter penalties for drug crimes and immigrants, although he expressed little understanding of the details. "My administration stands proudly with America's sheriffs, deputies, and law enforcement officers. And we stand, also, 100% with strong law and order. We want you to just keep doing your job as well as you're doing it," he said at one 2018 roundtable.

He argued that police officers should be physically rougher with criminal suspects, echoing far-right claims that "the laws are so horrendously stacked against us, because for years and years, they've been made to protect the criminal." In 2020, thirteen people on federal death row were executed over the roughly six months just before Trump left office, in violation of COVID protocols, including many who had severe mental health disorders.

The irony is that Trump cared very little for the law throughout his life. News media and prosecutors have uncovered that Trump cheated on his taxes and leveraged his assets for inappropriate financial gains. During his presidency—leaving aside January 6 and his efforts to overturn an election— Trump engaged in self-dealing by mixing his business with his political role. He has been criminally indicted in two states and by the Department of Justice for crimes related to January 6. He has been convicted of thirty-four felonies in New York and still faces dozens of felony charges for exposing government secrets and attempting to subvert democracy. He has suggested that, if reelected in 2024, he will use his position as president to take revenge upon prosecutors and other law enforcement officials he feels have persecuted him.

Trump was truly the sheriff president, not the law enforcement president. Trump cared nothing about the law per se, and his comments about policing were somewhat of a caricature of how law enforcement might see themselves in a world full of bad guys. In 2017, for example, Trump spoke to a crowd in Long Island and implied that some brutality against suspects was okay, even admirable:

> When you see these towns and when you see these thugs being
> thrown into the back of the paddy wagon, you just see them
> thrown in, rough. I said please don't be too nice. Like when you
> guys put somebody in the car and you're protecting their head,
> you know, the way you put your hand over? Like don't hit their
> head and they've just killed somebody. Don't hit their head. I said
> you can take the hand away, okay?

In my view, this was part of the appeal for sheriffs, who have long relied on nostalgic ideas about law enforcement's role in the community. Historians have noted since the mid-nineteenth century that sheriffs have the discretion to arrest or not arrest someone based on their personal or political ideals. It's difficult to track a failure to investigate or arrest. In some instances, a sheriff may exercise discretion based on the individual—say, another police officer or local politician or businessman. In others, sheriffs might ignore whole swaths of crime. A historian writing in the 1950s noted that for one Illinois sheriff, the theft of agricultural equipment simply did not amount to a "crime" and did not lead to arrests.

It's less clear whether this abundant discretion leads sheriffs to abuse their office more than other officials, but it seems probable. While there is no systematic tracking of sheriff (or police) misconduct, the available information suggests that sheriffs are more likely to be charged, accused, or convicted of misconduct related to their office. In South Carolina, sheriffs in nearly one in four counties have broken the law in the past two decades.

Because the office of sheriff is relatively independent, it is easier for sheriffs to abuse their authority, and, anecdotally, they do so often. A common problem—one shared by Trump—is the use of public funds and insignia of the office to campaign. Sheriffs have used the labor of people in their custody as well as deputies in their employ to help campaign for reelections. In Nevada, one sheriff was sanctioned for wearing his uniform while endorsing a candidate who, like Trump, tried to overturn the 2020 election.

Sheriffs are also notoriously difficult to remove from office, another echo of the Trump presidency. In Los Angeles, for example, one-term sheriff Alex Villanueva gained the nickname of the "Trump of Los Angeles" because of his refusal to comply with requests for transparency, even when ordered to do so by a court. He was voted out of office but has not faced any consequences for his actions during his term. (Villanueva made a run for the Los Angeles Board of Supervisors in 2024 but lost.) In Maryland, a longtime far-right sheriff has been charged with federal crimes relating to illegally obtaining machine guns for a political supporter. Even as he faces a criminal trial, the sheriff has returned to office and says he intends to remain there.

Maintaining such a regime demands loyalty from subordinates, something Trump also valued. He tended toward cronyism and fired and replaced federal officials with alarming frequency. In almost all cases, the sheriff has ultimate authority over hiring and firing and can dismiss deputies who oppose their political viewpoints. In some states, courts have ruled that sheriffs can even fire deputies if they fail to contribute to their political campaigns.

Trump embraced the avatar of the American sheriff as an ideal symbol of how he saw himself: a maverick with a badge who fights lawlessness without fear of reprisal from bad guys or good. Trump declared himself the "chief law enforcement officer" in the nation after granting clemency to political allies and firing government officials who testified in his first impeachment trial. In 2022, after being called out by the January 6 committee for fomenting insurrection against the government of the United States, he issued NFT trading cards depicting him as, among other things, a sheriff.

One of Trump's earliest and greatest fans was the ex–Arizona sheriff Joe Arpaio, who was one of the first public figures to endorse Trump before he even received the Republican nomination. Perhaps he sensed an affinity between himself and the reality television star. "Donald Trump is a leader. He produces results and is ready to get tough in order to protect American jobs and families," Arpaio told CNN in early 2016.

Arpaio first became the sheriff of Maricopa County—the most populous county in the state, which includes Phoenix—in 1993. He quickly gained notoriety in the American and international media—including publications like *Rolling Stone* and the *New Yorker*—for abuse of power. He built a jail using tents that he nicknamed "Tent City." He proudly told the press, which hung on his every word, that he forced people inside his jail—most of whom were not convicted of any crimes—to wear pink underwear and eat starvation-level rations. He used his post to harass Latinos under the guise of immigration policing. He supported SB 1070, the "show me your papers law," which gave local law enforcement leeway to detain and arrest people with brown skin on the suspicion that they might be undocumented. One night, he sent his deputies into Mesa to round up people who were working as janitors as they exited public buildings like libraries, under the guise of arresting those in violation of immigration laws.

Worth noting here is Arpaio's manipulation of the press. Many outlets published story after story repeating Arpaio's self-made moniker "America's Toughest Sheriff" with a mix of admiration and amusement. GQ published a celebrity profile, calling Arpaio an "anti-immigration firebrand," and CNN called him a "controversial figure." Even stories that were critical of Arpaio begrudgingly admired his tactics. His public information officer, Lisa Allen, a former local newscaster, was key in helping Arpaio plan many of his over-the-top media events. Allen helped to stage Arpaio's press conferences, and she was probably behind the creation and marketing of Tent City.

When Arpaio was sheriff, he followed Trump straight into the "birther" movement, which claimed, falsely, that Barack Obama was not born in the United States. Trump publicly spead this conspiracy theory; among sheriffs I have spoken with, some still believe it. Initially spurred by Tea Party activists, the lie was one of Trump's favorite talking points, one he repeatedly raised in television appearances even after Obama felt obliged to release his birth certificate to the public to pacify conspiracy theorists.

Inspired by Trump, Arpaio continued to claim that the document appeared fake. He even sent members of his volunteer posse, on taxpayer dollars, to Hawaii in an attempt to confirm his theory. In 2012, Arpaio spoke at an early CSPOA conference for nearly an hour, during which he claimed to have obtained shocking evidence of his investigation into Barack Obama's birth certificate. (Arpaio did not produce any actual evidence.) After he lost his bid for reelection in 2016, Arpaio claimed to have the results of his five-year investigation. Standing with the leader of a crack detective team he named the "Cold Case Posse," Arpaio gave a press conference in which he called Obama's birth certificate a "fraudulently created document." At that point, even Trump had given up on the conspiracy.

Importantly, Arpaio's rise to power coincided with the mainstream GOP's move toward nativist politics as they were being tested in Arizona, the result of many years of work. Despite initial inaction on the part of state and federal officials, Latino organizers worked to document Arpaio's abuses, which led to a successful court order in 2013 that forced Arpaio's office to end the illegal racial profiling of Latinos at traffic stops. In 2016, Arpaio was again ordered by a federal judge to stop racially profiling Latinos or face contempt of court, a misdemeanor punishable by six months in jail. His action cost the county nearly $70 million in court fines and fees related to his misconduct.

The election of Trump gave Arpaio hope that he would not face time behind bars even as the sheriff continued to argue that he had not disobeyed the judge intentionally. He plainly saw Trump in himself. In an interview he gave before the Republican primary in 2016, he told the *Guardian*, "I'm not trying to say [Trump] copies me. It just so happens we see eye to eye. . . . He's somewhat like me. Or I'm like him. I don't know which way it goes."

———

Phoenix was 107 degrees on the August afternoon in 2017 when Trump held his first rally after the Unite the Right rally in Charlottesville, Virginia, where white supremacists carrying tiki torches chanted, "You will not replace us" and a counterprotester named Heather Heyer was killed by a man who drove his car intentionally into a peaceful crowd. Trump had responded, only reluctantly, with a comment about there being "some very fine people on both sides."

The mayor of Phoenix had begged Trump not to come, worried about violence, and told him a pardon for Arpaio would exacerbate tensions in the city. During the day of Trump's rally, protesters and counterprotesters filled the streets. A young multiracial coalition chanted, "Hey Hey. Ho Ho. Donald Trump has got to go!" Signs said "No Trump! No KKK! No fascist USA!" Before the end of the night, police assaulted the protesters with riot gear, tear gas, and batons.

Inside the convention center, Trump spoke for seventy-seven minutes, unscripted and free-ranging as usual. He emphasized the large crowd inside, dismissing the protesters outside as a small group. He complained about the reporting around Charlottesville, which he felt unfairly accused him of empathizing with racists. He blamed the media for "trying to take away our history and our heritage" as the crowd chanted, "CNN sucks!"

Finally, as Trump turned the topic to the "border wall," he asked the audience, "Do the people in this room like Sheriff Joe?"

People cheered and a woman standing next to Trump gave a thumbs-up and mouthed an enthusiastic yes. "Pardon him!" people cheered.

"Was Sheriff Joe convicted for doing his job?" Trump asked. Then he went on. "He should have had a jury, but you know what, I'll make a prediction. He's going to be just fine, okay? But I won't do it tonight because I don't want to cause any controversy. But Sheriff Joe can feel good."

Throughout the speech, protesters outside grew restless. Police would later claim that some people on the street were throwing rocks. Just as the speech ended, police unleashed tear gas on the protesters, ordering them home.

Joe Arpaio eagerly watched as the moment he had hoped for finally arrived. Trump announced his intention to pardon the ex-sheriff.

Finally, on the night of August 25, a Friday, Trump followed through on his promise. He held the press conference just as Hurricane Harvey hit landfall in Texas because Trump figured people were watching TV news. This was a direct blow to the advocates, communities, and federal judicial system who had at last prosecuted Arpaio and voted him out of office. Arpaio went on to support Trump, appearing at Trump rallies in Phoenix in 2018.

––––––

Arpaio did not carve his "toughest sheriff" image out of nothing. In fact, sheriffs have long been something of a cross between a politician, law enforcement, and celebrity personality. It is telling that if you ask someone to name sheriffs, they will think of fictional ones first. Sheriff Andy of Mayberry. Sheriff Rosco in *The Dukes of Hazzard*. Woody of *Toy Story*. Little Bill Daggett in *Unforgiven*. This legend of the sheriff has served the position well. It has also allowed mainstream politicians to appeal to far-right causes under the banner of American heritage and history, even if that history is largely fabricated.

As media figures, sheriffs are generally freer to express political opinions than nonelected officials and, as a result, wade into waters that appear unrelated to their jobs. For one thing, sheriffs cannot be removed from office for what they say because the law considers their speech to be a form of political campaigning, so they could flock to Trump.

Sheriffs earned political support from a president who understood media and how to get attention. A photo with Trump meant something to sheriffs, especially those running in Republican areas. Sheriffs all over the country, ones who had never before allied with the federal government, much less campaigned as part of the presidential entourage, held rallies and events with Trump flags behind them. To elect a sheriff in many places was to show your support for Trump.

Trump's behavior mimics that of sheriffs—his TV-ready antics, inflammatory rhetoric, and machismo. They are a natural fit. His admiration for Arpaio stemmed from his desire to be seen as a man who would flout liberal niceties with toxic masculinity. But while Trump's rhetoric, behavior, and strongman tendencies were reminiscent of sheriffs and gave them permission to act the same way, he was accelerating and emboldening a movement that had already existed for decades. Trump did not invent the idea of the populist sheriff, but it was convenient for him to have a posse of them to back him up.

One particular issue on which Trump and the vast majority of sheriffs aligned was the issue of immigration and border militarization, including Trump's campaign promise to build a border wall, which did not materialize, as well as his policies designed to reduce immigration significantly overall. The ex-president paired extremely anti-immigrant views with a great deal of racist disdain for Black and Brown people. He spoke openly against Latinos, going so far as to criticize a Latino judge, and described all immigrants from Central America as gang members affiliated with MS-13. Trump described immigrants as coming from "shithole countries" and "countries we don't even know about," and he enacted the Muslim ban to block immigrants from certain regions altogether.

Alongside Trump's appointees like Stephen Miller and Jeff Sessions—both of whom had long harbored anti-immigrant animus—county sheriffs were a useful contingent that Trump could easily weaponize through preexisting programs to arrest and detain more noncitizens. Because sheriffs are generally both arresting officers and run jails, they have ample opportunities to interact with immigrant populations living in the United States when people are pulled over or arrested for any type of crime, even the most trivial. Further, because the U.S.-Mexico border lies mostly in rural counties, which are largely patrolled by sheriffs and their deputies, Trump found a ready contingent of "border sheriffs" who were familiar with the territory and viewed migrants crossing into their counties as an unwanted incursion as well as an opportunity to declare their MAGA bona fides. Many of the sheriffs who were eager to work with Trump had already been part of various other anti-immigrant movements that were rumbling at the county level.

In 2017, Trump met with sheriffs as part of a roundtable related to border security, at which he praised sheriffs as willing to stand as a bulwark to prevent the dreaded "invasion" from the south. During that session, Trump promised one sheriff that he would "take care of" state officials who were blocking his ability to properly police the border. In 2018, Trump held a meeting with law enforcement in which a sheriff asked Trump to "indemnify sheriffs" when they make immigration arrests. In early 2019, Trump held a roundtable that began with a prayer, again surrounded by sheriffs.

In another 2019 meeting, which happened during a government shutdown caused by Trump's request for $5.7 billion for the border wall, Trump held forth about "stopping bad people" with the proposed barrier. The sheriff of Victoria County, Texas (which is just outside Corpus Christi), described to Trump an incident in which a group of nineteen migrants died inside a tractor trailer. Cameras snapped photos as the sheriffs talked. "You are the very first president . . . to support local and federal agencies," the sheriff said.

The next month, Trump said he started a "big, big portion of the wall" as he stood surrounded by sheriffs in uniform, whom he used as a small chorus of agreement for his monologue. "Fantastic people. Fantastic men and women!" he said, praising law enforcement. He demonized migrants, calling them "convicted felons, people of tremendous, big problems." He then pulled out a sheet of paper and read off numbers of arrested immigrants from DHS as the sheriffs looked on, rapt. "We don't want murderers and drug dealers, MS-13, coming into our country," he added. At the time, Trump still faced political obstacles to funding for the wall as well as a shortage of jail space to hold immigrants; he had just implemented the "remain in Mexico" program, which forced migrants seeking asylum to wait for their hearings in Mexico, not the United States.

Sheriff Hodgson of Massachusetts, standing next to Trump, added that he was "very concerned about people being released that should be held."

"The president is absolutely right," he added.

"This is what we do. This is where we engage. If you do anything to undercut ICE funding, our communities will be at risk," a Texas sheriff added. "Our hats are off to the president!" Three hundred sheriffs presented Trump with a letter sent to Congress advocating for more space in jails for ICE detention. Later that same day he went to El Paso for a rally.

Trump, with the support of his attorney general, Jeff Sessions, also railed against the sanctuary city movement, Democrat-controlled cities that vowed to protect immigrants already in the country by refusing to cooperate with ICE. (At one point, Trump proposed sending immigrants to sanctuary cities as punishment.) The State of California also implemented a sanctuary policy that prevented sheriffs from cooperating with ICE. The California State Sheriffs' Association issued a letter disagreeing with the policy, and their message was later used by Thomas Homan, Trump's then acting ICE director.

It's worth remembering that not every sheriff agreed with Trump's anti-immigration agenda. Not only did some sheriffs win elections in major cities based on promises to limit interactions with ICE, but many sheriffs who had lived on the U.S.-Mexico border most of their careers did not see the advantage of a border wall and did not want much to do with Trump's priorities.

Trump's immigration policies necessitated additional jail facilities, so he reduced the federal standards for incarceration and doled out lucrative contracts with ICE to hold immigrants who were awaiting deportation under Trump's draconian policies. Between 2018 and 2019, Trump's administration nearly doubled the number of people in ICE detention, which added costs without substantively changing the number of people who were removed from the country.

----

Local elections have low turnouts; often less than one-quarter of eligible voters choose the county sheriff. They are also much more low-information than presidential elections. The advent of Trumpism, however, now means that sheriff candidates can connect themselves to Trump and create an association that moves beyond specific promises or experience.

Just as far-right sheriffs still rely on boogeymen like the Clintons and Obama to inspire loyalty from their constituents, Trump also, with his claims to "drain the swamp," claimed a personal and ideological authenticity that distinguished him from the political and pundit classes. Many of these tactics resembled the ways in which sheriffs themselves made claims to authenticity that transcended their political role.

These sheriffs were drawn to Trump not just because of his law-and-order stance; they also sympathized with his overt opposition to immigration, his dalliance with white supremacists, and his stalwart defense of the Second Amendment. Even with him out of office, many still see Trump as their role model: his lack of accountability, his brashness, his rejection of science and expertise, and his disdain for federal government and regulations. They have also embraced his contempt of so-called liberal cancel culture, which presents a variety of topics—from immigration, to drug legalization, to policing, to books—as battles in a vast culture war between the "left"— which includes Big Tech, academia, and the media—and the "true patriots."

Even before he ran for president, Trump's uber-masculinity, lack of restraint, and conspiracy-driven political ideas pushed him toward many of the far-right notions that motivate sheriffs, especially those in the constitutional sheriff movement. Trump seemed to view America's sheriffs as his own private posse, a curious evolution from the days when the federal government was often in opposition to local sheriffs.

Trump was a unique opportunity. Not only do sheriffs represent an idealized working-class America as depicted by Andy Griffith but they also represent a type of law enforcement that meshed with Trump's idea of the world and his view on policing: virulently racist, anti-government, profit-seeking, anti-academic, and quasi-vigilante. Trump sought, and sheriffs delivered, the type of populist policing that Trump believed was in line with his vision of the world.

Long secure in the knowledge that the laws are just recommendations, patronage is a right, and masculinity is a virtue, the humble county sheriff, that American icon, became the soldiers in Trump's culture war. It's no coincidence that sheriffs as a group are almost entirely white men and tend to have more powers in rural counties, places where Trump overwhelmingly won in 2016 and 2020.

Even if Trump does not return to office, his actions on policing and his emphasis on the county sheriff as the preferred mode of policing have left a lasting influence on the far right and the future of sheriffs generally.

# FOUR

# "AN OLD-FASHIONED CONSTITUTIONAL REVIVAL"

## *COVID and the Constitutional Sheriffs*

AT ALL OF THE CSPOA EVENTS, INCLUDING BATTLE MOUNtain, I was struck by the number of women attending—mostly women around my age, many with children in tow. They were in many cases less likely to carry military-style weapons (although a lot carried sidearms) and their concerns echoed those of many parents in the COVID era—they were worried about the impact of closed schools, of COVID vaccines, and of a frightening sense of disorder.

A part of me could understand. As I listened to the women speakers in Battle Mountain, I thought about my own elementary school–age child, who was, at the moment, wearing a mask to school and forced to play at recess a safe three feet from her classmates. In lieu of climbing a play structure or pushing each other on the swings, my daughter and her friends were getting creative, challenging each other in jump rope competitions from their socially distant spaces.

It seemed to me that COVID galvanized women, especially women who identified as mothers, in new ways, a hunch that was later borne out by increasingly raucous school board meetings in 2022. I began to notice that many anti-masking groups centered around schools were touting far-right sheriff ideologies. As a prelude to the "parental rights" movement that would create groups like Moms for Liberty, Facebook groups formed to talk about COVID restrictions in schools as well as suggestions on how to talk to county sheriffs about resisting masking orders and business closures. They mirrored the rhetoric of constitutional sheriffs, in particular a distrust of the federal government. The pandemic and related health protocols sent women to sheriffs—a trend the sheriffs courted—as they became interested in challenging COVID protocols in schools.

There is a long history of women involved in far-right movements, much of it involving jokes about "little old ladies in tennis shoes" who did the footwork for groups like the John Birch Society. Certainly, women led many of the local protests in the 1970s and '80s over the secularization of public schools. Additionally, the role of women in such movements has always gone beyond the stereotypically feminine focus on family and spiritual well-being—people like Phyllis Schlafly were as public-facing and political as their male counterparts. But what felt different to me was the fusion of militia-style movements that have long regarded sheriffs as particularly important with recent conservative movements largely centered on schools and children. Before 2020, most of the people far-right sheriffs targeted were men. Now women were seeking them out as a source of power and authority.

One such group present at Battle Mountain was Mamalitia—an anti-vax California-based prepper-style group formed in 2020—whose founders, Denise Aguilar and Tara Thornton, spoke passionately against the COVID vaccine and encouraged the women in the audience to "take charge of their lives." At a September 2021 "empower boot camp" held on the lawn outside the capitol building in Sacramento, members distributed information on fighting tyranny. While their speech had the by-then-familiar tones of outrage, they looked like women I might see at school drop-off, wearing scarves and trendy shoes with professional blowouts.

The two women had created a survivalist-style militia that promoted homeschooling and food sovereignty with a patina of female empowerment. According to its website, the group was a "community of constitution loving women that recognize our empowerment comes from fully engaging in our children's educations, our wellness, food and financial sovereignty, and over-all skills." Aguilar, like many of the new recruits to the constellation of far-right movements Mack courted, did not look like one of the "little old ladies" you might associate with conservatism. She is Latinx, has a neck tattoo, and—before Meta kicked her off its platforms for misinformation—used to post a variety of video confessionals in which she expressed her disdain for vaccines, California Democrats, and the federal government.

Most of Mamalitia's work focused on lobbying the California legislature to drop vaccine mandates and other health rules, like masking in hospitals. In the spring of 2020, the group staged a protest in Sacramento against COVID policies. Aguilar also argued in favor of household self-sufficiency—like *Little House on the Prairie*, she said in Nevada—ideas that pointed toward the growing parental rights movement that would rise out of the COVID-era advocacy.

Richard Mack saw the potential in women rallying to the constitutional sheriff cause despite his extremely traditional view of gender roles. For one thing, adding women both increased membership numbers and made far-right sheriff meetings seem less testosterone-filled. Women were just not associated with violence the way men were. Even though many women were present at the Capitol on January 6, the most famous of them, Ashli Babbitt (who spent fifteen years in the army), became a martyr to the cause after a Capitol police officer shot her and she died.

In one 2022 meeting with the California Federation of Republican Women, Mack suggested a distinctively feminine tactic.

"Bring cookies," he said, giving advice to women meeting with their local sheriff. "Not donuts, because that is too stereotypical. But cookies. With nuts." Preferably walnut or pecan, he added.

The day after the Patriotic Social Gathering in Battle Mountain, a county commissioner for neighboring Elko County named Rex Steninger wrote an email to Mack. Calling the rally an "inspiration," he said people in his county were asking for the same thing. "I was really impressed with the rally and also really liked your idea of taking back our country one sheriff at a time," he wrote.

A few days later, Steninger gave a rousing speech in support of joining the CSPOA, just like his neighbors in Lander County. He reiterated what he'd told Mack in his email, that he was inspired by the Battle Mountain rally—"frankly, it was jealousy," he said in an interview with the Family Research Council—and wanted to plan one just like it for Elko County.

Steninger's family has a long history in anti-government movements. They owned, managed, and operated the *Elko Daily Free Press*, the only local news source in rural Elko County from 1910 until they sold it in 2001. During that time, the family used the paper to push anti-government ideas, expressing support for causes like the Sagebrush Rebellion, a loose coalition of Western ranchers who opposed the federal ownership of land during the 1970s and '80s. Their activity, consisting of resistance to federal authority by refusing to recognize federal limits on public land grazing, was a precursor to similar movements by ranchers like Cliven Bundy against the federal ownership of land. (The federal government owns around 80 percent of the land in Nevada, the highest percent of any state.)

Like the publication, far-right politics were also a family tradition; Rex's father, Melvin, was involved in a lawsuit against the State of Nevada for enforcing a federal fifty-five-miles-per-hour speed limit before the state legislature approved the change. Steninger himself described his paper as a "champion for personal liberty and adherence for the Constitution." He has written and continues to write supportive stories about ranchers resisting federal regulation.

Steninger, now in his sixties, with bright blue eyes framed by intense gray brows, has lived his whole life in the same rural region, raising cattle at the foot of the Ruby Mountains. He is unabashedly anti-abortion and pro-gun. He told me over email that he fears "society's inevitable slide to liberalism." He said, "I have long held the belief in government overreach, most of my adult life, in fact. How about when President Carter tried to tell us what temperature to set our thermostats at or the 55 mph speed limit." He referred me to a speech he gave that separated people into "warriors" and "parasites." "We need to reject overreach," he concluded.

When Steninger raised the idea of repeating the Battle Mountain rally in his own county, he gave a lengthy oration listing the concerns of many rural Americans. "This pandemic had really brought to mind how far we have sunk as a nation. The First Amendment gives us the right to freely exercise religion and the right to freely assemble. Yet, the governors across the nation ordered us to stay in our homes and not socialize with our friends. They even told us to close our churches and not celebrate Thanksgiving and Christmas. . . . Most of us complied and obeyed. Most of us shouldn't have obeyed, complied; in retrospect, we should have revolted." The room burst into applause.

Members of the community, including the Elko County sheriff, Aitor Narvaiza, and Jesse Watts, the Nevada sheriff with the "We the People" tattoo, leaped to contribute money to cover the costs. Steninger claimed to have raised $1,200 that day alone.

He felt so strongly about the cause that he sent a letter to every county commissioner in Nevada's seventeen counties, asking them to join. "I've included a draft resolution you can use," Steninger wrote. "If you do decide to join the CSPOA, try to get your resolution passed before June 20 and join us in Elko for the patriotic rally. The rally is being held in conjunction with the national tour of Robert David Steele. . . . Either way, sign up as members of the CSPOA as a first step of taking back control of our country."

"I hope it prohibits future directives from the governor; that would be my strongest hope. . . . We're the rural counties and they don't pay much attention to us," he said in a later interview, explaining why the CSPOA resolution was so important to him. "We want to retake control of our government one sheriff at a time. Sheriff by sheriff. County by county. State by state."

---

When COVID first appeared in the United States in early 2020, nearly every politician, including Trump, encouraged schools and businesses to close. By the end of March, Trump had restricted travelers from China as a way of limiting COVID spread, formed the White House Coronavirus Task Force, and approved the Coronavirus Aid, Relief, and Economic Security (CARES) Act that provided $1,200 in benefits to most individuals as a way of alleviating the economic toll of business closures.

Very quickly, even as Dr. Anthony Fauci became a mainstay on television and ambulance sirens roared through the streets of the nation's towns and cities, Trump and other Republicans wavered on COVID restrictions. Trump began to tweet about "reopening" businesses and schools; other Republican leaders followed suit. In May, the president appeared unmasked at a large public gathering, sending a clear signal to his followers that the use of a face mask to prevent the spread of COVID was a political marker, not a public health necessity.

The nation entered an era of polarizing political divides. Democratic governors and legislatures kept masking and school closures in place to prevent the spread of COVID; Republican leaders like Florida governor Ron DeSantis relied on documents like the Great Barrington Declaration—a proclamation written by three scientists that encouraged government officials to end COVID mitigation measures, sponsored by the American Institute for Economic Research, a libertarian think tank that also supports climate change denialism—to question the reliability of the scientific consensus about COVID, including conspiracy theories that some officials were either faking COVID deaths or presenting unreliable statistics.

Through the spring of 2020 and beyond, so-called lockdown protests roiled much of the country, especially in rural regions, where far-right sheriffs were already entrenched. Mack took advantage of the new group of far-right sheriffs who sought political direction in solving the age-old dilemma: How to appease constituents while also avoiding negative backlash? He began to hold conference calls in which he railed against sheriffs who enforced business closures and masking orders and praised sheriffs who refused. This was, he said, interposition in action.

Sheriffs across the country began to oppose COVID health mandates, often comparing the regulations to Gestapo tactics and contributing to the spread of misinformation. Sheriff Scott Nichols Sr. of Franklin County, Maine, said he was "siding with American ideals" against "Nazi tactics." This came after Nichols took to Facebook on April 1 to state he would ignore Governor Janet Mills's stay-at-home executive orders. "We will not be setting up a Police State. PERIOD," Nichols wrote. "The Sheriff's Office will not purposefully go out and stop vehicles because they are on the road or stop and ask why people are out and about. To do so puts our officers at risk. This is not Nazi Germany or Soviet Russia where you are asked for your papers!"

Mack and the CSPOA argued that the federal and state government had exceeded their authority with COVID health measures, agreeing with county leaders like Steninger. Mack was able to assemble a quorum of county sheriffs who faced extremely outspoken voters already protesting COVID rules and looking for additional justification and support. He found that his anti-government ideas were more and more popular, especially among white rural and suburban residents, who were impatient with business closures and naturally distrustful of experts in Washington, D.C.

Mack held conference calls with other sheriffs and concerned members in which people called in and asked about the role of sheriffs in enforcing lockdown measures. He also used these events to expound on his own anti-government ideas and promote his organization. Throughout the summer during these group calls, Mack provided a litany of examples where sheriffs had successfully "interposed" between government agencies and communities.

For example, he praised law enforcement officials like Don Barnes, the sheriff of Orange County, California. Barnes put out a statement on April 30, 2020, saying he would not enforce the county beach closures mandated by the state. Mack described Barnes as "the good sheriff standing and doing his job and standing against the tyrant." Mack's rhetoric became more and more inflammatory. He also compared the enforcement of health regulations to the Gestapo and Hitler's regime. And, he claimed, sheriffs would be the ones to fix it.

Additionally, in discussing an anti-vax mother activist in Idaho who was arrested for refusing to leave a playground closed because of COVID, he said, "The gestapo is alive and well in America." Mack continued, "We have sheriffs starting to wake up. . . . Which sheriff do you want? The one in Wisconsin that had his little thug officers going to people's homes and harassing them, threatening them and saying you better not let your kid outside to play? . . . Do you, the American people, do you want that kind of sheriff in your community?" He contrasted such a stickler for the rules with a constitutional sheriff, who would not have arrested the mother in Idaho, just like he would not have arrested Rosa Parks. "That's what we do at the CSPOA, we create that," he said.

When asked if he was suggesting that Americans should ignore health orders and disobey the government, Mack admitted that he was and called on law enforcement officials to do the same. "We do not believe in violence," Mack said on that call, but he added that "it might come to that."

A particular source of ire for Mack was the closure of churches. "My biggest concern is how the churches are groveling before the government," he said. He fiercely criticized sheriffs like Chad Chronister of Hillsborough County, Florida. Chronister arrested Pastor Rodney Howard-Browne on March 30, 2020, for holding in-person services at his megachurch outside Tampa in defiance of Florida's pandemic orders.

In contrast, the sheriff of rural Sierra County, New Mexico, allowed a church to remain open. In an event memorialized by a 2023 documentary called *Noncompliant 2: The Sheriff*, Pastor Caleb Cooper of New Hope Revival Church in the town of Truth or Consequences refused to pause in-person services when ordered to do so in 2020 to stop the spread of COVID. He received an official cease-and-desist letter from the state as well as a visit from state troopers.

Sheriff Glenn Hamilton came to Cooper's aid and deputized the entire congregation, allowing the church services to proceed. According to Hamilton, the mass deputization meant that the church services were performing "law enforcement" activities, which were exempted under the state's COVID orders.

Cooper describes himself as a "revivalist" operating in the "Apostolic and Prophetic." One of his books is called the *Battle-Ready Remnant*, which is "a practical biblical guide in spiritual warfare as the revival remnant contends in the last days to gain victory in the invisible realm. We do not wrestle against flesh and blood but against demonic powers in the unseen realm." For Cooper, the sheriff plays a role in this battle, standing between his loyal church attendees and the government seeking to shut them down.

The documentary about Cooper and Hamilton was created and produced by KrisAnne Hall, a onetime Florida prosecutor who styles herself as a "constitutional attorney." Like Mack, Hall first gained notoriety in 2010, when she began to give seminars about how everyday citizens could resist government authority by ignoring the laws. Like Mack, she opposes taxes, federal regulatory agencies, and firearm regulation.

Hall's interests intersected with those of constitutional sheriffs, and she began to tout the sheriff as a law enforcement authority who could protect local citizens from state and federal governments. "The sheriff is the ultimate local check and balance on the abuse of power in all government," she says in her documentary. "If the sheriffs of this country will just unite and be unified in keeping their oath of office and defending the American people against oppression and abuse of government, we could take back our country tomorrow." Her talk is the source of sheriff memes online.

———

In late September of 2020, as the death toll from COVID reached a million people in America and it became increasingly clear that people of color were most at risk, Mack took a more besieged tone: "Statistics on coronavirus have been fabricated and falsely made higher," he said, echoing Trump's claims that COVID rates were being inflated. "The mask is a precursor to social engineering to make sure all of us will take the vaccination." He urged his listeners to "go to the local gun shop" to locate potential sheriff candidates who would not support COVID business closures or masking.

Mack also held an in-person conference at Liberty University in Lynchburg, Virginia, that September, at which sheriffs, law enforcement officers, and other supporters assembled maskless. The conference was not widely attended and mostly featured the most faithful among Mack's coterie.

By November of 2020, Mack's rhetoric had increased in belligerence and tone. He slandered "mainstream Republicans who did not support Trump," arguing that they "lie, cheat, steal, and sometimes murder," calling on "revolutionary war times."

He began to argue that more violent measures might be needed, despite his generally peaceful stance as a cop, Mack continues to claim he never shot anyone with his service weapon. "Religious liberty is being destroyed in our country. All of you know I don't advocate violence. But we gotta do more than just voting," he concluded, citing "all the voting fraud going on."

---

After the Liberty University conference, which was one of the few places where Mack could hold an indoor, in-person event in 2020 due to COVID restrictions, he went on the road again, not just holding large outdoor rallies like the one in Battle Mountain but also conducting more intimate "law enforcement training" sessions that catered to sheriffs, deputies, and other law enforcement–curious people.

I have attended a few of Mack's training courses, and they follow a general pattern. Most are held in churches or midrange hotel ballrooms, and any member of the public can attend for a fee of around $40. They generally feature Mack, eyes ablaze, exuding passion for Rosa Parks "the tax resistor" and a recitation of "his" Supreme Court case (even though his name is not actually in the case caption). There is often a segment for "law enforcement only," which consists of Mack's interpretation of the Bill of Rights and how sheriffs should enforce them.

In February 2021, the day after a three-day winter storm left millions of Texans without power and resulted in the deaths of at least 246 people, Mack launched what he would call the "Texas Tour" with a two-day event in the Woodlands, a suburb just north of Houston. The event remains one of his largest training sessions to date. It also set the template for how Mack would attempt to recruit sheriffs to the far right by tapping into already-existing networks as well as the discontent fueled by anti-lockdown protests.

About one hundred people—including about forty elected county sheriffs and the same number of chief deputies—sat around circular tables in a

windowless conference room at the Woodlands Resort, which advertises itself as a "special place" where "harmony and nature awaken the spirit and
reveal a serene sanctuary to unwind and escape or explore and experience a
myriad of worthwhile pursuits that beckon at every turn." The hotel complex
includes two "championship" golf courses. But these lawmen weren't there
for an ordinary business conference, nor were they there for pleasure. Some
sought companionship and maybe some ideas on how to handle their constituents. Others were looking for enlightenment.

The master of ceremonies was a man named Kirk Launius, who is the
Texas chair of the CSPOA. Launius has run unsuccessfully for sheriff of the
very Democratic Dallas County multiple times as the GOP candidate. Once,
he got within spitting distance of winning, at the height of Tea Party politics
in Texas.

That day in the Woodlands, Launius's bald head reflected the powerful
overhead lighting, making it look greased. He self-importantly introduced a
Texas pastor wearing full American Revolutionary–era regalia—white curl-
ing hair, stockings, breeches—as George Washington.

After "Washington" spoke and prayed, Rand Henderson, the local sheriff, took to the podium to praise Richard Mack, the leader who had brought
all of these people together. He explained that, over the past year, he was not
sure he had perfectly embodied the "constitutional sheriff" principles, especially when it came to COVID health orders. "I think I maybe got a B mi-
nus," he said, referring to his initial compliance with the orders.

He said that Mack had endorsed both of his runs for sheriff and spoke
about his struggles enforcing pandemic-related business closures and mask
mandates. "I took a step back and went back to what I had been taught by
Sheriff Mack. . . . Look to the Constitution first," he said. He explained it
was a learning process for him: "Thank God that we got someone like Sheriff Mack who is out there helping us with that."

Mack spoke next and called the crowd an "army of wonderful people here to set other people free.

"We have never and we will never advocate violence of any kind," he said, name-checking Martin Luther King Jr. and Gandhi. "The backdrop of this entire conference is, what is government's role?" Mack continued. "We've gone too far," he said, referring to church closures.

"We have sheriffs who will interpose. Stand in the way. And make sure we are not victimizing our citizens all in the name of 'It's for your own good,'" he said.

Two "constitutional lawyers" also presented: KrisAnne Hall from the documentary and Michael Peroutka, a fixture of the far-right circuit who supports Southern secession. An open advocate for Christian nationalism—his group, the Institute on the Constitution, advocates for a "biblical world-view of the founding fathers"—Peroutka was a board member for the League of the South, a neo-Confederate organization. In a 2012 YouTube video, Peroutka leads fellow group members in a rendition of "Dixie," referring to it as the "national anthem." In 2022, Peroutka became the Republican nominee for Maryland attorney general. When he lost the election, he refused to concede and alleged voter fraud.

A proponent of interposition, Peroutka told the group, "When a peace officer refuses to enforce an unconstitutional enactment or order, the peace officer is not breaking the law. He is upholding the law." Applause filled the room. "He's actually validating the law. He's actually vindicating the law."

He later referred to his "friend in Alabama," Roy Moore, the judge who was forced to leave the Alabama Supreme Court because he refused to remove a copy of the Ten Commandments from his courtroom. More recently, Moore ran for the U.S. Senate and was accused by multiple women of sexual assault and harassment incidents that occurred when they were minor girls and Moore was an adult.

Mack even introduced one of his favorite sheriffs at the 2021 Woodlands event: Pamela Elliott, who was elected sheriff of Edwards County, Texas, in 2012 and had just lost her primary bid for a third term. His 2014 book, *Are You a David?*, features Elliott on the cover as a David facing Goliath in the form of the Obama administration, which he portrays as being opposed to the Constitution and liberty.

A self-proclaimed constitutional sheriff, Elliott used her office to harass and intimidate local Democratic Party meetings with the purpose of discouraging Latino voters, according to advocates who asked the Department of Justice to investigate. The playbook now sounds eerily familiar. A Texas elections lawyer described her harassment of Democratic voters as "abuse of office" and potentially a "criminal offense." She worked with a local militia, the Edwards Plateau Rangers, to intimidate school board members and other officials. In 2014, she posted deputies inside polling stations. She was accused of campaign finance violations. She botched a murder investigation. In 2020, Elliott lost the Republican primary to the current sheriff, J. W. Guthrie, but faced no other consequences and now works as a detective for another sheriff agency.

An additional core member of the CSPOA team at the Woodlands and other Texas events was Gary Heavin, the former CEO of Curves, a fitness chain for women, and a Texan. Heavin's background is very much rooted in the evangelical Christian movement; he told the Christian Broadcasting Network that he became born-again at the age of thirty-two after experiencing a business failure that led to bankruptcy and jail for failure to pay child support. He reinvented his life, remarried, and started the Curves fitness chain. (Heavin recently sold Curves.) Heavin says he has a ranch near Crawford—as does former president George W. Bush—and has dedicated himself to various philanthropic causes that align with his religious and political worldview. According to the *Wall Street Journal*, Heavin donated $10,000 to the Oath Keepers. Mack said that Heavin "helped with some of our funding" and called him a "tremendous patriot and true American." (Mack told me Heavin is no longer associated with the CSPOA but did not say why.)

As he spoke, Heavin pointed out the journalists in the room and said that most of the people were carrying firearms. "At least fifty firearms by the women alone!"

This Woodlands event was a turning point for Mack and the start of a far-right coalition in Texas, joining mostly rural and suburban county sheriffs with local officials, evangelical ministers, and local militia groups. The combination of these elements would prove corrosive to the fabric of Texas politics, pushing the state further to the right.

Later, Sheriff Randy Hargrove of Houston County wrote of the conference, "What this CSPOA training is, in reality, is a good, old-fashioned Constitutional Revival!"

After the Woodlands conference, Mack held over a dozen CSPOA trainings across the state, attracting at least fifty elected county sheriffs as well as dozens of deputies, constables, police officers, and other public officials. The advertising flyer read, "The training is absolutely guaranteed to provide irrefutable evidence that sheriffs and local officials of each county or parish possesses the power and duty to protect their constituent from ALL enemies, foreign and domestic."

To make the trainings more attractive, Mack's team received permission from the Texas Commission on Law Enforcement to grant continuing education credits for law enforcement attendees. The trainings were all sponsored by county sheriffs' offices, and Mack occasionally flew from place to place on a private plane owned by Gary Heavin, a "CSPOA Life Member." (Mack eschewed the requirement to wear masks on flights, so he avoided travel on commercial planes when masks were required.)

I spoke with a few sheriffs who attended CSPOA trainings in Texas. Many told me that they did not believe in everything Mack said but tended to think that Mack had some good ideas. One sheriff, Trace Hendricks of Bosque County, told me he had gone to three CSPOA trainings over the past two years. He was reluctant to speak with me because, he said, the media was "trying to make sheriffs look like fools." He said he didn't "understand the hype" and certainly didn't think that the sheriff could overrule federal law enforcement. While Hendricks said he identified as a constitutional sheriff, he added, "[Mack's] got a couple of points that I disagree with. I didn't go and join any cult." He concluded our call by telling me, "People should be grateful that there are law enforcement officers who want to take the time to learn their constitutional rights and protect them from violations of their constitutional rights."

The CSPOA training events attracted Texas politicians like Attorney General Ken Paxton and the agricultural commissioner, Sid Miller, as well as people running for office, like Don Huffines, who launched a bid for Texas governor, running to the right of Governor Greg Abbott. (His billboards railed against immigrants and advertised his campaign promise to put "Texas first.")

———

Steninger's attraction to Mack and the constitutional sheriff movement surely stems from his position as a rural conservative, steeped in the politics of the West. The modern-day embodiment of the Jacksonian ideal, Steninger feels rooted to the land—evident through the generations of ranchers in his family—and is extremely skeptical of the federal government, all administrative regulations, and scientific expertise.

When he first assumed public office, Steninger was himself a part of the many revolts by ranchers against the Bureau of Land Management. The BLM basically balances the use of around 620 million acres of federal lands for environmental, agricultural, recreational, and industrial purposes, most of it concentrated in the West. Ranchers typically pay grazing fees to feed their cattle on parts of federal land not designated national monuments or protected environmental areas. Steninger and other Sagebrush Rebellion supporters believed states should assume control of the land, which would allow localities more say in how lands were used, especially when it comes to environmental regulations. This was supported by Trump, who appointed a head of the BLM who backed more grazing on federal land; the idea of reducing federal regulation of public land is also a component of "Project 2025," a plan hatched by multiple far-right organizations for Trump's theoretical second term in office.

The use and control of federal land has long been an uneasy tug-of-war between businesses and environmentalists, with the government's priorities somewhere in the mix. The Bureau of Land Management was created in 1946 through the combination of the U.S. Grazing Service and the General Land Office, specifically to assist in logging, mining, and ranching. Only later did the BLM become involved in environmental and cultural preservation as well as in designating specific areas for camping and hiking. With the passage of the Endangered Species Act in the 1970s, environmentalists had a new tool to limit extractive industries like logging and ranching on public lands. As a result, the BLM was forced in many cases to preserve federal lands for wildlife, which meant reducing recreational and agricultural use of the land.

Steninger would have known about Richard Mack as the sheriff who stood with Nevada rancher and far-right icon Cliven Bundy, who, in 2014, orchestrated an armed standoff against the BLM. Bundy, who had been (and still is) grazing his cattle on public lands for years without paying the fees, faced an ultimatum from the federal government—either pay around a million dollars or have his cattle seized. The rancher's far-right views had been heavily influenced by the same roots of Mack's philosophy: the writings of W. Cleon Skousen and the so-called White Horse Prophecy that portrayed the Constitution as "hanging by a thread." As a result, Bundy did not think that the federal government had the right to charge him any fees at all. After multiple attempts to collect the debt through legal means, the BLM sent dozens of agents to Bundy's ranch in southern Nevada to round up the cattle. They were met with armed militia members, who had heard Bundy's calls to fight the federal government. The BLM backed off. Bundy declared victory, not for the last time.

Mack made mainstream news by appearing onstage with Bundy and declaring, "We were actually strategizing to put all the women up in front. If they're going to start shooting, it's going to be women that are going to be televised all across the world getting shot by these rogue federal officers." He criticized the Clark County sheriff for refusing to stand with Bundy and insisted that a sheriff's job was to support militias and other anti-government groups in conflicts against the federal government.

Bundy's ranch was over seven hours southeast of Elko County, yet Steninger felt a comradery with Bundy and the militias that joined him during the infamous standoff. As a fellow Mormon, Steninger would also have known that Bundy relied upon the White Horse Prophecy and the teachings of Skousen to argue that he had the authority to declare himself sovereign from the federal government. In echoes of Skousen, Bundy made additional headlines when he said that Black people were "better off" during slavery.

Possibly inspired, Steninger used his county position to support a local ranching couple, Dan and Eddyann Filippini, who were protesting the closure of BLM land for grazing. In 2014, around two dozen ranchers from Elko and the surrounding counties led the Grass March, which traveled on horseback from Nevada to Washington, D.C., in protest. Elko County commissioner Grant Gerber, then seventy-two, made the trek and died when he fell from his horse. The governor appointed Steninger to finish Gerber's term. In 2015, Steninger helped the Filippinis herd their cattle onto BLM land, violating regulations. The event made the *Elko Daily Free Press*.

People like Steninger provided the key for Mack to spread his message and create a demand for his traveling show. Elko County held its own Patriotic Social Gathering in mid-June. Steninger played the role of emcee and spoke about his devotion to preventing "the spread of liberalism."

He began with an apocryphal story of a Saudi "sheikh" with the moral that "hard times make strong men, strong men make easy times, easy times make weak men, weak men make hard times." He blamed the stimulus payments for "intentionally creating a nation of parasites so we will meekly follow them down the road of socialism." Thanking the sheriffs of Nevada who attended—much the same as at the Battle Mountain rally—Steninger concluded on a sorrowful note: "This pandemic has really illustrated how far we have fallen."

------

On July 9, 2021, the ARISE USA! tour stopped in Yankton, South Dakota, after a brief rally at Mount Rushmore. The crowd was much thinner, the podium less elaborate compared to the one in Battle Mountain.

Steninger wore a white cowboy hat and gave a speech, talking in his quiet, listless mutter. "We can't change this government unless we have a grassroots uprising from the people," he began.

He explained how he was inspired to make Elko County a constitutional county after attending the rally in Battle Mountain. "It was truly an extraordinary rally," he said. He added that he had contacted the CSPOA and pushed a county resolution through. "The reaction to it was absolutely amazing," he said. "People want their leaders to stand up and say, 'We are not going to take these abuses any longer.'"

On the front of the podium behind which Steninger stood were photographs of six Native Americans, noble in profile, wearing traditional clothing and headdresses. "People desperately want to return to our founding principles," he said, but he was referring to his dedication to ranching and the history of manifest destiny. He was not talking about the people who had been displaced so that the ranchers could fence off the land.

The residents of Lander County continued to raise the "constitutional county" specter when chastising the county commissioners for not doing enough about election fraud. Eventually, the commissioners agreed to spend a quarter of a million dollars to switch from Dominion voting machines to another company's. Their chief official in charge of elections resigned after the 2022 midterm, one of five Nevada election officials who quit that year.

"I am convinced the last election was stolen and have been involved in every way I can think of to reveal the steal and fix the system," Steninger wrote in an October 2021 email obtained by the *Nevada Independent*. The legacy of the constitutional county was just the beginning of a new rural rebellion.

# FIVE

# THE AMERICAN SHERIFF

## *Arizona's Mark Lamb*

IN JULY OF 2021, I WENT TO MEET SHERIFF MARK LAMB OF Pinal County, the third-largest county in Arizona, with a growing population of five hundred thousand and multiple state prison facilities. He was less than one year into his second term and, after the swearing-in of Joe Biden as president of the United States, had started a new sheriff association called Protect America Now that took the far-right ideology of the constitutional sheriff movement and transformed it into MAGA-appropriate language.

Its slogan: "Organize an army of patriots." The mission: "[Educate] Americans about how our Sheriffs and the law enforcement community are standing for our Constitution and law and order."

I met Lamb in Florence, a town about an hour from Phoenix, where the sheriff has his office. The diner he chose was Western-themed, decorated with horseshoes and silhouettes of cowboy-hatted men. Lamb, dressed in Western sheriff chic, fit right in.

Lamb had spent the past few years honing his brand, which could be described—and he does describe it so—as "American Sheriff." Conveniently, the phrase is his social media handle, the title of his self-published memoir—*American Sheriff: Traditional Values in a Modern World*—the name of his brief-lived charity, and the name of a now-defunct, subscription-based streaming series modeled after *Live PD* that he named *American Sheriff Network.*

According to his book, Lamb was six foot three and 240 pounds. When he stood to greet me, he seemed to tower over the room with his Justin cowboy hat, which makes him look both younger than his age (early fifties) and timeless, as if he had walked straight off the TV set for *American Sheriff Network.* He wore jeans, cowboy boots, a button-down Western-style shirt, and a leather belt with "Sheriff Lamb" tooled across the back—it was a gift from a friend, he told me.

He was confident but also aw-shucks, and he spoke colloquially, talking about how Biden's immigration policies "suck," calling certain liberal ideas "stupid," and describing his attempts to lose weight "for the camera." He ordered only a side of bacon. "I'm on a diet," he explained.

Also present during our interview was Corey Vale, a Republican public relations expert who worked at the time for the Lincoln Strategy Group, a "blue-chip" Republican political strategy firm. Vale, who is from Brooklyn, was pale and bookish, with wisps of light hair and glasses. While he presumably shared Lamb's politics, he didn't share Lamb's demeanor. His main job appeared to be keeping Lamb the actual sheriff and Lamb the "American Sheriff" separate and apart, which struck me as a full-time job. He informed me that the first twenty minutes Lamb had spent in the café, which I had missed, were full of more handshakes and greetings.

Vale's boss at Lincoln Strategy was Nathan Sproul, an Arizona Republican and leader in the Arizona Christian Coalition, a GOP political organization founded by Pat Robertson, the televangelist. Back in 2012, three of Sproul's employees pled guilty to voter registration fraud; Vale denied these claims were true, and Sproul himself was never charged. He also ran Kanye West's short-lived but very expensive presidential "campaign" in 2020. Vale joked that his boss was concerned that speaking to me would create bad press because I was a liberal journalist writing a piece for *Politico* at the time. "For him," Vale said, gesturing to Lamb, "it's all good."

Lamb's new group, Protect America Now, echoed the language of Posse Comitatus and the CSPOA, extolling God, closed borders, and the original Constitution, dog whistles for right-leaning, pro-gun, pro-militia, anti-progressive movements across the country. At the time we met, their presence had already made a mark through a special news segment on "border security" filmed by Fox News in April 2021, which featured a dozen sheriffs walking in the Arizona desert next to a portion of the border wall. Many of the sheriffs were from places as far from the southern border as South Dakota and Massachusetts.

At its founding, the membership of Protect America Now was around two dozen sheriffs. It has fluctuated since then and, at its height around 2022, listed as many as eighty sheriff members. Unlike Mack's CSPOA, the group was open about its membership, posting a list online, complete with pictures. As of early 2024, the website was no longer active and the Facebook page no longer showed new posts.

Like the CSPOA, Protect America Now espoused the far-right ideas that lay at the core of the constitutional sheriff movement. The organization opposed gun restrictions, immigration, and "those who want more government and want to raise our taxes to the point where we become a socialist country." It also had a distinct Christian nationalist bent, although it stopped short of saying that the Constitution represented God's natural law, as the CSPOA does. The PAN website instead said that the group "support[s] Sheriffs and law enforcement members that believe in God, Family and Freedom." Lamb often repeated that phrase—"God, Family, and Freedom"—and I could hear the capital letters in each word.

What made PAN different was its use of media, especially online videos. In fact, everything it did appeared to be related to generating media headlines, producing slick videos for Instagram, and setting up the sheriffs (mostly Lamb) as talking heads on Newsmax and, occasionally, Fox News. PAN did not offer training for law enforcement, nor did it focus on recruitment per se. Instead, it appeared positioned to make the constitutional sheriff movement look hip and palatable.

Protect America Now projected a glossy image, represented by Vale, who for all practical purposes stood for the GOP Arizona mainstream. Yet Vale was extremely cagey about explaining the structure of PAN. The organization solicited donations in the amount of $17.76. Through my own research, I found out that PAN was registered as an Arizona corporation and had initially borrowed money from Lamb's political campaign coffers—he ran unopposed in 2020—and received money from other local business donors. But Vale refused to tell me whether Lamb or anyone else received payments from the entity, nor did he ever say how many people had donated to the cause.

Vale did tell me that PAN came about because of Biden's election, something like "sheriffs for Trump" once Trump was out of office. Vale also insisted, despite all appearances, that PAN was not just about Mark Lamb. All of the priorities, he said, were discussed as a group, and he vehemently denied that there was a single individual in control. It was plain he did not want me to get the impression that Lamb made all of the political decisions, even though he was far and away the most online individual in the organization, as well as the one with the most political ambition.

Lamb described PAN as an organization for sheriffs who "just want to serve our people," a rather bland description for a group so stridently anti-Democrat. Protect America Now was not, he insisted, a political organization, but, rather, the political nature of the organization—whose media relentlessly targeted Biden's immigration policies, supported open carry legislation, and mocked Black Lives Matter activists—was a necessity created by the political moment. The group, per Lamb, was "standing for what [sheriffs] feel is right and correct. And unfortunately, it's viewed as political sometimes."

There was no question that, in this neck of the woods at least, Lamb was a celebrity. Throughout the two hours we spent in the diner, passersby kept stopping at the table and clasping Lamb on the shoulder, prompting a handshake and a Hollywood smile. In other media, Lamb has extolled the character of the people in his county, describing them as "true Americans" with conservative values. This seemed borne out by the patrons. Diners kept turning around to look at our table, where plainly something important was going on.

Another patron of the diner walked by. "Can we start calling you Senator?" he asked.

"No, no. Please don't. Sheriff's good with me," Lamb said, looking abashed like any good politician should.

––––––

Much of Lamb's background is detailed in his 2020 book *American Sheriff*, in which he succinctly describes his peripatetic childhood as growing up "all over the world," which included stints in Panama, Hawaii, and Chandler, Arizona. A member of the Church of Jesus Christ of Latter-day Saints, Lamb served his two-year mission in Argentina and moved to Utah, later returning to Arizona after he married. "I was a minority," he told me, describing his childhood years in Hawaii. "We learned to be tough and defend ourselves."

He has quite a lot in common with Richard Mack and claimed at one point that they were distantly related, which I could not confirm. Lamb told me he comes from a long line of Mormons descended from an early Mormon convert named Daniel W. Jones, who chronicled his migration to Arizona in a travel memoir, *Forty Years Among the Indians*. Jones was part of the great migration of Mormon settlers who fanned out from Utah and settled in what is now Mesa, part of the Mormon mission to spread their religious beliefs and escape persecution.

Lamb's personal life was substantially less dramatic than his forefather's. In Utah, Lamb and his wife, Janel, ran a series of businesses, eventually declaring bankruptcy after a paintball business went under. The family, which by then included five kids, moved to Arizona, outside Phoenix. Janel wrote her own book—*The Sheriff's Wife*, which was largely based on Mormon principles centering on family, children, and "enduring gossip"—in which she said she was a flight attendant for many of these years. From her book: "Statistics show it's harder to become a flight attendant than to get into Harvard."

Around the mid-2000s, Lamb was running a pest control business when he became intrigued with the idea of law enforcement. He had never served in the military or had any police training, but he was, he said, "into guns." "I was doing pigeon control," he told me, which meant being on the roofs of houses in 110-degree heat.

One day, Lamb went on a ride-along with a neighbor who worked for the Salt River Police Department, and he described with self-deprecation the adventure of the night: "So, we show up, and I get out of the car, and I'm armed with courage and a flashlight, walking around with the deputies looking for this guy. . . . Amongst a bunch of trash and clothes, I see what I thought was about a quarter size of skin."

It was clear he had told this story before. Lamb formed a circle with his thumb and forefinger, demonstrating how much skin he saw. "So, they dragged this guy out, and that morning I came home, and I told my wife I was gonna be a cop." He slumped back into the diner booth.

His decision to go into law enforcement was, if anything, also a story of the failing American social safety net: "So if you're self-employed, you don't have insurance, right? I have five kids. So, the thought of having insurance, the steady job, my wife was like, 'Let's do it.'" Further, compared to climbing on the roof all day, he said, being in law enforcement seemed safer. (The Bureau of Labor Statistics' job-safety ranking considers roofer, number 4, as much more dangerous than police officer, number 22, so Lamb had a point.)

His first law enforcement job was with the Salt River Police Department, where, he says, his ancestor Daniel Jones's book is required reading. Knowing that he wanted to be sheriff, Lamb took a job with the sheriff's office, but then quickly quit to run his campaign.

"I had this deep, burning desire to run for sheriff," he explained at a 2020 CSPOA event. "I knew it was the Lord speaking to me and telling me I had a path."

The path that Lamb took, despite his protestations to the contrary, treated the office of sheriff as both a content-creation business and a springboard to higher office. Unlike most candidates for sheriff, during his first campaign, Lamb didn't focus on his experience or how he would reform the office, which had been badly mismanaged by the prior sheriff, Paul Babeu. Instead, he talked about his values and labeled himself a "constitutional conservative." His political ads described his platform as "pro-life," "pro-gun," and "pro-religious freedoms." One of his first moves was telling voters that he did not believe in abortion rights, even though, in 2016, that was not part of the job description of sheriff. He later told me that, while some people criticized him for being "overly political," he was just being honest. "I'm an open book," he said.

An early 2016 campaign video, titled "The Progressives Are Coming," featured clips of Hillary Clinton talking about regulating gun sales intercut with video of Lamb and his family visiting a local gun store run by one of the county commissioners. A vote for Lamb, the ad implied, was a vote against Clinton and a vote "for your values," as he said in another campaign ad, which featured photos of Lamb and his large Mormon family.

His actual plans for the county and its sheriff's office—the third-largest in Arizona, with around five hundred employees and a $40 million budget— remained vague. Lamb's ads were poorly produced and appeared homemade, featuring footage of the candidate proudly putting up his own campaign signs along the side of the road and confessional-style videos in his truck asking people to send in their early ballots.

In his quest to get elected, Lamb paid homage to longtime civil rights pioneer Roberto Reveles, now in his nineties, who lives in a retirement community in Pinal County, at the foot of Superstition Mountain. Reveles has dedicated his life to Arizona politics. While he is officially retired, Reveles still exerts a great deal of influence on Pinal County politics and was extremely critical of the previous sheriff, Paul Babeu, who was running for Congress and giving up the sheriff post, leaving the office under the cloud of a $2 million budget deficit.

Reveles may have been a lifelong Democrat, but Lamb knew he still had to impress. On the day of their meeting, Reveles spent over two hours chatting with the ambitious candidate, sitting in a modest living room decorated with Reveles's art, including a bust Reveles made of Raúl Héctor Castro, the first Latino governor of Arizona.

"I expressed my concerns," Reveles explained to me years later. He told Lamb that he was "only ensuring law enforcement was not being politicized" and added that, so long as the sheriff-to-be adhered to "professional policing," Reveles would not criticize him in public.

As we spoke, Reveles paused, and his lips turned up in a wry smile.

"That was my start getting to know Mark Lamb," he told me.

---

In 1845, John O'Sullivan, the editor of the *New York Morning News*, coined the term "manifest destiny" to describe the belief not just that the United States was fated to acquire more territory but also that its citizens would spread a specific form of democracy rooted in agrarian culture and white supremacy. In speaking of the annexation of Texas to the country, O'Sullivan wrote, "It was our manifest destiny to overspread the continent allotted by Providence for the free development of our yearly multiplying millions."

Not every politician was a fan of O'Sullivan—Abraham Lincoln was a notable critic—but he captured the sentiment of the era, the idea that America was headed toward a uniquely bright future that necessitated Anglo expansion into the West. In an essay titled "The Great Nation of Futurity," O'Sullivan wrote of the "boundless future" Americans faced, one unburdened by a history of European aristocracy and its consequent ill-advised wars, which pitted the few against the many. Instead, America and Americans were destined for greatness, physically manifested as an unlimited expanse of land and horizon: the "noblest temple ever dedicated to the worship of the Most High" under a roof of "the firmament of the star-studded heavens" in which "hundreds of happy millions" lived "governed by God's natural and moral law of equality."

Arizona was part of the Western territories the United States acquired in the aftermath of the Mexican-American War, which ended in 1848. Anglo settlers had already been moving into the territories, forcibly removing the Native Americans and Mexicans already living there. Because the desert was not good for farming, the federal government pushed more Native tribes into Arizona to clear the land to the east, which was more fertile. There was a sense that the West was empty, waiting for conquest.

Arizona was long seen as undesirable, just an unforgiving desert full of snakes and scorpions on the route to the riches of California. Richard Josiah Hinton published a travel guide to the Arizona Territory in 1878, describing both the landscape and the people as unwelcoming and brutal: "Arizona became a shelter for desperadoes also, and it had long been a shelter for the Mexican gambrusinos, mine robbers, horse thieves and cut-throats." He goes on: "No civil law existed." Thus was set the template for the West and Arizona as an ungovernable place, almost as if nature intended it to be that way.

The job of the Western sheriff involved both facilitating the displacement and genocide of Mexicans and Indigenous people and managing the influx of mostly men who came west to work on the railroad and find their fortune, described as the "golden age of the sheriff as peace officer." In particular, white male itinerant workers, often labeled derisively as "hobos" or "tramps," were seen as unmoored from the responsibilities of a family and, as a result, a threat to public order.

As with all sheriff lore, the history of the Western sheriff is largely a construction of people looking backward, imbued with all of the biases and myths that color much of popular American history. A 1933 treatise mourns the Western sheriff as both a pinnacle of law enforcement and short-lived. "The western sheriff holds the stage for a generation or more," the author writes. "For the first time in history, and perhaps the last, he stands before us as a personally active agent for law enforcement." Rather than serve as a boring administrative functionary, the Western sheriff's job included "rounding up cattle thieves, leading a mounted posse in pursuit of desperados, or engaging in gun-play with tough characters." Yet, even in 1933, historians and criminologists cataloging such things noted that sheriffs, even Western ones, rarely lived up to the excitement of movies and were more often than not engaged in "prosaic functions."

One reason why there was this distance between the fantasy Western sheriff and the reality stems from the lack of uniform standards and guidelines for all law enforcement before the 1900s. In the first instance, sheriffs were Anglo transplants who lacked knowledge of the terrain; they relied on violence to compensate. There also weren't a lot of qualified applicants for law enforcement. One book laments that sheriffs were "compelled to deputize men with shadowy backgrounds" for want of other choices. The post of sheriff paid better than many other civil service jobs because sheriffs worked on a fee-for-service model. Holding people in jail, serving papers, and delivering a horse thief all entailed fees that the sheriff collected. As more people moved to the county, the sheriff made more money. According to one historian, there were even claims of local voter fraud because sheriffs would recruit itinerant workers to register to vote.

While the West represented opportunity, it was only opportunity for Anglo settlers. During the Civil War, Confederates, seeking more power and more citizens to tax, tried to claim Arizona by taking over Tucson. The ensuing battle, the Battle of Picacho Peak, was later memorialized by neo-Confederates who moved to Arizona in large numbers after World War I in an effort to mint the Western state as an extension of the Confederacy. There is a war reenactment at the spot each year.

As a result of the Confederate influence, Arizona, like much of the West, adopted the politics of the South, particularly as white Southern Democrats moved there for jobs in extractive industries and transportation. When Arizona became a state in 1912, there was only one representative of Mexican descent invited to the statehood convention (who refused to sign the charter to make Arizona a state). The politics remained racially divisive. White women in Arizona were granted the vote in 1912, nearly a decade before ratification of the Nineteenth Amendment, but literacy tests and other forms of voter suppression prevented many women of color from voting for another fifty years.

Since then, sheriffs have played an important role in Arizona's politics as tamers of the frontier and enforcers of the ethnic divide. Their role as mercenary, jailer, and frontier general made them ideal for policing wide-open land with no police and a federal government with not enough resources to protect burgeoning railroads from thieves. It is not coincidental that the myth of the heyday of the American sheriff takes place against a backdrop that juxtaposes freedom and violence, expansion with oppression.

Today, the Arizona sheriff's job duties are largely defined by statute. They include to "preserve the peace" and "prevent and suppress all affrays, breaches of the peace, riots and insurrections that may come to the knowledge of the sheriff." Because so much of Arizona outside Tucson and Phoenix is rural, with large portions of federal and tribal land, sheriffs there tend to exert more political power than they do in geographically smaller Eastern states.

More to the point, tourists still visit Tombstone to see mock historical gunfights, and fans of Westerns still thrill to tales of outlaws-slash-lawmen like Wyatt Earp, a vigilante gunfighter who became the law. The myth of the Arizona sheriff endures in the state and, arguably, has been influential in the constitutional sheriff movement. Mack was an Arizona sheriff. Additionally, the idea of manifest destiny was central to many of the claims of W. Cleon Skousen, William Gale, and other forebears of the constitutional sheriff movement. A course at the National Center for Constitutional Studies explains that manifest destiny was "God's will" and not about conquest.

———

Sheriffs have generally both been wary of publicity and sought it. A sheriff handbook compiled by an Illinois ex-sheriff in the 1990s points out that having a media presence is important for sheriffs in the modern day, particularly because the sheriff is seen as a politician as well as a leader who can exert a positive influence on the moral character of the community. The handbook advises sheriffs that the "key to success of the sheriff's social role is . . . the tact and discretion he exercises in working with the many social groups in which he is immersed."

Being in the media can help a sheriff. One recent study found that almost half of all voters knew their sheriff, more than any state-level politician other than governor. Sheriffs have often created their own brand through uniforms, slogans, and insignia that vary from sheriff to sheriff. (There are no coherent rules or guidelines to govern uniforms, slogans, or other branding.) Joe Arpaio claimed to be "America's Toughest Sheriff." In Kentucky, a handful of sheriffs borrowed the image of a kneeling Knight Templar for their patrol vehicles to signify service. Now sheriffs are more likely to use digital-age technology, producing slick videos that often feature land, air, and sea patrols. Some sheriffs use social media aggressively, posting the mug shots of people with open arrest warrants or making fun of arrestees. One Florida sheriff did a series of memorable TikTok videos featuring his SWAT team in full gear, their faces covered.

At the same time, the development of television in the United States also led to the ineffective sheriff character, like Sheriff Rosco P. Coltrane on *The Dukes of Hazzard*, or Sheriff J. W. Higgins, who starred in a series of television commercials for Dodge. A handbook mourns that such shows "portrayed sheriffs as either corrupt, lazy, minimally involved in law enforcement, stupid, inept, or come combination of the above coupled with other evil traits." These stereotypical Southern sheriffs emerged in popular culture at a time when urban policing was on the rise, and the good old boy sheriff was fast becoming a relic. (As discussed later in this book, the stereotypes were neither unwarranted nor were they relegated to popular media, as a series of more academic-style articles also began to question the role of the Southern sheriff in particular.)

When Mark Lamb became sheriff, he wholly embraced the public aspect of his job. Over his first few years, Lamb transformed from the red-polo-shirt-wearing civil servant into the social-media-ready sheriff, "a patina of professionalism," Reveles called it in our interview. Lamb began to wear his personal uniform: a Justin cowboy hat, jeans, cowboy boots, a flap-pocket Western shirt, and his "Sheriff Lamb" belt. Often, Lamb wears his flak vest, a tactical-style vest that says "Sheriff" across the front.

As I watched the videos of Lamb appearing regularly in front of the county board of supervisors, who approve his budget and must also approve any media that involves county equipment or infrastructure, I felt as though I was watching the evolution of a character, like a reiterative process of generating a sheriff from a man who ran to be sheriff. The sheriff as character. The sheriff as politician. The sheriff as county executive.

In 2018, Lamb started filming a season of *60 Days In*, an A&E network show that, much like its hit *Locked Up*, featured the county jail as a dangerous place that legitimate law enforcement needed civilians to infiltrate to subdue the criminal element. Lamb's season aired in 2019 and introduced the sheriff, the new Lamb, to the world. In the first episode, titled "New Sheriff in Town," Lamb exits his black Chevy Silverado as the camera pans from the landscape to his face, set in a grim, serious look. "It's the real Wild West out here," he intones in a voice-over by way of introduction. "I am all about God, guns, and freedom. Every day it's a fight to protect them," he says directly to the camera, smiling his telegenic smile that appears to be chemically enhanced.

Also in 2019, Lamb became a host of *Live PD: Wanted*, a spin-off from the popular original, one of the most-watched police shows in the country. *Live PD* purported to show American policing in "real time," which meant car chases, searches, and arrests of people who often appeared to suffer from substance-use disorders. In essence, it was to policing what *The Apprentice* was to entrepreneurship. Lamb's spin-off focused on catching fugitives, like a father who kidnapped his child and a teenager who robbed a street vendor.

In June of 2020, A&E canceled the entire *Live PD* franchise, including Lamb's show, following a well-publicized incident in Texas. Deputies from the Williamson County Sheriff's Office were caught on camera tasing a man named Javier Ambler multiple times. Ambler died as a result. In response to the incident, Texas passed a state law that forbade law enforcement agencies from partnering with reality television shows. The George Floyd protests during the summer of 2020 put the final nail in the show's coffin. Thus ended one of Lamb's main sources of free political advertising.

Nonetheless, Lamb endured. By 2020, he had fully adopted his American Sheriff persona. Lamb started a charity, American Sheriff Foundation, using his *Live PD* popularity to sell T-shirts that said "American Sheriff" on the front. (A news report found a variety of discrepancies in the foundation's accounting and it is no longer operational. Lamb said it was an inadvertent error.) He advertised and helped to sell American Sheriff–branded firearms.

The website AmericanSheriff.com, which once belonged to the nonprofit, was redirected to the streaming network, which stopped producing new content by 2022. In 2023, the network was sold to TruBlu, a true-crime streaming service.

Lamb framed the television show as giving sheriffs a "voice." "We just felt like it was important to give them their voice back. And not only that, it's a voice that the people in America want to hear," he said.

"We really just want to showcase real sheriffs, real stories," Lamb continued, borrowing the network's tagline. The trailer for the new network featured lots of shots of Lamb—his profile against a desert sunset as the camera panned slowly over the shadows of cacti. He flashed his trademark smile as he talked about "the shine on the badge."

Lamb expressed sorrow about the "cancel culture" he blamed for ending the *Live PD* franchise. "You know, *Live PD* was the number one show on TV and gone overnight."

The COVID pandemic and ensuing partisan divides over masking and vaccines provided Lamb another opportunity to make the national news. Early in the pandemic, Lamb became a media sensation when he refused to follow business closure or mask mandates. Then, in the summer of 2020, he caught COVID himself, which he says he discovered when he went to meet with then-president Donald Trump and was tested. On the local news, he argued for "personal responsibility" in managing the virus.

Once COVID vaccines became available, Lamb issued a video in which he said he would not require vaccines for his employees, sworn or otherwise. "As long as I'm your sheriff, we will *never* mandate the vaccine," he said in the video, which went viral and ended up on Fox News. One Instagram post from his account reads, "No vaccine, no mask . . . I did test positive though for Americanitis!" underneath a photo of Lamb leaning back on a bench and smiling. I asked Lamb if he was vaccinated, and he told me to print exactly this: "That's nobody's damn business."

That summer, Lamb also decided to form a citizens' posse to protect the people against Black Lives Matter protesters. There were no large-scale protests in Pinal County, but the posse became something of a symbol in an era during which membership in militias was steadily climbing. Lamb said that in the first week he received hundreds of applications.

In Lamb's telling, the posse was about giving people a productive outlet at a time when police morale was low, a way for some people to "squelch some of the frustration that they're feeling right now." The Arizona far-right Republican legislator Kelly Townsend spoke in praise of Lamb's posse as a form of militia organizing in response to the protests in Kenosha, Wisconsin. "No longer are Americans going to sit by and watch a town burn to the ground," she told her audience in a video.

For his resistance to state and federal health guidelines, Lamb garnered the praise of Richard Mack, the CSPOA founder, who called him a "good constitutional sheriff." He was also praised on Fox News, Newsmax, and the podcast of Sebastian Gorka, Trump's short-lived deputy assistant to the president. Appearing at the maskless CSPOA meeting held at Liberty University during the fall of 2020, Lamb stood in front of a series of murals depicting Jesus after the crucifixion—removed from the cross and carried away. Then Jesus rises.

"For those of you who don't know, the Constitution is hanging by a thread," he said, gesturing to the paintings behind him and referring to Mormon prophecy. "The thread is the sheriffs of this great country."

---

Arizona has a tradition of bombastic sheriffs who make splashy headlines, plus a well-known harsh and punitive criminal legal system. In fact, one of the original architects of the state's penal system was Sheriff Frank Eyman of Pima County. In 1953, Eyman arrived at the state prison in Florence to help end a protest caused by overcrowded conditions. According to a news account, Eyman ended the insurrection with a flood of tear gas and lined suspected ringleaders against the wall. "We don't care how much blood and guts we have to spill," he threatened. His actions were violent but effective in their way, which pleased state leaders. A short time later, Eyman took over the prison and spent almost two decades as head of the state prison system. He set the template for the state's penal system today by instituting incredibly tough, military-style discipline, including a rigid codebook. Under his control, the prison "operated as an efficient, nearly complete self-contained village."

Eyman's purely punitive model of incarceration set the template for county sheriffs, who largely expanded on his ideas of rigorous discipline and harsh violence. To take the most famous example, Joe Arpaio's ideas were not particularly innovative, because they were already the practice in many Arizona state prisons. Many of Arpaio's early initiatives targeted people in his custody and were sold as cost-reduction measures—"tough and cheap," as criminologist Mona Lynch writes. As Lynch goes on to explain, one impact of the rise of Arpaio in the press ended up being the legitimization of violent and aggressive state penal practices that reformers were trying to eliminate.

That violence became the intent behind Arpaio's media stunts. When the county refused to fund a new jail, Arpaio held a press conference outside his "tent city" jail in August that made the front page of the *Arizona Republic*. Reporters noted that the outside temperature was 101 degrees; inside the tents it was hotter. When Arpaio created a posse of volunteer deputies, he paraded them in front of reporters at every opportunity. Same with the "chain gang." He marched seven hundred people, handcuffed together, wearing only pink underwear and pink flip-flops, for the cameras. One inmate was forced to cut a pink ribbon.

Arpaio never missed a chance to be in the spotlight. When Mack started the CSPOA, he joined, seeing it as another opportunity for a captive audience. Arpaio called himself a constitutional sheriff and praised Mack's mission. He also praised Mack's 2009 book: "[Mack's] lawsuit and subsequent victory at the Supreme Court proved once and for all that the Sheriff is indeed the ultimate law enforcement authority in his county and in this country. He is not a bureaucrat and he does not answer to one. He answers to his boss, the citizens."

Lamb himself invites the inevitable comparison to Joe Arpaio. Vale reassured me that Lamb was nothing like Arpaio and confessed conspiratorially that he found Arpaio to be mean. He implied that Lamb tried to avoid him. Less than a year later, a photo appeared on social media of Lamb standing chummily next to Arpaio at a GOP event.

————

The ethics surrounding sheriffs and their role as politicians versus their role as law enforcement are incredibly muddy, even though incumbent sheriffs must campaign for office as they attend to their day-to-day jobs. In many states, sheriffs cannot campaign in their official uniforms, but they can hold press conferences to announce their political positions while wearing their uniforms. Even when sheriffs are not wearing their official uniforms, they can wear signs of the office, like cowboy hats, sidearms, and shirts that say

"Sheriff." Lamb's flak vest is not official, but it says "Sheriff" across the front. Such markers of the office still represent authority and legitimacy, and the official day job provides an automatic audience with politicians, voters, and potential donors.

---

One of the most common criticisms, one that Lamb deeply resents, is that he spends more time being "American Sheriff" than "Pinal County sheriff," which is less glamorous but more relevant. The subject came up during his first term when Lamb asked the board of supervisors for permission to enter into agreements with production companies. Community members, including Reveles, critiqued Lamb for spreading himself too thin with all of the American Sheriff–themed products. The county board largely approved all of these projects, although they did not approve a television show that would have been about drug smuggling in the county. (They felt it would make the county seem dangerous.) Pro-police propaganda, however, was generally fine.

Like the county board, Lamb sees his extracurriculars as a service to the profession. Vale told me that Lamb had received messages from across the country from viewers, "the kind no one ever sees." I tried to follow up with Vale for specific examples of viewer feedback, as well as detailed data on how many subscribers and the income Lamb derives from the show. He said he could only tell me that there were "thousands." He was similarly vague on whether Lamb derives a profit from the network, which is organized as an LLC, with Lamb as one of the partners.

Reveles, the advocate, eyed Lamb's thirst for media as part of his politicization of the office to the detriment of those people most likely to be detained by the police. "It is fair to say over the years . . . he has become an extreme anti-immigrant, pro-Trump advocate. . . . My concerns have been exacerbated by all of his activities that take him outside his official sheriff's duties." Pinal County is over an hour from the U.S.-Mexico border. Reveles continued, "He clearly has politicized law enforcement, and that covers a lot of territory. Self-centered, extremist, anti-immigrant individual. It's something that I don't tolerate."

From what I can tell, Lamb is not violating ethics rules or any other regulations governing sheriffs and their office—because they don't really exist. The National Sheriffs' Association, of which Lamb is a member, does have a nonbinding model code of ethics for sheriffs that prohibits using the office for "private gain," among other things. Patrick Royal, a spokesperson for the NSA—who took time to praise Lamb and called him a "unicorn"— told me that while the code of ethics is the "basis of an organizational creed," sheriffs generally rely on their state laws for legal guidance. In fact, Royal said he wished more sheriffs were like Mark Lamb, at least in terms of their media savvy.

No rules require Lamb to report profits he makes, either in his appearances at gun shows, as a speaker at rallies, or through his product branding. Lamb would not disclose that information. I asked Sean Kennedy, a professor at Loyola Law School who is on the oversight commission for the Los Angeles County sheriff, about Lamb's involvement with Protect America Now, and he said he believes Lamb's behavior violates the NSA's code of ethics. Kennedy pointed to the provision about private gain, as well as one requiring equal protection of all citizens, without allowing "personal opinion, party affiliations, or consideration of the status of others to alter or lessen this standard of treatment."

Lamb said he keeps a strict division between his work as the Pinal County sheriff and his image as the "American Sheriff." Vale added, "All of his activities, both as sheriff and in his private time, are vetted through the [Pinal] County attorney."

During my visit, I was not allowed to set foot inside the official Pinal

County Sheriff's Office; I was not even allowed in the parking lot of the building. I was, however, permitted to sit in the sheriff's gigantic black pickup truck, which has a workstation in the center console and is the site of many of the sheriff's television appearances.

In 2022, Lamb permitted a French documentary crew to see the inside of his office, whose interior reflected the ways in which Lamb had embraced the American Sheriff as a media figure and a politician. The lobby showed Pinal County deputies executing tactical moves on a video loop. Inside his office, Lamb had a movie poster depicting himself that he said was a gift. It showed Lamb grinning, assault rifle in hand. Prominently displayed next to the poster, and much smaller, was a profile of Donald Trump in the style of the Apple logo. Behind his desk hung an antique firearm.

Pinal County supervisor Jeff Serdy owns a gun shop in the county and has been extremely supportive of Lamb. I asked Serdy whether he had concerns about Lamb's many roles. Was he worried it was unmanageable? "As long as the job is being done, then we support it," he answered. He added, "You could not ask for a better advocate for the Second Amendment than Sheriff Lamb."

But this concern expressed by residents in Pinal, which Lamb interpreted as about his abilities and time, is less about how many hours are in a day—although that is a valid question—but about whether there is a contradiction in being a sheriff who openly supports certain rights and being a sheriff who is required by law to protect everyone's rights, all the time. The job of sheriff, I have been told many times over, is unique because of the closeness between the sheriff and the voters. The National Sheriffs' Association says, "The Office of Sheriff protects the Public from undue political influence on a day-to-day basis." This contemplates that the people need protecting from other politicians. But who is supposed to protect the public from the politician who is the sheriff?

I had suggested that we go to a shooting range because I knew that was Lamb's favorite pastime. His wife, Janel, is also fond of shooting and appears on social media frequently with Lamb at gun ranges and gun shows.

We don't go to a shooting range as much as an open sandy field that Lamb said belongs to a friend of his. Pinal County is 5,400 square miles, the size of Connecticut, and most of it is sand. It was hot. The week before, the temperature had been a newsworthy 110 degrees–plus. The day I met Lamb, it was closer to 100 and a faint wisp of cloud floated in the sky, daring itself to cover the blazing sun. Lamb loved it. He wore Wranglers, worn cowboy boots, a black shirt with rolled sleeves, a fully loaded tactical vest, and his "Sheriff Lamb" belt. He barely seemed to sweat.

The back of Lamb's black Chevy Silverado 2500 HD contained his workaday weaponry, an AR-15 SBR, which is the weapon of choice for many mass shooters. The SBR stands for "short barrel rifle," which means it's shorter than the usual AR-15 rifle, making it more maneuverable if you were, say, negotiating narrow hallways. On his person, Lamb had his Glock, plus a long knife, a Taser with the Punisher logo on it, extra rounds of ammunition, handcuffs, and a patch that says "Sheriff." There were probably other weapons on his person that I didn't know about—because why not?

Lamb taught me how to shoot his AR-15, which allowed the user to adjust between semiautomatic and burst or automatic fire. (This is generally only legal for law enforcement and military.) That basically meant it fired lots of bullets really fast. Lamb emphasized to me earlier that Protect America Now was about the rule of law, except if that law was unconstitutional. One of the things he found unconstitutional was gun regulation. On this, he provided some context: "The Second Amendment is for people to be able to protect themselves. And it even says in there, even against a tyrannical government. And that's what the Second Amendment is about. . . . More people die by hands and feet." (This is categorically false.)

He went on. "We continue to ignore evidence and facts, and we play on emotion and politics. And that's, you know, I think that's dangerous when it comes to the Second Amendment. [Democrats are] attacking something, yet they don't have the statistics to support it."

Sheriff Lamb, like most of Arizona, loves the Second Amendment. Arizona is one of a growing number of states that allow "constitutional carry," which means that any eligible adult can carry a firearm without a permit, either openly or concealed. About thirty states have some form of open carry laws, many of which were passed since 2022.

When we left the gun range and stopped by a gas station to get some water to ensure we didn't die of dehydration, we again ran into fans. A man with tattoos and well-groomed blond facial hair wearing a "Proud American" T-shirt sold by the ultraconservative shock jocks the Hodge twins ran across the parking lot for a photo with the sheriff. When I excused myself for being in the way—really, the whole entourage was in the way—another man walking by said, "The sheriff is a good dude." A group of kids gathered around Lamb's truck for a sheriff-branded sticker. Lamb embraced the moment and gave me a "Sheriff Lamb" Velcro patch for my nonexistent tactical vest.

Interestingly, Lamb was quite willing to wax poetic on what he called the "rule of law." He told me, in reference to the many protests across the country opposing police brutality and racism, "The rule of law is being undermined in this country. And the rule of law is what has made America strong for so long. . . . But we're losing that. We saw it last year with the riots and looting. It feels most people—the constituents I talk to—feel like if you are of a certain party, you're not gonna be held accountable. And it's starting to be more and more apparent."

During our conversation, when I asked Lamb about January 6—didn't that violate the rule of law?—he volleyed back with objections to the treatment of Black Lives Matter protesters in Portland and Minneapolis, arguing they had never been held accountable: "I don't think that Black Lives Matter is productive for the Blacks. I don't. Because if they were, they'd be in Chicago, raising hell over these kids being killed."

But, I pressed on, wasn't January 6 an example of people violating the rule of law?

Lamb rejoindered. "I would have to view video. I would have to see evidence of a [law] being broken. . . . It's not my job to investigate, you know, what happened on January 6. And if I found that crimes were committed, then, yeah, you'd have to hold those people accountable. Just because somebody was there doesn't necessarily mean they're guilty. And I think we have to be very careful that we don't turn that into a political investigation." Later he added, "Because I guarantee you those people are very loving, Christian people. They just happen to support President Trump a lot."

I kept asking Lamb whether he felt he had an obligation to ensure that his fans, all the people watching the *American Sheriff Network* and reading *American Sheriff* and buying American Sheriff T-shirts, that those people didn't become more violent.

"I never said [Biden] wasn't president," Lamb said, at once saying that he didn't think there was election fraud while also suggesting that perhaps it was a possibility. He told me he believed that the media was overplaying the January 6 investigation. Pressed about the role of a sheriff, of someone that I watched people all day claim to know and respect, Lamb was remarkably, well, political. "I'm a very pro-freedom person. I believe in letting people live the way that they feel like they need to live," he concluded.

And while Mark Lamb's name isn't (yet) as common as Matt Gaetz, Marjorie Taylor Greene, or Stephen Miller, that's by design. As Lamb takes pains to point out, sheriffs are elected by the residents of a county, the most basic unit of government that applies to every single inch of land in America.

"It's not like Congress. . . . You can actually effect change as the sheriff. And you can do it in a timely manner. And I like that. I think there's, there is a beauty to that," he told me.

"I've never had a desire to run for Senate or Congress. I'm a patriot at heart. I love America. And I will serve the people where I can," Lamb confirmed. He propounded on the role of a sheriff, saying, "The sheriff is designed to protect the people from the bad guys. And I always say the sheriff is also there to protect the people from government overreach."

Lamb became a daily talking head on Fox News and Newsmax, deriding Biden's "failed" immigration policies and mocking Kamala Harris. He has a 13,800-member fan club on Facebook, impressed the ex–Trump adviser Sebastian Gorka by killing a rattlesnake in the desert, and spoke at Charlie Kirk's 2021 Turning Point USA Student Action Summit in Phoenix, where he quoted Shakespeare and Thomas Paine ("Tyranny, like hell, is not easily conquered") and promised that "the sheriffs are going to hold the line" in the fight against imaginary voter fraud. He represents a new strain of far-right sheriffs who are taking the idea of a "constitutional sheriff" in a decidedly Trump-y direction. As a reality TV star, he built up a network that validated the sheriff as the most important and praiseworthy law enforcement officer in the nation. All of this makes Mark Lamb an important figure to understand as the country decides how to deal with the legacy of January 6 and a Republican Party intent on ignoring the fact that the last president tried to take over the nation by force.

Clearly, Lamb is trying to refashion himself into the sheriff-politician, with a lot of Trump in the mix. He has remained a steadfast Trump supporter despite the ex-president's multiple indictments. And, like Trump, he has no qualms about using his office to court voters for his Senate campaign. Just as all of Lamb's endeavors run together, it can be hard to separate Lamb the candidate from Lamb the sheriff.

For example, a 2023 investigation by a local news outlet found that Lamb may have misused over $200,000 in inmate welfare funds, which come from incarcerated people when they purchase items from the commissary or make phone calls. Under state law, such money should go toward improving jail conditions, but he used the cash for firearms. Lamb angrily defended the spending at a Board of Supervisors meeting, arguing that he was entitled to purchase weapons as part of his job protecting those incarcerated in the jail. He called the story a "hit piece" aimed at him because of his political positions.

His latest gigs have gotten higher up the totem pole in terms of Republican politics. In the fall of 2021, Lamb was a featured speaker at the American Priority Conference, an event that is basically the equivalent of a right-wing Coachella, where he appeared alongside people like Michael Flynn and Roger Stone.

Lamb appeared at Trump's first rally in Florence, Arizona, in 2022, where tens of thousands of people camped in the desert for the chance to see the onetime president kick off another campaign. Before Trump took to the stage, Lamb waved to the crowds and received thunderous applause.

When Trump came onstage, he said, his tone petulant, "Mark Lamb, he's popular. Sheriff, would you like to run for another office?"

# SIX

# "I PAID FOR YOU TO KILL MY SON"

## *Sheriffs as Jailers*

ON A TUESDAY IN MAY OF 2015, TWENTY-SEVEN-YEAR-OLD Lamar Johnson was driving through the suburbs of Baton Rouge, Louisiana, to pick up his grandmother from dialysis treatment. Before he got to his destination, a police officer pulled him over, saying that his car windows were tinted too dark, a common pretext for pulling over Black drivers.

His mother, Linda Franks, told me in an interview that her son, like all Black men, had learned early on to be careful around the police: "We understand, and we try to prepare our kids that this is a fact of life for you."

According to police reports and body camera footage, Johnson was polite and accommodating. He would have normally just received a ticket, but the arresting officer found that Jackson had an outstanding warrant from 2011 in Jefferson Parish. As a result, the officer told Johnson he had no choice but to arrest him on the outstanding warrant and take him to the East Baton Rouge jail (which is named the East Baton Rouge Parish Prison, or EBRPP) to sort it out. Franks said her son called her when he got to the jail to "let me know that he was okay, not to worry. It was a minor traffic thing, and it was going to be fine."

Jefferson Parish is just outside New Orleans and about ninety minutes from East Baton Rouge. Normally in this situation, Johnson would have been transferred to the Jefferson Parish jail because that was where his warrant was entered. But there were delays in contacting Jefferson Parish authorities, so, until the transfer was finalized, Johnson had to stay in EBRPP.

In Louisiana, once someone is booked into jail, the law requires that the sheriff bring them to see a judge within seventy-two hours for what is often called an "initial appearance" or "arraignment," depending on the court. During the initial appearance, the arrestee is informed of the charges against them, and the judge sets bail, which is the amount of money someone is required to pay in order to be released from jail pending trial. Bail amounts are intended to ensure that a person charged with a crime returns to court, but often people are unable to pay any bail, so they must stay incarcerated until their case is resolved. About 30 percent of arrestees nationwide cannot afford to pay any amount of bail and are thus incarcerated without being convicted of any crime.

Johnson was caught in a tricky situation. He couldn't see a judge in East Baton Rouge because his case was in Jefferson Parish. But he also could not control when Jefferson Parish decided to initiate his transfer. These were decisions all left up to the county sheriffs, which often means long delays, especially on weekends or holidays.

Franks spent the week calling the East Baton Rouge Sheriff's Office repeatedly to see if she could pay her son's bail so that he could come home, but she was told there was nothing to pay because the warrant was from Jefferson Parish. She told me that holding people in jail, even when unnecessary, as in Johnson's case, is a common practice of Louisiana sheriffs. "One of the real unique features of Louisiana," she said, "is how the sheriffs freely swap prisoners and charge each other [for holding people]. There are lots of stories of overcrowding, and [sheriffs] ship people hundreds of miles away from lawyers and families. The longer they stay, the more [money] the jail makes."

EBRPP is run by Sheriff Sid Gautreaux III, who has been in office since 2007. Johnson told his mother on a phone call that the East Baton Rouge jail was overcrowded and dirty, with feces on the walls. Open-air dorms held around one hundred men, supervised by only one or two guards. Fights broke out frequently.

Finally, on Friday, the Jefferson Parish Sheriff's Office agreed to pick up Johnson on Monday. Monday morning, Franks drove to the Jefferson Parish jail expecting to pay her son's bail and take him home.

"Oh, they didn't tell you?" a deputy asked her. Over the weekend, Johnson had been hospitalized. He had attempted to die by suicide. According to the sheriff's office, Johnson had a psychotic episode caused by synthetic marijuana, which was widely available inside EBRPP.

Franks sped to the hospital, but when she got there, deputies wouldn't let her see her son. "The jail told me I needed to bring verification that Lamar was my son," she said. She found his vaccination records and his high school diploma; only then was she allowed to see him. He was shackled to the hospital bed, barely alive.

The next day, Johnson lost consciousness, and mere days after that, his family removed him from life support. He died the day his daughter graduated from kindergarten. "I thought they killed him," Franks told me. "They did something to him. . . . I am a taxpayer, and I paid for you to kill my son."

―――――――

Almost every state, through legal code or constitutional mandate, grants county sheriffs the ability to control local jails, like the one where Lamar Johnson died. Today about 85 percent of local jails are controlled by sheriffs, which makes jails the only carceral institutions in this nation that are run by elected officials. Sheriffs control everything in a jail, from the type and quantity of food, how medical care will be doled out, what the housing looks like—double cell, dormitory style, or solitary confinement—and what sorts

of necessities people will be permitted, everything from phone calls, to com-
missary, to an extra blanket when it is cold. Sheriffs are even in control of
transporting people from jail to court or to the hospital for treatment (and
make the decisions whether or not to do so).

Despite this near-absolute power, sheriffs have resisted change and oversight in their jails. Many politicians and other local leaders also ignore the
jail unless there's a problem that attracts the press (like an escapee). The
history of jails helps to explain why this is so.

For one day on the internet in the summer of 2020, people were fascinated by an old house in Missouri. Built in 1875, the house was on sale for
$350,000, with a hardwood floor and new fixtures in the bathroom and
kitchen. It also had a nine-cell jail attached, via a door in the kitchen. The
owner apparently thought that the jail would make a great "escape room" or
"haunted house."

While people reacted with a mixture of amusement, shock, and horror,
this was indeed how most jails in America existed for the bulk of the country's history—informally and largely relying on the labor of a sheriff's wife
and children to keep it running. This was particularly true in rural regions,
where the population was sparse and sheriffs could act based on personal
financial incentives and prejudice, unencumbered by questioning eyes.

During the 1800s, many county jails were just small rooms attached to
the sheriff's house or, sometimes, abandoned mining shafts. Inmates were the
sheriff's personal responsibility, and they were incentivized to keep their
wards alive and healthy because they were paid a per diem fee for each person.
(Sheriffs also did not want to consolidate their jails because it would mean
losing the fees.) Sheriffs' wives did the cooking and cleaning for the inmates,
without pay, of course. Women and children, who were rarely incarcerated,
were generally the wife's responsibility, and they were treated like members
of the household. Men were held in the same room regardless of why they
were there; witnesses, debtors, and suspected murderers all mixed together.

A sheriff's greatest challenge was ensuring that detainees did not escape or else he would lose his promised compensation. As one nineteenth-century sheriff treatise explained, "The sheriff or his jailer is bound to have sufficient force to prevent a breach of the prison, for nothing but the act of God, or an accidental fire in the jail, or the act of the public enemies, will excuse an escape, after one has been committed to prison."

Perhaps such warnings rang so true because escapes and armed rebellion were common. Walls were straw or wood, easy to infiltrate, and generally unguarded. In addition to being the cooks and cleaners, wives sometimes had to pick up firearms and defend their sheriff husbands when things turned violent. A newspaper article from 1900 praised a sheriff's wife who helped defuse a potential riot in the attached jail. "She did not scream and she did not faint," the writer explained, preventing further violence until help arrived. Another wife made the papers for fighting alongside her husband to rescue their toddler, whom a jail escapee had taken hostage. The sheriff held a gun and the wife a broom.

While many rural jails were mom-and-pop operations, by the mid-nineteenth century, cities were building dedicated structures to detain people. Some larger urban centers like Chicago and Los Angeles constructed what amounted to congregate jails, little more than casually governed large rooms. In Chicago, such a jail was built below the county courthouse in 1853. In 1869, a man tried to set it on fire by using his pipe to set the straw mattress aflame. The fire consumed the entire room, and, according to the *Chicago Tribune*, "everything combustible in the cell was soon on fire, and the inmates literally stood in the flame." When a guard finally opened the door, the men ran out, their hair on fire. All of them died. The *Tribune's* writers did not think the idea of setting the jail on fire was necessarily a bad one, calling the facility "an abomination in the sight of man; a pest house in which the living decompose."

By the twentieth century, jails were an obvious site of disease, violence, and chronic abuses across the country, urban and rural, West, South, and East. Author and policing expert Frank Richard Prassel wrote, "Sadism, personal gain, and simple indifference turned the jails into incredible human jungles of depravity," which he blamed on the fee system: "Collecting fees for care of prisoners from various governmental units, [sheriffs] could then provide food and other items for prisoner use at unconscionable prices. By hiring guards, maintaining buildings, and supplying meals at the lowest possible actual cost, profits could be maximized."

One way to keep people out of the jails, as sheriffs learned early on, was to rent them out as labor. This overcame the practicalities of holding people in a room for weeks or months, but it created other abuses. It also coincided with a boom in jail populations. Before the Civil War, sheriffs would occasionally hold enslaved people who had been trapped by slave catchers, either collecting fees from the white slaver or, if no one came, selling the enslaved person and keeping the profit for themselves. But the number of people in jail was relatively small.

After Reconstruction, sheriffs, alongside law enforcement more generally, began to arrest and jail Black people for violations of Black Codes, laws that governed how and where Black people could assemble or travel and set long jail sentences for petty theft. Once a person was arrested, sheriffs participated in the practice of convict leasing, which allowed them to profit from those they jailed. This was the beginning of jails as big business.

Convict leasing was a system where jailers leased out the labor of incarcerated people, which both relieved them of caring for them and meant that the jailer could make, not spend, money. The lessees, who were told that they needed to work off their sentence, participated in all manner of private industry, including mining, farming, and factory work. This practice continues today, albeit now the workers receive some compensation, ranging from a few cents to a dollar or two an hour. Sheriffs send their incarcerated populations to work at many types of businesses, from fast food to chicken processing to public works, like cleaning up trash and tending the grass on roadsides.

Most Southern penal institutions participated in convict leasing, but jails were especially notorious for physical abuses. John Henderson, a Texas judge in the late 1800s who was a prominent critic of leasing, argued that the worksites and living conditions run by county sheriffs ranked even lower "in the scale of degradation than the state convict camps," even though the people confined there had admittedly committed "lesser crimes." In many cases, Henderson pointed out, these were men who owed fines, and thus were sent to work on local farms because they were poor. Plus, there was the danger of having young boys who were "housed and worked with hardened criminals," which would only school these innocent youth in crime. Those being held in county lockups were often unable to make their voices heard. In Liberty County, Texas, a man complained of living in an "eight foot cell" and watching those around him lose their teeth thanks to scurvy.

As time went on, states abolished convict leasing, but jails remained unregulated and dangerous. Most of the people held in jail had not committed serious crimes and many were guilty of no more than being bad or disorderly. Historian Melanie Newport, in her study of the Cook County jail, *This Is My Jail*, also emphasizes the fact that jails were thought to contain the "rabble," not criminals, as the basis of her argument that jails have been historically used to define racial differences, with political demands changing the meaning of jails over time.

In 1957, jails were described as containing "heterogenous conglomerations of humanity spewed from the gutters." Many of the people held in jails were labeled as "drunkards" or, more generally, people that society did not feel like dealing with. The thought was that the jail was for people who needed to be removed from the community for a short amount of time but not punished for their behavior. In 1967, a survey of a city jail found half of the people were there for "drunkenness."

In one of the few early books written about jails, *Jails: The Ultimate Ghetto of the Criminal Justice System*, attorney Ronald Goldfarb (who was part of LBJ's task force tackling poverty) remarked that jails are for, in essence, poor people. He cited another policing expert who called jails "the traditional dumping ground for the untried, the petty offender, the vagrant, the debtor and beggar, the promiscuous or the mentally ill." Goldfarb described his visit to a jail in Atlanta and his shock at the conditions, which he compared very unfavorably to those of state prisons. "I was shocked to discover conditions so horrible I could not believe them. . . . Inside a relatively modern exterior in a modest, busy part of town was a cramped, dark, dank interior. Large, four-sided cages each held sixteen men. . . . [I]nmates are kept inside these cages twenty-four hours a day. . . . [T]here is no privacy and no activity at all."

As jail populations grew in the 1970s, people like Goldfarb thought that this assortment of people were not, in fact, "real" criminals but were unfortunate. The jails were now large edifices, built as modern accoutrements for bustling cities, made of concrete blocks and conceived of with complicated architectural plans. Yet, at the same time, jails provide little if no opportunities for rehabilitation. This is not what they were designed to do.

John Irwin's 1985 *The Jail: Managing the Underclass in American Society* remains one of the main scholarly treatments of jails as an institution. Irwin argues that "the jail, not the prison, imposes the cruelest form of punishment in the United States." The concern about jail conditions coincided with an explosion of the incarcerated population, particularly in jails. Between 1955 and 2008, jail admissions in the United States increased from less than 1 million to a peak of 13.6 million.

———

Today, jails are an integral part of the criminal legal system and incarcerate huge numbers of people in near-constant flux. According to the Bureau of Justice Statistics, the country's three-thousand-plus local county jails receive nearly 9 million admissions every year. An analysis by the Prison Policy Initiative found many people were admitted more than once; at least 4.9 million individuals were booked into jail one or more times in 2019. Many law enforcement officials refer to this as the "revolving door," by which they mean that people are booked into jail, released, and then frequently rearrested within days or weeks. About seven hundred thousand people are in county jails on any given day, and the population of any individual jail can range from a dozen to thousands of people. For example, the Los Angeles jail system, the nation's largest, regularly holds an average of thirteen thousand detainees on any given day.

Jails are still treated like a temporary holding place for people on their way somewhere else—either court, prison, or home. Many more people see the inside of a jail than the inside of prison. Most people in jail have been arrested but not yet convicted of a crime or are serving shorter sentences, under a year. Others are there awaiting a transfer or court hearing. Sheriffs also hold people for ICE or the U.S. Marshals, generally for a fee per day. (More on this later.)

More recently, however, jails are holding large numbers of people who should be in state prisons, which means people are in jails for years, not days. As mass incarceration boomed, jails became a key part of relieving prison overcrowding. In Louisiana, the state pays sheriffs $26.39 per day to hold a single state prisoner, which is not quite enough to improve care or conditions. Around half of the state's prisoners are held in local jails.

The problem is that county jails, which were never intended to be long-term-care facilities, don't have the resources and infrastructure to take care of high-need people for long periods of time. Sheriffs, who are not required to have experience in medicine or management, often deal with the situation by claiming that they need more money; however, because of the independence of the office, states struggle to oversee how sheriffs spend that money.

In California, the state was ordered by the U.S. Supreme Court in 2011 to reduce the population of the state prison system. The program, called "realignment," returned more incarcerated people to the control of the county sheriff. While sheriffs received grants in exchange, there were no rules governing how the money was used and came with little oversight. An investigation by ProPublica found that the increase in the jail population at the Fresno County jail led to eleven deaths in one year. Many of the jails in the Central Valley have seen increased violence because they are simply unfit to care for incarcerated people, especially those there for longer sentences. Nor are sheriffs required to take steps to separate long-term inmates from those awaiting trial. The Fresno sheriff met allegations of insufficient care with callousness, describing these deaths as "inevitable." (The Fresno sheriff was one of the sheriffs who met with Donald Trump while he was president.)

While sheriffs no longer receive fees for jailing people, they do have the option of charging those in their care with various fees and additional fines, which amounts to a transfer of wealth from the most poor to the sheriff's office. Abuses are common and result in meaningful hardships for the victims, not the sheriff. In states like Michigan, people held in jail must pay the sheriff for their "room and board," fees tacked on after their jail sentence is completed. Sheriff Thomas Hodgson of Massachusetts described himself in 2012 as a "pit bull on your pant leg" in his efforts to collect fees from people incarcerated in the Bristol County House of Corrections. In Louisiana, sheriffs regularly "lease" the labor of detainees to public entities, like the county, or to private companies. In 2019, one man died working for a concrete company as part of Louisiana's labor program; his family has still not been able to get the result of the autopsy.

In Alabama, where the state allocates a paltry $2.25 a day per detainee for food, sheriffs were allowed to retain any excess money from this amount. This led to sheriffs starving inmates for savings, resulting in enough cash that one Alabama sheriff used the money to buy himself a beach house. Another infamously fed his inmates only corn dogs so that he could keep the surplus. The notorious "corn dog sheriff" managed to squirrel away $212,000 over three years; he ended up spending a day in jail when he ignored a judge's order to improve the food quality. Many such abuses (which are often legal) were discovered by intrepid advocates and journalists and, while Alabama has since passed a law forbidding the abuse of funds, many more abuses go unnoticed and unregulated.

Sheriffs also decide how people inside the jail are punished when they break rules, decisions that are made without the intervention of a judge or attorney and are meted out without any hearing or due process. These decisions can have serious consequences. People are placed in solitary confinement for months at a time. Sometimes sheriffs can impose what appear to be bizarre rituals designed to humiliate and, sometimes, stroke their own ego. In one Georgia jail, the sheriff forced the incarcerated men to engage in marine-like physical drills, march in formation, and praise the sheriff in mandatory chants. He also used a restraint chair—a chair with straps used to pin the victim down in uncomfortable positions for hours, usually with a hood over their head—to punish people. In 2023, a federal judge sentenced this sheriff to eighteen months in prison for civil rights violations.

Experts agree that jails, even more so than the infamous supermax prisons, are the most dangerous places in America. At least one thousand jail deaths occur per year, falling under the jurisdiction of sheriffs. In their role as jailers, sheriffs are entrusted with the most vulnerable populations. Medical experts universally acknowledge that the first forty-eight hours after arrest are the most dangerous in terms of a person's mental state and health. Jails are on the front lines of mental illness and disordered substance use, which gives sheriffs even more power over people who are largely ignored by society and who lack the resources to get help outside of the criminal legal system. It is not uncommon, for example, for people to endure painful withdrawals in jails and die without ever seeing a medical professional.

There are especially unique challenges for pregnant people. While no reliable figures exist on the number of births in jail, the general neglect and inconsistency of services means that a pregnant person is at the mercy of the sheriff. For one thing, sheriffs can determine whether or not a woman in the jail can receive abortion care, even if she asks for it and even if it is legal in her state. Ex-sheriff Joe Arpaio used to routinely refuse to transport women for abortion care until he was sued by the ACLU and forced to comply. In Tarrant County (Fort Worth, Texas), a woman gave birth in 2020 on the floor of her solitary jail cell. Staff did not notice until after the infant was born, despite her cries for help, according to a federal lawsuit. The infant died. The sheriff, Bill Waybourn, said the woman "never made a sound," and, thus far, no one has been held accountable for the infant's death.

As the public eye has turned toward reforming prisons nationally, advocates have increased their scrutiny of county jails. The challenge is immense because there are so many jails across America and no consistent reporting requirements. With widespread newspaper closures, there is precious little information on how these jails operate or how safe they are. People inside the jails struggle to communicate with the outside world because their interactions are policed, their calls recorded.

Even when those in jail are eligible to vote—in most states, only those with felony convictions are completely barred from voting—they do so at the mercy of the sheriff. In some cases, sheriffs have excluded volunteer groups who help incarcerated people fill out their voter registrations to qualify for absentee ballots. Stricter laws governing absentee ballots also impact incarcerated people. In Texas, for example, the time between requesting and submitting an absentee ballot is so short that an incarcerated person often cannot send their ballot back in time to vote.

––––––––

As Linda Franks tried to figure out what had happened to her son, she learned just how difficult it can be to get information from a county jail. Her experience—finding out much too late that her son was near death—is not uncommon. One of the major issues with jail deaths is accessing information because sheriffs both prefer the secrecy and have little to no oversight forcing them to do otherwise.

As Franks began to uncover what happened to her son, she learned that many of the records were incomplete or misdated. What appears to have happened, according to a combination of jail records and the testimony of other men who were there, is that her son, Lamar Johnson, probably got into an altercation; he had approached a guard and told him that he was concerned about his physical safety. He was pepper-sprayed, handcuffed, and thrown into solitary confinement. After that, his mental health deteriorated, although it's not clear that anyone tried to provide him treatment or other assistance. The medical staff did not seem to think he might be suicidal. On Saturday morning, EBRPP records indicate that Johnson was found with a blanket around his neck.

Franks did not believe the sheriff's story. "Lamar was optimistic and upbeat. [The sheriff's office says] he had a psychotic breakdown. There was nothing in his file. Nothing that would have caused long-term problems. We just couldn't figure it out." She believed that if her son did have access to drugs, it was through the sheriff's deputies, who often smuggle in drugs and other contraband to make extra money on the side.

EBRPP, it turned out, was one of the most dangerous jails in Louisiana, which is one of the most dangerous places to be incarcerated in the whole country. In the three years before Lamar died, fourteen people had died in the same jail; there is still no official cause of death for nine of them. A 2018 report by the Promise of Justice Initiative, a New Orleans–based criminal justice nonprofit, found that the EBRPP death rate "far exceeds the national average because of inadequate medical and mental healthcare and a failure to properly train and supervise staff." The report goes on to cite specific health-care deficiencies, understaffing, and severe overcrowding that led to the neglect of people in the sheriff's care.

While most deaths documented by the PJI report were related to medical conditions, some were due to violence. Seventeen-year-old Tyrin Colbert was choked to death by his cellmate. Guards ignored his cries. In 2018, I interviewed a man who was held at EBRPP after his arrest who described being hit in the face with a heavy object that injured his jaw. It took weeks for him to get medical treatment. He told me he was glad to eventually get to Angola Prison, where he felt safer.

The same year the PJI report was released, Franks formed the East Baton Rouge Parish Prison Reform Coalition with the explicit goal of ensuring that the community knew about the people who had died there. The vast majority of people in leadership were connected to victims of the EBRPP. The coalition appeared at county meetings and pushed for transparency, accountability, and changes to health care and staffing. The group also led a grassroots movement to oppose a tax increase that would have given more money to the sheriff's office.

"Outside of resurrection there's nothing they can do for me," Franks said. "Lives are being lost. No attention is being put on that. When these incidents happen, [the sheriff's office] will approach families and intimidate them. But there have been hundreds of these incidents, and they are supposedly hanging themselves."

One major factor that inspires families to pursue advocacy is that they do not receive any information about their loved ones' deaths. People often die (or get very sick or injured) in jail without anyone outside being notified. The bodies of the deceased are considered part of the investigation, so family members are not allowed to view or bury the bodies as part of their grieving process. Information about a jail death is deemed confidential—usually as evidence in an investigation being carried out by the same sheriff in charge of the jail—so family members are not even told how their loved one has died. This means that people learn the facts months or years after their loved one's death, not only delaying their grieving process but also hampering their ability to seek justice through the courts in cases of wrongdoing.

Most important to movement leaders like Franks is that people understand the toll such a death takes on a family: "It leaves you hollow. I struggle with bitterness and anger and rage. And not having the resolution [of Lamar's death]. People don't consider the horror of that."

The impact of jail deaths on family members is profound. Such neglect appears consistent even when the sheriffs themselves are committed to reform. In Houston, I spoke with two mothers whose sons died in the Harris County Jail, which was run by Sheriff Ed Gonzalez, a Democrat who has embraced many reforms to the system, including cite-and-release, a practice that keeps people charged with crimes like drug possession from even entering the jail. Unlike a lot of sheriffs in this book, Gonzalez is humble and dresses like his deputies, in a dark uniform, no cowboy hat to be seen.

Yet, his jail has seen a relatively high number of deaths. The Harris County jail system holds around ten thousand people, one of the largest in the country. In 2022, at least twenty-eight people died in custody; according to advocates, more people have died just after their release from jail. Releasing sick and injured inmates is one way sheriffs can conceal deaths. When I examined the data in a story for the Appeal, I found that more people had died from homicide per capita in Harris County than in any other jail in Texas.

In 2021, Dallas Garcia's nineteen-year-old son, Fred Harris, was killed by a twenty-five-year-old man named Michael Paul Ownby, who had recently admitted to attacking a guard and was awaiting trial on domestic violence charges. Ownby was about twice the size of Harris, who had been in jail for less than a month. According to eyewitness accounts, incident reports, and a lawsuit, Ownby smashed Harris's head into the concrete floor, kicked him in the head, and used a sharpened utensil to stab him until he was fatally brain damaged. Forty minutes later, Harris, unconscious and not expected to recover, was sent to Ben Taub Hospital, which is one of the busiest trauma centers in America. (In 2023, Ownby pled guilty and was sentenced to fifty years in prison.)

Garcia had been concerned about her son because he had special needs. She kept calling the jail to ensure he was getting his medications. "He needs his medication. And he's special needs. And I'm like, 'His IQ is really low, he probably does not understand what's happening here.' . . . And I was like, you know, I'm afraid for him. I don't know, you know, because he's, he's very childlike. And these are adults. And I don't know what their charges are. But I know his charges are pretty bad charges. And I was just, I was afraid, I was so afraid. I was so afraid. I called. I called again."

According to Garcia, she found out Harris was in the hospital two days after the attack when the chaplain called her. She said she was told that Harris had been in a "fight" and that he was in the hospital. "[The chaplain] said Fred was injured. . . . She said that he was in ICU, and I was immediately upset. . . . I thought it was a prank."

When she went to the hospital to see her son, however, Garcia said that it was clear he had been stabbed and seriously hurt; this was no ordinary fight. "'Injured' wasn't even the word for it. It was like he had no bones in his face standing. . . . There was just lacerations on his head. And they just weren't consistent with him being in a fight." According to Garcia, there was tension between herself and the officers assigned to watch Harris as he lay in a coma. "We had people from the sheriff's office threatening to take him off life support, that he was still a ward of the state. Basically, they were saying that I had to pull the plug," she said. She said that she and the deputies present were yelling at each other, with the guards saying she needed to "pull the plug" or else there would be no investigation. She was also not allowed to grieve properly: "I mean, they gave me twenty minutes with him before he passed. And that was it. And [the deputy] told me, 'I was only supposed to give you fifteen.'"

Larhonda Biggles's son, Jaquaree Simmons, also died in the Harris County Jail in 2021. He was in jail for an alleged parole violation and was put in a solitary cell, allegedly because of COVID. Frustrated, he plugged up the toilet with his clothing and flooded the cell. Deputies came, took his clothes, and left him naked.

In a report filed with the attorney general's office at the time, officials say that Simmons tried to hit a deputy with a meal tray, causing a fight that ended with a deputy punching Simmons. Later, an investigation showed that a dozen deputies had punched, kicked, and slammed Simmons's head against the floor. He was left unconscious there and died. None of this was captured on video.

Biggles said the chaplain called her and said, "Okay, well, there was an accident with your son today, where he was found unresponsive in his cell. We proceeded to give him CPR, and rushed him to the hospital, where unfortunately . . ."

When the chaplain said "unfortunately," Biggles said she threw the phone across the room. Her daughter picked it up to finish the conversation, and Biggles heard crying and screaming. She was not allowed to see her son's body because of an internal investigation. No one explained what happened to Simmons for months, not until the sheriff gave a press conference a few months later and announced he had fired eleven deputies for "very serious policy violations" and suspended seven more. He said that these deputies had "betrayed my trust and the trust of our community" and that he was personally "upset and heartbroken."

---

Given the state of county jails and the way they are run, it's hardly a surprise that COVID-19 presented an unprecedented threat to incarcerated people, especially those in jails.

One of the unique features of county jails is something experts call "churn," meaning the movement of people in and out of the facility. Jails see a lot of churn. Not only are people coming in and out for work, but people are constantly being moved to other facilities and released into the community, all while new people are still being booked into the jail.

Lawyers and public health experts immediately saw that this churn, added to the already deplorable health care and lack of sanitation, meant that the pandemic would hit jails particularly hard.

At the time COVID shut down businesses and schools, I wanted to help assemble a coalition of sheriffs who would agree to release a large number of people from their jails. Most people in jail are there pretrial, meaning that they have not yet been judged guilty of whatever crime for which they were charged. While there are some people held pretrial without bail—someone accused of capital murder, for example—most are eligible for cash bail, meaning they can pay an amount of money and be released into the community until their trial. So long as they return to court on the appointed day, people accused of crimes have the right to go home. But often they cannot afford to pay even minimal bail amounts as low as $100.

Some sheriffs, I thought, might be willing to set an example for others by signing a letter promising to release certain groups of people: the elderly, the medically fragile, those who were simply unable to pay bail. A group of left-leaning prosecutors, who are also elected, agreed to do so. Medical experts in Washington State had released a series of official protocols recommending the release of large numbers of people from custody. Many sheriffs were already using cite-and-release to prevent new arrests. But getting sheriffs to agree proved difficult. Many were waiting to see what other sheriffs were doing. They were unwilling to judge others and worried about getting bad press.

To be sure, county jails admitted fewer people during COVID, and law enforcement released some people who were particularly vulnerable and awaiting trial for low-level offenses. Cops also arrested fewer people, issuing tickets in many cases, and fewer people on the street meant fewer traffic stops.

The Vera Institute of Justice studied jails in the months post-COVID and found that jail populations overall dropped by about 25 percent, with some places releasing more and some none at all. Over time, the institute found that many jail populations began inching upward, although most remained below pre-pandemic levels. Sheriffs were some of the people most in favor of increasing jail populations, despite the dangers to their own staffs.

---

It became obvious that it was difficult, if not impossible, for people to avoid getting COVID in jail. Incarcerated people did not have access to face masks, hand sanitizer, or soap. Some created their own face masks out of T-shirts or bedding in an attempt to avoid the virus. Social distancing was impossible. In many places, incarcerated people sleep hardly a foot apart. In one instance, a sheriff argued that lying head to toe was sufficient for social distancing because it met the "six foot" requirement.

Sheriffs were suddenly in charge of deciding how to respond to a pandemic, which most were ill-equipped to handle. Many focused on ending family visits but were reluctant to release people from custody. Others were unsure how to treat those who showed COVID symptoms. A lack of COVID tests and uncertainty meant that some sheriffs simply ignored coughing and wheezing; they told their employees to come to work even if they thought they might have been exposed to the virus.

Ironically, while sheriffs often claim they have absolute control over their powers to arrest, many sheriffs refused to use the release powers they did have under statute. Law professor Aaron Littman at the UCLA Law COVID Behind Bars Data Project compiled statutes that permitted the release of people from jail, but sheriffs seemed loath to use it, despite their talk about power.

Advocates filed dozens of lawsuits seeking the release of vulnerable people from jail as well as asking courts to force sheriffs to follow health orders to protect people in their custody. In August of 2020, in a shadow docket decision, the Supreme Court ruled in favor of the sheriff of Orange County, California, overturning an injunction that required the sheriff to ensure that his jail facility complied with public health mandates. In her dissent, Justice Sonia Sotomayor wrote, "The District Court found that, despite knowing the severe threat posed by COVID-19 and contrary to its own apparent policies, the Jail exposed its inmates to significant risks from a highly contagious and potentially deadly disease. Yet this Court now intervenes, leaving to its own devices a jail that has misrepresented its actions to the District Court and failed to safeguard the health of the inmates in its care."

In addition, jails tended to foster conspiracy theories and distrust between those incarcerated and the guards running the jails. Those who were incarcerated, cut off from the world, and unable to see visitors or their attorneys—courts had come to a standstill so no one knew when they would get their legal situation resolved—became fearful that COVID would overtake the facility and no one would know. In many instances, people were put into isolation or moved, but because they were not told the reasons behind it, some incarcerated people worried about being put into a space with COVID-positive people without knowing if they were sick or not. Sometimes, people just disappeared because they had died. In the Bristol County, Massachusetts, jail—run then by Thomas Hodgson, the sheriff who gave Trump the plaque—a group of detainees objected to their treatment and demanded explanation. In return, the sheriff unleashed dogs and a SWAT team, injuring many. In an eventual report, the state attorney general found that the sheriff had engaged in systemic abuses in his jail that were partially responsible for the incident.

As the pandemic wore on and Donald Trump began to push governments to return to business as usual, many sheriffs, who are overwhelmingly more likely to side with Republicans and have a conservative ideology, were suspicious of Democratic state governments, who, in their eyes, seemed to want everything to come to a standstill indefinitely. These attitudes impacted how sheriffs chose to treat people with COVID as well. In most jails, sheriffs outsource health care to private corporations, which has led to multiple lawsuits and accusations of poor care.

But even when they do not outsource their medical care, such contracts are up to the discretion of the sheriff with input from the county commission. The general instinct is to keep down costs. In Arkansas, the sheriff of Washington County hired a local health-care provider, Dr. Rob Karas, to oversee the medical care in his jail. Starting in November 2020, Karas said he treated 254 incarcerated people with ivermectin for COVID. The issue only came to the attention of county leaders when a jail employee complained that Karas had given him the dubious cure for COVID. According to a lawsuit filed by five people held in the jail, the treatment was given without consent, often called "vitamins" or "antibiotics." One man told CBS News:

"We were running fevers, throwing up, diarrhea . . . and so we figured that they were here to help us. . . . We never knew that they were running experiments on us, giving us ivermectin. We never knew that."

The county settled the lawsuit and the state medical board took no action. Karas kept his contract with the jail. In fact, the county passed a resolution praising him for a "job well done."

---

Linda Franks transformed her tragedy into an opportunity to organize with other local advocates, lawyers, and impacted people to bring together specific policy demands and collective memory. By sharing her story and listening to others, often in her cozy hair salon, Franks has helped to bring the humanity of those who die in jail into the public consciousness.

The hardest parts for family members left behind are the opacity of the system and the sense of being alone in their grief. Krishnaveni Gundu, the cofounder and executive director of the Texas Jail Project, which advocates for those who have been abused or whose loved ones died in jail, told me that sharing stories is an important way to build solidarity and community. "People get to see that they're not alone," she said. "It becomes an organizing tool, a movement-building tool."

Andrea Armstrong, a lawyer, law professor, and recipient of a MacArthur Fellowship, has undertaken the task of creating a database of people who have died in custody in Louisiana. Her first project was naming every single person who died in the New Orleans jail. With a team of researchers, Armstrong constructed a database that is overwhelming in its numbers and sheer humanity. The information did not come easily: Armstrong and a team of law students from Loyola University New Orleans College of Law requested public records from every prison and jail in Louisiana. The same team painstakingly collected information about the individuals who died.

Reviewing the database of names, I was struck by how jail deaths are generally not memorialized. One section of Armstrong's project, "In Memoriam," humanizes the data her team collected: what people loved, what they liked, what they were looking forward to doing after jail. Bryant P. Johnson died in the New Orleans jail in 2000; he was twenty-seven. Researchers found a news article about his death, but there was little other information. They managed to reach his brother and sister, whom they found by searching library archives for Johnson's obituary.

By talking to Johnson's relatives, the researchers filled out the facts that make a life. He finished a culinary arts program and had recently taken a job working offshore. Johnson's third child was born months after his death.

According to official records, Johnson died by suicide, but his family never believed it. He was arrested for having an open container, a law no longer on the books in Louisiana. His family had been unable to see Johnson's body for two weeks; they were sent from the jail to the hospital before being told they had to wait until the investigation was complete. Once they were able to, Johnson's family hired a pathologist to examine the body. He concluded that Johnson had been beaten by guards, thrown against the wall,

and probably choked. But the jail concluded that Johnson had died by suicide, so that is what appeared on the death certificate, and there was nothing
left to be done.

It is difficult to force compliance in reporting, never mind ensuring such
reports are accurate. In 2017, Texas passed legislation that required independent investigations into jail deaths. In most cases, that independent investigator is the Texas Rangers. The Texas Commission on Jail Standards also
started tracking jail deaths in an attempt to hold sheriffs accountable for
what happens to inmates in their care.

This process, however, can take years and, as documented by the *Texas
Observer*, often fails to hold sheriffs accountable through a lack of enforcement
and no consequences for failures. Jails can fall out of compliance with state
standards, but they are not closed. The paper's analysis of years of Texas
Rangers' investigations showed repeated instances where jailers ignored people's calls of distress or failed to adhere to the minimum standards of care.
Even when guards had broken the law or falsified records, they were rarely
charged or faced employment consequences. Some sheriffs skirted the investigation requirement by releasing people to the hospital before their deaths.

When I spoke with Larhonda Biggles and Dallas Garcia, the two women
whose sons had died in the Harris County Jail, they had differing experiences
of the system. For Garcia, prosecutors had swiftly moved to charge the inmate accused of killing her son. For Biggles, whose son had been killed by
deputies, the resolution was less satisfying. Ed Gonzalez, the sheriff, disciplined a dozen deputies, but none have been charged with a crime. Biggles
told me, "You know, I think about it a lot. I think about how [the deputies]
feel now that it's done, and, you know, do they care?"

———

For decades, criminal justice organizations have focused on state and federal
prisons as sites of reform. But over the past few years it has become obvious

that county jails—run almost entirely by elected sheriffs—have remained dangerous, outdated, and resistant to reform. Many of these efforts have been led by smaller grassroots groups, like those in Texas and Baton Rouge. Certainly, these efforts have faced strong headwinds.

For example, the EBRPP Reform Coalition ran a grassroots campaign to oust Sheriff Gautreaux from office, which he has held since 2007. Political party seemed to matter little: Gautreaux ran as a Democrat in 2007 and switched parties in 2011 to run as a Republican, winning both times. In 2019, grassroots organizations found a candidate who was willing to consider reforms and backed his run for office, but the effort failed, largely because the incumbent sheriff, Gautreaux, was able to raise over $400,000. The same thing happened in 2023: both times Gautreaux won with over two-thirds of the votes cast. An analysis of Gautreaux's donations revealed that many came from vendors and others who benefited from contracts with his office, including $10,000 from two Dallas gun shops and $10,000 from the bail bonds industry, alongside tens of thousands from contractors and construction firms. No laws prevent sheriffs from taking donations from entities or people with whom they may have a conflict of interest, so sheriffs take campaign money from gun ranges, correctional health-care providers, construction companies, and other vendors.

Sheriffs, for their part, argue that they are not responsible for jail deaths because the people in jail are already at risk. They point to the use of illegal drugs, undiagnosed mental illnesses, and untreated physical ailments. To some extent, many people end up in jail because of policies in other parts of the criminal legal system. In Houston, for example, the district attorney had sought extremely high bails for defendants, which made the jail more crowded. Hence, as law enforcement says, jails are "de facto mental health institutions" because so many people in desperate need of services end up there.

While they are not wrong, the concept points to a challenge inherent in reforming jails: getting people to care. Gundu told me that it was important to create meaningful accountability for jail deaths to show that all lives have value. "We have to make conditions better because it's a reflection of our culture and what we hold dear as a society," she said.

Armstrong, the law professor, has also spoken many times about the problem of getting people to care about the lives of those incarcerated. The incarcerated people are disproportionately Black and Latino across the country, which is reflected in the disproportionate number of deaths. Armstrong has written extensively about the need to think carefully about jail conditions as part of any comprehensive system of criminal reform. Too often, she argues, reform focuses on reducing mass incarceration but neglects the conditions of those confined.

Both Armstrong and Gundu talk about the importance of improving jail conditions alongside improving access to care in the community. Jail, Gundu said, "is not built to mitigate harm. It's built to perpetrate harm." The problem is a lack of accessible mental health care, housing, and other services in the community, including Medicaid expansion, which Texas has not adopted. "We have all these studies and data and evidence-based solutions on what actually keeps us safe," she explained. "And it's not jail."

When I talk to people who have been forced to confront the harms caused by sheriffs, I see how it is necessary to both envision a society where services are provided before people are ever at the point of going to jail and to ensure that people in jail can go home. Norris Henderson, founder and executive director of Voice of the Experienced, a grassroots organization in New Orleans run by formerly incarcerated people fighting for criminal justice reform, told me that people "just want to come out of jail no worse than they went in." Not better, he emphasized, but just not worse. Armstrong has written the same in her work:

"At a minimum, people should not end their judicially set sentences of incarceration worse off than when they entered."

Sheriffs say they are trying to implement programs inside jails, and the National Sheriffs' Association highlights jails with successful education and work programs. Sheriffs tend to fixate on the idea that jail can distinguish the worthy people from the unworthy, allowing some to leave jail with high school credits or a job. Yet, they don't lobby in favor of state oversight of jails even though twenty-one states have no oversight or regulatory commission at all. Further, these rehabilitative programs simply show just how invested sheriffs are in their jails to ensure that they remain an important part of the community. Sheriffs could advocate for community programs, not bigger jails. Yet, few do.

On a national level over the past few years, sheriffs have faced more scrutiny because of high-profile jail deaths. While the vast majority of jails do not see any deaths in a single year—only around 20 percent of jails do—there is no repository of accurate data. In 2013, Congress passed the Death in Custody Reporting Act, which empowered the Department of Justice to collect data and issue findings on jail and prison deaths. But state departments of corrections and local county jails frequently do not report their data, and there is no mechanism to force them to comply. No comprehensive report ever emerged from the legislation. The last federal report counting jail deaths from the Department of Justice was for the year 2019.

Journalists reporting on jail deaths encounter roadblocks, and the lack of information leads to inadequate reporting, namely because most jails do not issue press releases when people die inside their walls. Two reporters in Pennsylvania attempted to construct a database of people who died in the state's jails, and in addition to problems obtaining data and reports, they found that, in many cases, sheriffs had released people just prior to their deaths to avoid reporting a "death in custody." (I and others have found similar instances in other states in the course of reporting.)

In the fall of 2022, Representatives Jon Ossoff of Georgia and Ron Johnson of Wisconsin held hearings on jail and prison deaths, which featured families of those who had died in East Baton Rouge Parish. Louisiana does not require that parish jails notify the state when people die pretrial; those deaths are only reported to the local coroner. The deaths of people serving sentences—about 50 percent of Louisiana's state prison population is housed in parish jails run by sheriffs—are reported to a state agency, the Louisiana Department of Public Safety & Corrections, which publishes only limited data.

One of the people who testified was Vanessa Fano, whose brother, Jonathan, died by suicide after spending three months in solitary confinement in EBRPP after he was arrested during a mental health crisis. "We trusted the system," she said, explaining that she and their mother had had almost no contact with or information about Jonathan until his death. Dr. Homer Venters, a physician who oversaw care at Rikers Island, examined the records relating to Jonathan's death and wrote, "Systemic failures and gross deficiencies in the health care system for detainees at EBRPP directly contributed to the death of Mr. Fano."

---

County jails are an important reason why sheriffs remain powerful and difficult to hold accountable. As one sheriff said, bemoaning a time she had to release people because of a lack of funding, "Being a peace officer, you know, you want to keep people locked up."

Sheriffs both complain about jails—they are generally a sheriff's greatest liability—and use them as a way to gain political power. Sheriffs have incredible influence on the construction of new jails, which means that they have immense control over not just the lives of the people inside but also exactly how many people they can arrest and incarcerate in the first place.

Once they are built, jails are a significant budget line item and involve a large number of vendors, especially in more rural regions, where jobs may be scarce. The bulk of a jail's budget—around three-quarters of the cost—are the salaries, benefits, and retirement for those who work there. In a sense, sheriffs are job creators as well as jailers. As a result, sheriffs have lobbied for larger jails, more funding, and more staff to both bolster their reputation for election and ensure that their departments keep growing. In more rural areas, sheriffs and sheriff hiring impact a significant percentage of the community, and the county jail is an important driver of economic success. Federal agencies like the Department of Agriculture help fund county jails as part of rural infrastructure, as did programs like COVID relief funds, which largely went to law enforcement agencies and jails. Keeping a jail economically viable ensures that a sheriff can run on a platform as a job provider.

After reporting on sheriffs who are focused on national politics and broad ideas about the Constitution, I was struck by how the job sheriffs imagine for themselves differs from reality. Jails are one of the sheriff's core functions, and, from my point of view, one that most do not do very well. A few even seem to delight in cruelty. Think of how much emphasis far-right sheriffs place on the fight for the Constitution as compared to the lack of care for those who most need it. The dismal state of county jails may be the best signifier of how much sheriffs have built a myth for themselves that significantly conflicts with the truth.

SEVEN

## "KEEPING THE PEACE"

*Sheriffs and Guns*

DURING THE 2022 SUPER BOWL GAME BETWEEN THE LOS
Angeles Rams and the Cincinnati Bengals, Arizona U.S. Senate hopeful Jim
Lamon—the founder and former chairman of a solar power company owned
by Koch Industries—paid over $100,000 for a campaign advertisement. In
the commercial, Lamon, along with Pinal County sheriff Mark Lamb and
the president of the National Border Patrol Council, Brandon Judd, is dressed
as a spaghetti Western gunslinger. Lamon wears a white cowboy hat and a
sheriff's star pinned to his chest. The men take aim at Nancy Pelosi, Joe
Biden, and Mark Kelly, the Democratic senator from Arizona, chasing them
out of town.

That year featured multiple political advertisements with firearms, including another by fellow Arizona U.S. Senate hopeful Blake Masters shooting a
gun into the desert. Lamon lost the Republican primary (and Masters lost to
Democrat Mark Kelly in the general election), but the message about gun
ownership—that good guys with guns are vital to the American character—
remained. How did we know Lamon was the good guy in the ad? Well, he
had a sheriff's star. In the director's cut, he even rode away on a white horse.

Go to any cheesy Old West–themed amusement park and you will see some version of the sheriff with a gun on his hip. It's a fantasy, of course, since it's not clear that nineteenth-century sheriffs regularly carried firearms, and even if they did, it's not clear they were the good guys. But the image endures and has become an important part of how sheriffs see themselves and how Americans see sheriffs.

The myth of the American sheriff embodies many of the aspects that gun-toting Americans appreciate, like rugged individualism, masculine virtue, and adherence to a code of honor. As discussed earlier, for those reasons, far-right movements like Posse Comitatus, which glorified guns, latched on to the sheriff as the political figure most likely to support civilian firearm possession by white men in particular. Both the far right and the gun lobby (and, in the case of Lamon, the GOP) have courted sheriffs specifically because of their legitimacy as law enforcement. It is easier to stomach widespread gun ownership when a trusted authority on state violence gives permission, and, of course, it's not a coincidence that these dedicated gun owners and their sheriffs are mostly white men.

Sheriffs have supported these groups by using both political channels, which includes testifying in state legislatures and writing letters, as well as informal channels, like engaging in political protest bordering on insurrection by vowing not to enforce democratically passed gun laws. They use the language of interposition and nullification to express their support of gun owners, even when state and federal governments try to impose regulations in the wake of horrific mass shootings. Constitutional sheriffs across the country have promised to interpose—stand between—their constituents and any government agency, whether Democratic lawmakers, RINOs (Republicans in Name Only), or the Bureau of Alcohol, Tobacco and Firearms, that threatens to impinge in any way on unregulated firearm possession. In exchange for their support, sheriffs have benefited financially, politically, and sometimes personally. Gun owners are such an important part of any sheriff's constituency that they are obligated to cater to the extremely pro–Second Amendment crowd.

It's not a coincidence that sheriffs came to see the Second Amendment as a right worthy of interposition. The history of the sheriff is deeply entangled with the history of firearm ownership in this country. Historically, the sheriff was charged with "keeping the peace," which often meant breaking up groups of armed men who might be intent on causing harm. Even today, sheriffs in many counties control the process of permitting firearms, issue concealed carry licenses, and, in most places, confiscate firearms as ordered by a judge either through "red flag" laws (emergency laws that allow the removal of firearms because of an imminent threat) or because of a domestic violence protective order.

No one owns more guns than Americans. Twenty-nine states allow qualified individuals to purchase and own firearms without a permit or training—also called "constitutional carry" by the pro-gun contingent—as of early 2024. Almost every state allows any legal gun owner to carry their gun in public. Over the same period of time, gunshots became the leading cause of death in children, and homicide is the leading cause of death for pregnant women in America.

Sheriffs have played an important role in this movement to deregulate guns and have helped to wholly rewrite how the entire country must think about firearms and violence within the span of just a few decades. As I traveled across the country trying to understand the far-right sheriff movement and how it has changed politics as we know it, it became impossible to ignore the guns. Everyone, everywhere, was armed.

---

In February of 2023, I went to a Second Amendment—"2A" for shorthand—rally in Phoenix. Arizona has some of the least restrictive gun laws in the country. Anyone can purchase or carry a gun, open or concealed, without a license, so long as they are over eighteen and have not been convicted of a felony. Everyone at the rally was carrying a gun, and most of them were military-style weapons, long guns slung across chests and over shoulders, loaded with heavy cartridges containing enough rounds to take out the entire scene, causing their carriers to sweat in the perpetual desert heat.

I was there because Sheriff Mark Lamb was planning to announce his Senate campaign. After claiming in our interview that he had no interest in national politics, Lamb was running against Kari Lake—the GOP candidate for governor in 2020 who never conceded defeat—to become the Republican candidate for the Senate seat occupied by Kyrsten Sinema, who chose to run as an Independent. While I had doubts as to whether Lamb's persona could outmatch Lake's, who was the GOP favorite, I was not surprised that he was using this moment to make his announcement, even though his son, his son's fiancée, and their child had recently died in a car crash in December of 2022.

The people attending this rally were his people, the kind of voters he hoped to bring to the polls. Near the stage, the white-hatted Lamb glad-handed members of the Proud Boys, who wore black polo shirts with a yellow crest, some displaying their role in the organization—"president," "treasurer"—on their sleeve. Many wore long sleeves to hide distinctive tattoos, as well as dark glasses and hats, attempts to avoid photographers and journalists like me. On the internet, legions of lefty advocates were collecting pictures at protests just like this one to identify and create rosters of men who belonged to these far-right militia-style groups.

The Proud Boys were one of the groups that led the attack on the Capitol on January 6, 2021. Created in 2016 by VICE Media cofounder Gavin McInnes, the group began as "Western chauvinists," less militia-minded, more weird fraternity. Members were anti-feminist, anti-Black, anti-Muslim; they appeared at nativist protests, as counterprotesters at Black Lives Matter rallies, and as anti-LGBTQ protesters. Jason Kessler, a onetime leader, helped organize 2017's Unite the Right rally in Charlottesville. In 2023, Enrique Tarrio, the leader after McInnes stepped down, was sentenced to twenty-two years in prison for his role in the events of January 6.

The 2A rally here is an annual event, replete with corporate donors and an official sponsor, RidersUSA, a right-wing motorcycle club whose members were older veterans wearing leather vests covered in patches and headbands with the Arizona sunrise logo. There was a sense that people came regularly. I spoke with two men from Phoenix who said they attended every year. One was disdainful of journalists and told me that last year a major media network had put his photograph, in which he carried his friend's child's teddy bear, on the front page just to make them "look bad."

The 2020 rally, which numbered around 2,500 people, was the largest one the organizers had seen. Held in front of the Arizona capitol building, the spectacle of thousands of men in military gear carrying weapons frightened many and created fears of violence. After January 6, the idea of a small army in front of the capitol building no longer seemed like a good idea to the leaders of Phoenix.

As a result, the 2023 rally remained in sight of the capitol building but was moved to Wesley Bolin Memorial Plaza, a pleasant tree-covered sculpture garden mostly dedicated to military veterans as well as a six-foot-tall granite monument to the Ten Commandments. Again, like at Battle Mountain, I found myself at an event that could be described as family-friendly despite the presence of firearms. It was a clear day, and there were booths for the John Birch Society, Turning Point USA, and firearm-friendly insurance policies. There were a few Confederate flags among pro-Trump flags. People grabbed BBQ and tossed beanbags in games of Constitution-themed cornhole. Kids flung their bodies onto squishy inflatables with abandon in the "Junior Patriot Park." A dad carried his daughter's abandoned princess doll and his sidearm without irony. A group of young men proudly wheeled around a homemade guillotine that they said "works."

The opening prayer was presented by the Tipping Point Academy Warriors, a dozen students from a private Christian school in Phoenix that teaches "Bible-based Constitutional Education." Cade Lamb, Mark Lamb's eldest son, appeared early to sing the national anthem before the speeches began. Cade had recently separated from the army after five years and ran a far-right podcast that appeared inspired by Joe Rogan's but was even less journalistic. Cade has interviewed Kyle Rittenhouse and the people behind True the Vote as well as a variety of tactical weekend warrior types, plus his dad. He told "the one and only" Rittenhouse he was "really jealous" that the teenager had been "out there getting action"—read, killing people—while Cade said he had not, despite having been in a war zone. Cade doffed his cowboy hat and sang the national anthem a cappella style, dreadfully out of tune, with a crooning voice that let you know he meant it.

Here the Second Amendment was about more than gun ownership. Guns were the higher principle that protected all other rights. Sure, every attendee identified as a "responsible gun owner." There were discussions on guns as tactical weapons to protect a man's castle as well as being just plain fun to shoot. But the rally was about more than guns; it was about how all other rights should be interpreted in light of the Second Amendment, with a great deal of emphasis on "the right of the people to keep and bear arms shall not be infringed." No one seemed willing to consider the consequences of having a populace so highly armed. Instead, the sense among everyone I spoke with was that weapons were an essential part of the Constitution as well as a God-given right that should be protected even at the expense of life.

"The Constitution doesn't create or grant rights. It protects rights that already exist," the opening speaker explained.

"The Second Amendment is the great unifier," another speaker said. "And why is that? It's so simple. It's because we all want to protect what we love. And the Second Amendment protects our right, our God given right, to protect what we love. We love freedom, and we love our family."

While it would seem that there wasn't much to protest, given the state of the law—the U.S. Supreme Court had just ruled in favor of gun owners during the summer of 2022—gun rights groups kept their members in a frenzy by reciting worn conspiracy theories and pointing to modest Democrat wins at the state level. In 2022, Arizonans had elected a new Democratic governor and attorney general who supported sensible gun regulation. There had been a recent change to ATF regulations on pistol braces, attachments that allow a handgun to be fired like a rifle. Even though this was a small adjustment to registration requirements, it was enough to evoke the specter of massive disarmament.

The sense of persecution gave gun owners a higher calling. Guns were vital to self-sufficiency and individualism, even though no one looked like an individual in the sea of tactical gear purchased from one of hundreds of online outlets. One speaker said that "God, guns, and gold" were the keys to being free, and then went on to talk about the gold standard, related to a far-right conspiracy theory that awaits the collapse of the American economic and financial system. Another argued that "Jesus would support the Second Amendment," quoting the Bible verse about the "cloak and the sword."

Phoenix bike police were present, but they stayed on the sidelines, opting not to interfere or interact with the many armed people at the rally. Snipers stood at their stations on the roof of the capitol building. "They are our guys!" one of the speakers said, gesturing toward the men, who were dressed in black and looked suspiciously to me like militia members, not cops.

At one point a young man in fatigues began to argue with other militia members. The police simply watched as the veterans from RidersUSA separated the men to prevent a fight. One bearded man took the angry guy aside to talk him down; he was yelling about family court. I wondered what would happen if a gun were to fire accidentally. Everyone was so heavily armed, it was hard to imagine no one would die.

I engaged in conversation with some of the attendees, trying to gauge just how far they were willing to extend guns above other rights.

One of the Riders said he knew Mark Lamb from his pest control business. He asked me if I found shooting "empowering." I told him I wasn't sure I was good enough to be confident. He described taking his granddaughters to shoot and called guns a "tool." He admitted that he could see some of the people at the rally as "intimidating," but, overall, he thought it was the safest place in America.

Another older man affiliated with the Riders, who said he had participated in a border militia but remained frustratingly vague, told me ex-sheriff Joe Arpaio was his "hero." "I'm not opposed to immigration. I'm opposed to illegal immigration," he said.

In speaking with some of the attendees, I found that few were willing to acknowledge any instance in which an individual might be, well, afraid of guns. Many men were impressed I didn't "freak out" when I saw their rifles or excessive rounds of ammunition. One man, who told me he worked as a private security guard, expressed concern about so-called red flag laws that seek to remove firearms from individuals who pose a threat to others, often used to protect victims of domestic violence. He gave an example of a hypothetical woman who sought to have her partner's firearms removed because he punched a wall "near her head."

"Can't a man be angry?" he added.

I thought of a meme I saw on Facebook posted by one of many gun rights groups. Called "How Red Flag Laws Actually Work," it begins with Jane, "a bitter ex" who reports "Randy" for "posting mean things about her" on social media. The police "find his gun posts, posts criticizing the president, and distrust of government." The story ends with a SWAT raid (to take the man's guns), and "Jane enjoys a glass of wine." The message is clear: women who fear violence from their partners are lying and, even worse, cooperating with the enemy.

Just then, Lamb took the microphone, wearing a white cowboy hat and his bulletproof vest with "Sheriff" across the front.

"Who thinks this new wrist brace decision is garbage and unconstitutional?" he began, referring to the aforementioned ATF rule. He went on to argue that the ATF "is not a legislative branch of government. And this is a slippery slope to allow them to start making decisions like this," a view of federal regulation that is consistent with constitutional sheriffs as well as a variety of far-right groups who have long used the ATF as a punching bag.

"Do not give an inch on your Second Amendment right," Lamb told the crowd. Then he went on to tell a confusing story.

"Take the guns out of it," he said. "I wouldn't allow you to change the Second Amendment, just as I wouldn't allow them to change the First Amendment," he went on, talking about individual firearm ownership as "a protection the Founding Fathers gave us to protect our God-given rights."

Lamb then announced he was "seriously considering" running for U.S. Senate, a decision he confirmed a few weeks later by officially entering the race.

As he wrapped up, a man in a "Kyle Rittenhouse did nothing wrong" T-shirt yelled, "What are we going to do about the farmer?"

He was referring to George Alan Kelly, a seventy-five-year-old Arizona rancher who, less than three weeks before, had allegedly fired his AK-47 into the darkness of the desert, killing forty-eight-year-old Gabriel Cuen-Buitimea, a Mexican man who was crossing Kelly's property to enter the U.S. Kelly had previously written a self-published book about a rancher who needed to kill migrants in order to protect his property from dangerous cartels. He was being held on a million-dollar bond and charged with first-degree murder. Far-right groups would shortly fundraise to free Kelly pending his trial. (In 2024, Kelly's case ended in a hung jury, and the prosecutor declined to recharge.)

"What I can assure you is that the bond seems a little bit excessive,"

Lamb said, and exhorted people to "make their voices heard," which was odd, to say the least, in a situation in which a man may or may not have shot another man in the back, facts that were currently being disputed in a court of law, where Lamb did not hold any sway. But nevertheless. Perhaps Lamb meant that the people should make their voices heard here, in this place, and that by "voices" he meant voices raised in support of guns. In other words, people should not be deterred from celebrating the 2A, even if it meant one man died and another was in jail.

Many of the speakers were even more strident than Lamb, with rhetoric rife with pro-MAGA and anti-media messages—the "other side that hates our freedoms." One of the speakers who later endorsed Lamb's Senate run was Lindsey Graham—not the senator but a woman known on the internet as "Patriot Barbie." Graham has full, pouty lips and a penchant for yelling about liberals. She says that she was radicalized during the pandemic when her Oregon beauty parlor, Glamour, shut down, like many others, as a result of executive orders related to the coronavirus. She made a "call to arms," summoning militia members to patrol Salem with her. The state fined her, and she sued and lost. After moving to Arizona, Graham used her earnings as an influencer to buy two homes and start a new business, which largely seems to exist online.

She now touts firearm ownership and absolute gun rights as a vehicle for Christian salvation. Graham may have committed sins in her past, evidenced by her fading tattoos and an abortion that she regrets immensely, but she is now saved. Graham's mission is to save others who might be like her former self: lost and unarmed. In 2022, Graham turned her focus to anti-trans advocacy, using her platform to dress as a cat and mock a transgender school board member during a public meeting. The public official filed a restraining order against her when Graham continued the attacks, and Graham said she was going to appeal the order.

Wearing a hat reading "Lioness," Graham said that guns were the last thing she had to protect herself and her daughter from the threat of trans women. "We've got to protect all of these rights that they are infringing on," she said. "And as much as it seems like men using the women's locker room has nothing to do with the Second Amendment, it does now. Because areas where we think we wouldn't need our Second Amendment rights . . . they removed our women's rights"—by which she meant allowing trans women to use women's facilities—"and we do."

———

Constitutional sheriffs like Richard Mack and his CSPOA crew argue that the Second Amendment should be interpreted literally, and, as Lamb does, they will recite the text as if it were an incantation. "A well-regulated Militia, being necessary to the security of a free State, the right of the people to keep and bear Arms, shall not be infringed." Sometimes it's yelled. Sometimes there's an emphasis, as Lamb did at the 2A rally, on "shall not be infringed!"

Initially, I was bewildered that the recitation of the Second Amendment, with all of its confusing commas, was used to convey so much. I now find it useful to think about this extreme textualism in terms of religion. The religious history scholar Catherine Wessinger frames the use of legal jargon by sovereign citizens—one of the far-right groups to emerge from William Potter Gale's Posse Comitatus—as "magic." Wessinger explains, "Magic consists of rituals (often involving speaking or writing words of power) that are believed to have the power to effect changes in the physical world."

Wessinger suggests that, for sovereign citizens and other far-right groups, legal words and documents take the form of magic in the sense that saying them or repeating them manifests a change in the world. When Supreme Court justices do it, it's called "textualism," which relies on the plain meaning of the text to divine the intent of a written law. Far-right movements, from the Ku Klux Klan to neo-Confederates to constitutional sheriffs, have utilized similar methods, repeating bits of legal text as if those words themselves, the act of repeating them, of rolling the sounds in the mouth, will bring about power. In the case of the Second Amendment, that power is, in many ways, the ultimate power, the right to wield weapons that cause massive death and destruction.

The constitutional sheriff movement is very clear that it believes in a completely unlimited right, framed as race-neutral and rooted in history, to own all kinds of firearms. But the history of the Second Amendment and gun ownership in America is inextricably intertwined with race; it is also a lot more complicated than the far right would have most people believe.

To start, there are multiple historical interpretations of how the Second Amendment came to be. While the constitutional sheriff movement claims to rely on history and tradition, many contemporary historians now believe that the Second Amendment has its roots in white supremacy. In her book *The Second: Race and Guns in a Fatally Unequal America*, historian Carol Anderson posits that the founders intended for the Second Amendment to be anti-Black, intentionally excluding Black people, free and enslaved, from owning firearms, lest they should rebel and fight against slavers. In a recent book, legal scholar Carl Bogus agrees that the Second Amendment was worded to reassure the colonists that they could quell slave rebellions through armed forces: "My thesis is that, in the main, [James] Madison drafted the Second Amendment to ensure that Congress could not disarm the militia and thereby undermine the slave system in the South," Bogus writes. In other words, the yeoman farmers who epitomized the American Revolution were white and armed.

While pro-2A sheriffs rely on the text of the Second Amendment, despite its ambiguities, the same sheriffs also ignore the history of gun regulation, including how law enforcement helped to regulate guns for the purposes of public safety. Localities may have regulated firearms on a case-by-case basis, and gun laws, such as they were historically, varied from place to place. Sheriffs, as conservators of the peace, were often in a position to both use and regulate guns, although it was not a core component of their job. Some older state statutes penalized sheriffs for failure to disperse angry mobs or to disarm potentially dangerous people. Such laws were probably subject to discretion and point to the historical reality that, while many people did own guns in the eighteenth and nineteenth centuries, they were not central to law enforcement.

Laws regulating firearms did not exist on the federal level until 1934, when Congress passed the first modern gun control legislation. Those laws set up a regime of gun permits for owners and forbade people with felonies on their criminal records from possessing guns. More gun control provisions were enacted in 1968, which expanded restrictions on who could own a gun, influenced by a variety of events like the assassination of John F. Kennedy, civil unrest in Black communities caused by over-policing and discrimination, and the rise of the Black Panthers, who adopted assault rifles as a sign of Black resistance to white supremacy. It's worth noting that most sheriff associations, alongside police associations and even the National Rifle Association, supported gun control throughout this era. Sheriffs even drafted a statement in support of gun restrictions in the 1960s.

Carol Anderson connects this regulation regime to continued anti-Black animus, pointing out that the Second Amendment de facto excluded Black people and preferentially treated white firearm owners as entitled to use their weapons as they saw fit. Most laws that required arrest or the confiscation of guns were written to prevent Black people and other immigrant communities from possessing weapons that might cause them to sustain successful popular uprisings. Even today, current gun laws that protect an individual's right to defend themselves—often called "stand your ground" and "castle laws"—are used with more success by white men to justify shootings, while courts often reject the same arguments when used by Black men or women.

Ronald Reagan, a lifelong NRA member, was the first president to address the future 2A movement, uniting two common ideas that many pro-2A advocates hold: individual gun ownership and fear of crime. He wrote a 1975 column for the magazine *Guns & Ammo* in which he explicitly linked a rise in crime with firearm ownership that would become his presidential position: "In my opinion, proposals to outlaw or confiscate guns are simply unrealistic panacea." He argued that, instead, people who used firearms to commit crimes "should be given mandatory sentences with no opportunity for parole. That would put the burden where it belongs—on the criminal, not on the law-abiding citizen." In his framing, guns are used to commit murder, which is a crime, but in some cases, he indicates without saying explicitly, it might be okay to murder someone in the event it was necessary to prevent a crime from occurring. In his 1980 presidential campaign, he promised to roll back gun restrictions, pairing the ownership of guns with a desire to fight crime, not commit crime, a foreshadowing of the "good guy with guns" to come.

Reagan did not change his rhetoric despite surviving a 1981 assassination attempt. In 1983, he told attendees of a GOP fundraising dinner, "You won't get gun control by disarming law-abiding citizens. There's only one way to get real gun control: Disarm the thugs and the criminals, lock them up, and if you don't actually throw away the key, at least lose it for a long time." Later that same year, he gave a speech to the NRA, saying, "It's a nasty truth, but those who seek to inflict harm are not fazed by gun controllers. I happen to know this from personal experience."

Despite the talk, however, Reagan did not deliver massive change. He signed only one gun bill that tweaked existing legislation, the Firearm Owners Protection Act of 1986. The NRA called it "the most sweeping rollback of gun control laws in history" because it lifted some of the stricter gun laws prohibiting sales and transfers. It was vigorously opposed by ten law enforcement organizations, including the National Sheriffs' Association. The bill was revised to include a ban on automatic assault rifles to obtain enough support for passage.

Within just a decade, sheriffs as a whole would switch their position from supporting gun control measures in 1986 to aligning with the NRA and other even more radical pro-gun advocacy groups. Much of this is due to some sheriffs aligning with far-right movements like Posse Comitatus, as well as the growth of the constitutional sheriff movement, which is deeply linked to opposition to gun control. In recognition of this shift, gun lobbyists, like the NRA, and gun manufacturers began to provide political and financial support to sheriffs, who agreed to lobby against gun control and even go so far as to promise to interpose between their constituents and federal regulatory agencies. As the U.S. Supreme Court similarly shifted its jurisprudence on the Second Amendment, moving toward an individual right to possess firearms, sheriffs were able to use gun rights as a platform that appealed to an important bulk of their support: white men.

The transformation began when, in November of 1993, President Bill Clinton signed the Brady Bill, federal legislation that required background checks on firearms purchases. The bill had a troubled history. Named after James Brady, Ronald Reagan's press secretary who was paralyzed in the assassination attempt on the president, the bill bounced around for seven years and faced vigorous opposition from the National Rifle Association before finally becoming law. The far right and gun rights advocates opposed the provisions, some seeing it as an additional federal incursion and evidence of the "New World Order." This despite the fact that Reagan actually wrote a *New York Times* op-ed in favor of the Brady Bill, arguing that a "cooling-off period" would prevent gun violence.

One of the provisions of the Brady Bill required local law enforcement, including sheriffs, to conduct background checks for firearms purchases. This was already a practice in some states and was intended as a stopgap until the creation of the National Instant Criminal Background Check System (NICS), a database of gun owners and relevant criminal history that was formally launched in 1998. Until the NICS was completed, however, the Brady Bill contemplated that local law enforcement would review applications to purchase firearms to ensure the buyer had never been convicted of a felony in another state or wasn't, say, subject to a restraining order.

Enter Richard Mack of the CSPOA, who would engage in the Supreme Court case that made him famous.

According to Mack, he learned about the Brady Bill at a meeting of Arizona sheriffs and was immediately outraged. He alone among his fellow sheriffs objected to the Brady Bill's provision that required local law enforcement to conduct and enforce background checks for firearms purchases. "They are violating the Constitution and asking me to help. I won't do it," he told the *Washington Post* at the time. Describing it as the "biggest miracle" in his life, he said he went home to ask his wife what he should do.

While Mack casts his decision to oppose the Brady Bill as stemming from a heartfelt sense of betrayal of his religious sensibilities, he was part of a nationwide effort by the NRA to dismantle the Brady Bill in court. In his book *Gunfight*, Adam Winkler points out that Wayne LaPierre, then the new and more aggressive head of the NRA, turned to the courts to challenge the Brady Bill because congressional support was too powerful even for NRA dollars. Ultimately, six sheriffs filed lawsuits, aided by gun rights organizations, in Mississippi, Vermont, Arizona, Montana, Texas, and Louisiana, all challenging the same provision of the Brady Bill on background checks.

The case that made it to the Supreme Court was titled *Printz v. United States*, named after the sheriff in Montana, Jay Printz, who joined Mack in his lawsuit. After hearing the case, in a majority decision written by Justice Antonin Scalia, the court overruled the provision of the Brady Bill that required local law enforcement compliance. The decision generally fits into what are called "anti-commandeering" strains of jurisprudence—basically, case law that makes it unconstitutional to require states to use their resources (including people) to implement federal law.

In terms of Second Amendment case law, the *Printz* decision was dwarfed by later SCOTUS rulings, including Scalia's 2008 majority opinion in *District of Columbia v. Heller*, which formally recognized an individual right to own firearms. Much has been written by legal scholars on the evolving jurisprudence of the Second Amendment, and, given recent legal developments, it is still changing. But the basic holding of the *Printz* decision in 1995—that the federal government could not force local law enforcement to conduct background checks—is now a nonissue because records are computerized and centralized. In some places, increasingly fewer ones, sheriffs do issue gun permits, but the background checks happen automatically at the point of sale. The *Printz* holding was fairly limited and does not say anything beyond the applicability of the Brady Bill. To Mack, however, the case is everything.

After the SCOTUS decision, Richard Mack became the NRA's Law Enforcement Officer of the Year, and he has since based most of his reputation on the *Printz* case, which he still sells as a small pamphlet that he carries in his breast pocket. His typical stump speech includes a version of "I fought the Clintons and lived," with a laugh, which he recites waving the pamphlet that contains the *Printz* decision. "Every one of you should have this," he said at one event. "This is miraculous." Mack has argued falsely that the *Printz* case applies to COVID-19 health orders, Obamacare, and the IRS.

While Mack frames his lawsuit as an act of individual courage, he was connecting the rise of far-right movements and their focus on gun ownership as a civil right with both an increase in firearm availability and the rise of gun rights "stars" like Larry Pratt of Gun Owners of America and LaPierre of the NRA. All three men, in fact, published books about gun rights in 1995, the same year as the Oklahoma City bombing, which itself reinvigorated fears that Democrats would seek to restrict firearm access. After the bombing, LaPierre wrote an infamous six-page fundraising letter that called federal agents "jack-booted government thugs" and went on to say, "Not too long ago, it was unthinkable for federal agents wearing Nazi bucket helmets and black storm trooper uniforms to attack law-abiding citizens." The pro-gun vibes were already in ascendance when Mack came on the scene.

In Mack's ideology, firearms stand for the protection of the rights of white men and literally give those rights physical force through the ability to commit violence. He has written at least two books against gun regulations alone. One 1996 book, titled *From My Cold Dead Fingers: Why America Needs Guns*, features his wife's carefully manicured hand holding a pistol on the cover. The book is very much a work of its time, rooted in what Jennifer Carlson, a sociologist and MacArthur Fellow, calls the "citizen-protector" model promoted by pro-gun lobbyists and many on the right. Mack recasts a variety of sensational events, like the 1984 shooting of four Black teenagers in a New York City subway committed by Bernhard Goetz, whom Mack describes as "a responsible American under threat of personal harm or injury."

Reminiscent of Reagan's pro-gun rhetoric, Mack argues that the only solution to criminal activity is for everyday citizens—"responsible Americans"—to arm themselves and be prepared to defend their lives or property. He racializes crime and argues that "Black-on-Black crime today is pervasive . . . It is a social ill and has nothing to do with the constitutional right to keep and bear arms." Government regulation of guns is a precursor to tyranny and annihilation. As examples, he cites the Nazis in Germany, the Native Americans ("annihilated" because they were "left defenseless"), and Mormon settlers in 1819 Missouri. Gun owners as "good guys with guns," ready to help law enforcement prevent crime and other lawless disorder.

———

Just before his death, the historian Richard Hofstadter identified the rush for firearms ownership and the identity that went along with it as an important project for the right. He coined the term "gun culture" to describe

Americans' stubborn attachment to firearms, or, as he wrote, "that the people's right to bear arms is the greatest protection of their individual rights and a firm safeguard of democracy."

From what I saw at the Phoenix 2A rally, constitutional sheriffs and their supporters have moved far beyond the "citizen-protector" model and have embraced firearms as a means of protecting other, unrelated rights as interpreted through an anti-federal lens, like free speech and the right to assemble, especially the right to hold religious services during COVID, and property rights, as seen in the use of guns by counterprotesters in the summer of 2020.

Thanks to the influence of far-right movements that glorify the county sheriff, sheriffs tend in increasing numbers not just to see civilian gun ownership as a force multiplier—more "good guys with guns"—but also as a necessity given the threats of government overreach. As a group, sheriffs support gun ownership in much greater numbers than police chiefs and the general public. In 2013, the National Sheriffs' Association, which had supported gun control under Reagan, issued a statement blaming gun violence on "media violence, drugs, gangs, [and the] breakdown of the family" and affirming that sheriffs "strongly support our citizens' protected right to bear arms under the Second Amendment and . . . do not support any laws that deprive any citizen of the rights provided under the Constitution and Bill of Rights."

Further, a survey of more than five hundred sheriffs conducted by the political scientists Mirya Holman and Emily Farris in 2021 showed that, as a group, sheriffs were much more permissive of gun rights than the population as a whole: around 75 percent of the sample thought that gun laws should be "less strict," and very few found them too lax. This held true for all sorts of gun regulations, from "red flag laws" that remove firearms from individuals deemed dangerous to bans on assault-style rifles. By way of comparison, the nationwide polls find about half of all voters think the current gun laws are too lax, and most surveys show general support for red flag laws.

Sheriffs' current stance in favor of more gun ownership contrasts sharply with the sentiment of police chiefs, which tends to be anti-gun. In 2016, a sniper in Dallas killed five police officers during a BLM event. The police chief, calling for stricter gun regulation, commented at a press conference, "We don't know who the good guy is versus the bad guy when everyone starts shooting," a play on the "good guy with a gun" pro-gun slogan. In Texas, 75 percent of police chiefs opposed a 2021 law that made open carry permissible. That same year, police chiefs all across Texas also opposed "constitutional carry," which eliminated licensing and background check requirements for assault-style rifles. In contrast, Texas sheriffs did not voice opposition to the 2021 change in the law. (According to work by Jennifer Carlson and other scholars, rank-and-file police may be increasingly more likely to support individual gun ownership as politics have polarized.)

There are a few explanations for why sheriffs even now support more gun ownership despite the links between guns and violence. Sheriffs are much more likely to be white, male, and conservative, much more so than the people they serve. Because sheriffs are more powerful in rural communities, they also are elected to serve in communities where gun ownership is more popular. In Texas, for example, when a sheriff arrested a group of men for standing outside a business with assault rifles, a pro-gun group staged a rally and the leader said, "This guy needs a lesson. He needs a big lesson, and we need to go out there and teach him."

It's also important to consider how the county-level system of government gives sheriffs and county officials more say in political matters than their population would suggest. For example, in 2023, when around 80 percent of Illinois sheriffs said they would not enforce new gun regulations, that high figure made the laws appear unpopular. But those sheriffs only represented around 40 percent of the population of the state. By assembling en masse, sheriffs can create the appearance of disprorportionate political power than their population warrants. Most researchers overlook this aspect because sheriffs, as law enforcement, have the appearance of legitimate authority, rather than simply being political actors looking to bolster their chances in the next election cycle.

Unlike police chiefs, who are appointed, sheriffs are elected and express their political views more freely; there are no rules that forbid them from talking about policy questions—although they may face electoral consequences. And there is the influence of groups like the National Rifle Association, which has specifically sought to recruit sheriffs and other law enforcement officers to their side.

Since the formation of the CSPOA, Mack's greatest recruitment moments tend to come when Democrats call for gun regulation, often in the aftermath of a mass shooting tragedy. Mack uses these opportunities to seize on far-right conspiracies about Democrats confiscating guns to encourage sheriffs to interpose on behalf of gun owners. Under Mack's theories, sheriffs can, and are in fact constitutionally required to, protect gun owners from federal regulation.

After the 2012 massacre at Sandy Hook Elementary School in Newtown, Connecticut, in which twenty young children were murdered along with six school staff members, Mack recruited around five hundred sheriffs to sign a letter opposing all gun regulation. The alliance included groups like Gun Owners of America and the Oath Keepers. Mack describes the moment as a "miracle" because, he says, sheriffs across the country contacted him about the proposed gun regulations being floated by Congress and the president. A form letter that Mack sent to sheriffs across the country included language that indicated any gun regulations would be the equivalent of starting a war, with overtones of the racist rhetoric the right used when talking about then president Obama.

We are the generation who will decide whether we continue as the constitutional Republic as designed by the Founders, or will we succumb to the temptation to "fundamentally change America" into another socialistic regime? Many of your citizens have much at stake and deserve to know the truth. They are afraid and do not like what they see. Many feel this is the most critical time in our nation's history since the Civil War.

Each letter included a "pledge" for the sheriff to sign, promising to "oppose and disallow, any and all attempts to further erode the rights of the citizens of our counties and parishes. Accordingly, we oppose the current gun control scheme being proposed and any attempt to register gun owners or their firearms."

As the pledge shows, Mack argued that sheriffs are in a unique position to advocate against gun control on a local level because they can use the power of nullification; basically, Mack says, sheriffs can ignore gun laws with the justification that he believes they violate the Constitution. Remember that under his theory of nullification and interposition, sheriffs are theoretically able to stop federal or state agents from enforcing firearm regulations, which basically amounts to insurrection and paves the way for individual gun owners to believe that they have a right to resist gun control on their own terms. Mack is a Second Amendment purist—he does not believe in any regulations on gun ownership, including for those with criminal histories, nor background checks, nor age limits. Mack is particularly suspicious of the ATF, a wing of federal law enforcement heavily involved in firearm regulation.

The "constitutional" theory of Mack's philosophy generally is limited to ideas that coordinate with the far right: ensuring unrestricted firearms, libertarian economic policies, eliminating federal regulatory agencies, and a "color-blind" view that ignores the Fourteenth Amendment. I asked Mack, for example, whether nullification could apply to abortion bans, and he was vehemently opposed to the idea. He wrote:

> Our job as sheriffs, and all government in America, is to protect
> Life, Liberty, and the Pursuit of Happyness [sic]. "That to secure
> these rights, governments are instituted among men." (Dec. of
> Ind.) Thus, sheriffs are not within their rights to protect the kill-
> ing of unborn children.

Mack's explanations tend to generate huge confusion in the media. When-ever sheriffs appear, there follows a spate of stories about sheriffs "ignoring" laws "they don't like." While true in a sense, it undercuts the real goals of sheriffs aligned with Mack and his cohort: to promote a vision of the country that adheres to an extremely white, Christian belief system that focuses on protecting white citizens' right to own firearms and ignores the rights of mar-ginalized groups like women, immigrants, BIPOC, and LGBTQ+ communi-ties. Mack's incantations of the words of the Constitution, the Bill of Rights, and his own court case show that he does believe in the law, very deeply. He seeks to return the law back to an imagined history—the same history that revered the sheriffs and their role of summoning posse comitatus.

When Mack talks about guns, there is something reverent about his speech, not just about the object—which is also a fetishistic material good that many sheriffs raffle off to raise money—but about the religion of fire-arms based on the radical (and violent) change those weapons can bring about.

This may all sound overly abstract, but over the past few years, as gun restrictions are dramatically loosening and more people are dying from gun violence, it's hard to deny the very real impact of Mack's strategy. One tan-gible result is the partnership between the NRA and sheriffs, which has produced lobbying by sheriffs and their state associations as well as money and guns for sheriff's departments. Recognizing that legislatures are more likely to listen to their sheriffs than the NRA, the gun group has ghostwritten letters and op-eds for sheriffs to use. In New Mexico, emails showed that the NRA had helped sheriffs to draft their anti–gun control letters and offered support. The NRA has additionally funded sheriffs' offices, providing them with hundreds of thousands of dollars in weapons and support for community programs across the country.

Aligning sheriffs against firearm restrictions also creates an appearance that more people support unfettered firearm access than they do. According to the Pew Research Center, about half of Americans think that guns make people safer and over 60 percent think that it has become too easy to obtain firearms. Per the same survey, people in rural regions are much more likely to say that the right to own guns is "essential to their own sense of freedom" as compared to urban dwellers. Rural residents are also much more likely to own guns, which means that sheriffs, who rely on rural voters, largely overrepresent people who already support access to firearms.

Encouraging sheriffs to ignore firearm restrictions also taps into the history and power of the office, at least as perceived by sheriffs. While there is no legal basis for sheriffs to claim gun regulations are unconstitutional—one law professor called the notion "a controversial one at best"—it does create an appearance among far-right groups that there are people in political office who support their vision of the world. This can be extremely powerful, as the election of Donald Trump showed, by providing legitimacy and shifting the discourse further to the right. It also frustrates and stalls discussions at the state and federal level about firearm regulation, since lawmakers who know that sheriffs will mount massive resistance to gun regulation might hesitate to get into a power struggle, particularly since there are no mechanisms to force sheriffs to enforce gun laws. The best most governors can do is use other law enforcement, like state police, to enforce the laws sheriffs will not. Because this solution is so politically distasteful, many politicians seek to avoid the issue altogether.

Since 2019, this has happened repeatedly as states seek to enact gun reform and sheriffs lobby against the regulations and vow not to enforce such laws. Sheriffs from Washington State to Colorado to Virginia have since proclaimed their fealty to the Second Amendment and say they will not enforce federal or state gun restrictions. It's not a coincidence that this movement grew steadily throughout the two terms of America's first Black president. In New Mexico, one sheriff described proposed gun laws as being pushed by "gun-grabbing socialists" and dismissed the connection between domestic violence homicides and guns, with twenty-five out of thirty-three sheriffs calling their counties "Second Amendment Sanctuaries." In 2019 alone, most of the counties in Colorado, New Mexico, Virginia, and Nevada made themselves "2A sanctuaries." In Tazewell County, Virginia, the 2A sanctuary resolution cited a clause in the Virginia Constitution reserving the right to call a militia to the county—which they threatened to use—as justification for their decision. One sheriff in Colorado said he would rather go to jail than enforce a gun law. He cited as inspiration Rowan County, Kentucky, clerk Kim Davis, who went to jail because she refused to sign same-sex marriage certificates. By mid-2021, over 60 percent of all counties were sanctuary counties (almost two thousand counties). In contrast, there are fewer than two hundred places designated as immigration sanctuaries.

BLM protests in the summer of 2020 only heightened concerns about the need for "law-abiding citizens" to arm themselves for self-protection, as illustrated by the iconic photo of Mark and Patricia McCloskey standing outside their fancy home in St. Louis with an AR-15 and a handgun, brandished in defiance of the protesters seeking social justice. The pandemic and nationwide protests against police violence only accelerated an ongoing trend toward viewing gun ownership as a necessary prerequisite—both symbol and tool—for white men to remain in power. For those who oppose Black Lives Matter, carrying a firearm is a physical demonstration of their political ideology.

––––––––

In the fall of 2019, a new Democratic majority had taken over Virginia's legislature, driven by vast demographic changes in the state. Alongside the Democratic governor Ralph Northam, these lawmakers promised to enact meaningful laws that would limit access to guns. Many of the measures were relatively noncontroversial. For example, one proposal was a red flag law, which would make it easier for law enforcement to temporarily remove firearms from the possession of people deemed dangerous in a judicial hearing. Another proposal included universal background checks for firearm transfers, closing what is sometimes called the "transfer loophole"; another limited handgun purchases to one a day. In all, they were fairly commonsense proposals that, according to statewide polls, most people wanted.

On the January day that most Americans celebrate Martin Luther King Jr., a group of firearm aficionados in Virginia celebrate Lobby Day. The Virginia Citizens Defense League (VCDL) is a nonprofit group that lobbies for gun rights and is most famous for their aggressive founder, Philip Van Cleave, a onetime reserve deputy sheriff, who became famous when he was duped by Sacha Baron Cohen into doing a parodic ad for "Kinder Guardians," firearm trainings for kids. For the past two decades on this day, members have assembled at the state capitol in Richmond to agitate in favor of bills that make it easier to own firearms and against bills that seek to limit gun ownership or use.

Nonprofits that monitor extremists and the Department of Justice were extremely concerned about violence on Lobby Day 2020. Rumors circulated that some of the alt-right groups that appeared at the 2017 Charlottesville Unite the Right rally would also participate. Governor Northam used his "state of emergency" powers to forbid firearms within the capitol perimeter. The FBI arrested some neo-Nazis, who said they planned a "race war." One Democratic legislator threatened to send in the National Guard to enforce compliance with gun laws.

On January 20, the crowds were energetic, but there was no violence and only one arrest. Alex Jones of InfoWars popped out of a $300,000 Terradyne Gurkha (an armored vehicle on a Ford F-550 chassis that he calls the InfoWars Battle Tank), yelling into a megaphone. People waved Gadsden and pro-Trump flags. They wore military fatigues. Those with long guns were confined to a space off the capitol grounds. Trump tweeted, "That's what happens when you vote for Democrats, they will take your guns away." An NBC reporter called it a "white nationalist rally" in a now-deleted tweet, which was roundly mocked on Fox News. Van Cleave claimed he'd expected a peaceful demonstration all along, despite his support for militias. And it mostly was.

Of course, the sheriffs were there, supporting the pro-gun protesters. Sheriff Richard Vaughan of Grayson County said, "If the bills go through as proposed, they will not be enforced. They are unconstitutional."

In the run-up to Lobby Day, Sheriff Scott Jenkins of Culpeper County— who had his election funds seized in 2023 by the Department of Justice as part of a corruption investigation and lost reelection—vowed to make everyone in his county an "auxiliary deputy," thereby allowing them to possess firearms. "I plan to properly screen and deputize thousands of our law-abiding citizens to protect their constitutional right to own firearms," he wrote on Facebook. While he did not ultimately follow through, his office did have dozens of civilian deputies, many more than permitted by statute. (The new sheriff ended the civilian deputy program.) In a now-deleted Facebook post, Jenkins wrote, "An elected Sheriff answers only to the citizenry. I will always respect the rule of law but I don't need to wait for a court to interpret my duty for me."

At Lobby Day, Jenkins took to the stage set up in front of the Virginia capitol building after Dick Heller, the respondent in the Supreme Court case *District of Columbia v. Heller.* He appeared hatless and broad in his brown uniform with gold epaulets, a sheriff's star pinned to his chest. "As a Virginia sheriff," he began, "I know full well the authority vested in all our sheriffs. You the citizens directly elect us to office." He said that sheriffs are "the final line that says no encroachment on your Second Amendment rights."

After reiterating his famous claim—"I will choose to deputize thousands of my citizens to see that they're able to keep their lawful legal firearm"—he added, "Law enforcement is on your side." The message was clear: law enforcement, even the state police who were there that day to protect state property and ensure that protesters did not carry their firearms onto capitol grounds, were on the side of the gun owners.

VCDL bases much of their advocacy on the theory that permissive gun laws are a crime deterrent. Along with lobbying against gun regulation, it also lobbies against criminal justice reforms, arguing, for example, that local gun control in Richmond led to a rise in crime. The group joins other pro-gun advocates who have called up faulty research that links gun ownership to a decrease in crime.

Van Cleave, president of the VCDL, affirmed the group's commitment to the police by praising the officers there and adding, "Virginia has some of the best sheriffs around."

The sheriff of York County and Poquoson, Danny Diggs, who became a state senator in 2023, wore an orange sticker that read "Guns Save Lives"— a play on the orange T-shirts and signs used by advocates for victims of gun violence—in addition to military insignias. First, he evoked the patriotic ideals of the Revolutionary War: "We struggled against a tyrannical government and gained our independence in 1781. It's been about 240 years, and we are now faced with tyranny again. We should not have to struggle to win our freedoms again."

"He has even disarmed law enforcement," Diggs said, referring to Governor Northam, again drawing a connection between the people protesting gun regulations and law enforcement. Diggs relied on the traditional division between the "good guy" with a gun and "criminals." "Disarming law-abiding citizens does not make us safer from emboldened criminals," he said.

In Virginia, sheriffs are "constitutional officers," meaning that their role is enshrined in the state constitution. Virginia sheriffs enjoy a degree of independence that is greater than in some other states. While most states do define the office of sheriff in the state constitution, the position is also governed by a vast network of legislation that outlines everything from compensation and term limits to removal procedures. Virginia sheriffs, on the other hand, have previously argued, mostly successfully, that the state cannot legislate their activities, a fact that has excluded sheriffs from statewide police oversight. But this does not mean that sheriffs are qualified to interpret law on the level of courts and judges, at least according to experts like Mary McCord, a law professor and the executive director of the Institute for Constitutional Advocacy and Protection at Georgetown University Law Center, and the then attorney general of Virginia, Mark Herring, who, in 2019, wrote an advisory opinion explaining that local constitutional officers "cannot nullify state laws."

---

As I saw at the Phoenix gun rally, the pro-gun movement has become a mainstay of the GOP, moving beyond ex-military and law enforcement to include everyone, while it has also become ever more consumerist.

Lamb loves guns, even though he never served in the military. Unlike Mack, who says he never used his firearm as a sheriff and is never pictured holding one, Lamb made his reputation largely as a firearm influencer—"marketing and branding," he says in his first book—before he became sheriff.

I learned myself just how powerful the symbol of a firearm could be. When I interviewed Lamb for *Politico*, we went shooting in an empty field. A professional photographer took pictures of Lamb posing with his short-barreled assault-style rifle in the desert. When *Politico* published them with the story, some readers were upset and thought that it glorified firearms. In a move that made me feel even more wary of the photos, the sheriff used them for promotional purposes, and the NRA even adopted the photos to use on social media. Lamb has also continued to use the photos for various social media posts.

Lamb's social media is splattered with firearms. Fridays, Lamb shoots gigantic machine guns into old car carcasses. He hunts boar with his son. In an online video, Lamb crosses the street with an assault rifle in one arm and a framed copy of the U.S. Constitution in the other, accompanied by a quote from Thomas Jefferson, "Free men do not ask permission to bear arms." (According to historians, this is not a quote by Thomas Jefferson but was invented for the internet.) In a Sunday video, Lamb placed his sidearm, a Bible, and a copy of his self-published memoir on a bench. (The Bible is one that Lamb advertised on social media. The book included the King James Bible as well as "America's Founding documents," the same one Donald Trump would hawk in 2024.)

Even his office is a display of firepower. In the lobby, there are television screens showing films of deputies performing military-style maneuvers. Behind his desk, underneath an American flag, an old "cowboy rifle" that was a gift from his wife and pistols with "3:10 to Yuma" grips. A fake movie poster with Lamb in full combat gear and a cowboy hat, with the title "Lawman: Calm. Dedicated. A Hero." A skateboard with a portrait of Lamb and his assault rifle.

In a French documentary, Lamb says his position on guns is "about standing up for what the Founding Fathers set up, the freedoms we have, our

God-given freedoms, which are secured by the Constitution. . . . The Constitution doesn't give you rights. The Constitution secures rights given to you by God. The ability to own guns is a Godly right. That is something you are blessed with."

Guns function as both a weapon and a tool as well as a signifier of an identity. The sheriff has auctioned off multiple assault rifles, some emblazoned with "American Sheriff." He even held an event that cost $500 a person to join "Second Amendment Defenders" for "an evening of shooting, food and fun," including "private gun range access & shooting an AR15." The website for Lamb's Senate campaign features the candidate shooting into the desert. Under "Protect Our Second Amendment Rights," it says, "The Second Amendment is a God-given right. The right that protects all other rights."

Sociologist Jennifer Carlson describes two phenomena in her book *Policing the Second Amendment* that summarizes the tactics sheriffs use to oppose gun regulation. Gun militarism integrates racist ideas of criminality to promote the notion that law enforcement needs firearms to show that they cannot be outgunned. Sheriffs emphasize this when they describe shootings as "bizarre crimes" and "heinous." Lamb went on a podcast and described shootings as the result of the "mentally ill," arguing that "something real needs to be done," even though the evidence supports the opposite: those with severe mental illness are more likely to be victims than perpetrators.

The other ideology, gun populism, is a cultural identity wholly centered around gun ownership and Second Amendment absolutism and is manifested in everything from camouflage and military clothing, expensive military-grade weapons, and bumper stickers praising firearms. Carlson points out that these "good guys with guns" are seen as supplements to law enforcement. Many sheriffs attend gun shows, taking pictures with notable pro-gun advocates like Kyle Rittenhouse. At Shot Show, a large, flashy gun show in Las

Vegas, Lamb poses to promote a variety of gun businesses. To Carlson's theory, I would also add the rise of Christian nationalism, which imbued firearm ownership as a "blessing," in the words of Sheriff Lamb.

The dangers of gun populism have escalated and the association with militias who are on the side of law enforcement—posses—has increased, largely because social media has made it easier to recruit groups of people quickly to a specific location. Kyle Rittenhouse, who was seventeen when he shot and killed two men and severely injured a third at a protest in Kenosha, Wisconsin, in 2021, perceived at the time that he was in a militia serving local businesses. He called himself a "medic," assumed authority over "civilians," and believed, like others with him, that he was working to provide security. Rittenhouse's lawyer called his client "a Minuteman protecting his community when the government would not."

───────

In 2022, the Supreme Court decided the case *New York State Rifle & Pistol Association v. Bruen*, which knocked down New York State's gun licensing regime and created what legal experts call a new standard to assess gun regulations that relies on a historical interpretation of the Second Amendment. Many states are being forced to substantially change gun regulations that were previously constitutional. That same year, firearms became the leading cause of death for children. A mass shooter killed nineteen children and two teachers at an elementary school in Uvalde, Texas, using an AR-15–style rifle as dozens of law enforcement officers watched and waited. Yet all indications show that sheriffs are even more opposed to gun regulations than they were a decade ago, and "no-compromise" 2A positions are becoming common among people who identify as conservative.

As legal scholars are debating what this means for gun regulation in this country, sheriffs have insisted that gun rights are still under attack. All across upstate New York, sheriffs vowed not to enforce gun regulations passed by the Democratic governor Kathy Hochul. While they generally relied on their discretion, the sheriffs pointed out that they could not be forced to enforce the law and make arrests. Washington State sheriffs similarly said they would not enforce certain gun regulations. The New York State Sheriffs' Association also opposed the regulations.

Red flag laws rely on cooperation with local law enforcement, and there is no law that would create mandatory use of such laws, since they rely on a determination regarding a person's dangerousness. Often sheriffs who promise to nullify gun laws hesitate to use red flag laws. The man who opened fire in a Colorado gay nightclub in November 2022 had previously been accused of making bomb threats, calling himself the "next mass killer." Despite this, the El Paso County sheriff, who had previously expressed his view that the state's red flag laws were unconstitutional, did not use the existing laws to remove the shooter's guns. (The sheriff argued that the laws were vague.)

On July 4, 2022, a shooter opened fire on a parade in a Chicago suburb, killing six and wounding two dozen. In response, the governor of Illinois, Democrat J. B. Pritzker, proposed limits on assault rifles. Around 80 of the state's 102 sheriffs signed a letter indicating their view that the proposed legislation was "unconstitutional" and that they would refuse preemptively to enact the provision, even though there was nothing required of local law enforcement. The law bans the sale of certain new assault rifles and requires current owners to register theirs.

The letter was based on a template from the Illinois Sheriffs' Association, which was working with a county commissioner to coordinate strategy with the CSPOA and Richard Mack. Mack also tried to have a CSPOA training session, relying on the "Texas strategy," in which he crisscrossed the state and recruited local sheriffs, but Mack was too ill to attend and only two sheriffs showed up. He sent out an email blast to all sheriffs using a list he had purchased, and one sheriff told him to take his name off the list.

"The reason we don't have sheriffs on board is because they are ignorant," Mack later said on his weekly "seminar" for CSPOA members. "We got our foot in the door. . . . We did the best we could."

Yet, at the same time, there has been almost no discussion about the Black men who are serving prison time for illegal firearm possession. Prohibiting people with felony convictions from owning firearms remains one of the very few gun restrictions that sheriffs support. Not only does this bolster support for the "good guy with a gun" theory, it also tracks with the attitudes of white supremacy inherent in the support for gun rights.

In Illinois, as an example, many of the young Black men in prison are there for illegal firearm possession. The laws for felony gun possession are incredibly punitive, sending people to prison for up to a decade for possession of a gun unlawfully. According to a 2021 report out of Loyola University Chicago, the vast majority of people convicted for felony gun possession in Illinois are from Chicago and 35 percent are Black teenagers and men up to twenty-four years old. Sheriffs and their allies are happy to blame Chicago—especially Black residents of Chicago—for gun violence, all while arguing that their "law-abiding" communities don't need gun control measures. Guns appear to be bad only when the people wielding them aren't white men.

The issue of firearms in this country is unlikely to come to an end anytime soon. Not only are more people purchasing firearms but also the GOP has embraced unlimited gun ownership as a core principle. As presidential candidates uplift vigilantes who have claimed self-defense, there is a great disparity between who feels permitted to carry guns and who is arrested and charged for gun possession.

# EIGHT

# "THIS ISN'T A BADGE, BUT A SHIELD"

## Sheriffs and Militias

SHERIFF DAR LEAF OF MICHIGAN MADE NATIONAL NEWS when, in the fall of 2020, he defended a group of thirteen men, all associated with two Michigan militia groups, who were arrested and charged with federal and state crimes related to an alleged plan to kidnap Governor Gretchen Whitmer. On camera, the sheriff gave an outrageous-sounding justification for the alleged plot, arguing that the scheme to arrest the governor actually had some legal basis. It was, he said, legal under Michigan law for these men to enact a "citizen's arrest" of the governor—or any elected official—for violating the U.S. Constitution with her COVID stay-at-home orders. In his bumbling way, Leaf said, "A lot of people are angry with the governor, and they want her arrested. So, were they trying to arrest, or was it a kidnap attempt? Because you can still, in Michigan, if it's a felony, you can make a felony arrest."

This clip went viral and linked Leaf, one of Mack's most stalwart constitutional sheriff followers, to militias and the potential for political violence. The reality of the prosecution would turn out to be more complicated than initial reports made it seem, but journalists and pundits began to report on constitutional sheriffs in earnest, shocked that legitimate law enforcement would defend accused criminals.

For me, this was not shocking. The links between sheriffs and the far-right militia movement—paramilitary groups that believe their legitimate authority comes from the Constitution—have a storied history that comes from many of the same roots as Richard Mack's constitutional sheriff movement.

William Potter Gale, the father of the Posse Comitatus movement, first gave militias legitimacy by linking them to the Constitution, appropriating the term "unorganized militia" to refer to paramilitary groups. This gave militia followers a patina of legitimacy and claims to lawfulness that author Daniel Levitas calls "patriotic constitutional vigilantism."

The militia movement really picked up steam in the 1990s, especially after the 1993 passage of the Brady Bill, the first comprehensive federal firearms legislation in decades, which also had the effect of linking militias with the Second Amendment as an organizing principle. Like constitutional sheriffs and other far-right groups, the militia movement was further radicalized by the standoffs at Ruby Ridge (1992) and Waco (1993). Both of these incidents, which involved federal law enforcement officials and a number of questionable civilian deaths, radicalized the nascent militia movement in opposition to federal authority. Thus, members embraced a version of states' rights and localism that gave individuals the right—indeed the duty—to protect so-called constitutional values like individual liberty and Christian morality without the burden of sticking to laws. Mark Pitcavage, a historian who has written about the far right for decades, described the militia movement as "sanctioned by law but uncontrolled by government," which feels like an apt way to capture the contradiction.

The militia movement would not have come about, however, were it not for additional cultural and political trends that brought firearms and tactical

training into the day-to-day life of more American men. A series of wars—
the Vietnam War and the Gulf Wars—led to an expansion of the U.S. military, which meant that many more men, particularly working-class men,
were experiencing the violence of war as well as tactical training. Those same
veterans brought their desire for tactical gear home, a commercial movement
that coincided with more affordable guns and ammo starting in the 1970s.
War-style games like paintball became popular as well as magazines that
displayed military-style gear for purchase alongside movies like *Rambo*,
which featured highly trained men who yearned to use their special skills in
daily life.

Perhaps the most ideal militia man of the era was Bo Gritz, a Vietnam
veteran and a 1992 third-party presidential candidate. During the 1992
Ruby Ridge standoff, Gritz served as an intermediary between the federal
government and white supremacist Randy Weaver, eventually persuading
him to surrender peacefully. Gritz, who had a larger-than-life persona rife
with exaggerations and falsehoods, also claimed to be the inspiration behind
Sylvester Stallone's Rambo character. Gritz and his supporters brought together neo-Nazis, white supremacists, survivalists, tax protesters, and other
far-right groups with a promise of masculine dominance using military-style
force all under constitutional authority.

This combination of groups, many openly racist and anti-Semitic, has
always raised the issue of whether to categorize militias as all white supremacist. Historian Kathleen Belew argues in her work *Bring the War Home* that
the militia movement, like Posse Comitatus, acted as part of the broader
white power movement. Sociologist Amy Cooter, however, roots the militia
movement in nostalgia driven by perceived social changes and reliant on a
more subtle form of white supremacy.

Cooter's more nuanced view matched what I saw and, to me, is more
useful to explain how militias and constitutional sheriffs can claim to be

both "race-blind" and have ideas deeply rooted in white supremacy. The militias I saw in Nevada standing for sheriffs, for example, had Latino members as well as white ones. One of the most well-known constitutional sheriffs in Nevada is Aitor Narvaiza, who immigrated from Spain as a child and has argued for stricter immigration limits. Both constitutional sheriffs and right-wing militia groups embody what Cooter calls the "more subtle forms of racism [which] are very pernicious and problematic and embedded in our political system."

A less examined, but extremely important, aspect of the militia movement includes their general embrace of conspiracy theories, which began with Posse Comitatus but grew to encompass all sorts of conspiracies about public health, the environmental movement, and elite politicians. While the flavor of conspiracy has changed with the times, there were always the same elements of infiltration and invasion, fears that perfectly slotted into the idea that able-bodied men needed to prepare for war. In the 1990s, far-right groups feared the incursion of the Bloods and the Crips, who, these conspiracy theorists argued, were being paid and supported by the federal government to generate a kind of societal takeover through violence. Other conspiracies, like the black helicopters allegedly sent by the United Nations, recalled fears of globalism and New World Order–style thinking. Now the fears include Chinese infiltration of infrastructure, migrants crossing the U.S.-Mexico border, and COVID vaccines; some militia-adjacent groups even cite the October 7, 2023, Hamas attack on Israel as a sign that the United States needs to remain vigilant to outside invasion.

Amid this swirl of ideas, the militia movement of the 1990s always looked to the sheriff as an important symbol and a real-life example of how law enforcement could operate as honest "community police," especially when juxtaposed with overbearing federal law enforcement. One of the major militia leaders in Michigan was Norman Olson, cofounder of the Michigan Militia. In 1995, he testified in front of a congressional committee:

> We will defer to the lawful historic authority, which is the
> county sheriff. He indeed is the commander of the local mili-
> tia. And when a situation erupts, in which we would be
> deputized . . . he cannot [join us] of course because of his polit-
> ical nature. . . . Knowing the historic role of our sheriffs, in the
> event that the county would be endangered, he could deputize a
> ready posse and form the militia to defend the people.

Olson went on to explain that federal law enforcement agencies, in contrast, were seen as threats. He proposed legislation that would require federal
agencies to seek permission from the sheriff before entering a county, because
the sheriff, in Olson's mind, could be trusted as an honest broker with community members and constituents.

As Olson's words indicate, militias, like Posse Comitatus before them,
respected the county sheriff as the only legitimate authority because the sheriff was elected and, thus, in their minds, more likely to be aligned with constitutional values. As the federal government invested in policing, providing
local police with more military equipment designed for counterinsurgency
tactics in cities, militias felt justified in their distrust of police and federal law
enforcement. The contrast between sheriffs—white-hatted, riding a horse or
driving a pickup truck, attending church, knowing the names of neighbors—
and federal police agencies was emphasized by this perceived militarization,
which was only highlighted by events like the Waco siege.

After a period of relative quiet for the militia movement—9/11 brought
nationalist fervor into the mainstream and militias felt less necessary when
the biggest threat was outside the U.S.—the election of Barack Obama in
2008 reinvigorated militias alongside the constitutional sheriff and Tea Party
movements. All three of these far-right movements used fears of firearm
confiscation to rally support. They were not, these groups asserted, reacting
to the election of the first Black president, but instead they were concerned

about a socialist takeover. The focus also turned to nationalized medicine ("Obamacare") and immigration, especially migration at the U.S.-Mexico border and Muslim immigrants, the same topics that preoccupied the GOP, which helped to shift many of the ideas behind the militia movement into more mainstream politics, including the (short-lived) presidential runs of Ron Paul, whom both Richard Mack and Stewart Rhodes supported.

The number of militias quadrupled by the end of the first year of the Obama administration, which concerned law enforcement because of militia groups' reliance on firearms as both a signifier for constitutional rights and a method to threaten violence. In 2009, less than three months after President Obama took office and the same year Rhodes formed the Oath Keepers, the Department of Homeland Security released a brief report on right-wing extremism titled "Rightwing Extremism: Current Economic and Political Climate Fueling Resurgence in Radicalization and Recruitment." While the report admitted that, at the time, there were no indications of planned terrorist activity, it argued that the "economic downturn and the election of the first African American president present unique drivers for right-wing radicalization and recruitment." It also pointed to militia recruitment of military veterans and police.

The report had the opposite effect to that intended. As soon as it became public, Republicans pushed back against the idea that there was a growing problem with people adopting such ideologies and took particular umbrage at the implication that veterans might join such movements. They argued the report was anti-American. The document was posted on the Oath Keepers' website and forwarded to members, used as proof that the Democrat-led government was attacking them. Military leaders and veterans, in particular, were insulted; plus, there were still ongoing wars in Iraq and Afghanistan. Janet Napolitano, the secretary of Homeland Security, quickly backtracked. Despite her experience in dealing with far-right movements—she had worked on the Oklahoma City bombing case as an assistant U.S. attorney general in Arizona—she apologized and erased the mention of "right-wing extremism" from the department's vocabulary to pacify the GOP and military.

Far-right sheriffs benefited from the Obama administration's failure to pursue militia groups as a national security priority. Militia supporters nursed a sense of persecution, and far-right politicians weaponized that grievance to organize far-right groups locally. Discontented veterans of the long-running wars on terror turned to local far-right grassroots groups and county sheriffs. General Michael Flynn, now an ardent Trump supporter and QAnon adherent, was one such ex–national security official who left the federal government and became virulently anti-government, bringing more legitimacy to militias' fears of threats from within and abroad because of his experience in overseas war.

Around the mid-2010s, I witnessed far-right sheriffs supporting militia activity largely in the service of anti-Muslim policing. Sheriffs across the country hired John Guandolo—an ex-FBI agent who holds openly anti-Muslim views—to train their deputies on how to spot Muslim "terrorists" in their community. In 2014, Guandolo told Frank Gaffney, a notable Islamophobe, "I always focus on the sheriffs because the sheriffs are the most powerful law enforcement officers in the country. Get them to understand this. . . . I believe that it's at the local level that this has to be handled."

In 2015, a group of armed men led by Jon Ritzheimer, a member of the Three Percenters and a former Oath Keeper, held a demonstration outside a mosque in Phoenix. Both then sheriff Joe Arpaio and the then county attorney Bill Montgomery (who is now on the Arizona Supreme Court) condoned this Islamophobic display. While this event was nonviolent, it signaled the willingness of far-right militia groups to display their role as protecting white Christians from foreign encroachment. Later that year, a young man with openly racist views and connections to the far-right movement massacred nine congregants at Charleston's Emanuel African Methodist Episcopal Church. In 2017, President Trump issued the "Muslim ban," an executive order that blocked immigrants from Muslim-majority countries from entering the U.S.

To be fair, the vast majority of law enforcement officials opposed political violence as well as open bigotry. But two things set the stage. First, law enforcement in general ended most far-right protests without violence, treating white anti-government protesters delicately, probably out of fear of another Waco or Ruby Ridge. And second, sheriffs found themselves politically aligned with these groups, whether because of expediency—militia members vote, after all—or because of shared opposition to Obama and Democrats.

The permissive attitude of sheriffs has remained remarkably consistent. Even sheriffs who do not agree with militias have generally been able to tolerate their presence and perceive that their grievances are legitimate. One reason could simply be identification: sheriffs, who are mostly white men, see militia members, also mostly white men, as similar to them. Black protesters or immigrants, on the other hand, appear less sympathetic. Sheriffs bent over backwards to respect the constitutional rights of militias, including their right to assemble and to use firearms. One Michigan sheriff said of the local militia in 1994, "They're not violating any Michigan or federal law at this point, and I don't expect them to." Sometimes sheriffs even called upon militias to assist in times of natural disaster or search for missing people.

It should be said that every state nominally outlaws paramilitary groups. The Institute for Constitutional Advocacy and Protection at Georgetown Law defines "unorganized militias" as "groups of armed individuals that engage in paramilitary activity or law enforcement functions without being called forth by a governor or the federal government and without reporting to any government authority." At the same time, many militia activities—holding meetings, discussing political ideas, and shooting guns—are perfectly legal and the statutes are vague. As a result, there have been no prosecutions of militias with the exception of those whose members have engaged in overt acts of violence or other crimes, like illegal firearms possession.

———

The election of Donald Trump and the COVID pandemic presented a unique opportunity for militias to participate in legitimate political discourse, often alongside county sheriffs. They protested business closures. They came out in support of Second Amendment sanctuaries, often providing public testimony in support of such declarations. And later they would seek to assist law enforcement during the 2020 racial justice protests and with election security, both of which relied heavily on conspiracy theories propagated by GOP politicians. Rather than outlaws, militias saw themselves as "super citizens," in the words of Amy Cooter.

Here is where we return to Dar Leaf and his defense of local militia members.

In May of 2020, around one hundred Michiganders gathered for a maskless rally in Grand Rapids to protest the COVID public health orders issued by Governor Whitmer, a Democrat. Dubbed the "American Patriot Rally—Sheriffs Speak Out," the attendees wore dun-colored hoodies and caps and waved American and Gadsden flags alongside the same Three Percenter flags I saw in Battle Mountain, a Roman numeral III in a circle. Some carried signs condemning "Whitler"—a portmanteau of "Whitmer" and "Hitler"—blaming the governor for their dissatisfaction. They gathered in Rosa Parks Circle, a location chosen intentionally by the organizers to reflect their belief that their protest was part of a tradition of civil rights.

The militias came newly invigorated. Two weeks earlier, many of the same militia-aligned people had stormed the Michigan capitol building, threatening legislators with military-style rifles and carrying a Confederate flag and a noose. A few days before the rally, the Michigan Liberty Militia had helped a seventy-seven-year-old Owosso barber reopen his shop in opposition to the governor's orders and oblivious to the dangers of COVID.

The May rally began with two tween girls doing a short dance among rows of fluttering American flags as the song "Bleed the Same" by Mandisa (a song the artist said was inspired by the problem of racial violence) blared from a temporary sound system. One of the first speakers was Ryan Kelley, a former real estate broker and onetime candidate for governor of Michigan. Kelley would be sentenced to sixty days in jail for his role on January 6. He took to the stage accompanied by chants of "USA! USA!" He called Whitmer a "dictator." Next to him stood Phil Robinson, aka Warrior of Odin, the leader of the Michigan Liberty Militia, a gloved hand on the assault rifle slung across his chest, gnashing something between his jaws. He wore his gray beard in two large braids.

"Who runs this state?!" Kelley called. Robinson looked on silently.

"The People!" the audience cheered. This call-and-response punctuated every few sentences of Kelley's speech.

"We have elected sheriffs speaking out today against the illegal executive orders," he said to applause. An audience member waved a handwritten sign that said "MI Sheriffs Stand Against Tyranny."

Kelley continued: "Our message here today at the American Patriot Rally is very clear. We are here to encourage all Michigan law enforcement to uphold the Constitution of the United States of America and not to enforce the illegal executive orders by our governor!"

The featured speaker and only sheriff present was Dar Leaf, who was elected sheriff of Barry County in 2004 and has run unopposed in every election since then, including in 2020. (He bragged once that his approval rating has never dipped below 65 percent, which I could not confirm.) Squat and ruddy, with a shock of unruly whitish hair and a bristle-comb mustache, Leaf has long been an outspoken proponent of Mack, conspiracy theories, guns, and militias.

Leaf took the stage with members of the Michigan Liberty Militia and the Wolverine Watchmen, another militia group, and free-associated for about twenty-five minutes. "Could you imagine Rosa Parks?" he began. "What if she didn't go to the back of the bus?" he contemplated, taking a page from Richard Mack. "What if a deputy told her she could sit wherever you want?"

He compared the Owosso barber to Rosa Parks then, calling them both "rebels." "It really ticked me off, when they were trying to shut him down. The amount of force they were using," he went on. He explained that he told his deputies to handle such things "with a phone call."

"Most of us here are Christians," he said. "We are supposed to be praying for our leaders." He then added that prayer was working to reopen the state, county by county.

Leaf was funny, bawdy (he made a joke about rectal thermometers), and incredibly sincere. "If we are enforcing an unlawful law . . . we could be sued!" he said, arguing that if he were to enforce COVID health regulations, he would be setting himself up for a lawsuit.

Toward the end of his rambling talk, which covered schools, taxes, and the mental health toll on police officers, Leaf plucked at the Barry County sheriff's badge pinned to his chest and said, "This right here. This isn't really a badge, it's a shield. It represents the old times when the knights were protecting their kingdom. They had their shields. They had their swords. That's what that represents."

At this point in the rally, a group of audience members approached the stage. Some held actual foam shields. One was labeled "federal government"; one "state government"; and one "Barry County." It was a demonstration.

The federal government, Leaf explained, was there to "protect our borders." The state government's job was to "protect us from an overreaching government." The local government was there, Leaf said, to protect people from the state. Then the militia members moved to the front of the stage as the audience cheered and chanted, "U.S.A."

"It's called the militia," Leaf said. "A well-regulated one at that, these beautiful men up here." He then began to recite the Second Amendment, the militia members mouthing the words along with the sheriff.

"A well-regulated militia. Being necessary to the security of a free state," Leaf recited, and stopped there to explain that a militia was the "last home defense" for when local government fails.

"I'm lucky you got my back," he joked to the men onstage—two of whom were later arrested for the alleged plot against Governor Whitmer—adding that Hillary Clinton was more of a "domestic terrorist" than the militia was. Leaf later described that moment as "one of those speeches where you just knock it out of the ballpark." His speech included all the anti-federal and pro-gun ideas that now have come to define the modern far-right sheriff movement.

It would not come as a surprise, given this event and how Leaf viewed his role as sheriff, that he would later defend the accused men. After a CNN headline reading "Sheriff Spoke in Defense of Accused Domestic Terrorists," other Michigan sheriffs condemned him. Matthew Sexton, executive director of the Michigan Sheriffs' Association, which represents all the sheriffs in the state, issued a statement saying, "His comments were dangerous, and let me be clear, there is nothing about this alleged plot that could be construed as legal, moral, or American."

While you might think this would have repercussions for Leaf, it didn't. Leaf ignored calls to resign. No one could fire him, and he easily won reelection less than a month later. The contest was not even close.

Even further, the prosecutions of the Michigan militia members mostly proved Leaf to be correct. Evidence revealed the work of multiple FBI informants, raising allegations of entrapment. Five of the thirteen were convicted, five acquitted, and the rest pled guilty.

Leaf expressed his vindication: "I actually had people calling me up and thanking me for speaking up about the Constitution, because they are going after these guys," he said in 2023, connecting the defense of militia members with constitutional rights. As for those calls to resign in 2020? "Why would I resign when I'm right?" he asked hypothetically.

———

Both sheriffs and militias claim the same historical legitimacy rooted in the history of America and a strict reading of the Constitution. While it is true that militias played a role in the nation's founding, like sheriffs, they also rely primarily on a mythologized history that sidelines inconvenient links to white supremacy and a law that is much more contentious than the far right would have people believe.

Like sheriffs, militias have their roots in seventeenth-century England, when King Charles II passed the Militia Act of 1662, taking guns from anyone "dangerous to the Peace of the Kingdom" and leaving them in the hands of qualified militia members only. Perhaps as a result of this history across the seas, firearm possession became a symbol of power for Anglo settlers in the Americas. Colonial laws typically required all white men between sixteen and sixty—"militia eligible men"—to own "at least one cutting weapon" and some sort of firearm for use when they were called upon to serve. These laws did not contemplate the purchase of multiple firearms, because mass consumer culture was not around yet. Instead, the laws often required the colonial government to provide militia-eligible men with firearms, implying that the militia was a required form of service.

When the colonists unlawfully took up arms against England—in their eyes, overthrowing tyranny—they formed militias to fight British rule. But the results were considerably more nuanced than the far right admits. Militias were more often seen as ragtag and undisciplined. George Washington famously complained, "I am wearied to death all day with a variety of perplexing circumstances, disturbed at the conduct of the militia, whose behavior and want of discipline has done great injury to the other troops."

In his book *To Shake Their Guns in the Tyrant's Face*, historian Robert

Churchill points out that colonial and early America had a strong tradition of militias. Leading up to the Revolutionary War, the British monarchy imposed strict taxes upon the colonies, which triggered noncompliance, which, in turn, metastasized into armed resistance.

One influential proto-militia figure Churchill points to is Jonathan Mayhew, an eighteenth-century minister who preached libertarian self-determination. He believed that God demanded men resist tyrannical and oppressive government through violence. If despotic rulers demanded compliance with laws that "transgress the will of God," Mayhew said, such demands were "null and void," and "disobedience to them is a duty, not a crime." Mayhew's idea remains relevant for modern militias, particularly the notion that a higher law motivates members' actions, again legitimizing armed resistance.

To explain the text of the Second Amendment, some lawyers argue that the militia clause refers to state militias, not the ability of individual citizens to form their own militias, taking away the constitutional authority the militia movement believes legitimizes it. Historian Roxanne Dunbar-Ortiz has argued in her work that the colonial conquest of America involved systemic violence against Indigenous tribes across the continent. Militia violence was an important aspect of the colonial settler regime before there was government (or sheriffs). Dunbar-Ortiz explains that "the voluntary militias described in the Second Amendment entitled settlers, as individuals and families, with the right to combat Native Americans on their own." Sheriffs, similarly, are associated with the mythos of the "frontier," a lawman who helped to support colonial-settler violence and enable the continued seizure of land.

Militias reappear throughout American history, sometimes with links to law enforcement. After the Civil War, there were Black militias that sought to defend their communities from oppressive extrajudicial violence; these groups were vilified by Southern Democrats to justify more violence. The

KKK in its various incarnations was a militia dedicated to white supremacy and often supported legitimate political processes on a local level even as they expressed anti-federal views. Churchill similarly points out that the far-right movement that emerged in the 2000s utilized both legitimate political processes, like elections, get-out-the-vote drives, and protests; and illegitimate processes, like terrorist attacks, mass shootings, and threats of violence against politicians. In other words, they helped to elect sheriffs who supported their organizations while also being unafraid to use extrajudicial violence to achieve their goals.

Today, it could be argued, the difference between the two is collapsing: sheriffs coordinate with militia groups, and the Oath Keepers declare themselves Trump's private strike force. Sheriffs hold trainings for firearm owners to act as church defense forces in the event of a mass shooting. As civilian firearm ownership and use becomes more common and deregulated, I saw that sheriffs were willing to see everyone on their side as part of their potential posse.

In September of 2023, Leaf spoke at a CSPOA training course in the farthest western point of North Carolina, a town named Murphy. Deep in the Nantahala National Forest, Murphy is two hours from Chattanooga and Atlanta, making it a rural town perfectly equidistant from two other states in which the CSPOA was hoping to recruit.

The part of North Carolina where Murphy is located has long been considered a hotbed of militia activity. The most famous far-right figure of the region is Eric Rudolph, who bombed the 1996 Atlanta Summer Olympics as well as abortion clinics in Georgia and Alabama in the 1990s. In Atlanta, one person died and hundreds were injured; the abortion clinic bombings killed a police officer and wounded many others. Rudolph hid in the forest of western North Carolina for five years before he was caught by the FBI in

Murphy while he was looking for food in a dumpster. It's not completely clear what ideology motivated Rudolph, but most experts who have written about him think that he was part of the militia movement associated with Christian Identity, the white supremacist movement supported by William Potter Gale.

Leaf was the keynote speaker. He was not flashy or charismatic. His Midwestern accent was thick, and he swallowed the endings of his words. Because of his demeanor, he deftly blended wild conspiracy theories—for example, he told me that he still thought that Barack Obama was not born in the United States—with amusing, self-deprecating tales. By the time I had untangled what he was saying—*He can't possibly think that, can he?*—he had moved on to talking about hockey.

In his speech to a roomful of mostly civilians and about a half dozen sheriffs from rural Georgia and North Carolina, he talked about how the press had pursued him relentlessly since the rally at Rosa Parks Circle. In his eyes, he explained, he was only defending the Constitution from those who would deviate from its principles of liberty. "If I shake my head," he said, "it's because I always thought that was treason."

Those who have possibly committed treason, in Leaf's view, were part of a long list that included "globalists," Supreme Court justice Sonia Sotomayor, Governor Whitmer, and the media. Their crimes involved taking away "property rights," forging Obama's birth certificate, spreading misinformation about the effectiveness of masks against COVID spread, denying the biblical influence on the Founding Fathers, and other things that they "must not teach in college anymore." His hero was Joe Arpaio, who, he said, "took on the eagle" and investigated Obama's birth certificate, promoting the far-right "birther" conspiracy.

He also managed to name-check so many conspiracy theories, it was hard to count them. There was "Agenda 21," a United Nations global sustainability report that some on the far right argue was really about harming American dominance. There was COVID, which he posited might be "from a foreign country," and the government's response, which he said involved putting infected people into elder-care homes on purpose.

As evidence of the long reach of Mack's ideology, Leaf credited CSPOA seminars, which he has attended regularly since the organization began, with helping him discover that the sheriff gets his power from the people. He supplements CSPOA propaganda with his "own research" on the true meaning of the Constitution, reflecting how Mack's ideas propagate and generate even more radical rhetoric as sheriffs dig into additional materials, often spread through the same networks as militia groups and the CSPOA, that reflect their worldview.

"Our own government is supposed to leave us alone and is supposed to protect us being left alone," he said. This is what he argued happened to the local militias. They were "pushed" by government agents into "stupid talk" about threatening to kidnap the governor, which, he posited, was probably a "trap." They were, he said, tried by the media and "unlawfully detained." "How about habeas corpus?" he said. He claimed he received death threats for defending the militia members from what he viewed as illegitimate attacks by the media.

He went on to describe the posse as the local militia led by the sheriff. "You are the commander in chief of your posse," he told the sheriffs in the room.

Leaf's view of the militia—and indeed of the entire structure of government—flows from his dedication to a biblical interpretation of both the Constitution and U.S. history as a whole, to which he credits lessons from Michael Peroutka's Institute on the Constitution, the pro-Confederate lawyer who occasionally tours with Mack. It is a form of Christian nationalism—like many who identify as Christian nationalists, Leaf does not tout any particular religious affiliation publicly—that flavors his entire view of the world, everything from politics, to the U.S. Supreme Court, to health care, to relationships between men and women.

"I got news for you folks," he said at one point. "They used a lot of Bible quotes when they were writing the Constitution."

He concluded his hour-long stream of consciousness with a call to sheriffs to stand by their principles: "Hold tight. A sheriff's gotta have courage. When you show courage, your people in your community will get behind you or beside you." His evidence was his reelection and his faith in the CSPOA. "There's a bad, bad movement going on, folks. And it's up to all of us to kind of stay on that path here in the United States."

———

After his speech, I managed to buttonhole Leaf, and we spoke in the parking lot. He was friendly and later invited me to sit down with him for the locally provided BBQ lunch offered for training attendees.

During his talk that day, Leaf reiterated that during the time of King Alfred the Great, each county was called a "shire." "What's happening is the Danes and Vikings are coming into Great Britain and are being very, very successful," he said. All of the shires got together, and then all the kings got together and appointed a "commander in chief." This, he says, is just like the American system of government today. The idea of preparing for an invasion is not incidental. "They took their country back," he concluded.

Here, Leaf was referring to the familiar "King Alfred" history of the sheriff's office that tasked sheriffs with maintaining small militias, sometimes called posses or "musters." (Stewart Rhodes also used the term "muster" to refer to a gathering of Oath Keepers, in keeping with this tradition.) This glorification of a mythic past, indeed one with all the trappings of knighthood and legends, fits with both the idea of the "sheriff" as a figure above and beyond the role of mere law enforcement officer as well as the sort of white, masculine justification of violent displays in the name of the public good. It extends the idea of a "good guy with a gun" to an exalted status, not only good because he is protecting the flock but because he is blessed, beloved, and chivalrous. Not just righteous but also chosen.

I asked Leaf to explain the difference between a militia and a posse. "Well," he said, "it depends on what you are mustering them up for." A militia, he explained, would be "mustered" by an official "under military law," which places them under the control of a governor or the president. "When I call them up," he went on to clarify, "we call it a posse."

He then referred me to a presentation he uses titled "The American Sheriff: At the Common Law."

Men, he said, have to be "armed and ready" for the posse or the militia. "People go and say, 'Oh, "militia." It's a dirty word.' Have you ever done jury duty? That's militia duty. That goes all the way back to the twelve tribes of Israel. You're protecting not just your land, but you also protect your laws," he said.

"'Militia' is not a dirty word. It's a duty," he continued. In his presentation, one slide reads, "The Militia are your neighbors, friends, and relatives in your county. They are of all occupations and walks of life. When crisis comes, all that is needed is wrapped up in your local militia (doctors, nurses, engineers, businessmen, merchants, farmers, carpenters, builders, farmers, butchers, bakers, candlestick makers)."

Leaf told me something similar: "It means that everybody's a militia. Everybody's a posse. Okay? If you're able-bodied, I can call you on up if something happened right here and you're in my county. I say, 'You got to help me out here.'" He was referring to the people who had just attended his talk. They were not necessarily all armed now, but Leaf, as sheriff, supported their right to become battle-ready. It struck him as natural that a church basement would serve as a proto–training ground. Faith in the Constitution and the Bible were fundamental building blocks to militia membership.

Then he went on to discuss the role of history, including the Bible, specifically the first chapter of the book of Numbers, which describes the Twelve

Tribes of Israel. In the passage, God tells Moses to "take a census of the whole Israelite community by their clans and families" and "count according to their divisions all the men in Israel who are twenty years old or more and able to serve in the army." These are the tribes—the militias in Leaf's thinking—who help Moses fight for Israel.

Leaf's discussion, ranging from the Bible to the Constitution, reflects how the militia movement became part of Christian nationalism, or the belief that the United States should be a Christian nation. Strains of Christian nationalism run throughout the constitutional sheriff movement; take, for example, Mack's strong views that the Constitution protects "individual liberty" and gun rights but not LGBTQ+ people or abortion rights for women. For this reason, the CSPOA-aligned sheriffs' idea of nullification—sheriffs who ignore federal or state laws because they are contrary to their interpretation of the Constitution—is not a both-sides issue. Instead, it's quite clear that nullification refers to rejecting laws that are inconsistent with a biblical interpretation of the Constitution or with a libertarian view of government. ("The right to be left alone," in Mack's words.)

Leaf went on to explain that he was not anti-government but rather wanted people to understand the role of the different branches of government. Which made sense in some way. But then he began to talk about domestic violence, specifically the Lautenberg Amendment, a federal law that criminalizes gun ownership by people with domestic violence convictions. "I'm kind of flabbergasted," he went on. "Who gave the federal government authority over all the guns?" "Shoving," he contended, did not count as abuse. "They say it's a crime of power. Liquid power, I think they mean," he said, referring to alcoholism as a cause of domestic violence. (In 2023, the U.S. Supreme Court heard arguments in *United States v. Rahimi*, in which the respondent argued that criminalizing firearm possession by individuals with a domestic violence protective order violated the Second Amendment.)

Interestingly, even though he trains people in the use of firearms, Leaf himself did not cite gunplay as a skill he used in the course of his job. Instead, he praised his problem-solving abilities and attempts to communicate with people, connecting himself to the folksier stereotype of the neighborhood sheriff, not at all the commander of an army.

But who benefited from his style of community policing? For example, he told me he was called to one domestic violence incident where he gave a man a cigarette to calm him down and avoid a violent encounter. In another tale, Leaf had successfully proven that a young woman's accusation of domestic violence was untrue. The accused man avoided arrest.

"Did you arrest the woman?" I asked.

"Oh yes," he said, "I charged her with a felony. Because she lied."

---

Later, Leaf pressed into my hand a small booklet written by a man named Brent Allen Winters, who, according to his website, is an "American geologist, Bible translator, common lawyer, author, and teacher of comparative law." Winters practices a type of law he calls "common law," which is a form of sovereign citizen ideology, people who believe in a sort of pseudo-law. He also teaches a class on the history of the sheriff ("The Constitutional Sheriff") with Leaf as part of an array of courses that include topics like "Drafting a Common Law Asset-Protection Trust" and "The Good Book Uncooked" (referring to the Bible).

Winters's one-hundred-page booklet, *Militia of the Several States*, explains, in prose littered with nonsensical yet formal legalese, that both the U.S. Constitution and the Bible intended for militias to exist. (Over half of the booklet consists of Bible passages with lengthy footnotes.) I found it disorienting to read because it did not conform to what I (or most people) understood as law. Through a series of anecdotes, Winters writes that the U.S. government should hew closer to biblical principles. One of those principles is the militia, as Leaf told me, through the Twelve Tribes of Israel.

One chart explains that "God is the well-spring of all true right," "The People are direct creations of God," and "The Militia is those able-bodied men of the People." In sum, while the Constitution is a product of people, the militia comes directly from God, not the Constitution, and is, therefore, a super right, a form of citizenship beyond U.S. citizenship—it is the birth-right of all "able-bodied men." The militia should defend the Constitution against "its enemies—both foreign and, of even greater danger, domestic (among us)."

Sovereign citizens are best known for their use of fake legal documents, which they present to courts. Many don't believe in state identification, birth certificates, or taxes. Leaf justified his positions on what sovereign citizens call "common law," another legal term borrowed for its Anglo-Saxon roots. Both Leaf and Winters also believe in the right to form "citizen juries," which are like courtroom juries but are not assembled in courts of law by judges; rather they are assemblages of like-minded individuals, vigilante-style. Once such a judgment has been issued, in this scheme of thinking, the militia executes the decision.

———————

The potential value of militias to sheriffs became apparent during the summer of 2020, after the murder of George Floyd. Throughout that summer, large multiracial groups of (generally) young people protested in the streets, in some places for weeks on end, occasionally clashing with right-wing counterprotesters. A big difference between these uprisings and prior years' Black Lives Matter movements was their ubiquity. Smaller towns and cities across the country—not just on the coasts—saw people in the streets. Even though most of these uprisings were nonviolent, there were a handful of cities where so-called antifa groups—loosely knit but heavily armed left-wing protesters—clashed with right-wing militias or street gangs such as the Patriot Front.

While some militias initially marched with Black Lives Matter protesters, most became disillusioned by repeated displays on right-wing media of burning buildings and destruction of property, taking advantage of the fact that there was a perception among some people—especially Republicans—that antifa posed a particular danger. Trump added fuel to the fire by saying, "When the looting starts, the shooting starts."

Mainstream and far-right sheriffs alike amplified the GOP messaging. While there were some law enforcement officials who joined marches or otherwise facilitated protests, many sheriffs used the opportunity to blast progressives, especially once the protests' demands crystallized around the slogan "Defund the Police." Bob Songer, a dedicated CSPOA-aligned sheriff in rural Washington State, declared Black Lives Matter "a terrorist group" that wanted to "turn us into a communist country."

Inspired by this rhetoric, militias began to organize with counterprotesters, nominally to protect property and ensure orderly conduct. Groups of mostly men, armed to the teeth, dressed in fatigues, showed up at protests against police violence. Sometimes they just directed traffic or tried to defuse street brawls. Sometimes they said they were defending the community from outsiders. To many, they looked like an occupying army. And many of them were either encouraged or tacitly endorsed by their local sheriff.

One such confrontation happened in Minden, Nevada, a town of less than four thousand people in Douglas County. The politics of Minden are unabashedly conservative; the county overwhelmingly voted for Donald Trump, and its residents supported unlimited gun ownership and resisted COVID health mandates. Until 2023, Minden was one of the few towns with a "sundown" siren that blared at five o'clock every evening, which was historically used to warn Black and Native people to leave town before dusk or else face arrest or violence.

Nevada has a history of far-right activity, ranging from the aforementioned Sagebrush Rebellion to violent extremists like Jerad and Amanda

Miller, who, in 2014, shot and killed two cops, a bystander, and themselves after covering the cops' bodies with swastikas. Earlier that same year, Jerad Miller had appeared in a photograph with Mack taken at a local sheriff's debate.

At the same time, Minden, like many towns across America, had a significant number of people who were sympathetic to the calls for racial justice. One of them was Minden's head librarian, Amy Dodson, a middle-aged woman with a red streak in her blond hair. Dodson had been working in Minden for over six years and has been a librarian all her life. When the American Library Association, a nonprofit whose mission is "to promote library service and librarianship," urged libraries to "center the voices and experiences of Black library workers, the Black community, support the broader Black Lives Matter movement, fight against police violence, and help the cause of racial justice," Dodson was in full agreement.

Working with her staff, Dodson drafted a proposed diversity statement to "make everyone feel included" that she posted on the library's Facebook page for public comment before making it official. The page-long text of the proposed statement (called a "possible diversity statement") read in part, "The Douglas County Public Library denounces all acts of violence, racism, and disregard for human rights. We support #BlackLivesMatter. We resolutely assert and believe that all forms of racism, hatred, inequality, and injustice don't belong in our society."

The statement went into a packet of materials for the next library board meeting, scheduled for July 28, 2020. Within "less than twenty-four hours," Dodson told me, the chief deputy district attorney for Douglas County, whom Dodson described as "pretty conservative," called her and inquired about the statement. "He called and told me to take it down. And I didn't," she said.

Shortly thereafter, Douglas County sheriff Dan Coverley posted his own statement on Facebook. It read, in part, "To support [the Black Lives Matter] movement is to support violence and to openly ask for it to happen in

Douglas County. . . . Due to your support of Black Lives Matter and the obvious lack of support or trust with the Douglas County Sheriff's Office, please do not feel the need to call 911 for help. . . . I wish you good luck with disturbances and lewd behavior, since those are just some of the recent calls my office has assisted you with in the past." Coverley's language echoed a letter that various Republican attorneys general and two sheriffs sent to Congress asking for "assistance in tempering the anti-police rhetoric."

Dan Coverley was elected to office in 2019 after serving nearly two decades as a deputy in the Douglas County Sheriff's Office. He's an extremely military-looking man with cropped hair; he lacks the air of the Western cowboy that many Nevada sheriffs have adopted. Coverley did not contact Dodson before he posted his response, and she said that she learned about it as it spread around the internet.

"The whole world kind of exploded," she said. Despite that, Dodson remained steadfast. "So, I felt like, I shouldn't take it down. As you know, before all that happened, I just thought it was something really important that we needed to do, and we needed to tell everyone that, you know, we're anti-racist, and that we're welcoming everyone and that we are a library, a place of free speech, free expression.

"It came across as a very childish response," she said of the sheriff's letter. After she learned about it, Dodson told me she called back the chief deputy DA and told him that the sheriff was threatening her. "And I'll never forget his response," she said years later. "He said, 'No, he's not really threatening you per se. . . . He's just saying that you shouldn't bother contacting them.'" She described the interactions as "patronizing and mansplaining." "He immediately defended the sheriff," she added, even though his role as an attorney was to advise the library, not the sheriff.

The sheriff's response to the library letter set off protests from more liberal groups. Even though the sheriff walked back some of his comments a day later—arguing that he would respond to a call from the library and was just reacting to a "difficult time to be a law enforcement professional" without apologizing—there remained a sense in the community that a standoff was imminent.

Dodson is not a firebrand; she now lives with her dog and husband in Illinois, where she is a head librarian at a more liberal library system. When we spoke, two years after the incident itself, she had gained more perspective and it was clear to me that she felt strongly the importance of maintaining the library as a safe space. I asked Dodson why she felt the statement was important to keep posted, despite the warning from the county. In addition to being a previously discussed issue at the library, she told me, "there were just a lot of protests going on around the country, a lot of people taking a stand on various issues related to racism and related to diversity and so on. And, so, it was a very natural time to do that. And I felt like it was too important, and it needed to be said. I knew that I lived in a conservative place. It's a very Republican county, but I had no idea how bad it was until all this happened."

By "all this," she was referring to a standoff exacerbated by the presence of militia groups as well as a sheriff who supported them.

Almost immediately, community members contacted the sheriff to voice their support of his actions. In one email, a resident wrote, "Coverley is another word for courageous. . . . Keep my name on the list of locals ready to respond to support Dan wherever, however, and whenever he need [sic] it," the writer concluded.

The controversy made national news and a group of multiracial young Nevada residents affiliated with Black Lives Matter planned a protest for August 8. Predictably, the rumors of the protest spurred a flurry of counter-protest activity. Notably, there was a community meeting that provided the impetus for local militia groups, including Three Percenters, to rally. A few days before the protest, some militia leaders sent out a mass email to

Coverley supporters: "Douglas County residents, it is now the time to stand up for our Sheriff's Office and our town. . . . Every able-bodied citizen needs to show up in solidarity with the Sheriff and kindly walk those interlopers OUT OF TOWN. If we don't run them out, they will stay and continue to come and turn Minden & Gardnerville into Portland, OR."

Another email said that the groups have "reached out to the Sheriffs dept., they are well prepared and the Northern Nevada Militia is backing them up."

These emails were all sent to the sheriff's office. When the town manager, John Frisby, inquired about the militia presence—he worried that it would deter families from using the water park in town on a hot summer day—Coverley's chief deputy, Ron Elges, wrote back, "Hi . . . yeah . . . I am not sure . . . they called I said we are good . . . this is what they want to do . . . we can't control the public spaces . . . sorry."

On the evening of August 7, militia members, armed with rifles and decked out in full fatigues and bandannas as face masks, patrolled the streets of Minden as a prelude for the next day. Some carried baseball bats, stun guns, and knives.

Many of the BLM protesters—who lived in Reno and Carson City—aware of the danger, decided not to go at the last minute. Those who did tried to brace themselves for an assault.

County officials were well aware of the increasingly hostile situation as well as the large number of counterprotesters, who seemed ready for a fight. On August 6, the Douglas County Board of Supervisors posted a statement that included the following message: "We respect each individual's right to peacefully assemble. However, Douglas County will not tolerate violence or the destruction of property." This was interpreted by some as expressing support for the BLM protesters, which in turn triggered the militia groups into thinking that the sheriff might cave in to liberal demands.

A sample exchange in the comments:

COMMENT: We know our sheriff will protect the property of
   our community and citizens.
RESPONSE: if the police can't the citizens will.

The words recalled those of Mike Beach, a leader of the Posse Comitatus movement, who respected sheriffs as the ultimate law but also thought that if the sheriff was not willing to back the militia, then he should be removed from office. Gale, in such an instance, wrote that it was okay to hang the sheriff at high noon. Most important, all these men believed, the militia will complete its mission because the Constitution justifies this response. Coverley had activated a potentially violent group of supporters who might not heed his authority.

On the morning of Saturday, August 8, Coverley and his deputies were greeted by the cheers of at least a thousand supporters holding signs and chanting, "Stand with Dan!" Ensconced behind a podium emblazoned with the sheriff's star and the words "A Tradition of Service," the sheriff addressed the counterprotesters. "I want to say that I love this community. My focus has always been and always will be protecting it," he began. He reasserted his respect for the library and added, "We respect each individual's right to peacefully assemble. . . . I believe everyone should feel safe in his community." He concluded by saying that the "relationship between the sheriff's office and its citizens is extremely important to me."

Many of the counterprotesters brought lawn chairs and beer, as if it were a festival. One man with a white beard, dressed in fatigues, a helmet, and armed with a pistol at his waist, an automatic rifle across his chest, and a four-foot metal rod on his belt, addressed the crowd: "Militias are a group of people who want to keep the community safe," he said in an even tone. "We're not racists. . . . We are always recruiting. We are always looking for people of all skill sets and all backgrounds."

At the same time, a group of roughly twenty Black Lives Matter activists arrived for their march, which went down the main street to the city hall. The counterprotesters not only outnumbered the young group thirty to one; they were also heavily armed. One witness testified later that at least two out of three counterprotesters were armed with long guns. Another told me that the counterprotesters pointed their firearms at the youngest marchers, blew air horns, and spat in their faces. One of the BLM protesters said he was "surrounded, harassed, assaulted, and chased around town."

In a radio interview, a counterprotester explained that they were worried about "antifa" and the potential for destruction of property. His explanation reflected the goals of the militia movement and their belief in the Constitution, which was positioned as in opposition to the BLM marchers, who were liberal intruders accusing the residents of Minden of being racist. "What we feel is that the BLM movement has demonized white people," he said, describing himself and the other counterprotesters as "good-hearted patriots."

Despite these claims, videos and eyewitness testimony show that the counterprotesters were fairly aggressive. "The counterprotesters were extremely heavily armed," a law enforcement officer later testified, adding that they were older and mostly white. A local lawyer who was observing described the scene as "very frightening," pointing out that the group of BLM protesters was "very tiny" and unarmed except for one man, who was a military veteran and wore fatigues, there to protect the protesters.

In a video shot by local journalist Kelsey Penrose, a female voice from the militia side shouts, "We died for you!" (referring to combat veterans) as a BLM protester walks by with a sign reading, "Police accountability is not a radical demand."

Eventually chants of "Blue lives matter" and "All lives matter" overpowered any speech from the BLM group. The protesters made peace signs with their fingers in response. "Some guilty white girls," a man said of the protesters.

Finally sparks flew in the combustible environment. A young man named

Timothy Moore drove his black pickup truck into marching BLM protesters, hitting two teenage girls. The truck, while moving very slowly as Moore laid on the horn, appeared to intentionally target the marchers. Upset, a BLM protester threw an empty water bottle at the truck. Then a group of militia members swarmed another BLM protester; one counterprotester struck him repeatedly as an AR-15 dangled from his shoulder. "They wanted to kill these kids," a witness told me.

The video shows how the spark grew into a flame, and the tenor of the protest changed. The BLM protesters headed for a park, heckled by the pro-sheriff side. "Get the fuck out of here!" some of the counterprotesters screamed. "Remember, this is Nevada!" "Get out of town!" "Go home!" A man biked by with a Trump 2020 flag draped across his back. "Blue lives matter," the crowd began to chant again.

The BLM protesters were trapped in a crowd. Law enforcement officials stood nearby but did little to intervene.

Before any further violence occurred, law enforcement from Carson City arrived and escorted the BLM protesters away. "There would have been a massacre," Penrose, the journalist, told me, describing this day as the scariest protest she had experienced.

Ilya Arbatman, a progressive activist who grew up and lives in Reno, told me that the assault resembled the vigilante violence he now associates with the January 6 insurrection. "The sheriff abandoned a small group of peaceful protesters to be swarmed, threatened, spat on, humiliated, and assaulted," he said. Sheriff's deputies did not intervene as the militia surrounded the protesters; they sat on the sidelines and watched. The entire situation was dispiriting. "Local militia groups enjoy a fair amount of community support, and there is no acknowledgment, outside of activist circles, of the danger they pose and their ideological ties to white supremacy," Ilya added.

Penrose told me that it was clear to her that Coverley's office did nothing to stop the counterprotesters from becoming violent and agitated. "They respect cops," she said about the counterprotesters, and told me that she thought if Coverley's deputies had told the counterprotesters to separate from the BLM group, there would have been less violence. "I was so furious that these deputies in riot gear were walking across this parking lot like a gauntlet at a football game," she added, describing how Coverley's officers paraded to cheers and applause. "Every single deputy was working. They were there to be applauded."

After the event, a deputy wrote to Coverley and his command staff, "Apparently BLM did not feel overly welcome here in Douglas County." Deputy Elges responded, "Thank you . . ."

Moore, the man driving the truck, was convicted of "failure to yield" and served a month of weekends in jail after a short trial; he also was fined $640 and assigned forty-eight hours of community service. Moore's lawyer was from the law firm of Joey Gilbert, the man who appeared with Mack in Battle Mountain.

Because the event was publicized and on video, the Democratic attorney general of Nevada, Aaron Ford, opened an investigation into Coverley's failure to intervene. It was, after all, Coverley's job under state law to "suppress all insurrections." Ford also appeared at an August meeting of the library board to make a public comment in support of Dodson's diversity statement, noting that "no government official should issue a threat to withhold public service" because of support for BLM. Yet, there was no real consequence for Coverley, which irked Dodson. She told me, "Well, we're both publicly funded, we both serve the same citizens. But he can say and do whatever. And there's no repercussions."

The sheriff has not really showed any remorse for the incident. In 2022, Coverley was investigated for an ethics complaint that alleged that he wore his uniform that year to campaign for Adam Laxalt, a Trumpian candidate for the U.S. Senate. And in 2023, Coverley attended a law enforcement training at the Claremont Institute, which strongly opposes the Black Lives Matter movement, calling it a "revolutionary movement fundamentally opposed to the American Way of Life."

As for Dodson, she resigned in July of 2021, telling me that her job had become impossible even though she thought most people were generally supportive of the library. The library board subjected her to an independent investigation, which found nothing and cost the county around $30,000.

More important, Dodson said the incident altered her perception of law enforcement and the town she considered home. "When it all started, you know, I was in fear for a long time, I just lived in fear. My husband didn't let me go anywhere by myself anymore, because he was afraid of what might happen. I was terrified of getting pulled over on the road, I was scared of law enforcement for the first time in my life. And because it's a small town, and they see my name, and, you know, see red. All of law enforcement hated my guts, basically, in that county."

———

Sam Bushman, who became the CEO of the CSPOA in 2022, hosts a daily far-right two-hour radio show in which he defends Mack against groups like the Southern Poverty Law Center and discusses the legal underpinnings of constitutional sheriff ideology. "I encourage people to join posses, not militias," he said. "One has the proper role of legitimate government . . . that's slightly different from militias." He added that the Second Amendment "sanctions" militias, and "posses are the answer to that."

David Kopel, a pro-gun law professor who works for the Cato Institute, a libertarian think tank, and has written dozens of briefs related to Second Amendment cases, has argued that the right of posse comitatus is linked to militias and that sheriffs are "intended third-party beneficiaries" of Second

Amendment rights. "As a general policy," Kopel writes, "it is often best when posse members have the same types of firearms as those carried by a full-time certified sheriff's deputy." In essence, he makes the same argument Mack and Bushman do: putting sheriffs in charge of militias prevents complete anarchy.

Events like the one in Minden generated national press and pushback from the left to regulate militia-style groups without running afoul of extremely liberal gun laws and the First Amendment. This effort was aided by the Department of Justice's January 6 prosecutions of major militia leaders, which fragmented national associations like the Oath Keepers. But there is a concern that constitutional sheriffs will continue to support militias, especially when faced with a situation in which local militias claim to be on the side of law enforcement. Georgetown Law professor and former federal prosecutor Mary McCord testified before a House committee in December of 2022 that "[militias] have recruited and sought favor from active-duty law enforcement. And they have aligned themselves with 'constitutional sheriffs,' a movement of elected sheriffs who believe they are the highest law of the land, answerable only to the U.S. Constitution as they interpret it."

Part of the problem is that there have been few consequences for sheriffs who cooperate or support local militias in their counties. Technically, they are not breaking any laws—law enforcement is not legally required to defend protesters from attacks—and sheriffs have wide leeway to use their discretion and political influence as they see fit. Far from being disciplined, these sheriffs, like Coverley and Leaf, receive praise from right-wing media and the GOP. They are given more attention and political support for their position, not less.

Far-right sheriffs identify readily with the goals and aims of militia groups, whose members see themselves as law enforcement adjacent. Their elaborate gear and weaponry are an intentional signifier of their perceived legitimacy. The growth of militias, combined with an increasing far-right influence on law enforcement, could become an ever more frightening mix should tensions rise again. As later chapters will discuss, the resurgence of support for far-right sheriffs in circles beyond the CSPOA, including mainstream right-wing organizations, is bound to bring about more instances of militias feeling emboldened to take the law into their own hands.

# NINE

# KEEPING THE COUNTY WHITE

## *The Southern Sheriff*

THE TOWN OF NEW IBERIA, LOUISIANA, HAS BEEN DIVIDED by railroad tracks for more than 150 years. On one side lies Shadows-on-the-Teche, a plantation home converted into a museum nestled behind a wrought-iron gate among grounds covered in verdant gardens. There's a charming downtown marked by historical plaques as well as the office of the local newspaper, the *Daily Iberian*, which has been in business since 1893.

Drive across the railroad tracks and you'll find an unassuming neighborhood where kids ride their bikes in the street. In front of 500 French Street, an old house owned by the Iberia Parish Federal Credit Union, there is a plaque honoring a group of Black professionals—Eddie L. Dorsey, Ima Pierson, Howard C. Scoggins, and Luins Williams—and a date: May 17–18, 1944.

"Along with leaders of the newly formed NAACP chapter," it reads, "Drs. Dorsey, Pierson, Scoggins, and Williams were violently expelled from Iberia Parish on May 17–18, 1944, because they supported Black workers, who successfully petitioned the federal government for a welding school."

The four doctors honored on the plaque, alongside other Black professionals, were members and leaders of the local NAACP chapter in the 1940s.

They were thrown out of New Iberia so violently that one man died from his injuries inflicted by then sheriff Gilbert Ozenne, a man who was well known for his racism, and the sheriff's sidekick, a man under his command with the ominous name of Gus "Killer" Walker.

Public historian Dr. Phebe Hayes—her doctorate is not in history but rather in communication sciences and disorders—was one of the main people responsible for the placement of the plaque, which marks the type of violence that was all too common in the Jim Crow South, but one that remains rarely discussed.

Hayes is soft-spoken but does not mince words when she has something to say.

"I had colleagues who came here, and they questioned, 'Well, where are the Black people in this story of New Iberia?'" she said, explaining how she began researching, assembling, and then honoring the history that went unacknowledged by the local historic sites, the museums, even the local paper, which was in print at the time of the expulsion but did not publish an article about it. The results of her work reflect not only the role of sheriffs in the American South but also how hard other institutions worked to protect their misdeeds.

―――――――

Before his death in 1987, James Baldwin wrote one of his last major essays, "To Crush a Serpent," in which he compared the white evangelical ministers of the Reagan era to Southern sheriffs. They have "the same lips, the same flat, slatelike eyes, the same self-righteous voices." Baldwin continues, "Both believe that they are responsible, the one for divine law and the other for natural order. Both believe that they are able to define and privileged to impose law and order; and both, historically and actually, know that law and order are meant to keep me in my place. . . . The minister and the sheriff were hired by the Republic to keep the Republic white—to keep it free from sin."

As Baldwin's writing reflects, the post–Civil War Southern sheriff has a particular place in the American collective memory, one filled with equal amounts of nostalgia and disdain. Unlike other elected officials in the South, sheriffs had both symbolic power—in most counties, sheriffs sat atop the local political and social hierarchy—and actual power, like the ability to arrest or not arrest, to jail or not jail. How sheriffs opted to use that power was a source of contention in the South, a place where labor and power were deeply dependent upon a racial hierarchy.

One of the main ways that sheriffs used their state-sanctioned power to deploy violence was to work with both elected leaders and extrajudicial racist terrorist groups like the Ku Klux Klan to ensure that Black Americans remained subservient to white Americans. In some cases, sheriffs were using their discretion to enforce the law through arrests, beatings, and jail. Other times, sheriffs intentionally ignored instances of violence or illegal segregation in education and public services because they knew that blocking the economic and political upward trajectory of Black people was essential to creating and maintaining the social, economic, and political status of elite whites. In other words, the sheriffs served an important role in maintaining the white supremacist social order locally.

This is not a new concept for those who, in the past decades, have sought to emphasize the ways in which modern police descend from slave patrols, groups of militarized posses who ranged from professional slave catchers hired to locate enslaved people who had run away to deputized civilians. In the United States, one of the earliest Southern police forces emerged in Charleston, South Carolina, as a slave patrol in 1702. The historian Jill Lepore compares them to the posse comitatus because they were a quasi-militia group of conscripts who used the "hue and cry" to summon others when needed. Other states followed. North Carolina created a "patrol committee" specifically in response to fears of Black rebellion. Around the 1900s, police became more standardized; they wore uniforms and received salaries.

They took their inspiration from the military and shifted toward orga-nized top-down structures, away from the rabble of the unorganized militia or posse.

In contrast, because of their specific history and elected status, county sheriffs played a slightly different role in preserving the racial caste system. Most of the time, a sheriff's power was limited to their county and restricted their activities to preserving the peace—preventing local uprisings—and keeping people in jail. In the South, sheriffs, like other countywide positions, were local white elites. So-called suspects captured by slave patrols would sometimes be turned over to the sheriff, who would house and feed them until either their enslavers arrived to claim them (and pay the sheriff for the costs of room and board) or a year had passed, after which the sheriff could auction the enslaved person and keep the profit for himself, as mentioned in chapter 5.

The potent power and wide discretion of sheriffs led newly enfranchised Black voters to seek control over the position in the post–Civil War era. While later revisionist historians sympathetic to the lost cause—the idea that the Confederacy was a noble endeavor—would claim that Black com-munities were unable to hold on to powerful elected positions, this is just not true. Black Republicans used their new political power to win elections, while Southern Democrats tried to overthrow legitimately elected leaders through a series of violent insurrections.

In the time period of 1865 to about 1877, often called Reconstruction, Black men sought office and were elected to federal, state, and local positions in large numbers, as were white Republicans who supported the end of chat-tel slavery. The office of sheriff was seen as particularly important for Repub-licans because it was "atop the pyramid of local power," and Black people hoped to seize the legitimate use of state-sanctioned violence to benefit for-merly enslaved populations, who faced daily terror from organized white terrorists. Sheriffs were also instrumental in lynchings, either directly or through negligence, feigned or otherwise. According to one historian, three out of four lynchings in Louisiana involved a sheriff. For a Black man, to be a sheriff was to hold and hopefully reform a position that had been instrumental in racist oppression.

Even further, the sheriff, as local law enforcement, was entitled to carry weapons, which Black people had been forbidden to do before the Civil War. The symbol of a newly free Black man wielding a weapon was powerful and challenged the racial hierarchy. Laws strictly forbade Black people from possessing guns, so to carry a gun as a legitimate agent of the state was a form of empowerment.

There were also practical reasons why the office of sheriff was desirable. For one thing, the sheriff was one of the few elected offices that paid an annual salary as well as substantial fees, a helpful inducement for those who were not monied property owners. A Mississippi politician called the job "the best paying office in the state." The role of sheriff was also tied to the right to vote because, in many Southern states, the sheriff registered voters and, in some cases, refused to register Black men or threatened violence to those who tried to register. Black citizens who tried to vote were "threatened, beaten, jailed, 'run out of the parish,' or slain."

These same qualities made the office of sheriff contested for the ex-Confederates, who did not like the idea of Black men controlling a position with the power to make arrests, especially the arrests of white men. According to historian Eric Foner, the loss of local control was even more distressing to Southern Democrats than the loss of state power because of the direct impact such officials had on residents' daily lives.

Accustomed to dominating communities through white patronage, Southern Democrats used violent means of extrajudicial terror to remain in power as well as other political trickery. For example, the role of sheriff required a bond, or the payment of cash as a kind of insurance to ensure the official was responsible with public money. Few Black aspiring sheriffs were in the position to pay this fee up front. Certainly, the violence was one of the main deterrents. The Equal Justice Initiative estimates that, conservatively, at least two thousand Black people were killed through white supremacist violence in the Reconstruction years. Louisiana alone accounted for around one thousand of those deaths, many related to attempts by Black men to access the vote. While the eighty years after Reconstruction saw thousands more lynchings, there were more per year during that brief period than during any other post–Civil War year.

As a result, there were not a lot of Black sheriffs when compared to state representatives in particular—just a small handful in the South. In 1874, a Mississippi county elected a Black sheriff, but he was not allowed to take office because he was removed by local white political figures. When the Black community protested, a white mob killed fifty Black people.

At the end of Reconstruction, the federal government withdrew its support for anti-slavery forces and white Confederate rule reinstated itself in the South, resulting in widespread racial terror and disenfranchisement through legal mechanisms like poll taxes and literacy tests. Locally, white leaders used all sorts of methods to disenfranchise Black voters. They purged voter rolls and permitted local employers to threaten their workers with the loss of their livelihoods unless they voted Democrat. Much of this happened with the blessing of the local sheriff.

One such insurrection happened in Iberia Parish in November of 1884, called the Loreauville Riot. Republicans held most of the important offices, including those of police jury (the equivalent of a parish council), sheriff, and judge. Ex-Confederate Democrats rigged the election by stuffing the ballot box and kicked the Republican officials out of office. The Republicans appealed to the state government, and the governor sent the state militia to intervene.

Republican Theogene Viator, the ousted sheriff who had properly won the election, assembled a militia of Black men and physically retook the courthouse, which served in those days as the main seat of local government. The self-proclaimed Southern Democrat sheriff, a man named P. A. Veazey, assembled his own militia and kicked Viator and his men out of the court-house. After a few days, the promised state militia of about two hundred men finally arrived, but they sided with the ex-Confederates, not Viator. Together, those who had supported slavery and did not want to see Black men in power took over the courthouse, captured Viator, and put many of Viator's men in jail.

Rumors swirled that more Republican militias were coming. Viator was released and reassembled his mostly Black militia to interrupt a Democratic political meeting in the town square. The two groups fought, but it was far from a fair battle. White men, the Democrats, ran home, grabbed their shot-guns, and began shooting at the Black men under Viator's command at ran-dom. Black men ran; some were shot. Others jumped into the bayou to escape, drowning instead. One news report said that they "fled in all direc-tions, leaving their hats, shoes, horses, everything." The armed white men chased them down and killed as many as possible, leaving their bodies in the water.

In an example of how the press downplayed racial violence, the *Times-Picayune*, the local newspaper in New Orleans, published a story arguing that the Black residents had been "told so many wild stories about the Democrats that they verily believed the day of doom had come." The paper called the idea that Black people had been killed running away "false." The official death toll was eighteen people, sixteen of them Black, but this is probably a gross undercount. Weeks later, residents were still finding the bodies of those who had run in an effort to escape death.

The white-run news transformed this event from a coup that overthrew an elected Republican government into a horror story of armed Black men, turning the massacre into a legitimate act of white self-defense. The *Shreveport Times* described the event as "the most deplorable and bloody affray ever perpetuated." Years after the event, white Democrats would periodically fearmonger about a Black militia that would return to overthrow the government, blaming power-hungry Republicans.

The massacre did effectively end Republican local rule, which meant sheriffs, along with county judges and prosecutors, were Democrats from that point on, white people sympathetic to the cause of the ex-Confederates. The incident sank into history; there was no report, no investigation, and almost no literature written about it. But you can hear the echoes of this story in the calls of the county leaders in Battle Mountain to defend their patriotic social gathering against Black Lives Matter protesters, even though no such protesters ever came.

Iberia Parish, Louisiana, feels far from the city of New Orleans. As I drove into New Iberia, the main town, I saw a man working in a field under the morning sun. It was only May but already sweltering hot.

The main crop in the region is sugarcane, and the role of sheriffs in this laborious and dangerous job reflects how these elected county officials served an important purpose in maintaining industry after chattel slavery ended. Without sheriffs in the post–Civil War era to force Black residents into laboring for white plantation owners, the industry might have collapsed. Transforming sugarcane into sugar requires a great deal of effort, and men, women, and children were grievously injured producing a crop that was profitable for the plantation owner but life-ruining for those who did the hard work. As a result, there were always rebellions and work stoppages, most of which are infrequently taught in an effort to keep the myth of the grand plantations alive.

For the historian Phebe Hayes, white supremacy and the control of capital served not only to keep Black families from upward mobility; it also created a false history where whites were always in charge, including serving as sheriff. "It was all a big lie, a conspiracy, you know, to take away the history and the culture of a people," she said.

Hayes, along with Jordan Richardson, a Black public historian focused on digitizing historical materials, met me at the Iberia African American Historical Society Center for Research and Learning. Its building is across the street from Shadows-on-the-Teche. The Center plays an important role in the ongoing efforts to remake the former plantation into a museum and cultural center that more accurately portrays the history of Black communities in New Iberia.

The Center is a second act for Hayes, who grew up in Iberia Parish and was a speech pathologist in Iberia public schools in the 1980s and '90s. She was also a faculty member at the University of Louisiana at Lafayette as a professor in communications and served as dean of the College of General Studies at the University of Louisiana at Lafayette until she retired in 2013.

Hayes began her public education in segregated schools and finished high school in an integrated school. After her retirement, she dove into her family history, and through that research she found a suppressed record of successful Black business owners, community leaders, teachers, and doctors in Iberia Parish. In 2017, Hayes founded the Center "for the purpose of researching, disseminating, preserving, and commemorating the history of African Americans in Iberia Parish." She sought to honor Black historical figures in New Iberia through public markers that would remind residents and visitors alike of Black history. Yet, as I walked through downtown New Iberia, I was struck by all the commemorative plaques and small monuments—in addition to Shadows-on-the-Teche—that honored white history.

One of her first projects was a marker for the first Black female physician in Louisiana, Emma Wakefield-Paillet, who was born and raised in New Iberia. Hayes told me that at a certain point she realized that Black people in

New Iberia "have to write our own story. But first, we got to do our own research. So that's part of what piqued my interest in this work."

All this work happens in the shadows of Shadows-on-the-Teche, the plantation, which is the dominant historical site in New Iberia and has been a museum since 1961. The old house is still draped in Spanish moss and concealed behind a lush garden, but the historians at Shadows have engaged in a process of incorporating the history of racism and slavery, bit by bit. "The house remained in the same family for four generations," reads the Shadows website. "As a former plantation home, the story of the Shadows is as much about the hundreds of enslaved men, women, and children who lived and labored at the site as it is about the Weeks family."

The traditional interpretation of plantation homes used to be "evidence of the grand old South," as Hayes said, and often erased what enslavement meant. But she thought that most people "in this day and age" knew better. "There are more and more people who challenge those kinds of narratives being presented to the public as truth," she added.

She drew a direct comparison between white residents of the town who resist reforms to law enforcement and those who resist a revision of history that includes an expansive understanding of the Black community and its contributions. Hayes told me that some residents of New Iberia remain attached to the old way of telling history "because their heroes or their family's heroes were Confederate."

Those white people, she pointed out, seek to defend law enforcement now: "'I'm going to fight for their monuments to stay up. I'm going to fight for education and curriculum that reflects that they are heroes and that they protect me from those people over there.' So it's not local, it's statewide, it's national, that your sheriffs and your police officers are benefiting from a very racist past."

The original owners of Shadows, Mary and David Weeks, built the plantation house in 1831. Like many planters, they grew and harvested sugarcane on the banks of the Bayou Teche, a 125-mile waterway that was the Mississippi River's main course thousands of years ago, a welcome, if swampy, place for agriculture.

Sugarcane harvesting is one of the most physically difficult jobs, and white planters relied on the labor of enslaved people, who worked from dawn to dusk in the oppressive humidity, cutting their hands on thorns, and even losing limbs in the process. "When those [grinding] machines come on . . . they don't go off until the end of the grinding season. So, it's like October to December, sometimes January if the weather permits, and your enslaved workforces [are] working fourteen to sixteen hours a day," Richardson explained.

Women and children formed about 40 percent of the overall labor force in 1860. The sugarcane itself requires a great deal of processing before it comes close to resembling the white stuff on a kitchen table. After the cane was picked, the plant was squeezed for its juice, which was then boiled, producing coarse brown sugar. Enslaved workers would stand for hours over hot, boiling cauldrons, stirring constantly so the mixture didn't burn and ruin the product. Later inventions in the nineteenth century, including vacuum pans, allowed for better processing of the cane juice. This made it easier to produce fine, whiter sugar, which was in greater demand in Northern cities like New York and Chicago.

After the Civil War, white landowners bemoaned the loss of labor, blaming the new free men and women for being unwilling to work. They began to institute laws and economic systems that, as Richardson told me, "re-enslave[d] and control[led] Black bodies" in order to recapture the unpaid workforce they lost in the war.

The planter class solely focused upon restoring an economy that relied on enslaved labor. Refusing to modernize processes or change how they operated, white planters begged the federal government for aid to repair levees and other infrastructure, arguing that it would provide "moral influence in healing past dissentions." William Weeks, the son of the Shadows' first owner, wrote about the agreement he struck with the newly freed workers:

> During sugar making we agree to work 18 hours out of 24, two hours being allowed us out, this time for eating meals, & we further agree to make every exertion to save the sugar crop of the employer.
>
> No. 1 men $8/month; children 14–17 for food; house rent free; usual allowance of good wholesome food, higher wages for sugar makeing.

But it became obvious over time that the free men and women were not eager to return to the past. The physical labor of harvesting sugarcane was horrible and dangerous. Planters fretted over the loss of women and children as labor; newly freed families no longer wanted to do that thankless work, which only benefited the landowner. Instead, newly freed Blacks focused on forming their own farms to grow food, build churches, and educate their children. Just as Black communities sought to have their own interests represented in local law enforcement, they also wanted work that reflected their own priorities and families.

In reality, the economic problems post–Civil War had multifold causes: a crashing economy, changes in sugar production, and a workforce more interested in self-preservation and community building than working for former white slavers. When historians went back to review the lost-cause version of events, they found that the problem wasn't a lack of interest in labor by formerly enslaved people. "It seems that [the plantation owners] simply failed to recognize that labor productivity was higher under slavery for reasons having nothing to do with the workers themselves," a historian noted in 1976. The ex-slavers would turn to the sheriff to solve their labor problem.

Sheriffs were intimately involved in the creation of a labor force specifically designed to gain financial benefit for themselves and for wealthy white land- and business owners. The fee system sheriffs had relied upon since the creation of the office gave them a personal pecuniary interest in keeping a captive labor force because they could personally profit from the enterprise.

The discretion of sheriffs to decide who to arrest and who to jail became an essential tool in this project. The entire criminal legal apparatus targeted Black residents, mostly for property or other low-level crimes, and the laws were easy to enforce with a great deal of latitude. At the same time that sheriffs targeted Black men for re-enslavement, they also reverted to the system of white patronage. White elites could and did ask sheriffs to release particularly good workers, even if those workers had committed violent crimes. Crimes of violence against Black people, especially Black women, were largely ignored. And white people were rarely arrested and jailed for any crimes. Sheriffs, never really accustomed to solving major crimes like murder and rape, were an ideal enforcement mechanism.

After Reconstruction crumbled, sheriffs played a key role in the institution of convict leasing, literally kidnapping people off the street and forcing them to work without pay. Southern states passed Black Codes, many of which targeted "vagrancy," which was a broad category of behavior that could range from sitting, standing, or walking without express permission from an employer. One Louisiana town outlawed "any person pursuing immoral activities" or who used "obscene, boisterous or profane" language in public. A Louisiana state law allowed sheriffs to punish people accused of vagrancy with six months of hard labor, like improving streets or other public improvement projects.

As a sign of the intent behind the Black Codes, they were also used to quell labor rebellions. In the 1880s, labor riots rocked southern Louisiana, and the suspected ringleaders were arrested until everyone was "compelled to return to work under the conditions fixed by the planters." But white people who committed crimes against Black individuals, even serious crimes like murder and assault, often paid a small fine and were released.

For those Black workers whose labor was not leased out by the sheriffs, they often found themselves at the mercy of deputies anyway. Sheriffs, with the help of state militias, crushed attempts by local workers to organize during the 1890s. In one case, white militias, lawmen, and vigilantes murdered one hundred Black men for participating in a single strike.

Black men accused of violating Black Codes faced arrest and, once incarcerated, were sent to work on railroads and in factories, swamps, mines, and fields. The Thirteenth Amendment outlawed "involuntary servitude" except for one notable exception: "as a punishment for a crime." Sheriffs benefited financially from the practice, often earning a cut of the worker's "pay," all of which went to fines and fees for alleged crimes. The worker never saw any of it. In many Southern states, this practice was universal. South Carolina at one pointed leased everyone in its prisons out for labor. By 1914, convict leasing brought in tens of millions of dollars for state governments each year, or roughly half a billion dollars adjusted for inflation. One in four Black men doomed to this labor never returned home.

Ida B. Wells described convict leasing as a form of enslavement. It was. Like Baldwin, she blamed both white religion and white law enforcement. "The religious, moral and philanthropic forces of the country—all the agencies which tend to uplift and reclaim the degraded and ignorant, are in the hands of the Anglo-Saxon," she wrote, leaving Black communities without resources.

At the same time, Wells explained, "The judges, juries and other officials of the courts are white men who share these prejudices. They also make the laws. It is wholly in their power to extend clemency to white criminals and mete severe punishment to Black criminals for the same or lesser crimes. The Negro criminals are mostly ignorant, poor and friendless. Possessing neither money to employ lawyers nor influential friends, they are sentenced in large numbers to long terms of imprisonment for petty crimes."

Over time, the convict-leasing system came under fire when it became clear to white lawmakers that corporations were unjustly profiting from free or nearly free labor. By the 1900s, the convict-leasing system in Louisiana had formally ended, but in most Southern states, sheriffs were (and are) still white and held (and still hold) the reins of power.

Real change did not come until the passage of the Voting Rights Act of 1965, again emphasizing the importance of the Black vote in transforming the role of the sheriff. "Black and other minorities had no real influence on the sheriff," a historian wrote. "The sheriff's department, reflecting the dominant political structure of the community, saw Black demands as either irrelevant or something to be repressed."

This tangled history helps to explain why the Southern sheriff remains entrenched as an institution and has been hard to change. The sheriff was not just a law enforcer but also a political, social, and industrial nexus of power. In many counties of the ex-Confederacy, Black residents vastly outnumbered white ones. The sheriff with his proximity to money, power, and state-sanctioned violence was a vital component of keeping white supremacy intact for generations. Because sheriffs were able to control so many aspects of local life, including the local press, they went unchallenged and their powers unchecked.

———

Sheriff Gilbert Ozenne became the sheriff of Iberia Parish in 1940. When some well-suited Black professionals started an NAACP chapter in New Iberia, one of their first projects was to set up a welding school for Black people, since all the other professional programs in Iberia were for white people only. Edran Louis Auguster, who was then a principal at a Black high school in Iberia, described the atmosphere at the time for an oral history project at Duke University, saying, "But in New Iberia the city officials, parish officials and any other white that was in authority, they tried to keep any civil rights movement out of the city."

Ozenne warned Black community leaders that they would be "personally responsible for anything that may happen in New Iberia." He falsely told the FBI that the NAACP was stockpiling ammunition for a race war.

Ozenne, who saw civil rights organizations as outside agitators, decided it would be best to rid New Iberia of the NAACP in order to restore social order. One night, a black car containing four deputies kidnapped the chapter president, Leo Hardy, a bartender and insurance agent, and took him to see the sheriff. Two deputies pinned Hardy by the arms on the floor while the sheriff kicked and punched him. "Where do you want to go? East or west?" he then asked Hardy. Deputies grabbed Hardy by his necktie, threw him into their cruiser, and drove him to a deserted road. They told him to walk, fast, and fired a pistol to make sure he did not turn around.

Hardy ended up calling his friend Howard Scoggins to pick him up to drive him to the nearby town of Lafayette, where he ultimately died from his injuries.

Sheriff Ozenne repeated this process of expulsion with the other leaders of the NAACP's Iberia chapter. They were pistol-whipped, beaten, and stomped on the face, then driven out of town and dumped on the roadside. "Killer" Walker, who delivered most of the worst beatings, was the sheriff's right-hand man. News spread through the town, and Black leaders, many of them physicians and other professionals, left town before they could be beaten down and thrown out.

Auguster described how the sheriff chased people down one by one: "So while they were getting rid of Negroes they went and they got Dr. Luins

Williams and beat him and drove him out of town. We had another doctor here, Dr. Scoggins. They went to get him and they would go at night. . . . He put the lights out and opened the door and told them to come on in. They didn't want to go in, they wanted him to come out. So he said I'm not coming out there but you come in. So they left him. But Scoggins for his own safety moved away from here. . . . While they were getting rid of what they called agitators, they got rid of the doctors too."

The national chapter of the NAACP, with assistance from Thurgood Marshall, a future Supreme Court justice, pressured the FBI, then run by J. Edgar Hoover, himself a segregationist, to investigate. An FBI agent confronted Sheriff Ozenne in his office. According to historian Adam Fairclough, who studied the case, the FBI agent described the sheriff as "belligerent" and "armed to the teeth." Allegedly, Sheriff Ozenne showed the agent his firearm, then opened a cabinet to display an arsenal of weapons and ammunition, including tommy guns. The sheriff told the FBI that he was just clearing out troublemakers. No one, white or Black, wanted to talk for fear they would "be found dead in a gutter somewhere," according to one anonymous would-be witness. The resulting FBI report that went into the official file wholly ignored the racism of Sheriff Ozenne's actions, dismissing Hardy and the others as arrogant troublemakers.

Despite the inadequate report, the Department of Justice still brought the case against Sheriff Ozenne and Killer Walker to a grand jury, but it returned no indictments. The creation of a civil rights unit within the Justice Department in 1939 was supposed to end impunity for racial terror. By 1944, it had successfully convicted only one lyncher and three police brutality cases. There would be no accountability for Ozenne.

---

By the second half of the twentieth century, the "Southern sheriff" began to appear to many criminologists and policing professionals as a kind of provincial relic, a caricature of a corrupt, racist white man chomping on a cigar.

After the passage of the Civil Rights Act in 1964, Northern intelligentsia scorned the Southern sheriff while also using the entrenched racism of the ex-Confederacy as an excuse not to reexamine the role of sheriffs everywhere in the United States. The 1970s brought Rosco Purvis Coltrane of *The Dukes of Hazzard*, which showed a Southern sheriff who was embittered, hard-nosed, and haplessly chasing the Duke boys. That character stood in stark contrast to that of Sheriff Andy Taylor of Mayberry, who never shot his gun and didn't seem to worry about his pension.

"A Neanderthal image," two sociologists wrote of the Southern sheriff in 1980. They went on, "In the context of the media, the sheriff is clearly portrayed as an unprofessional redneck whose real role is to oppress minorities, often coupled with a good-natured tolerance of local folkways and social 'morality.'"

The office of sheriff has changed little in Louisiana since the days of Reconstruction, where the position is still a "constitutional" office and, therefore, considered exempt from legislative changes and attempts at oversight. According to the 1974 Louisiana Constitution, sheriffs are the highest law in the land and are the "chief law enforcement officers." A Louisiana sheriff "has more constitutional authority and responsibility than any sheriff in the fifty states," a video by the Louisiana Sheriffs' Association says. The then sheriff Jeff Wiley of Ascension Parish praised the office's "independence and a sovereign nature," which meant that sheriffs are "not subordinate" to any other office.

Louisiana's sheriffs together form a political force able to influence legislation by providing testimony and information to lawmakers. Each sheriff also has significant control over local politics and the economy. Sheriffs can accept political donations, make contracts with outside vendors, and permit both public and private entities to use people held in jail as labor, often through "work release" programs. In many parts of the state, people serving time in jail fix church roofs, mow grass along the sides of roads, and maintain airstrips for the small commuter planes that bring their wealthy owners from the bayou to the state capital.

"You just call up the sheriff, and presto, inmates are headed your way," wrote the *New York Times* in 2006, quoting the owner of the Panola Pepper Corporation saying, "They bring me warm bodies, 10 warm bodies in the morning. . . . They do anything you ask them to do." While some incarcerated people are paid minimum wage, they often must reimburse the sheriff for room, board, and clothing during their period of incarceration out of their wages. Business owners praise the system because the workers can be "put in cold storage," they told the *New York Times*, locking them up until their labor is needed.

In 2017, when the state legislature was considering a variety of laws to reduce the state prison population, a sheriff spoke up to bemoan the loss of labor: "In addition to the bad ones—and I call these bad—in addition to them, they're releasing some good ones that we use every day to wash cars, to change oil in our cars, to cook in the kitchen, to do all that, where we save money. . . . Well, they're going to let them out."

Perhaps the sheriffs in Louisiana are able to get away with so many abuses of office because the tropes about racist Southern sheriffs prevent outsiders from seeing opportunities for change. There's a deep rift between the way sheriffs see themselves as local centers of power and the way state and federal authorities see sheriffs as corrupt, inherently racist, and unchangeable. Even when the Department of Justice intervenes in particularly violent policing practices, they are reluctant to challenge the sheriff once they are on his turf.

———

Phebe Hayes told me that when she sees the portraits of all the white sheriffs of Iberia Parish, "I think about the roles they played."

Jordan Richardson interrupted. "Lynching," he said.

"I was about to say that. The roles they played keeping Black people in line. Intimidating. . . . The roles they played in the deaths of so many Black people, especially, and women and children. . . . It's abominable to me that people like that, their pictures are still on walls—I know it's a historical fact that is being demonstrated—but there were people that did horrible, horrible things to their neighbors. And then they went home."

"As heroes," Richardson said.

"No, no, no, they didn't let anybody know. Because they knew they did wrong. And they go to Mass. Yeah. And then they, they went back home. But they did horrible things."

The Loreauville Riot was just one example of the violence that raged across the former Confederacy. Roving bands of angry white mobs, including the Ku Klux Klan, attacked free people, stealing what little property they had and terrifying them into opting out of the political process.

This was in addition to the terror lynchings. The Equal Justice Initiative has documented over four thousand lynchings in the South from the end of the Civil War until 1940. According to the EJI report, Iberia Parish had one of the highest numbers of terror lynchings in the South.

In some cases, white terrorists organized and killed people en masse. In post–Civil War Iberia Parish, small vigilante groups of local white men patrolled the streets to catch rumored roving bands of highwaymen, and so-called White Leagues tried to intimidate Black voters, both with violence and by ordering that white planters fire any Black people who voted Republican. Sometimes, lynchings were used to punish Black men and women who were accused of crimes, especially since there were rampant white fears at the time that there would be violence and theft committed by Black men. In 1873, a white mob hung three Black men who were accused of robbing and murdering two white store owners. Such lynchings were seen as just punishment and used to enforce the racial hierarchy. During an 1873 meeting of ex-

Confederates, one leader said, "The white people have at least as many rights as the black . . . and if those having or claiming authority do not dispense equal justice to both races, we shall take care of ourselves."

As keepers of the county jail, sheriffs were key figures in permitting lynching. They would open the doors of the jail to allow murderous mobs to enter and stand by, if not assist the lynchers themselves. An anti-lynching advocate explained, "In most cases, the sheriffs and his deputies stood by while the mob did its work and later reported that the mob had taken them by surprise, or that, though aware of the impending danger, they were unwilling to shoot into the crowd lest they kill innocent men, women, and children." To most sheriffs, opposing a lynch mob simply wasn't worth the trouble, if they weren't in fact completely in approval of the lynching. These same sheriffs would then tell grand juries, if there were any arrests or investigations made, that they didn't recognize anyone at all.

As the same advocate wrote in the 1930s, this made sense. Sheriffs were and are elected by their constituencies, which, in the ex-Confederacy, would include only white men, thanks to Black disenfranchisement. There was social pressure to comply in addition to something akin to race loyalty. Sheriffs, as a result, worried about appearing too harsh with the crowd of lynchers and disliked calling on outside reinforcements to disperse the mob.

The NAACP and other anti-lynching reformers would explicitly target sheriffs as crucial participants in lynching and related racial violence—both to hold them accountable and to educate them as to their responsibilities. When Alabama rewrote its state constitution in 1901, it added a provision that made the sheriff responsible for preventing people in jail from being kidnapped and lynched: "Whenever any prisoner is taken from jail, or from the custody of the Sheriff or his deputy, and put to death, or suffers grievous bodily harm, owing to the neglect, connivance, cowardice or other grave fault of the Sheriff, such Sheriff may be impeached." If a sheriff failed to protect people in their custody, the sheriff could be impeached through a trial-like process.

By this point, many white people deplored lynching and found it distasteful and brutal as well as bad for the economy—it understandably chased away Black laborers and brought the unwanted attention of the federal government. They sought to end the practice, not because they necessarily believed the races were equal, but rather because they sought to avoid the negative press of such brutal spectacles. The proper process, these whites thought, was to use disenfranchisement, not gruesome violence, to subdue the Black population. As one historian explains, "Taking the vote from Black men, anti-lynching advocates argued, would lessen white anxiety and demonstrate that the white elite could control Blacks and protect white supremacy without the help of the rabble." To that end, the new 1901 constitution included poll taxes and a literacy test.

Sheriffs, these politicians thought, were a key link and should be held liable for failure to protect the people in their custody, which might include measures like taking someone secretly to another location or ensuring the presence of armed guards. The issue became a debate about local governance: Should the state be able to remove a sheriff? Or should local communities be left to police their own sheriffs?

In the 1890s, ex–Alabama governor and federal judge Thomas Goode Jones helped ensure the provision passed by reminding people of the failure of local communities to hold their own sheriffs responsible for misconduct. Northern publications praised Alabama officials for the change. The *New York Times* called it "an agreeable surprise."

When states applied adequate pressure on sheriffs, the law enforcement leaders did try to prevent lynchings, sometimes employing over a dozen armed deputies to protect Black men from mobs, at least in cases that were especially notorious. In their effort to reduce public lynchings, sheriffs and other parts of the criminal justice system sought legal shortcuts. Trials and executions happened quickly to satisfy bloodthirst. Sometimes lynch mobs threatened sheriffs themselves or engaged in exchanges of gunfire with deputies while trying to break into jails in order to seize prisoners, which led sheriffs and their deputies to mete out beatings to Black detainees as a way to show the white public that there was adequate punishment taking place. Sheriffs were still steeped in complicity with racism and violence, sometimes because of the pressure from their fellow white neighbors and voters, but almost always to the detriment of the Black community.

On September 24, 2006, the people of New Iberia were in the midst of revelry. It was the annual Louisiana Sugar Cane Festival, a three-day celebration of parades, music, and food, where the streets of the town are closed to traffic and become home to colorful marching bands and floats tossing candy to children in the crowds. The celebration has a long history in the region, whose dark, rich earth and muggy weather provide the ideal environment for growing vast fields of cane. A 1946 schedule for the festival includes a "Cavalcade of Cane," which tells the story of the sugar industry "with 500 actors in costume," alongside balls, orchestra performances, races of boats made from hollowed-out logs, and an agricultural fair displaying the newest innovations in cane-harvesting technology.

The culmination of the festival is a beauty pageant where judges select the Queen Sugar. Teenage girls in dresses with long trains, capes, wands, and glittery crowns compete for the title. A man, someone who "contributed to the sugar industry," is chosen to be King Sucrose, with much less glitter. And those who can trace their lineage back to the ancien régime dine outside in the balmy night on tables festooned with green and white ribbons and tablecloths, echoed by the festively decorated homes of families descended from plantation owners behind wrought-iron gates in the exclusive City Park.

On the other side of town, the largely Black neighborhood holds its own festival, located on land that had formerly been the Hopkins family's sugar plantation. Literally across a set of train tracks from the grand old homes, the West End was populated with many of the dilapidated quarters that housed enslaved workers and, after the war, sharecroppers, which the current residents continue to patch and repair against storms and floods that cause the bayou to overflow into the streets. During the formal Sugar Cane Festival, West End residents hold their own celebration that was once called the "Brown Sugar Parade," complete with a "Queen Brown Sugar." Now the festivities are less formal and resemble more of a block party, with families joking and dancing to the music of DJs, who play in the open air.

On that September day, hundreds of people flooded the streets of the West End in celebration. Delphina Walker and her husband, Edward Charles Walker, had come to work early that day to get ready for the party. They owned Gator's Barbecue, a joint at the corner of Hopkins (named for the infamous plantation owner) and Robertson Streets, and they had hired a DJ and were busy prepping hot dogs for the kids and ribs and chicken for everyone else. By late afternoon, the festivities were in full swing. Around five hundred people, including children and the elderly, were dancing, talking, and eating, flooding into the streets and the open lots that teemed with green despite years of neglect. As the food disappeared and the sun swelled orange and red on the horizon, Edward signaled to the DJ to play the last song. About a half dozen deputies from the Iberia Parish Sheriff's Office drifted in the crowd. No one thought much of it. "Everybody was just enjoying themselves," one attendee said.

Suddenly and without warning, tear gas enveloped the crowd. Delphina was inside the stand and saw from the window as the gas dispersed and the deputies began yelling for people to get out of the street. She panicked. "They shot at me. They were aiming at us. They knew babies were out there. Do you think they cared?" Delphina said at a town hall meeting the next week.

A teenager thought the noise might be fireworks, but he began running just in case. Delphina's sister, Cheryl Ann Hill, was already headed to her car with her eight-month-old grandchild in her arms. A can of tear gas hit her on the shoulder. All around her, people were screaming, crying, and choking. Cheryl couldn't tell where the gas had come from. To her, it seemed like a sudden assault. Clutching the baby to her chest, she ran.

Cheryl bumped into some deputies as she fled and asked them why they were gassing the crowd. The deputies threw more cans of gas into the crowd and told Cheryl that they had been ordered to "clear the streets." The deputies retreated to their cars as some members of the crowd began to shout and throw rocks. Officers said they were being hit with thrown bottles and broken glass. Before leaving, they set off more tear gas.

Later, the Iberia Parish sheriff, Sid Hebert, conducted an internal investigation of the incident and found no wrongdoing by his office. The official story was that the sheriff, concerned that the West End revelry was getting too "rowdy," sent a group of deputies to disperse the crowd, who were then attacked with thrown bottles. "They felt . . . they had the right to block the street," Sheriff Hebert's official statement read, justifying the ensuing violence by law enforcement.

For many West End residents, the events of September 24 were simply another example of the extreme brutality of the Iberia Parish Sheriff's Office, which had taken over the primary duty of policing New Iberia, the parish seat, since the town dissolved its police force in 2004. There were town hall meetings, and the local newspaper invited readers to write in and express their opinions on whether the sheriff's use of force had been excessive. One hundred sixty residents of the West End said they were injured, including Cheryl Hill's eight-month-old grandchild and an elderly woman who grew up under Jim Crow. They sued the sheriff's office, unsuccessfully.

The Reverend Raymond Brown, then a member of the New Black Panther Party and the Louisiana chair of the National Action Network, threatened to take to the streets in protest. "If [the sheriff] fails to correct the wrong he did and we hear of any more Black people or white people being gassed, the Black Panther Party is coming here. . . . If you want a real confrontation, call the Black Panther Party. . . . You can call that inciting a riot all you want, but I know the definition of self-defense." The *Daily Advertiser,* speaking for many white people in New Iberia, argued that Reverend Brown was stoking racial dissension. They urged a thoughtful and impartial investigation.

Neither of those came to pass. Sheriff Hebert reached an agreement, brokered by the Department of Justice's Community Relations Service in concert with local clergy and the local NAACP chapter, promising that his office would focus on community relations and decreasing crime in the West End. "The good Lord sometimes delivers his message in a sort of rough and tumble way," he said in a press conference.

In 2008, Hebert decided not to run for reelection, leaving the field wide open. One of the candidates was Louis Ackal, then sixty-four and a retired Louisiana State Police captain. He had a bulldoggish demeanor and an air of entitlement, an antihero who was also one of the people. Ackal had grown up in New Iberia, and his family has deep roots there. His ancestors had owned department and shoe stores after immigrating to Louisiana from Lebanon in the 1880s. There's a bridge that crosses the Bayou Teche named after Elias "Bo" Ackal Jr., who was in the state House of Representatives. Louis Ackal himself served in the Iberia Parish Sheriff's Office before moving on to the state police. He was a special investigator in the state Department of Public Safety before moving to Colorado for a two-year test of retirement's slow pace.

Ackal's time in the state police working narcotics investigations gave him a worldly air for the people in Iberia Parish. He presented himself as a reformer. In his campaign speeches, he said he was running not for glory but out of concern for his hometown. "I'm not a big fan of politics," he told a crowd. "The reason I ran was because people told me they were scared in their own homes."

He wanted to improve community relationships, saying that he had heard "horror stories" about citizens' encounters with law enforcement but thought that more visibility and deputy training would do the trick. He planned to establish "self-imposed performance indicators," which would track crime rates in New Iberia, and wanted to create an improved internal disciplinary system for misbehaving deputies. And for those who worried Ackal was too old, he said, "I'm not going to apologize for my age."

A few people remained skeptical. The year before, community activist Khadijah Rashad, who has been tracking law enforcement violence in New Iberia for over two decades, said, "I heard he had done some stuff," referring to Ackal's behavior as a deputy and state trooper. Other Black residents were also dubious and chafed at the way Ackal seemed to assume that the West End community would adore him.

Ackal ended up beating Sid Hebert's second-in-command, David Landry, in the election, but just barely, by two percentage points. "I am confident the new sheriff will turn things around," said then New Iberia mayor Hilda Curry, who was white. Ackal would soon show that his idea of reform was not the kind the Black community had in mind.

It became clear almost immediately that Ackal did not intend to make reforms designed to improve public safety. At first, he implemented modest changes that ruffled a few feathers. He put "In God We Trust" bumper stickers on brand-new cruisers and bought every deputy a new uniform. The bumper stickers upset the American Civil Liberties Union, but the people of City Park and the surrounding neighborhoods, the white people, trusted that the changes were good.

One of Ackal's main campaign pledges was to deal with the increasing crime rate. Since 2004, when the police force was dissolved, New Iberia had experienced rising crime rates, alarming residents on both sides of the tracks. There were also high-profile instances of violence that worried people. In 2009, the year Ackal took office, a thirteen-year-old girl was shot in a car on her way home from Walmart in the West End. Ackal took the view that the town needed harsher policing, blaming crime on "a rise in violent tendencies in society today."

Yet, Ackal's reforms appeared to make the crime problem worse. According to what official data is available, officers made arrests in 85 percent of murders in 2004, but that number decreased to 50 percent by 2008. Once in office, Ackal stopped tracking homicides altogether, so no one knew the crime rate. His public information officer told one reporter when asked, "These are not stats that we keep." He also dissolved the internal affairs unit, so there was no one to investigate complaints.

That choice was unsurprising because Ackal's main method to tackle the crime problem was a regime of incredibly oppressive and racist policing that disproportionately harmed Black residents. In 2010, Ackal formed the Increased Man Power Addressing Crime Trends (or "IMPACT") squad, which was sent to the West End to do what Ackal called "n——— knocking." The IMPACT squad would hit the streets of the West End, pulling people out of barbershops and restaurants, arresting people on their way home or to work. Black men were literally snatched and thrown to the ground, punched in the face or pistol-whipped, then either tossed in the back of a cruiser or sent on their way, told to warn their friends to take care.

Ackal's persona was always foulmouthed and plainspoken, but he fostered a culture of virulent racism in the department, particularly in the IMPACT squad. A former deputy named Jason Comeaux summed it up succinctly in later trial testimony: "They [Black residents] were animals, and they needed to be treated like animals."

"That was just to beat on us for any old reason," a longtime resident said of the IMPACT squad. During the 2011 Sugar Cane Festival, Ackal, just like his predecessor, busted up the West End parties with tear gas, this time announcing his deputies' arrival with the wail of sirens that sent people running for cover with hands over their ears.

The Black residents knew it was a double standard; they were treated brutally but did not receive any of the benefits of the tough-on-crime attitudes. "If you call and say there's a drug deal going on, they'll come right away. But if you call and say somebody's dying at the end of the street, they'll be here in 40," another resident told a local reporter.

In 2014, Ackal's office claimed that a young Black man named Victor White III had shot himself while handcuffed in the back of a sheriff's office vehicle. His family—his father was a pastor who had clashed with Ackal before—sued. (Pastor White would also be fundamental in organizing an unsuccessful campaign to have a recall election to get rid of Ackal in 2017.)

In New Iberia, the population of the county jail surged thanks to Ackal's brutal policing. Inmates were forced to sleep on the floor. The sheriff taught his deputies to treat the jail as a gladiator arena. Men were routinely stripped of their clothes, hog-tied, and placed in a circle facing a concrete wall as the deputies unleashed their batons and dogs. In one video leaked to the press, deputies watched a police dog maul a man as he desperately tried to crawl away, hampered by his shackled legs and arms. The other men in the room, also handcuffed, turned their faces away, worried that they would be next. There were also special rooms where there was no video surveillance, and men say they were dragged there for vicious beatings. When these men did go home, they nursed concussions, broken bones, brain trauma, and a deep well of humiliation.

Ackal modeled himself on Arizona's Sheriff Joe Arpaio and reveled in the power of demeaning people held in the Iberia Parish Jail through ways both petty and cruel. He put them in hot-pink jumpsuits and forced detainees to sleep in a pink cell called the "Flamingo Hotel," joking that pink was a "calming" color. He denied people ice during the hot summer and then laughed about it when the state inspector came calling. When civil rights groups or the "liberal media" criticized him, he put his boots up on his desk, chomped on a cigar, and snarled in a way that was endearing, if you were on his side, or threatening, if you were not.

———

In 2016, after repeated complaints from residents and the involvement of large advocacy organizations, the Department of Justice opened an investigation into Ackal, charging the sheriff and his deputies with crimes punishable by jail time. But just like the time the federal government intervened when confronted with the racist policing by Sheriff Ozenne, these prosecutions would not satisfy everyone or provide all the answers.

"I guess with Ackal being the sheriff, these guys thought they were above the law," said Anthony Daye, a man who says he was beaten by Ackal's deputies until he was unconscious and later testified for the Department of Justice. That same year, readers of the local newspaper, the *Daily Iberian*, voted Ackal "Best Elected Official" and "Friendliest Law Enforcement." One reader commented that the sheriff, then under criminal indictment, "gets the job done."

Deputies confirmed this when they testified for the federal prosecution. One deputy estimated that he and his crew had beaten people over one hundred times. Their testimony wove a story where the deputies were mafiosos and Ackal was their don. Ackal, they claimed, endorsed and promoted a culture of racism and violence. Three members of Ackal's office were sentenced to prison time for their role in abusing people inside the jail; ten others pled guilty.

During the federal prosecution, Ackal threatened to shoot the DOJ lawyer "between [his] goddamned Jewish eyes." Despite the plethora of evidence, Sheriff Ackal was acquitted by a jury, confirming for some Black community members that sheriffs evade the law just as effectively in the twenty-first century as they did in Ozenne's time.

Civil rights attorney Clay Burgess, who sued Ackal on behalf of dozens of people who were abused, severely injured, and killed by Ackal's deputies, recently described the office as a criminal gang "starting from patrol all the way to the jail." He described a time when he went to visit the Iberia Parish Jail and Ackal asked him to step into a room that he knew didn't have video surveillance. He told him no. "I wanted to come out alive," he said. I believed him.

In 2020, Ackal finally left office, but he was never forced to reckon with what he had done. Local activist Leroy Vallot told me, "This is so much deeper than Ackal. . . . They knew he was doing things wrong. It just impacted the African American community. Ackal does not exist in a vacuum."

The end result was that the West End community suffered even more. "The community lost out big time," Khadijah Rashad mourned in 2020. "We should have organized then." She was dubious about the potential for change, pointing to the history of Louisiana sheriffs. "They don't have to abide by rules and regulations," she said. After all, she points out, Ackal got to quietly leave office without a conviction or even a blemish on his record: "He gets to ride into the sunset. . . . People were terrorized and bullied, and he gets a clean slate."

---

Sheriff Ozenne died under mysterious circumstances in 1951, the same year he faced an ethics investigation involving financial kickbacks. The *Daily Iberian* said he died from a heart attack, but the rumor was it was by suicide.

Phebe Hayes talked to me about her own experience as a lifetime resident of New Iberia. Her great-grandparents are on the banners out in front of the Iberia African American Historical Society. "With history, it's great to study it because it can help us understand how things unfolded, and things that may have affected all our families. But even when I look at New Iberia, which is my hometown, I've grown up here. My family, all our roots are here. I can still see systems in place that support white supremacy, as I've told some of the city leaders. . . . It has to be said, you know, there are systems in place that support how things are done and continue to be done. There are still Jim Crow strategies that are used."

She pointed most directly at the local news, including what events were covered and which were not. "It's about power and control," she said.

"We are still a white supremacy community," she stated softly. But later she added, "Things are still not right. But I think we're better than we once were."

TEN

# BORDER WARS

### *Sheriffs and Immigration*

IN JUNE OF 2021, I DROVE TO A STRETCH OF PRIVATELY owned property near Naco, Arizona, to an event titled "Rally to End Biden's Border Crisis." Dozens of sheriffs from across the country were scheduled to be there. Their keynote speaker and lead organizer was Pinal County sheriff Mark Lamb.

The event was semisecret, and journalists were not welcome. But it was free. So I signed up as a private citizen and was promised an additional email that would reveal how to get to the site. I never got the email. Since I had already driven four hours from Phoenix to the U.S.-Mexico border, I figured I would drive around and, surely, would be able to see hundreds of vehicles and people standing in the middle of the desert.

This turned out to be more difficult than I anticipated. I first went to the border checkpoint in Naco, a town that spans the United States and Mexico. Nearby, I found two grade school–age boys standing outside in the desert heat. They wore cowboy hats and held a flagpole with both the American flag and a "Thin Blue Line" flag, which is a grayscale American flag with a blue line horizontally across the middle. I pulled over and asked what they were doing and whether they knew about the rally. They did not.

It's hard to exaggerate how unfriendly the desert is in that part of the world. There's almost no vegetation, just prickly shrubs. Driving up and down the highway at a crawl, squinting into the distance, I was pulled over by an Arizona state trooper. I considered asking him about the rally but thought better of it. Glaring at my out-of-state plates and driver's license and eyeballing an array of discarded snack wrappers next to me on the front seat, the trooper wrote an official warning for driving too slow and let me go. The encounter left me unnerved. Law enforcement in the region were always on the lookout for people who might be picking up migrants or delivering supplies.

Just as I was about to give up, I saw a small paper sign—"End the Biden Border Crisis Rally This Way"—pointing down a dirt road across the highway from a small diner. My little rental sedan could barely bump down the path. After about ten minutes of driving in the dirt, I encountered a checkpoint, guarded by men in militia-style clothing and carrying long guns. I gave my name; I was not on their list. I tried to keep my face neutral. A young man, heavily armed, waved me through, looking confused but not alarmed.

I had made it.

In front of me was a chunk of the incomplete border wall that was the backdrop for a stage, surrounded by tall lights that illuminated the scene as dusk fell. One section of the desert was now a parking lot. The rows of pickup trucks and SUVs carried flags: "Stop the Steal." "Trump 2024." The Gadsden "Come and Take It" yellow flag. And my favorite, "God Guns and Trump," with two semiautomatic rifles and a cross imposed upon an American flag.

Most of the attendees were white, about half were women, and almost everyone was wearing some form of patriot gear—Three Percenter T-shirts and patches, "Don't Be a Sheep" shirts, MAGA garb, and a group of men and women in their sixties wearing matching "America First" T-shirts. Many people had brought collapsible camping chairs and coolers, as if they were experienced hands at rallies in the middle of the desert. There were few children, but a handful of dogs panted in the dusty heat.

Many of the people there were plainly right-wing vloggers and assorted independent media. A man with slicked-back hair buttonholed important-looking people and stuck a microphone in their face. A woman wearing tight low-rise jeans livestreamed her experience; she kept grabbing attendees by the elbow to draw them into the frame with her. Many attendees were armed, so there were Glocks tucked into waistbands and revolvers in holsters, alongside a local militia acting as security, directing trucks into parking spots.

As far as the eye could see, the border wall stretched into the distance. Night came and the air cooled pleasantly. In the distance were mountains framed by a brilliant sky: rose, then poppy, then a deep purple.

The property is owned by a rancher named John Ladd, whose 16,400-acre plot happens to share 10.5 miles with the U.S.-Mexico border, a borderland covered in sand, grit, and sparse vegetation. Ladd's family first claimed the land as a homestead in 1896, and they have lived on it continuously since then, raising beef cattle. Ladd considered himself a steward of the land and belonged to a variety of rangeland conservation groups that advocate for development designed to prevent soil erosion. Part of his property abuts the San Pedro Riparian National Conservation Area, which protects a rare ecosystem, and he deeply resented being forced to consult with the federal government to make changes to the ranch property.

Since 2016, Ladd spoke regularly to the media about what he calls a "deluge" of migrants who walk across his property during their journey to the United States. According to the rancher, the migrants not only trespassed on his property; they also left behind belongings, damaged his fence line, killed horses, and, in one instance, killed a fellow rancher. That rancher, a man named Robert Krentz, was indeed found dead in 2010, but law enforcement never figured out who shot him.

As of 2021, Ladd thought the problem was Joe Biden. "The hands of the

Border Patrol are tied," he told a local publication. Ladd claimed there were about one hundred migrants crossing his property each day. "My family has lived here since before Arizona was a state—I won't be chased off by people who have no respect for our borders," he wrote in an affidavit for a lawsuit against the Department of Homeland Security for violating environmental laws by allowing migration across the U.S.-Mexico border.

The spotlights popped on around the stage, blotting out the stars. A crowd of sheriffs—about four dozen from around a dozen states—almost all wearing Stetson-style cowboy hats, stood in front of the stage, holding up a banner with pictures of people, mostly children, who had allegedly been killed in some way by immigrants—some in traffic accidents, some in shootings, and some because of fentanyl overdoses. They were martyrs for the cause of anti-immigration advocacy, their deaths a reason for xenophobia, even though all studies show that immigrants commit fewer crimes than citizens.

"Can you see me now?" the banner read across the top.

Lamb strutted onstage. He flashed his toothy smile as if to show how he earned the nickname "Hollywood." Lamb wore his cowboy hat pulled low to his eyebrows; below the hat, a trim goatee and mustache were visible.

He began, "We are standing up for the rule of law. We are standing up for fair policies. We are standing up for the Constitution."

The sheriffs came to the microphone one by one. Sheriff Tony Childress of Illinois, the only Black sheriff in attendance, called Joe Biden and Lori Lightfoot, the then mayor of Chicago, "losers." Sheriff Scott Jenkins of Culpeper County, Virginia, called his hometown the "MS-13 Capital of the East," referring to the Salvadoran gang infamous for violence and a frequent target of Trump as an example of "bad hombres." "Every county is a border county," Jenkins said.

Sheriff Jesse Watts of Eureka County, Nevada—the same one from Battle Mountain—took the microphone and said he was there "to make sure the wall gets finished."

Watts barely needed the mic: "Your county sheriff will not fail you! We are in the grocery store with you. Our children are in school with you. And that's the reason why we are going to stand up and be the voice of ya." He flashed his "We the People" tattoo like a signal when he wrapped up his short speech.

Most of the sheriffs were brief, waiting like penitents to approach the mic. One quoted the book of Matthew: "We are the salt of the earth." They came from New Mexico, Arizona, Oklahoma, Nevada, Iowa, South Dakota, Illinois, Pennsylvania, Massachusetts, and Texas. They praised God. All but one were white. All were men. Many had never seen the border, never mind the border wall.

"I am not sent to you by the government. I am sent to the government by you," said the sheriff of Sierra County, New Mexico, who had deputized a twenty-person church congregation in May of 2020 in order to allow them to gather in violation of coronavirus restrictions. He offered to deputize everyone present.

"The sheriffs will never fail their citizens," another New Mexico sheriff said.

Some sheriffs paid homage to the young people who died from drug overdoses. An Iowa sheriff referred to the murder of Mollie Tibbetts, a young college student, in 2018. A twenty-four-year-old farmworker from Mexico was convicted of her murder in 2021, and the trial was politicized by Trump as a reason for more punitive immigration laws.

After the sheriffs finished their procession, they crowded in around the stage. A man began to play "The Weight of the Badge" by George Strait. Every sheriff removed their hat and looked down, as if in prayer. The lyrics tell the story of a police officer who leaves his family only to get injured and wind up in the hospital, an ode to the "tempered strength" of the law enforcement officer who lays his life on the line. Lamb appeared in the official video, his hat blocking the setting sun, as Strait croons.

The sheriffs made their burden known. Migrants who did not come the "right way" were the kind of lawless un-American people that sheriffs were duty bound to stop.

———

The entire event was orchestrated by an anti-immigrant group called the Federation for American Immigration Reform, or FAIR. Ladd, the rancher, was a spokesperson for FAIR, which borrowed his folksy manner to show how real Americans were impacted by immigration. The banner of victims was part of FAIR's propaganda campaign. And the sheriffs were part of the plan, too; law enforcement representatives sponsored by and held up by FAIR as reliable spokespeople for their brand of xenophobia.

Just as the NRA took a nascent sheriff movement and amplified pro-gun sheriffs, anti-immigrant organizations like FAIR have used sheriffs as credible messengers, providing the lawmen with information on immigration trends and a forum to make their legislative demands known. FAIR is part of a constellation of Southern Poverty Law Center–designated hate groups called the "Tanton network," named after their founder, John Tanton. Tanton was a Michigan ophthalmologist who, in the late 1970s, had the idea to create a series of connected groups that would all advance an extremely restrictive anti-immigrant message. FAIR largely connects with law enforcement and produces reams of xenophobic media. The Center for Immigration Studies is a think tank that publishes anti-immigrant reports and serves as an expert for the news media. NumbersUSA is a grassroots organization that focuses on direct-to-voter mail. They all present the same anti-immigration message, which helps the sheriffs who want to advance an anti-immigrant agenda by providing tangible support in the form of data, lawsuits, and publicity.

Tanton's original interest in immigration restriction was environmental, based on the eugenics-based fear of overpopulation and a decline in white birth rates. The net results were extremely racist, and many of Tanton's early backers were avowed white supremacists and Nazi sympathizers. In 1988, the *Arizona Republic* published leaked memos that Tanton had written and distributed to like-minded colleagues. They reflected the nativist view that immigrants from countries like Mexico, Guatemala, and El Salvador would not adhere to traditional "American values."

In one leaked memo, Tanton contemplated an apartheid-like state: "In California of 2030, the non-Hispanic Whites and Asians will own the property, have the good jobs and education, speak one language and be mostly Protestant and 'other.' The Blacks and Hispanics will have the poor jobs, will lack education, own little property, speak another language and will be mainly Catholic. Will there be strength in this diversity? Or will this prove a social and political San Andreas Fault?"

Despite his words, Tanton wanted his network organizations to be race neutral on their face, which is evident in the rhetoric of both FAIR and FAIR-aligned sheriffs today, who avoid explicit race-based language and opt for messages focused on criminality and "American values." FAIR garnered some early fans like Warren Buffett, who were influenced by the environmental movement—foot traffic through the borderlands is often held up as a cause of environmental degradation and erosion. (Buffett distanced himself from FAIR around 1988 after the leaked memos were published.) FAIR scored a major win in 1994 when California voters passed Prop 187, which limited benefits for undocumented immigrants and required local law enforcement to cooperate in their arrest and detention. The group decided to turn its attention to sheriffs as good partners for this type of enforcement law.

Unsurprisingly, the first sheriff FAIR looked to was Joe Arpaio, the sheriff most infamous for his anti-immigrant stance. He became part of a FAIR-backed effort to pass a series of Arizona laws intended to be so hostile for immigrants that they would avoid the state. In 2005, Russell Pearce, a GOP state legislator who had also been one of Arpaio's most trusted officers, spearheaded legislation that criminalized giving rides or other transportation to migrants crossing the border (such as giving someone a ride to the hospital or a shelter). "What part of 'illegal' don't you understand?" Pearce exclaimed when asked about this law.

In 2006, Arizona passed legislation that denied undocumented immigrants bail, prohibited them from bringing tort claims if they were injured, and denied them in-state college tuition. That same year, federal lawmakers considered what was called the "Sensenbrenner immigration bill," which would have made illegal entry—returning to the country after being deported—a felony. That same year, FAIR told its members, "Creating coalitions with police and sheriff's [sic] departments all across the country to confront the issues posed by mass immigration has been a key FAIR goal for many years." But the fulfillment of that goal nationwide was still a few years away.

The series of laws Arizona passed in 2006 mobilized Latino activists, including Roberto Reveles, who would later express deep concern about Mark Lamb's policies as Pinal County sheriff. Reveles helped organize one of the largest pro-immigration marches in the country. That April, one hundred thousand activists marched to the state capitol. The group became Somos America Coalition, which translates to We Are America.

To contradict the implication made by FAIR and its allies that Latino immigrants were not law-abiding, Reveles encouraged marchers to carry the American flag and emphasized how most immigrants were hard workers who sought a better life from what was available to them in the countries of their birth. He believed in voting as a form of resistance. "Today, we march! Tomorrow, we vote!" was his rallying cry.

In a coup for FAIR, in 2010 the then-governor of Arizona, Jan Brewer, signed into law the state's most infamous anti-immigrant bill, SB 1070. The Support Our Law Enforcement and Safe Neighborhoods Act, better known as the "show me your papers" act, empowered county sheriffs like Arpaio to use their policing powers to arrest, jail, and deport immigrants. Mass racial profiling resulted, leading to a civil rights lawsuit and prosecution by the Department of Justice until 2012, when the U.S. Supreme Court invalidated many of the provisions of the bill. (That same year, the DOJ formally filed a civil rights lawsuit against Arpaio for a pattern of racial profiling and excessive violence.)

SB 1070 was drafted by FAIR and its legal counsel at the time, Kris Kobach, who later became the secretary of state and attorney general in Kansas. Kobach invented a new legal theory that paved the way for county sheriffs to become more involved in immigration. Since the 1800s, immigration law had been a decidedly federal issue, one to be determined by the Senate, the House of Representatives, and the president. Kobach thought that local government officials—like sheriffs—could legally be empowered to enforce immigration law.

Through FAIR, Kobach brought his ideas to other states, which passed laws like SB 1070 as well as a raft of legislation that required that all government agencies and schools use only the English language and refuse to provide social services and assistance to undocumented families. His ideas also enabled states to allocate funds and land for the construction of "border walls."

Kobach and the passage of SB 1070 set the stage for FAIR to recruit sheriffs to their cause, tapping into the already existing network of far-right sheriffs that Richard Mack was busy assembling at the same time. Unlike Mack, FAIR gained more widespread acceptance from sheriffs who did not necessarily identify as constitutional sheriffs. In 2011, FAIR produced a promotional video for the annual National Sheriffs' Association Conference. According to FAIR's annual report that year: "In 2011, we identified sheriffs who expressed concerns about illegal immigration." FAIR staff "met with these sheriffs and their deputies, supplied them with a steady stream of information, established regular conference calls so they could share information and experiences, and invited them to come to Washington to meet with FAIR's senior staff."

This began a series of events used by FAIR to more aggressively court sheriffs and present themselves as experts on immigration. By the end of 2011, a group of sheriffs calling themselves the "National Sheriffs' Immigration Coalition" met with FAIR representatives in Massachusetts with the goal of outlining how sheriffs and FAIR could better cooperate to achieve anti-immigrant objectives. The group was spearheaded by Thomas Hodgson, the now-ousted sheriff of Bristol County, who stood beside Trump and promised to send incarcerated people to help build Trump's border wall.

In 2012, FAIR held its first "border school" for sheriffs in El Paso. In the group's annual report it claimed, "More than 60 federal, state, county and city law enforcement officers from across the country participated." FAIR implied that the border school was sanctioned by federal law enforcement by including a DEA logo on the flyers; it was not. In one email, FAIR officials said, "We value the sheriffs we meet so we do all we can to roll out the red carpet." In 2015, Richard Mack of the CSPOA spoke at the FAIR border school, which included an event at Vickers Ranch, the home of an extremist border vigilante group called the Texas Border Volunteers. This militia group met a few times a month to conduct "border watches," using military gear and night vision goggles to detain migrants crossing through the property.

FAIR continues to hold various events for sheriffs, like the rally I attended. Every year, it holds a meeting in Washington, D.C., called "Hold Their Feet to the Fire," which features many of the same sheriffs I saw at the border wall rally. FAIR-backed sheriffs, like Lamb, also regularly appear as witnesses for various legislative panels and investigations, contributing "on the ground" experiential testimony that regurgitates many of FAIR's talking points, especially that immigrants are predisposed to commit crimes. (This is not true.)

Rachel Goldwasser, who analyzes far-right groups for the Southern Poverty Law Center, told me, "Any sheriffs or other law enforcement officers aligning themselves with such an organization, especially those whose jurisdiction lies inside border states, should provoke great concern."

County sheriffs have become useful avatars for the anti-immigration movement, but it wasn't necessarily a given that this would be the case. To understand how sheriffs are involved in immigration at all, we first have to explain how immigration law became connected to law enforcement.

Modern immigration law is relatively new, all things considered, and local law enforcement had nothing to do with the process until 1965. That year, the Immigration and Nationality Act established the modern-day immigration system, which focused on preserving family units and, as a result, favored those with American ties. This set the stage for what became the modern system for immigration policing.

Throughout the 1990s, the United States merged immigration enforcement with the criminal system, creating what some legal scholars call the "crimmigration" system. Individuals who had broken immigration law became subject to mandatory prison time because of changes to the code made in 1996, legislation called the Illegal Immigration Reform and Immigrant Responsibility Act. The IIRIRA was part of a raft of legislation signed by then-president Bill Clinton as part of his "tough on crime" agenda. A lot more people, almost any immigrant with a criminal conviction, became automatically deportable overnight. Sheriffs could use the IIRIRA to arrest suspected undocumented immigrants of relatively minor crimes, like drug possession, shoplifting, and drunk driving, and send them into deportation proceedings. "Today, it is often hard to explain where the criminal justice system ends and the immigration process begins," César Cuauhtémoc García Hernández, a law professor and the author of the book *Crimmigration Law*, wrote in a 2017 essay.

One of the main ways crimmigration brought sheriffs into immigration enforcement was as jailers. After the IIRIRA, the need for more places to detain immigrants exploded. Working with Immigration and Customs Enforcement—ICE, the federal agency tasked with enforcing immigration law in the interior of the United States—sheriffs became key to locating, jailing, and deporting immigrants already in the country. Because sheriffs operate jails and, as a result, regularly see people who have been accused of crimes, they are a convenient inflection point for ICE. Since the 1996 changes to immigration law, sheriffs' offices have screened people entering jail to see if they are undocumented or have been previously deported. If someone is flagged as being in the country without proper documentation— this can include an expired visa or even an error in the database—sheriffs notify ICE, which takes the person, jails them, and then initiates deportation hearings.

Over 70 percent of all ICE arrests start in this way, most of them with people who either have not been convicted of a crime or who have been charged with nonviolent crimes like driving without a license. In this way, every single person booked into any jail becomes a target for deportation, a process expedited by the 2008 Secure Communities program of President George W. Bush, which created an extensive biometric database of people entering and exiting the country. The assistant secretary for Homeland Security Julie L. Myers described how the program would be "a virtual ICE presence in every local jail." Another report bragged, "ICE knows who is in custody within an hour of when they are arrested through the live scan prints that are shared with the federal Department of Homeland Security."

The 1996 IIRIRA also created a pathway for sheriffs to act as immigration agents themselves, interrogating people about their nationality and determining whether deportation might be appropriate. Sheriffs can voluntarily join this program, called 287(g), to act as extensions of ICE. While the program has never been large—it does not provide any additional funding for sheriffs and, in fact, generally costs them money—it is a tool abused by sheriffs who want to politicize their anti-immigrant bona fides. Arpaio, for example, used his 287(g) authority to justify massive immigration raids until the federal government kicked the sheriff out of the program in 2011 for his overly aggressive policing.

The intent behind IIRIRA and 287(g) was to target and arrest immigrants thought to be transporting drugs into the country. But, in actuality, people who are arrested can be deported even without a conviction, if they are totally innocent, or if they are charged with a traffic infraction. In 2008, Jim Pendergraph, a former North Carolina sheriff who went to work for ICE in 2007, told an audience of law enforcement, "If you don't have enough evidence to charge someone criminally but you think he's illegal, we can make him disappear."

At its height during the Trump years, around 140 sheriffs participated in 287(g), called a "force multiplier" because it turns sheriffs into immigration agents; around 120 counties still participate, including most of the counties in Florida. While sheriffs do not need a 287(g) agreement to alert ICE when they arrest noncitizens, the agreement gives sheriffs' offices more authority to interrogate people at the point of arrest about their immigration status. It also allows them to hold individuals until ICE can pick them up, often through a process called a "detainer," which is just a piece of paper from ICE asking sheriffs to hold someone until an agent can arrive. Detainers have been disputed in court, and some sheriffs will not honor them unless they are accompanied by a court order from a judge. But there is not a lot of consistency in how sheriffs manage immigration issues, which means every new sheriff in every county can create a whole new system based on their own priorities.

Finally, above and beyond all this authority, sheriffs benefit from the massive immigration detention system because they can lease jail space to ICE for housing federal immigration detainees. All of these new criminal laws created a huge need for places to hold people awaiting deportation hearings. While some immigration detainees are held in private prisons, county jails run by sheriffs hold the vast majority of people pending their hearings or deportation. The pressure to reduce reliance on private prisons has caused this industry to explode for sheriffs. By the end of 2017, around 25 percent of immigrants in detention were held in county jails run by sheriffs, who get paid anywhere from $30 to over $200 per person per night.

All these incentives draw sheriffs into the business of profiling, arresting, deporting, and detaining immigrants. While the immigration priorities are set by the federal government, there is little oversight of sheriffs, who have wide discretion as to how they choose to enforce the law.

As such, abuses are fairly common when a particular sheriff makes deporting immigrants a priority. While Arpaio was well known, he was far from the only one, and this abuse of discretion by sheriffs extends well beyond states on the southern border like Arizona and Texas. Under 287(g), Sheriff Terry Johnson of Alamance County, North Carolina, used his immigration enforcement powers to inspire terror and line his pockets. In 2006, after he joined the 287(g) program, his office pulled over Latinx people at six times the rate of white people. (Traffic stops are a common mode of immigration enforcement because people can be arrested for "driving without a license" if they are undocumented and, therefore, unable to get a license from the state.) Johnson told his deputies to "go out there and get me some taco-eaters." In the five-year period between 2008 and 2013, 10 percent of the county's undocumented community members were deported.

Like many rural sheriffs, Johnson oversaw the construction of a county jail much larger than what the county needed in order to house more ICE detainees for a fee, which enabled him to profit from his biased policing. He justified his policing strategies by arguing that "cartels" were invading the county. With sheriffs across the country, Johnson links drug enforcement with immigration from Central and South America as a way to sow terror and division within the community. Just as sheriffs during Reconstruction used the Black Codes to justify the arrest and jailing of formerly enslaved people, sheriffs like Johnson use the "war on drugs" to rationalize their substantial role in the tough policing of immigrants.

Even when sheriffs are openly discriminatory, like Johnson (who was still in office as of the publication of this book), it takes years for government agencies to act. It is worth pointing out that immigration enforcement is one of the few areas where the federal government does have some say. Because immigration is a federal issue, presidential administrations can end 287(g) programs, for example, or set priorities for deportations, as the Obama administration did. At the same time, this is what makes far-right sheriffs so very dangerous under an administration like Donald Trump's. Once activated, sheriffs are already organized, prone to be anti-immigrant, and have internal networks that help them lobby for funding and more aggressive laws.

Civil rights organizations like the ACLU and coalitions of immigrants have lobbied for President Joe Biden to end 287(g). Even some left-leaning sheriffs agree. Dave Mahoney, who was the president of the National Sheriffs' Association and sheriff of Dane County, Wisconsin, which includes Madison, has argued that 287(g) agreements are bad for public safety because they make immigrant families afraid to contact law enforcement for fear of deportation proceedings.

———

Beyond all the immigration enforcement sheriffs can do inside their jails and counties, sheriffs in counties along the U.S.-Mexico border have also emerged as emissaries for the far-right media to produce images that scare viewers and stoke xenophobic panic. While there was no actual immigration enforcement taking place at the border rally I attended, part of the spectacle was to generate the impression that sheriffs were experts on immigration.

On Fox News, the panic is near constant, accompanied by videos of so-called migrant caravans crossing the U.S.-Mexico border. Red states like Texas have furthered the message by engaging in state-level tactics reminiscent of Arizona's SB 1070 to manage immigration. Operation Lone Star, which Texas governor Greg Abbott began in the spring of 2021, created a multiagency task force that included many sheriffs, who received extra state funding to arrest and detain migrants.

Sheriffs have served as useful messengers for the right-wing media, often because—unlike rank-and-file Border Patrol members, who must follow the orders of the presidential administration—they can say whatever they want to whomever they want. The deep irony is that no matter what the sheriffs say, they remain eligible for financial assistance from the federal government, which can be used for helicopters, surveillance equipment, ATVs, and other technology and manpower.

While sheriffs cannot arrest individuals simply for walking across the border—crossing into the U.S. without proper documents is not a crime but a violation of civil law—they often assist the United States Border Patrol, which is the military-style police arm of Customs and Border Protection. The USBP's mission is "Protect the American people, safeguard our borders, and enhance the nation's economic prosperity." The agents on horseback who were infamously photographed chasing after migrants in Del Rio, Texas, were Border Patrol. Border Patrol agents are also stationed at ports of entry into the United States. They make the initial assessments of asylum claims, detain people until they are released, and deport some people automatically by simply busing them across the border.

Sheriffs partner with Border Patrol often in situations where there are a large number of people or on search and rescue missions. Because many people walking across the U.S.-Mexico border cross desert and mountains, they often get lost, sick, or severely dehydrated. Sheriffs can also use their policing authority to conduct traffic stops in border counties and look to see if the passengers are transporting drugs or people—"trafficking," in sheriff parlance. Both of these are criminal, so when they catch someone trafficking, the sheriffs typically arrest the driver and turn the migrants over to Border Patrol for processing.

One of those sheriffs is Lamb, who has turned border security into media segments in support of his Senate candidacy. In October of 2023, right after announcing his campaign for Senate, Lamb filmed a political ad with his official department helicopter purchased with money from Operation Stonegarden, a federal grant program run by FEMA that gives money to local law enforcement to "support joint efforts to secure the United States' borders." The program, which distributes around $90 million annually, was cited in a 2017 report by the Office of Inspector General as having "not issued adequate guidance or conducted thorough reviews of proposed Stonegarden spending."

Part political ad, part marketing, Lamb filmed a highly produced mission in which he spies a "scouting location" from the air, which he says is where smugglers cross the border. He then lands the helicopter and talks to a group of migrants who are shown crossing into Arizona from Mexico. (A neighboring sheriff complained that Lamb was actually flying over his county without permission.)

Lamb has staked his career on agitating for increased border militarization as well as limiting immigration through what he calls a "closed border." As part of the DHS grant system, he also gets paid to purchase additional equipment, including vehicles, helicopters, and firearms, to "police the border," even though Pinal County is about one hundred miles from the actual U.S.-Mexico border.

All the equipment and trappings of the sheriff's office give Lamb's commentary on immigration the patina of authority, which he has used to spread well-trodden right-wing theories about massive human and fentanyl trafficking. In 2021, he told Fox News, "The people that come here, they're raping the women, they're using children as pawns . . . not to mention the drugs they are pouring into our communities. . . . We won't tolerate it as sheriffs!" He regularly takes politicians, including Representative Matt Gaetz of Florida, on "border tours" in which he shows them backpacks, shoes, and other debris as evidence of migrant crossings. "The coyotes bring the hard drugs. They're nasty," he told Gaetz, who was then under investigation for allegations of sex trafficking a minor. In late 2022, Lamb filmed a series with Turning Point USA called "Border Wars" in which he calls himself a "lion" protecting the "sheep" from "pure evil."

Even while he critiques the Biden administration, Lamb also profits from it. Through Operation Stonegarden, his office has received around $30 million over the past five years. Since Biden came into office, Lamb's office has received at least $16 million, more than twice as much as he did under Trump. This is part of the Biden administration's attempt to fund border enforcement to pacify Republicans, who would like for him to take a harder line on the issue.

As Lamb's exploits show, sheriffs have benefited the most from the militarization of the U.S.-Mexico border as well as the accompanying political debates. But this is all a relatively new phenomenon. Trump courted sheriffs to participate in his anti-immigration agenda. He held multiple roundtables with "border sheriffs" and touted his immigration policies, including the construction of a border wall. Under his administration, so many sheriffs joined the 287(g) program that it more than doubled in number.

Many sheriffs were eager to participate in more deportations, drawn to Trump's political message to be "tough on immigration." But his administration also cracked down on and vowed to prosecute the few sheriffs who refused to cooperate with ICE, and published lists of "noncooperative" sheriffs.

After Trump left office, however, immigration policy changed little. In fact, the Biden administration has poured more money into immigration enforcement at the U.S.-Mexico border than ever before, which translates into billions of dollars largely being distributed to sheriffs and other law enforcement to spend on more military equipment.

In the largely rural counties that border Mexico, county sheriffs are generally the chief law enforcement officers responsible for maintaining public safety. At the same time, sheriffs do not set immigration policy.

The physical site of the border allows for media-friendly visuals and tactics that sheriffs use to claim they are "humanitarians" both for rescuing lost migrants and for catching potential human traffickers. Sheriff Lamb posed wearing his hat and a tactical vest in front of whirling chopper blades and has produced videos purporting to show backpacks of drugs in the desert, dropped by fleeing migrants. One Texas sheriff claimed he found prayer rugs and "Quran books" on the border that he said indicated ISIS members were entering the United States illegally. "We'll send them to hell!" he promised CNN. There are even special "border schools," where sheriffs in the Southwestern United States invite politicians and other notables to tour the U.S.-Mexico border and see the terrain for themselves.

The pageantry of the videos helps sheriffs use their positions as elected law enforcement to advocate for stricter immigration policies. In essence, sheriffs as social media influencers create and disseminate propaganda to encourage Americans to see them as reliable sources of information on immigration. GOP politicians and advocacy groups have seized on this and made sheriffs their messengers. For most sheriffs, advocating for greater investment in border security increases the availability of grants and funding for equipment. And the truth is, very few people travel to the U.S.-Mexico border, so videos and pictures hold more interest, especially if they involve tactical maneuvers like an action movie.

———

At the Arizona rally, parents whose children had died—mostly from fentanyl overdoses—spoke. One after another they told their stories as the sheriffs held a yards-long scroll plastered with the faces of hundreds of young people, mostly teenagers, some chubby-cheeked kids, a display that is familiar to anyone who watched Trump's campaign. The group behind the banner— often called "Angel Families" or "Angel Moms"—are the parents of people who they say were killed by undocumented people, no matter how indirectly, as in the case of fentanyl overdoses. (It is difficult to verify the truth of these stories, but in many cases of fentanyl overdose, it is not clear how the drugs entered the U.S. Most illegal drugs enter through ports of entry, hidden in cargo.)

The industry of using victims as a propaganda tool has been exploited by a variety of anti-immigrant groups, many of which were involved in the border rally. One such group, Advocates for Victims of Illegal Alien Crime (AVIAC), is run by a California ex–entertainment industry guy named Don Rosenberg. AVIAC is interconnected with a variety of other anti-immigrant groups including the Angel Families, who appeared often with Donald Trump to bolster his policies. There's a personal story behind AVIAC as well. In 2010, Rosenberg's twenty-five-year-old son died when his motorcycle collided with a car driven by a man from Honduras in a horrific hit-and-run accident. Rosenberg found out that the driver didn't have a license but was in the U.S. on temporary protected status, which meant he could have gotten one. He was convicted of vehicular manslaughter. Rosenberg's anti-immigration quest started with a pursuit of people without driver's licenses, which he suspected were mostly undocumented people. This turned into a full-on push against immigration as he recruited other parents whose children had died, many from drug overdoses and others from shootings or car accidents.

At the rally, the rows of grieving parents presented an appealing picture and softened the face of anti-immigrant animus. Their stories, however, were not always as closely linked to immigration as one might think. For example, one parent lovingly described her son, who died as a teenager after overdosing on Oxy. "He only took it the one time," she said, explaining that her son had tooth pain from a dental procedure but was unable to fill his prescription because of a lack of health insurance. So he borrowed a pill from a friend. It's hard to fact-check mourning parents, and—knowing the toll of people who have died from overdoses—I could understand and sympathize with this tactic. But almost none of the parents I heard speak that day had a direct, provable link to immigration.

This has been a tactic of the anti-immigration movement—and an effective one, judging by the faces of the women around me. Most of them, like me, were mothers. They did not seem enraged or ready to storm the border fence. Instead, they appeared to believe that the line of sheriffs and a return of Donald Trump would bring them closure.

———————

Constitutional sheriffs and Richard Mack have not only partnered with FAIR and other related groups, they bolster anti-immigration policies, even though these sheriffs nominally oppose federal legislation. Their policy choices appear to be motivated by anti-immigrant malice, which includes conspiracy theories that the Democrats and liberals are intentionally permitting mass migration in order to impact elections in their favor.

In a "statement of positions" on the CSPOA's website, the group argues for something close to net-zero migration as well as offering its opinion about the Great Replacement theory: "We are a nation of laws, and our immigration laws are not being enforced. Further, immigrants are not assimilating into our culture as they once did. This results in devastating consequences culturally and economically."

The Great Replacement theory, promulgated by Fox News pundits like Tucker Carlson, argues that non-white immigrants will eventually "replace" white Americans and Europeans. The CSPOA often frames this as part of a plot by liberal elites to ensure that Democrats win elections. As Carlson said on his show in 2022, "Here's what we do know, for a fact: there's a strong political component to the Democratic Party's immigration theory . . . and they say out loud: 'We are doing this because it helps us to win elections.'" The eighteen-year-old who was charged with killing ten Black people in a Buffalo grocery store left a manifesto in which he claimed the Great Replacement theory legitimized his violent actions. So it's clear that these words have dangerous, real-world ramifications and the potential to lead individuals to commit violent acts even without the endorsement of the movement, the same way Timothy McVeigh was influenced by militia ideology but was not himself in a militia.

The CSPOA supports full militarization at the border, including preparations for an invasion that they believe is not only possible but imminent, immediate deportations, a border wall, and the right of states to police the border as they wish. The final policy solution as stated on the website: "County Sheriffs must use their authority to protect their citizens from abuse and violation of their rights by the invasion of illegal aliens."

Mack's organization also hosts a large number of nativist and anti-immigration advocates at their trainings. Much of the group's rhetoric echoes that of their predecessor movements, like the John Birch Society and Posse Comitatus, which were also virulently anti-immigrant and particularly opposed to immigrants of color. (The Claremont Institute also opposed immigration, particularly from non-European countries, and focused on migrants as threats to the American way of life.)

Mack personally told me via email that Texas sheriffs were interested in the CSPOA because of immigration. Almost all of the Texas sheriffs who participated in Operation Lone Star—Governor Greg Abbott's militarization of the Texas-Mexico border—have attended CSPOA trainings.

Perhaps more worrisome than the overlap with far-right sheriffs is the popularity of the anti-immigration message with a broad swath of sheriffs, both those who consider themselves "constitutional" and those who don't. Anti-immigration groups like FAIR have infiltrated mainstream sheriff groups like the National Sheriffs' Association as well as the offices of many sitting sheriffs. In 2021, the *Washington Post* reported that some sheriffs worked with FAIR and the White House to increase sheriff enrollment in 287(g). Many of those sheriffs faced allegations of racial profiling or poor jail conditions.

The day before the Arizona rally I attended, most of these sheriffs had been at the annual conference for the National Sheriffs' Association at the Phoenix Convention Center. This was not a coincidence. The NSA plays a vital role in connecting sheriffs with legislators to lobby for stricter immigration enforcement and more money to do so. The NSA helps to connect sheriffs with FAIR.

The NSA's current CEO and executive director is not a sheriff but a lobbyist named Jonathan Thompson, who worked for FEMA and DHS under President George W. Bush. Thompson was a featured speaker at the FAIR border school in 2015. FAIR and the NSA have also partnered on legal briefs filed to support an anti-immigration agenda. Shortly after Inauguration Day 2017, FAIR produced another ad featuring sheriffs, including NSA president and St. Charles Parish, Louisiana, sheriff Greg Champagne. The ad, "Sheriffs Standing with Trump on Immigration Enforcement," shows Champagne thanking the new president "for agreeing to stop illegal immigration and restore the rule of law."

Technically, the NSA is nonpartisan. Its previous president was Dave Mahoney, the Democratic sheriff from Wisconsin. But the group takes an extremely hard-right stance on immigration, among other issues, reflected in both the policies and the membership of their Border Security Committee. The leader of the committee, Arizona sheriff Mark Dannels, has received at least $7 million in equipment, including helicopters, from Howard Buffett, a son of Warren Buffett, a onetime supporter of FAIR. According to an investigation by the *Phoenix New Times*, Dannels allowed Howard Buffett to drive around in specially modified Ford Raptors and perform law enforcement tasks, like pulling over motorists and making arrests.

The convention featured a live horse in the lobby as well as a variety of panel discussions. Many were on immigration, including a panel called "Drugs, Death, Destruction and the U.S. Border," led by Idaho sheriff Kieran Donahue. Donahue has emerged as a strong anti-immigration proponent even though the nearest border to his state is with Canada. His nephew was killed, he told Fox News, by an undocumented person in a drunk-driving crash.

The center of the convention is the showroom, which features the booths of various vendors and organizations. Some are private companies that sheriffs can pay to provide services in their jails: non-internet-accessible iPads, food, laundry and, oddly, smokeless tobacco. There were a wide variety of vendors selling "protective gear," including a hermetically sealed container for drug evidence. There were model cars and trucks, even a helicopter. And there were firearms, including a virtual reality training simulation where attendees could stalk an invisible enemy inside an acrylic cube with a nonlethal firearm.

———

Trump made a concerted effort to place county sheriffs at the center of his immigration policies. Most of the meetings he held with sheriffs concerned "border security." As Republicans move toward dismantling federal law enforcement and administrative agencies, sheriffs may assume a larger role in immigration enforcement. Since Biden took office, sheriffs from both political parties have lobbied the federal government for more resources to militarize their border enforcement. This movement has not abated, and GOP politicians in the legislature have also found sheriffs to be useful allies in arguing for more restrictive immigration.

Sheriffs are particularly useful to politicians because, unlike Border Patrol, which is a federal agency and must be loyal to the president and his executives, sheriffs are unchecked in expressing political views. They can openly (and loudly) criticize the Biden administration, and since most sheriffs are Republican, sheriff coalitions present the illusion that their anti-immigrant views are popular.

The myth of the sheriffs goes a long way when immigration restriction proponents are looking for support; they represent the frontier and a world of self-made men who are acting to protect their families. This partnership presents deep concerns about whether sheriffs can police immigrant communities without prejudice. Sheriffs also represent the violence of settler colonialism, which they reenact by supporting anti-immigration policies and using their position of authority to spread unfounded information. The deep rift between those two visions of the sheriff epitomizes how politicized law enforcement can deepen divides locally and for the entire country.

# ELEVEN

# A MAN ON A MISSION

*Election Fraud*

IN MAY OF 2022, RICHARD MACK ANNOUNCED A PARTNERSHIP with True the Vote, a Texas-based organization with a mission to detect voter fraud that was founded by Catherine Engelbrecht, a right-wing firebrand, in 2009. According to Mack, after the release of Dinesh D'Souza's film *2000 Mules*, which made wild, debunked claims of massive voter fraud in the 2020 election, he contacted True the Vote "with the messaage [*sic*] that we wanted to help get more sheriffs to investigate the evidence *2000 Mules* presented in the movie."

In a note posted to the CSPOA website, Mack wrote: "The Constitutional Sheriffs and Peace Officers Association (CSPOA) is calling upon all Americans and law enforcement nationwide to come together in pursuit of the truth regarding the 2020 election. Considering the persistent allegations of election fraud since even before the 2020 elections began, and as a response to the perpetual polarizing effect this has had on the American people, the CSPOA would like to put this issue to rest. Our constitutional republic and peaceful future as a free people absolutely depend on it."

Just two months later, Mack convened a daylong "emergency training" session in a Las Vegas hotel ballroom to address the topic of voter fraud and talk about what sheriffs could do in the face of this threat. The audience included some two dozen sheriffs as well as another two dozen interested individuals. Among them was Rex Steninger, the county commissioner from Elko County, who was convinced there was substantial voter fraud in the 2020 election.

Right from the start, Mack asked for money, pointing to the jars in the middle of every table scattered throughout the hotel ballroom. "It's not a crime to donate more than once. It's a crime to vote more than once," he said to approving laughter.

He had strong words for sheriffs who did not feel that they should be investigating election fraud: "We hope the sheriffs in this country will reject any public official that says there was election fraud, but it wasn't enough to overturn the election. Any investigator that doesn't investigate a crime because it wasn't very bad. . . . That's like saying only a few people got raped." He urged sheriffs "who don't have to ask permission from anybody" to start their own investigations.

Mack also showed a CSPOA-produced video that purported to reveal the truth about ongoing and consistent voter fraud. The ten-minute amateur production used clips of popular shows like *Last Week Tonight with John Oliver* and news clips of liberals like Barack Obama to suggest that voter fraud is not a partisan issue. The voice-over then raised allegedly historical incidences of voter fraud, including the vote of 1888 and the Battle of Athens in 1946. Both were voting scandals involving corruption and bribery.

Then Mack invited Engelbrecht and her current business partner, Gregg Phillips, who claims he is an expert in "op sec" (operational security), to sit onstage with five sheriffs who had either investigated voter fraud in their counties or promised that they would do so. Behind them were the words "Election Fraud HAS HAPPENED."

Engelbrecht explained her reasons for recruiting sheriffs to their cause, which included the fact that no federal or state officials would cooperate with her group: "Once we had been burned by both the Federal Bureau of Investigation and state-level law enforcement, we realized we've got to take this more local. . . . As God would have it, at the same time, both Sheriff Mark Lamb of Pinal County, Arizona, and Sheriff Mack reached out. . . . All of a sudden, it's like the lights went on—it's the sheriffs. That's who can do these investigations. That's who we can trust." She had landed on sheriffs as messengers for her cause, politicians who carry a badge and a gun who were more than willing to engage in baseless fearmongering to drum up votes for the far right.

Three of the sheriffs onstage—Dar Leaf; Racine County, Wisconsin, sheriff Christopher Schmaling; and Johnson County, Kansas, sheriff Calvin Hayden—professed their concerns about election security and had each spearheaded an election fraud investigation in their home county. What went unsaid was that none of their investigations were fruitful—none of the sheriffs had found what local prosecutors deemed enough evidence to go to court. All three had also faced backlash from mainstream media as well as other public officials, who thought these investigations were a waste of resources.

Yet, the disapproval from others, especially those in the mainstream, only increased their sense of validation. Why would people object to an investigation if there was nothing to hide? Hayden, for example, claimed that he had opened two hundred investigations based on complaints from his constituents. He explained that residents of his county brought to him "volumes and volumes of all the information they've collected."

He went on. "I didn't know anything about elections. We were cops. We don't know anything about elections." After reviewing the evidence, Hayden claimed he had hired "a cyber guy" to use "geodata" to substantiate these initial complaints of voter fraud. The deputies in his department, he said, "are excited, and they are bird dogs." Hayden made it sound like his office was on the brink of an amazing discovery.

But his story completely fell apart upon the slightest scrutiny. Local news looked for the two hundred complaints but only found one. Instead of tracking down existing voter fraud, Hayden had tried to persuade county officials to allow his office to transport the ballots in unmarked vehicles and oversee the counting of them. Peg Trent, Johnson County's chief counsel, opined that allowing him to interfere this way would "give the appearance that the Sheriff's office is attempting to interfere with an election."

These far-right sheriffs would not find evidence of substantial voter fraud, nowhere close to enough to impact the 2020 election. But their goal was not to resolve outstanding cases or even to restore confidence in elections. Their goal was to use Trump's claims that he won the 2020 presidential election as a way to burnish their own far-right credentials and, along the way, seed conspiracy theories that would prevent people from voting. It's difficult to prove the existence of a negative, but luckily these sheriffs didn't have to in order to succeed.

Elections and election administration do not seem like traditional law enforcement concerns even though, as sheriffs will point out, election fraud is a crime. Election fraud, according to experts, is very rare. There is no evidence the 2020 presidential election was marred by fraud. And in cases of election irregularities, there are county clerks and voting commissions whose job it is to ensure the accuracy and integrity of voting. The involvement of the far-right sheriff movement in elections, however, is not about solving crimes.

Mack's posse against voter fraud has its analogues in the ways Southern sheriffs conspired with violent racist terror organizations to prevent Black voters from casting their ballots, which included everything from threatening Black voters with violence to actual examples of ballot box tampering. In March of 1965, Sheriff Jim Clark of Dallas County, Alabama, rounded up a three-hundred-man posse to meet a group of peaceful civil rights marchers, including John Lewis, at the Edmund Pettus Bridge. Lewis described Clark this way: "He was a very big man. He wore a gun on one side, a night stick on the other side and he carried an electric cattle prodder in his hand. He wore a button on his left lapel that said 'Never,' 'never' to voter registration. He was mean."

The ensuing violence on the bridge, called Bloody Sunday for a reason, had the effect of catalyzing the movement for voting rights as people watched nonviolent marchers get beat up on television. President Lyndon B. Johnson signed the 1965 Voting Rights Act only a few months later, which not only provided additional protections for Black voters but also required states with histories of voter suppression to preclear any new voting law changes with the federal government. This so-called preclearance provision was incredibly important in eliminating laws like reading tests or other pretextual excuses to prevent voter registration.

In May of 1966, Clark faced a challenger in the Democratic primary for sheriff. His opponent was Wilson Baker, the former Selma public safety director who had criticized Clark's openly racist hostility, even though Baker himself was "a segregationist." A record number of Black residents went to vote, all recently registered thanks to the Voting Rights Act.

Clark challenged the results of the election every step of the way. The local Democratic Party removed six ballot boxes from a primarily Black district, which Clark claimed were tainted by fraud. The 1,700 ballots were almost all for Baker. Clark lost the lawsuit. He then tried to run as a write-in candidate, handing out preprinted stickers with his name on them. Baker became the sheriff despite every effort of Clark to intervene.

In 2013, the U.S. Supreme Court effectively eliminated the preclearance provision of the Voting Rights Act in a case called *Shelby County v. Holder*. This ruling opened the door for states to enact new voter registration laws that previously would not have been allowed. In the eleven years since *Shelby County*, at least twenty-nine states have passed around one hundred laws to restrict voting, and turnout for voters of color significantly declined. Federal law prohibits voter intimidation, but the definition is fairly slippery. Some traditional practices, like voting inside the sheriff's office, are no longer allowed in most places. But sheriffs have continued to stretch the law by using their office to intimidate voters.

Historically, sheriffs have forced deputies to stump for their election. In 2022, the sheriff of Johnson County, North Carolina, parked a tank outside a polling location. His deputies handed out flyers supporting his candidacy. He won reelection.

Almost as soon as Trump lost the 2020 election, various conspiracy-minded right-wing groups looked to partner with sheriffs once it was clear that they had lost in the courts and with state officials. Sheriffs, who were already organized, prone to conspiracy theories, and liable to empathize with Trump, proved to be an excellent group to recruit. Some used the opportunity to reinforce their support for Trump to attract voters, many of whom believed in large numbers that the election was stolen. Others appeared to genuinely believe in the existence of massive voter fraud as part of a general swirl of anti-democracy conspiracies.

"Stop the Steal" slogans and themes immediately populated the far-right sheriff movement, especially in the places where Mack had already made inroads during 2020. The constitutional sheriffs were particularly distrustful of electronic voting machines, which they viewed as black-box mysteries, and many, including Richard Mack, argued for paper ballots, which a handful of rural counties have tried to implement. My hat at Battle Mountain did, after all, say "#UNRIG."

On December 4, 2020, Mack spoke at a "Stop the Steal" rally in Phoenix to protest Arizona governor Doug Ducey's refusal to help Trump steal the election. In his short speech, Mack argued that the answer to a clean election would be found locally. "What's left when no one will look at the evidence?" he asked. "State by state," he answered himself. Because sheriffs were a local office, their investigations by nature would be grassroots, focused on local voting.

"When you tabulate the vote using software and computers you pretty much know you are going to have voter fraud," he continued. "We just want to be able to verify the vote," he said, blaming the media for calling him "racist." "We've gone too far allowing voter fraud. We've gone too far allowing CDC regulations for COVID-19. . . . All of this is interlinked to the destruction of the Constitution and the destruction of America."

He also exhorted the police to support right-wing protesters. "Do not arrest common everyday American citizens. Stand down. . . . Keep your word!"

———

One of the most stalwart supporters of the Big Lie, and a "true believer" in the words of Richard Mack, has been Dar Leaf, the conspiracy-minded Michigan sheriff. His quest for voter fraud reflects what happens when sheriffs are permitted to abuse their power for political or personal purposes. A large part of his perpetual investigation reflects his conspiracy-minded views and the influence of the sovereign citizen movement, both of which are likely to increase in the run-up to the next election.

In September of 2023, when I interviewed Leaf, he said he was still investigating the 2020 election using state resources, including one deputy on election fraud full-time, out of only thirty deputies in his entire office. And no one could stop him.

"We're not gonna have a Constitution if we don't have secure elections," he told me.

I asked him if he really thought there was election fraud in Barry County, which has a population of around sixty-three thousand and voted two to one for Trump over Biden.

"I think it's . . . I think it's nationwide. If you got one of those computers, you're open to it," he said. He went on to explain to me that he had spoken with several "computer experts" and "operational security types," who were able to gather data to show that there had been fraud throughout Michigan, even in Barry County. He wasn't able to release the results of his investigation—I had been asking for years, like other reporters—but he felt confident something was there.

At one point he held out his hand and tried to explain how the rolling results of the 2020 election showed conclusively that there was voter fraud. It was inscrutable, but I realized asking more questions would not clarify the matter. His quest struck me as quixotic. I could see how he viewed it as noble. The more people doubted him, the more he pressed on. He did not seem worried about my questions, but he also did not express to me any doubt that he was correct.

Like all law enforcement, sheriffs have wide discretion to decide what investigations they want to do, how much resources they will dedicate, and, as Leaf shows, what the limits of that investigation are, all without oversight. As elected officials, sheriffs are not neutral arbiters of fact-finding, but, instead, a political body endowed with the ability to ask questions and demand answers, to pick and choose whom to interview, and, thanks to social media, to put the whole thing online for everyone to see even when news stations decline to air their press releases.

Even though Leaf said he did not use public resources or money for his multiple election-related court petitions, he has not hesitated to use the legal process as well as his office to pursue his passion, even going so far as to seize vote-tabulating machines. In the process, he has partnered with many of the figures who helped Trump attempt to overthrow the election. He has also spread the myth and panic of voter fraud throughout the state of Michigan, a swing state and one of the most segregated places in the country.

Leaf said that he was warned that the 2020 election would be fraudulent that July, and he felt as if everything else were laid before him like fate. Watching the results pour in on election night, he realized that "everything they said happened." In December of 2020, represented by Stefanie Lambert, a Detroit attorney who worked with Sidney Powell's legal team, Leaf filed a lawsuit to force an audit of voting data. Among other things, he raised concerns that voters had used Sharpie pens to vote and included handwritten affidavits from Barry County voters who believed they'd seen fraud. The judge promptly dismissed the lawsuit.

When this first lawsuit didn't work, Leaf decided that he needed to look at the machines themselves, but that is not allowed. He had the idea to create an "official" criminal complaint, a document that details the experience of a victim of crime. But this meant he had to find a victim. In the spring of 2021, a former Barry County deputy named Julie Jones helped Leaf by filing a criminal complaint based on information from Matthew DePerno, a pro-Trump attorney who had previously run for Michigan attorney general and had filed lawsuits related to voter fraud in a neighboring county. (They were all dismissed.)

With the "official" criminal complaint in hand, justifying his continued policing of the matter, Leaf sent a private investigator named Michael Lynch, who is connected to Lambert and DePerno, along with a deputy named Kevin Erb to question local election officials about the possibility that the Dominion voting machines had altered votes. Lynch seized one Dominion machine in Irving Township, reassuring the clerk that this strange investigation was "fine." It was later returned with the seal broken, meaning someone had tried to look inside.

Most of the other clerks were not so happy with Leaf's intrusion into their work. Rutland Township clerk Robin Hawthorne, who has been in her job for eighteen years, told me that Lynch asked her "a whole bunch of questions" about how the voting machines were programmed. She explained that, at the time, she was preparing for an upcoming municipal election and felt annoyed that someone was questioning her competence. She refused to divulge anything to the investigator.

Hawthorne told me that she generally did not have issues with Leaf, even though "I don't one hundred percent agree with his philosophies." She pointed out that the county voted two to one for Donald Trump in 2020. "Where's the money coming from? Who's paying for this?" she rhetorically asked with respect to the investigation and Lynch.

Leaf's attempt to question and harass well-established government employees throughout his community rubbed a lot of people the wrong way, and he was plagued by the question of who was paying for his investigations. He requested so many records from townships across the county that one demanded that he pay $1,300 in costs. "Per our lawyer, this request should never have been submitted," the letter reads. "We suggest you and your office concentrate on the law enforcement duties that our taxpayers elected you to do. . . . Potential legal actions are not something your department needs."

Leaf also upset Pamela Palmer, the Barry County clerk, who went to Julie Pratt, the Republican prosecuting attorney, around the spring of 2021. That July, Pratt went to see Leaf, who gave her two binders full of "evidence" that she reviewed. Also present at the meeting supporting Leaf was a former NSA official named Jim Penrose, who had assisted Powell's legal team in election lawsuits, as well as Lynch and Lambert. "It became a little contentious," Pratt described to me later.

Pratt said that she told Leaf there was "no probable cause" and asked him to "pause" the investigation, watching her words because, as she explained to me later, she could not tell the sheriff's office what to do.

Leaf continued on his path, hiring a deputy named Mark Noteboom, who requested reams of information from townships on voting records, again agitating other local leaders and disrupting the operations of the sheriff's office in Barry County.

Pratt said that in the spring of 2022 she became aware of Noteboom's work and reiterated her view that there was no criminal case, even sending Leaf an email. She explained that some people in the community who supported Leaf were highly critical of her decision. "It's okay. I didn't get into this for the fuzzies," she said later. In a 2022 county board meeting, Pratt defended her decisions and added that Leaf had asked her to charge the county health officer for "impersonating a doctor" as a way of expressing his disagreement with COVID health regulations. "Absolutely not," Pratt said. "I cleared her completely. . . . My job is not to charge everybody. My job is to seek justice."

Pratt was clear that she did not think any election officials were guilty of crimes, and she went on to critique Leaf's hiring of Noteboom, who was only working on election fraud to the detriment of solving actual crimes. "Voter fraud is a nonviolent case," she said. "I'm not saying it's not important." But, she added, there were not enough detectives working on cases that she felt needed to go to trial. "We are down to one," she said, "and when I say one, we are talking about one detective that deals with actual violent crime." (Leaf disagreed with this view when I talked to him.)

"So, we are now backwards," a member of the county board said.

"Please go out and vote," Pratt pleaded. "It's safe. There's no evidence of voter fraud in this county," she concluded. "And it's been a year and a half. . . . I'm just saying that we got stuff to do. Stuff to do that's really important. We got victims suffering."

When I talked to Pratt in 2022, she expressed frustration that Leaf was continuing to use his office's resources to fight windmills. Even though Leaf has asserted that he is not paying for Lynch's time, the office lacks sufficient detectives to solve rapes and kidnappings. Pratt, who is supportive of law enforcement generally and says she is "conservative on criminal justice," said the entire debacle was causing her to lose faith in the sheriff's leadership and impacting public safety in the county. Leaf's office is the primary law enforcement office for everyone in the county, and, with limited resources, it meant that Leaf's investigations into elections were causing cascading problems.

It did not seem that Pratt's pleading impacted Leaf's decisions. He, along with Sharon Olson, the township clerk who filed the complaint, has argued that the investigation warranted inquiry. "Also, we've had whistleblowers come up who were actually working in Venezuela," he told the county board, to laughter. This clearly irritated Leaf, and he continued to assert that "whistleblowers from all around the country" were giving him enough information to continue.

In a rare move, around June of 2022, Michigan attorney general Dana Nessel opened an investigation into Leaf and nearly a dozen others, arguing that they were part of a statewide conspiracy to secretly hide Dominion voting machines in a hotel room and attempt to dismantle them to prove that they had been hacked in some way. Leaf, in turn, filed his own lawsuit against the state with the assistance of Lambert, who is facing potential disbarment and criminal charges in Michigan. The sheriff argued that Nessel is preventing him from doing his job as law enforcement. He attached a handwritten affidavit to the court documents, prompting a spate of mockery.

In Leaf's telling, the state's investigation was simply a confirmation that he is fighting the good fight. By the summer of 2022, he said, "I'm a man on a mission right now. . . . We are still moving forward on it. We're not done with this. . . . I'm ready for the battle." He added that he questioned the results of the 2018 election as well, without evidence. And, ultimately, the AG's office did not prosecute Leaf (although it did indict DePerno and Lambert), which again filled Leaf with confidence. When I spoke with him in the fall of 2023, he told me that he felt the county leadership was coming around to his point of view and just needed to "see the forensic evidence for themselves."

Emails from a public records request show that in the summer of 2022, Leaf tried to recruit other sheriffs to join his mission. True the Vote came to see Leaf that fall, and he took them to multiple sheriffs' offices around the state. No one else decided to follow his lead, however. This prompted legal counsel for one county to complain that Leaf was "making everyone a fool," suggesting that he was simply falling prey to outside schemes so wild that no one was willing to join him.

Repeatedly, Leaf, like other constitutional sheriffs, insisted on the presence of voter fraud, yet failed to produce evidence of it. Because of the nature of the conspiracy theory and the mindset of these officials, that lack of evidence became evidence. And because they were sheriffs, no one could make them stop. Local officials gently tried to steer Leaf away from his cause, to no avail. The state attorney general decided not to charge Leaf, probably to avoid a controversy, since, after all, enough people had voted to keep Leaf in office with knowledge of what he was doing.

The other sheriff who partnered with True the Vote for a nationwide campaign was Mark Lamb in Arizona, a decision that ultimately brought the attention of Democratic advocates to call for more accountability from his office. While Lamb approached Engelbrecht and Gregg Phillips for a partnership, the move struck many residents as naked political opportunism. Even though the county voted mostly for Trump in 2020, over 40 percent of residents voted for Joe Biden, and the county was not so far from the diverse suburbs of Phoenix that many residents were concerned that their sheriff was repeating Trump's Big Lie.

While Engelbrecht appeared with Mack and other sheriffs in the summer of 2022, she seemed to have landed on Lamb as a more credible messenger for her cause. In a podcast, she explained that she was looking for "influencers" to help promote her message on a local level: "People are so fed up. . . . They are disillusioned with the whole process related to elections because where is law enforcement?" She continued, "We have our own experience with law enforcement because we started at the federal and the state level and they are all so politicized and weaponized against the citizens. . . . We think this is going to be just a groundswell of citizens across the country saying okay. This is how we are going to take our country back locally. Citizens working together with their sheriffs. . . . Sheriffs and local law enforcement helping to make sure those election laws are being upheld."

On a different podcast, Lamb said, "This was the most unsecure election, and there's a movie coming out called *2000 Mules*, and you're gonna see how unsecure it was. They have people. They track the phones of all these people ballot dumping into these ballot boxes every single day."

At a July 22, 2022, rally for Donald Trump in Prescott, Arizona, Lamb took to the stage after My Pillow's Mike Lindell, who has spent at least $40 million supporting false election fraud theories. Wearing his traditional cowboy hat, Lamb waved to the crowd, flashed his obscenely white smile, and announced his new partnership with True the Vote as part of his continued quest to ensure that America's sheriffs are enforcing the "rule of law." According to both Mack and Lamb, their two partnerships were established independently of one another.

"We will not let happen [the fraud that] happened in 2020!" Lamb exclaimed, talking about the 2022 midterm, after describing ex-president Donald Trump, whose Mar-a-Lago home was raided by the FBI two weeks later, as a man who "loves the rule of law."

Like many of Lamb's projects, the partnership was light on substance and heavy on vibes. In a promotional video, Lamb appears in his fully loaded flak vest and hat to talk about why "voters are frustrated," advising people to call a hotline and visit a website. "Elections have consequences," he told a small crowd. "America will not be saved in Washington," he explained, name-checking Mack and the CSPOA. "The sheriffs are your last line of defense for freedom." Then he asked for donations for additional public service announcements, which never happened.

Lamb and Engelbrecht set up a website called Protect America Dot Vote that was "about the rule of law" and connected to Lamb's sheriff group Protect America Now. There were many rhetorical parallels between the two groups, which made it hard to tell the difference. Just as Protect America Now focused on encouraging sheriffs to stand "against those who want to trample on our Constitution and reject law and order," Protect America Dot Vote urged sheriffs to "be ready to enforce the law, as well as protect their constituents from any form of illegal activity."

According to the now-defunct website, the organization had five main goals: "Connecting citizens and sheriffs," "Empowering sheriffs," "Open lines of communication," "Promote public service messages," and, of course, "Join our efforts," which includes a button to "contribute" cash donations.

While much of the material was public messaging and PR strategy, it also included a "National Election Integrity Voter Hotline" that promised to connect concerned citizens "to sheriffs' offices for quick evaluation of incoming information." It went live in the summer of 2022 with an email form that said it would "connect with your local Sheriff." A call to the hotline resulted in an automated message saying that operators were overwhelmed and directing callers to True the Vote to make a complaint.

Later, through public records, I found that the website generated a form letter to sheriffs with a pamphlet providing advice on preventing voter fraud. The letter included the "Protect America Dot Vote" header and Lamb's signature. It suggested that sheriffs patrol ballot drop boxes and install video monitoring: "Please consider increased patrol activity around drop box locations. Increased drop box patrol between 10pm and 5am is strongly encouraged." The letter offered grants for equipment and encouraged sheriffs to tell their constituents to contact "ProtectAmerica.vote" with their concerns. Finally, the letter emphasized "local control": "Sheriffs have control in their county. When other areas of government break down our local Sheriffs step in to make sure the law is enforced. Working with Sheriffs around the country we will raise attention in local communities and discourage law breakers from any organized effort to break voting laws."

The most important part of the project appeared to be the advertising. In a promotional video with Catherine Engelbrecht, the founder of True the Vote, Lamb said, "Where necessary, sheriffs can and will investigate when laws are being broken." He also took pains to cast the project as nonpartisan: "This is not about Republican or Democrat. This is an issue of the rule of law." This is also repeated on the website: "This is not a Republican or Democrat issue, this is about the right of the voters."

Lamb's increasingly extremist rhetoric alarmed residents of Pinal County as the line between his influencer status and his job blurred. While Lamb repeatedly claimed that his interest in election security was nonpartisan, citizens allied with Democratic organizations grew concerned that Lamb's partisan affiliations impacted the policing of the county. Democratic leaders attended meetings of the board of supervisors to express their growing concerns about Lamb and his desire to insert himself into election investigations.

Ralph Atchue, president of the Casa Grande Democrats and a onetime Democratic candidate for the Arizona Senate, told me, "Residents are growing more frustrated and are concerned their interests are not being taken seriously."

The problem became more acute because of a series of administrative errors during the August 2 primary that led to confusion, dismay, and additional fearmongering about "election integrity."

On August 3, dozens of county residents appeared at a board of supervisors meeting to complain about the election process; the elections director was fired and replaced by the county recorder, Virginia Ross. Speakers affiliated with both parties complained about the process and loss of trust in elections in the county, but many were there to express their concern that the sheriff's office was encouraging people to believe there was election fraud.

During the public meeting, Atchue said, "It is becoming apparent that Sheriff Lamb is crossing a line that we consider dangerous. Sheriff Lamb has put those of us who disagree with him on notice. He does not represent us, and we fear that he will not serve his oath of office to serve and protect us."

Roberto Reveles, the civil rights activist who has long been critical of Lamb, also took to the podium and renewed his calls for a "financial and performance review" of Lamb's office. He then shared his concern that Lamb was escalating by threatening his opponents: "I recently was subjected to intimidation when Sheriff Mark Lamb walked up to me and pointed at me and said, 'You and your fellow Democrats are destroying our country.'" Other citizens associated with local Democratic groups also told me that they were concerned about retaliation from the sheriff's office. "There's nothing to rein him in," a source said. It seemed that Lamb's very public display of anti-democracy goaded residents more than anything else. They felt that Lamb was trafficking in debunked conspiracy theories and was increasingly using rhetoric that insulted and demeaned people who were asking questions about his intentions.

The next day, Lamb posted a video to the Pinal County Sheriff's Office's Facebook page saying he was taking the concerns "very seriously." "As far as the sheriff's office goes, we are committed to making sure we look into this matter completely. . . . We will also be offering our services to help look at the voter rolls. . . . We will secure those ballot boxes. We will be watching the videos to make sure that nobody is breaking the laws." Lamb reiterated this claim about surveillance videos in another forum, saying, "I got in touch with my county recorder and said, 'I want video from all those boxes, I want to make sure there's video on all those boxes, and we will monitor those videos.'" (There was no evidence the sheriff obtained any video at all.)

Much of this appeared to be blustering. A representative from Virginia Ross's office wrote to me in an email, "Ms. Ross wasn't aware of the video that was posted by Sheriff Lamb. In the video, Sheriff Lamb is referring to the future. No discussions have taken place regarding voter roles [*sic*] or securing ballot boxes. . . . It is not normal practice to have Law Enforcement officers check voter roles [*sic*]." A representative from the Pinal County Sheriff's Office responded to a request for comment via email, "PCSO is not involved in this project, and no PCSO employees are assigned."

County Attorney Kent Volkmer, whose office referred me to the prosecutor's public comments in an August 10 special session with the board of supervisors, had taken the lead by hiring an outside expert to conduct a review of Pinal County's election processes. Then Volkmer said that he did not anticipate using the sheriff's office to investigate the August 2 primary—"We really don't want law enforcement doing it"—citing concerns of intimidation.

In a special session of the board of supervisors on August 17, Volkmer revealed that he had hired Brad Nelson, the prior Pima County elections director, to conduct the outside review. He also struck a more conciliatory tone about criminal investigations, mentioning that his office had been flooded with tips. "I have a sheriff ready, willing, and able to investigate any illegal actions," he said, largely in response to a flood of public comments filled with concerns about everything from using markers on ballots, to broken machines, to incorrect ballots, to outside funding.

Lamb confirmed Volkmer's assertion that he was involved only in "criminal matters," even though none existed—the only person arrested on their August 2 primary was a voter who was aggressively harassing election workers. Lamb used that arrest to justify greater police presence during the midterm election: "We will probably have more deputies roaming around. . . . We want to have a minimal presence . . . but we will have a little stronger presence roaming around."

Even still, Lamb managed to insert additional specters of voter fraud that remain unsubstantiated and unprosecuted: "We have a lieutenant in our agency who personally [said that] his grandmother and her husband both voted in the 2020 election, and they were deceased. . . . I should say their ballots were received per the secretary of state." (A PCSO spokesperson did not respond to a request to confirm this.) Even Kelly Townsend, the far-right Republican state senator who lost her reelection bid, appeared, discussed her failed injunction to prevent Pinal County from certifying the election results, and threatened the county with a lawsuit.

Lamb's political rhetoric outside official meetings remained combative. In an interview with Newsmax that week he said, "I'm trying to push for election integrity, which I think is not a partisan issue. Democrats and Republicans should want election integrity. But last week in the board meeting I had eight to ten Democrats show up and blast me because I believe in the Big Lie. . . . And it clearly shows that these folks don't care about election integrity. . . . They are turning this into a country that we just don't recognize. . . . They have taken exception with me on it. But you know that's not going to stop me from continuing to push for election integrity."

Similarly, in a True the Vote invitation-only meeting held in Pinal County on August 13—around 180 people were personally invited—Lamb doubled down on promising to review voter rolls and demand surveillance of ballot boxes. He even claimed he spoke with the board of supervisors about increasing his role in investigating elections. (Two members of the board of supervisors returned a request for comment and both denied meeting with Lamb outside of public meetings.)

Lamb also took time to lambaste those who have dared to speak against him again, exaggerating the story: "There was about eight people with masks there. . . . I'll let you determine based on their virtue signaling what party they were from. . . . They were there and those eight or ten people, they didn't get up to talk about the lack of ballots. They got up and talked about ME. And how bad I was, and how I politicize the office. What a giant turd I was."

He neglected to mention that one of those who cited concerns about Lamb was an elderly woman whose recently deceased husband was a longtime member of the previous sheriff's volunteer posse; she told me that after she spoke against Lamb, he told her she was "unfit" to wear her husband's old volunteer posse hat.

Atchue told me that he thought the line between Lamb's political views and responsibilities was "completely blurred." He said that residents are concerned that members of the Pinal County sheriff's posse will appear to police polling places.

Alongside other Democrat leaders in the county, Atchue feels frustrated about their options to rein in the sheriff. Noel Reck, another concerned resident of Pinal County affiliated with the Casa Grande Democrats who has similarly called for an audit of the sheriff's office, said he had approached multiple state and county officials but was repeatedly told they could not help him. He expressed his frustration to me over the phone. "The sheriff's budget is the biggest in the county. . . . [Lamb]'s got his fingers in a whole lot of things that raises questions. They're not taking care of the people."

Amid all of this political lobbying from inside the county, there was also pressure outside Pinal. I published a story about Lamb and True the Vote in August of 2022, which drew attention to the issue. That fall, Engelbrecht and Phillips were arrested for contempt of court related to a defamation claim by an election company. Around the same time, Dominion Voting Systems was suing Fox News for defamation, which put the network in the position of having to pay out hundreds of millions of dollars. (In April of 2023, Fox settled the case for $787.5 million.) Likely worried about similar fallout from his false claims, Lamb stopped talking about voter fraud and the website mysteriously evaporated. (This was also around the time Lamb began to explore the possibility of a Senate run, which may have also impacted his decision.) In a 2023 congressional hearing focused on "border security," Democratic representative Dan Goldman asked Lamb if he thought Trump won the election, to which Lamb said, "Well, Joe Biden is president now." He then tried to recast his advocacy for election denial as merely work on behalf of election security. "I believe there are a lot of Americans who have questions about election integrity," he said. He did, however, admit that there was no evidence of widespread fraud to question the election results.

Other sheriffs also distanced themselves from Lamb and Protect America Now, largely because they faced pressure from their constituents to distance themselves from the criminal indictments stemming from January 6. Loudoun County, Virginia, sheriff Mike Chapman, for example, claimed that he never officially joined Lamb's group and didn't agree with the election denial partnership. Through a representative, his office said, "The Sheriff is not a member of this organization nor engaged with them, and it would be inappropriate for him to discuss the group's mission, priorities or objectives."

———————

The focus of far-right sheriffs who pursued the slightest rumors of voter fraud can appear like inept attempts at politicking. But the threat of arrest and criminal prosecution leading to jail time was a very real concern for many people. GOP leaders felt growing political pressure to locate "real" instances of voter fraud to satisfy their constituents, around 70 percent of whom believed that Biden had not properly won the 2020 election. Florida created its own election police force. In some places, it was easier for sheriffs to find cases that could move forward, especially now that state lawmakers had passed increasingly extreme laws that were confusing for most people to understand.

Mack was able to point to one sheriff who had successfully pursued a voting fraud investigation: Sheriff Leon Wilmot of Yuma County, Arizona, whose investigations would ultimately lead to multiple prosecutions for voter fraud in San Luis, a small Latino community right on the border with Mexico.

Wilmot has been the elected chief law enforcement officer for the county since 2013 and is the sole police for many of the smaller municipalities scattered in the region. The sheriff has a long walrus mustache and a penchant for Vietnam War–era military vehicles. In part, his identity rests on his connection to his military service—he is a former marine—which colors how he thinks about the job. (Wilmot's office would not comment on these cases except to say he did not coordinate with Mack.)

Mack was happy to take credit for Wilmot's investigation, even though he had little to do with it. On May 11, 2022, the Yuma County Sheriff's Office issued a press release announcing that the sheriff and the Arizona Attorney General's Office were "working together to actively examine cases of voting fraud from the 2020 General Election and now a recent pattern of fraudulent voter registration forms leading up to the 2022 Primary Election," announcing specifically "16 voting/registration open cases." These cases became a right-wing sensation because they appeared to affirm the allegations of *2000 Mules*, which had made wild claims about "ballot harvesting" and because the cases involved Latino voters, which affirmed prejudices about illegal votes.

"People have been arrested there. And they are begging for plea bargains," Mack wrote me in an email.

The case involved a group of get-out-the-vote volunteers who were holding a voter drive on August 4, 2020. Guillermina Fuentes stood with a group of other workers wearing matching turquoise T-shirts at a table set up outside the Cesar Chavez Cultural Center in San Luis, a town so small and remote that most people did not have individual mailboxes. Fuentes, who had been the mayor of San Luis and owned a business, was answering community questions about voting and ballots.

Fuentes and her group attracted the attention of Gary Snyder and David Lara, two local politicians who had run for office in San Luis and called themselves the "vote hunters." They had been in conversations with the Yuma County Sheriff's Office for over a year about their long-harbored suspicions that the elections in the tiny town were "rigged."

Lara in particular had been concerned about voter fraud for over two decades. According to an interview he later gave to law enforcement, Lara believed that there was a group of voting advocates who pulled lists of absentee voters and then went house to house, helping them fill out their ballots. He described what these "professionals" do as "intimidation" and went on to explain that he also thought that these same people would "stuff" ballot boxes with "several hundred [and] even up to a thousand" ballots for their candidate of choice.

On August 4, 2020, on the advice of Lara, Snyder took surreptitious video of Fuentes at the voting drive.

In 2016, Arizona lawmakers made it illegal to do what is called "ballot harvesting." Ballot harvesting refers to the practice of depositing more than one absentee ballot at a time. It was not always illegal; in fact, it was common practice in many places, especially rural ones, for people to carry and deposit the ballots of neighbors and friends. Voting rights organizations challenged the legality of the Arizona law under the Voting Rights Act. The case made it up to the Supreme Court, which voted in 2021 to uphold the law, 6–3— conservatives versus the liberals.

In Snyder's August 4 video—it's fuzzy and jumpy—Fuentes takes ballots from a San Luis resident named Alma Juarez and appears to make a mark. In later interviews, Fuentes said she was probably writing the date on the envelope. At the time, Juarez testified that her sister had asked Fuentes to review her ballot to see if it was filled out correctly. The attorney general's office later characterized the video as showing Fuentes "running a modern-day political machine seeking to influence the outcome of the municipal election in San Luis, collecting votes through illegal methods." The video would become famous through True the Vote. Engelbrecht and Phillips used the clip to advertise their organization and it became a part of the eventual film *2000 Mules.*

By the afternoon of August 4, the sheriff's office had assigned Sergeant Jason Hemstreet to the case. Deputies seized the ballot box with the help of the county elections administrator and put it into evidence, calling the contents "fraudulent." Snyder walked to the sheriff's office with a copy of the video on a flash drive labeled "Evidence."

The next week, the attorney general's office got involved. According to public records from the AG's office, an investigator went to Yuma to meet with local law enforcement on August 13, 2020, a little more than a week after Snyder delivered his surreptitious video to the sheriff.

Initially, the two lawmen met with people who supported Lara and Snyder's suspicions that there was an ongoing voting fraud scheme. A local judge named Juan Guerrero told the investigators that there was a "ring" and that "he did not want to get attached to it or involved." Only a "selected group of people" knew about the plan, which was akin to a "pyramid scheme," he said.

Then the investigators widened their search to question everyone in the community. They not only approached Fuentes but also proceeded to interview around forty people, knocking on doors and asking about their ballots. In these interviews, armed agents asked voters whether they had voted and questioned them about Fuentes specifically, attempting to get a witness to identify her as someone who had come to collect their ballots. Anne Chapman, who represented Fuentes in her criminal case, said "the prosecution was racist from the start" and told me that her client was being used to make a political statement. She went on: "General deterrence happened when deputies went to forty San Luis community members' homes to interrogate them about their ballots. The attorney general's attempt to score political points is not a legitimate reason to prosecute."

Investigators also checked about forty ballots for latent fingerprints and sent those prints to a Department of Public Safety lab in Phoenix to see if they matched Fuentes's. Only four ballots appeared to have a partial print from her.

Public records indicate that Wilmot faced pressure to move the case along quickly, as right-wing groups intent on locating voter fraud asked his office for information on Fuentes's and Juarez's cases. Records also show that Wilmot was receiving other tips, including rumors of Latino advocates driving around with "boxes" of ballots, an allegation that was never sustained. He was also in communication with other Arizona sheriffs (namely of Cochise County) on the U.S.-Mexico border about the issue, although no other cases emerged. Lara and Snyder also continued to contact the Yuma County Sheriff's Office and the attorney general about additional concerns they had regarding alleged improper actions by community members.

In December of 2020, Arizona's then Republican attorney general Mark Brnovich indicted Guillermina Fuentes and Alma Juarez, charging them with "ballot abuse." Fuentes and Juarez both pled guilty. Fuentes served thirty days in jail and lost her right to vote or hold office for the rest of her life. Juarez served two years of probation.

At her sentencing hearing, the prosecutor and the judge used Fuentes's long history of civic service against her. Instead of an example of being connected to the community, her work getting out the vote was now a shadowy admission that she knew she was doing something illegal. "She understands the law," the prosecutor said, arguing for a stiffer jail term. "She was a leader and respected."

For other voting rights lawyers, Fuentes's prosecution was an attempt at racist intimidation fueled by far-right conspiracies that tainted law enforcement's views. Andy Gaona, an election lawyer in Arizona, told me, "The process works. Ms. Fuentes's prosecution has a racial overtone," and pointed to other, similar cases involving white voters who were not charged with crimes.

Gaona told me that the far-right push to aggressively hunt for voter fraud damaged trust in institutions and changed the way people think about election fraud. "Everything changed after [2000 Mules]. It was such an inflection point . . . a rallying point for people. This poorly made, poorly sourced thing became a new inflection point for conspiracy theorists."

There is no way to know for sure how much of this particular case in rural Arizona stemmed from the Big Lie and related election fraud conspiracy theories touted by far-right sheriffs. It does show, however, how sheriffs play an important role reinforcing far-right conspiracies using their political power, their law enforcement capabilities, and their lack of oversight. In multiple communities, people wrestled in different ways with how to deal with their sheriffs. Sometimes, other political figures helped provide a check. Sometimes, they reinforced the sheriff's beliefs. In all cases, the sheriff was plainly not acting as a neutral authority.

Not only do sheriffs have the ability to investigate crimes, compel witnesses to provide information, and seize evidence; they also hold a political position that comes with a ready-made platform they can use to tout their own policies and ideas. As a result, dissatisfied Trump voters flocked to local sheriffs, many of whom were already sympathetic to their cause, to demand investigations. Once those investigations occurred, no matter how flawed or incomplete, sheriffs took to social media and friendly news platforms to claim they had found voter fraud. This in turn gave legitimacy to what were essentially false rumors and conspiracy theories activated by Trump and his allies that are still in use as this book goes to print.

Once these investigations began, as in Yuma, law enforcement harassed already disadvantaged communities and took advantage of their legal discretion to prosecute individual voters and make people feel afraid and worried that they might face jail time. Minority communities, already concerned about the tremendous power of law enforcement, have few ways to stop these prosecutions once they are set in motion. And even when prosecutions fail, the damage has been done. Those already worried about running afoul of the law become even more terrified. Trust in institutions has been destroyed.

Because sheriffs cannot be removed from office for making political statements and because they can divert resources as they choose, there are no real mechanisms to stop them from investigating bogus voter fraud claims. Thus far, these sheriffs have largely not produced successful investigations because other public officials, from both sides of the aisle, have blocked them from moving forward. On the one hand, this provides an example of how checks and balances work on the local level. On the other hand, it magnifies the problem of how sheriffs can use their relatively unchecked powers to stifle democracy should the right combination of factors arise.

TWELVE

# REFORMING
# THE OFFICE OF SHERIFF

*"Don't Elect Me"*

ONE OF THE EASIEST AND MOST OBVIOUS WAYS TO REFORM
the office of sheriff is through elections. In fact, that's what sheriffs themselves say: if you don't like it, "don't elect me."

But how, exactly, should communities go about "unelecting" a sheriff?
During the civil rights movement of the 1960s, Black communities made
concerted efforts to elect Black candidates as sheriff both to end the reign of
racial terror caused by white sheriffs and to empower Black communities to
envision equal justice. In Lowndes County, Alabama, the role of sheriff was
traditionally feared. "If you were walking at night and you saw some car
lights, you better hit the ditch. It could be the sheriff," one Black community
leader said. Lowndes's population in the 1960s was 80 percent Black, but no
Black person had been elected to any local office since the end of Reconstruction. In fact, before the year the Voting Rights Act was passed, no Black
citizens were even registered to vote.

In 1965, Black residents, with the help of the Student Nonviolent Coordinating Committee, formed a third party called the Lowndes County Freedom Organization, in what historian Hasan Kwame Jeffries called a "great
experiment in democracy." Black advocates created a series of illustrated

comic-style books to introduce the slate of all-Black candidates as well as the jobs they would perform. For the booklet about the sheriff, one picture shows the sheriff "keeping the peace" by breaking up an "unlawful assembly" of KKK members in hoods; another shows a Black sheriff appointing Black election workers. As one civil rights worker explained, Black residents of Lowndes had never seen a Black sheriff before; the booklets gave people a vision of what the job required and how they could benefit from their own candidates in the office.

While the LCFO candidate, a World War II veteran named Sidney Logan, did not win that time, at the next election, in 1970, Lowndes County did elect its first Black sheriff, John Hulett, who had been a lead organizer for Black voter registration as well as chairperson for the LCFO. Two thousand Black people came to watch his swearing-in ceremony, guarded by armed Black men. (Hulett himself faced later opposition because of his decisions to compromise with white politicians. While he made the law more equitable by arresting whites who committed crimes, he also allied himself with white Democrats, including famous segregationist Alabama governor George Wallace.)

In the same vein, progressive groups ranging from the American Civil Liberties Union to grassroots community organizations have tried to encourage people to run for sheriff and, hopefully, win. Mimicking the same strategy many used for electing progressive prosecutors, reform-minded groups over the past decade have had successes electing sheriffs who run on platforms that promise to decrease jail populations, make fewer low-level arrests for things like broken taillights and minor drug possession, and sever cooperation with ICE. Max Rose, the executive director for Sheriffs for Trusting Communities, a nonprofit that supports grassroots organizers in sheriff campaigns, called elections "an important and limited tool."

Many of these electoral wins were spearheaded by communities of color and have led to more diversity across sheriffs. They are often hard-fought and take years of work. In 2016, for example, Latino organizers finally ousted Joe Arpaio from office through election. The process took over a decade and involved protests, public outcry, and, ultimately, a lawsuit by the federal government against Arpaio. The man who would eventually defeat Arpaio, Paul Penzone, ran against him in 2012 and lost. Only in 2016 did Penzone succeed, beating Arpaio by a margin of around 10 percent.

The anti-immigrant policies and racist rhetoric of Donald Trump's presidency motivated many local communities to seek sheriff candidates who would use their discretion to protect immigrant communities in particular. Most of these wins occurred in blue counties, where the voters strongly opposed Trump. One example occurred in North Carolina during the 2018 election when voters in the state's seven largest counties elected Black men as sheriff, all of them Democrats, many of whom ousted sheriffs who had been in office for a long time and were well entrenched. These sheriffs promised to end cooperation with ICE, make their jails safer, and reduce racist policing practices. In Wake County, for example, Democrat Gerald Baker, who is Black, beat the four-term GOP incumbent, Donnie Harrison, who is white. Harrison was a very conservative Republican who made deportations a key part of his crime-fighting strategy. Between 2013 and 2017, Harrison's policies led to the deportation of nearly 1,500 people. In another strange twist, Harrison attempted to run again for sheriff in 2022 but lost to the new Democratic candidate, Willie Rowe, who worked under Baker.

In 2020, two openly gay women in two different states were elected to the office of sheriff. Basing her campaign on the fact that she had been fired by her boss, the prior Trump-supporting sheriff, for complaining about discrimination and excessive force, Charmaine McGuffey ran for sheriff and won in Hamilton County, Ohio, a blue county in a sea of red. McGuffey contrasted herself with the prior sheriff, "a bully," who used excessive force on men of color. She used her own experience of discrimination as part of the pitch for her candidacy. In the video announcing her campaign, she walks toward a bathroom stall with a large sign: "DYKE."

In Charleston, South Carolina, another gay female candidate, Kristin Graziano, also replaced a longtime incumbent who had suspended Graziano when she declared her intent to run against him and who went out of his way to slander her before she took office. She is the first female sheriff in the state and, like McGuffey, used her identity as a selling point. When lawmakers in the South Carolina legislature considered a 2021 bill requiring that doctors performing abortions on rape victims must notify the sheriff, Graziano publicly opposed it. "I may be a new sheriff, but I'm not new at being a woman," she remarked.

Electing reform-minded, diverse sheriffs requires that advocates and voters overcome significant structural problems because of the nature of the sheriff's office. For one thing, it can be hard to find candidates for the job, especially in rural counties. One of the few requirements for sheriffs includes being a resident of the county where they wish to serve. In places where the sheriff's reputation looms large, it can be intimidating to run against a popular incumbent. Furthermore, because sheriffs can hire and fire at will, any challenger from within the office will likely be fired or demoted—as McGuffey and Graziano were—making the choice to run risky.

Even when they are successful, new sheriffs face a number of challenges, including an entrenched culture, preexisting lawsuits or construction plans, and harassment from political enemies. This reality has led many progressives to see sheriff elections as part of an overall strategy, rather than an end in and of itself.

---

In 2021, Susan Hutson ran for sheriff of New Orleans against Marlin Gusman, who had been in the office since 2004. Gusman had overseen the city's jail, then called the Orleans Parish Prison, through Hurricane Katrina in 2005, during which he refused to evacuate until the floodwater threatened to drown some of the people held inside. People recalled standing in chest-high water without electricity, food, or drinking water. There were also allegations of abuse by guards, who beat, ignored, and, in at least one instance, shot incarcerated people as they panicked during the storm. Gusman was elected as a reformer, and he presents as polished and educated, if a bit defensive, with degrees from the University of Pennsylvania and Loyola University in New Orleans. He has deep ties to the New Orleans political machine, which accounts for his success; he was the chief administrative officer for former New Orleans mayor Marc Morial and served on the city council for four years. His predecessor, Charles Foti, had been sheriff from 1974 until 2004, when he lost the election to Gusman. (Foti then ran and won the office of attorney general, which he held for one term. He ran again for sheriff in 2014 against Gusman and lost in a runoff.) Foti was responsible for a massive expansion of the jail, accepting contracts to hold people for other parishes and implementing a large work program that immensely profited the sheriff's office. The jail population ballooned to 6,500, making it the ninth-largest in the U.S.

But, under Gusman, the jail did not appear to become safer, despite a complete rebuild of a new facility called the Orleans Justice Center. In 2008, the jail was called one of the deadliest in the nation. In 2012, a group representing ten incarcerated men sued Gusman for unconstitutionally dangerous jail conditions, including endemic violence committed by guards. Incarceration Transparency, a project out of the Loyola University New Orleans College of Law, documented eighteen deaths at the jail between 2015 and 2021. Most of those people, like most of the jail population, were awaiting trial, often for nonviolent crimes.

Hutson was an unusual candidate for sheriff, not just because she was a Black woman (and would become the first Black woman to hold the office in

New Orleans). She had never been a law enforcement officer but instead served for over a decade as a police monitor for the city of New Orleans. (In New Orleans, the sheriff manages the jail, and the New Orleans Police Department conducts patrols, investigates crimes, and makes arrests.)

She has a background steeped in activism. When she was a teenager, she said, her grandfather was shot and killed by a sheriff in East Texas, which is where she grew up, an incident that Hutson credits for her inspiration to use her education and activism to fight racism. As a college student at the University of Pennsylvania, she was involved in political activism, protesting apartheid in South Africa and agitating for change after the 1985 MOVE bombing, when the Philadelphia police bombed an entire city block in a Black neighborhood, killing six adults and five children. After law school, she worked as a prosecutor and oversaw police in Austin, Texas, and Los Angeles before landing in New Orleans. "I'm not looking at it from [a cop's] perspective at all," Hutson said in an interview. "I believe that this system—this system has got to be fundamentally changed."

She gained the support of many longtime criminal system reform advocates in the city. Some of them had supported Gusman in the past. Norris Henderson, founder and executive director of Voice of the Experienced, a grassroots organization run by formerly incarcerated people fighting for criminal justice reform, who has worked with Gusman before, put it bluntly: "When you can't protect people inside of a jail, when you can't provide the quality of care inside of the jail, it's time to move on."

Hutson appeared not just to be committed to major reform, but she even expressed understanding for those seeking to abolish all jails. "I think we can get [to a world without jails] if we try. And so that's what I want to do. . . . Is it going to happen in my lifetime? I don't know. But I definitely want to do my part."

"I do not believe a single candidate can be our salvation," says Sade Dumas, executive director of the Orleans Parish Prison Reform Coalition

(OPPRC), a group that has long worked to reform conditions in the jail. "But I believe a progressive sheriff can make things less worse by refusing to enact regressive, harmful practices."

Dumas is a native of New Orleans and has worked for decades to decarcerate what she calls the "most incarcerated city in the most incarcerated state in the most incarcerated country in the world," quoting ex-mayor Mitch Landrieu. She is striking, with expressive features and long dark hair parted artfully on the side. Her brother was incarcerated for a nonviolent offense, which had made her aware of both the need to reduce jail populations and the importance of improving conditions inside the jail.

Dumas argued that reformers must focus both on reducing jail populations and on improving conditions, where she thought Hutson could play an important role: "We must work to reduce incarceration while improving conditions for people in there. Jail is not a place where people can thrive." Hutson, she added, was "not a politician and I think that's what attracts people to her."

Dumas had also worked with Gusman, pressuring him to reduce the jail population below his initial projections. OPPRC successfully strong-armed the city and sheriff to substantially reduce the size of the jail, so that now the incarcerated population is capped below 1,300, after a great deal of back-and-forth. Dumas and other advocates have claimed that Gusman never believed that the jail populations could be reduced, which led him to constantly thwart reform proposals.

Electing Hutson was the next step. Dumas became the cochair of PAC for Justice, a political action group that helped to elect Hutson despite the incumbent's entrenched financial resources and political support in the city. (Dumas also served on Hutson's transition team as a community coordinator.) In her victory speech in December of 2021, Hutson said, "We will not harm them, we will not kill them, we will help our neighbors."

But she faced a lot of obstacles. For one thing, she was not part of the good old boys' club—the media and her critics used misogynistic and racist tropes to mock her before and after the election. One community organizer told me that Hutson was honest to a fault, which sometimes hurt her ability to get things done in a city where nepotism and political dynasties matter a lot. "She really believes in fairness and transparent systems. She believes that government can function properly," she said. ("I'm not a great politician," Hutson confessed to me.)

Hutson also struggled to keep her campaign promises because of recalcitrant city officials and existing problems under Gusman. During the campaign, she called for the city to replace Wellpath, the health-care provider for the jail, which was blamed for many of the deaths. But there was no other eligible offer, forcing the city to return to the existing provider.

As for her major campaign promise—to stop the construction of a new $109 million jail specially designed to care for those who require special medical care, called "Phase III"—Hutson seemed to have lost the fight. The court denied a 2023 legal challenge, supported by Hutson, writing, "While we have been engaged in endless debate and hand-wringing, inmates in the care of the Sheriff have suffered and continue to suffer needlessly." The jail construction has begun, and the new sheriff seems to be unable to stop it. Dumas argued that even if Phase III construction moves forward, it should not be seen as a failure of organizers. Even worse, jail deaths did not stop. In June of 2022, a man jumped from the second story, breaking his spine; the next month, another died in a fight.

All these arduous efforts to elect reform-minded sheriffs reveal the fundamental truth: sheriffs are deeply intertwined with other aspects of the criminal legal system. They operate in connection with other county officials, the courts, and the constraints of arrest and incarceration. Electing sheriffs committed to reducing jail populations, arresting fewer people, and disentangling their departments from ICE has resulting in fewer deportations and fewer people in jail. In New Orleans, for example, the decades-long fight has led to a much smaller jail. But these electoral wins, hard-won as they are, remain entrenched in an old system, one where sheriff discretion is less effective and where most of the people who hold the office are determined to resist reform and keep the office the same as it ever was. (Louisiana has sixty-four parish sheriffs, and several endorsed Gusman. None endorsed Hutson.)

It would be easier if electing a new sheriff could be a lever that produces immediate effect. But, sadly, the discretion so valorized by the far-right sheriff's movement appears more difficult to extend to sheriffs attempting to make progressive change.

———

Certainly, electing new sheriffs seems like the most direct way to effect change, but is it enough? To answer that question, I talked to Anne Levinson, a Washington State lawyer, retired judge, and longtime police monitor who has been working on law enforcement reform for decades.

Levinson began her social justice career in college when she filed a Title IX complaint after the University of Kansas defunded and discontinued women's field hockey. In law school, she knew she wanted to focus on social justice issues and, after graduation, became deputy mayor for Seattle's first Black mayor. As a judge, she founded the first mental health courts and was one of the first openly LGBTQ+ public officials. In 2008, she organized a group of women to buy the Seattle Storm, the women's professional basketball team, from the Seattle SuperSonics. All of these experiences allow her to bring a bird's-eye view to the problem of sheriff reform.

Levinson emphasized that all of her experience has led her to think about "really giving voice to those most impacted." Many current processes to hold sheriffs accountable do not consider the community's needs.

It also so happens that Levinson is located in Washington State, which has long struggled with far-right sheriffs. This became particularly apparent during COVID. In 2020, a coalition that included public defenders and racial justice advocates tried to recall Adam Fortney, the sheriff of Snohomish

County, which is just north of Seattle. While this effort was not successful, Fortney was ousted from office in 2022 through election. The election might not have been possible had the recall not brought many of Fortney's abuses of office to light.

Fortney, who became sheriff in 2020, ran a campaign based on returning "law and order" to the sheriff's office, arguing that his administration would function as a "paramilitary organization" and promising to empower deputies to make more arrests. He attacked the prior sheriff, Ty Trenary, a Democrat, for engaging in "catch and release" practices by issuing citations in lieu of arresting people for small-scale crimes.

After taking office, Fortney not only followed through on his promises to allow deputies to make more arrests but he also made the questionable decision to rehire three deputies fired by Trenary for misconduct and excessive use of force. (The deputies in question also happened to be Fortney supporters.) Then, when COVID hit Washington State, Fortney was among the many sheriffs who refused to enforce state health regulations.

"As your elected sheriff I will always put your constitutional rights above politics or popular opinion," he declared via his Facebook page on April 21.

Shortly after Fortney's announcement, a local barber said he was inspired to open his shop—no masks, no social distancing—to the chagrin of others in the community. After a Snohomish man made violent threats against Governor Jay Inslee, the Snohomish County prosecutor, Adam Cornell, a Democrat, wrote that Sheriff Fortney's words were "akin to yelling 'fire' in a crowded theater." Cornell described Fortney's post as "a call to defy public health officials . . . a pronouncement that the medical science . . . is flawed and not to be trusted."

———————

Sheriffs are subject to some form of recall or removal in every state. There are three basic mechanisms to recall a sheriff, all of which are limited to circumstances in which a sheriff violated his oath of office or committed other types of misconduct. The first way, available in Florida and New York, is removal by a governor. The second way is for recall proponents to gather enough signatures for a ballot measure. The residents of the county can then decide by popular vote.

The third method is somewhat of a hybrid and involves some sort of fact-finding—either a judge or other authority evaluates the evidence for a recall—then there is a signature-gathering phase, then a recall election.

Because recalling a sheriff involves a lot of hurdles, it isn't done very often. I conducted a search of recalls, and while there are some examples in every state, many happened decades ago. This can leave communities unsure of what to do when their sheriff breaks the law. In North Carolina, for example, a sheriff hired a contract killer to murder a deputy who had recorded him making racist comments. The deputy planned to use these recordings to ruin the sheriff's political career. This seemed like obvious misconduct, but county leaders were stymied. The removal statute was ambiguous—it included removal for "willful misconduct" and "intoxication." The sheriff could also be removed if convicted of a felony. But what to do in the meantime, especially for something so egregious? Ultimately bowing to political pressure, the sheriff agreed to a suspension and was criminally indicted. While the situation was resolved, it did not result in a clarification of the recall procedure.

Beyond the confusion of the recall process itself, sheriffs can be recalled only for specific reasons that vary by state. Washington State law requires that a sheriff can be recalled only for "an act or acts of malfeasance, misfeasance, or violation of oath of office." The oath of office, which Fortney signed when he took office, states, "I will support the Constitution and Laws of the United States and the Constitution and Laws of the State of Washington and the provisions of the Charter and Ordinances of Snohomish County."

In 2020, Snohomish County advocates attempted a recall based on

Fortney's behavior in office, including his refusal to enforce COVID health mandates. In early June, after an extensive hearing in which both sides presented their case, a judge allowed the recall to proceed. Fortney appealed to the state supreme court, which agreed with the recall advocates.

In a written opinion explaining the decision, Justice Mary Yu, writing for the majority, pointed out that Fortney's "express refusal to enforce the law could be interpreted as a catalyst for action" and argued that, even though law enforcement can exercise discretion, their decisions must not be "manifestly unreasonable." "Fortney does not have the authority as Snohomish County sheriff to determine the constitutionality of laws. That is the role of the courts," she wrote in an incredibly rare legal moment.

Despite this historic win, the recall petition failed because organizers were unable to get enough signatures, which the recall advocates attributed to the challenges of COVID. After hundreds of unpaid hours and extensive effort on the part of community members, Fortney remained in office.

In 2022, Susanna Johnson, a longtime law enforcement officer who worked under the previous sheriff, ran against Fortney. She was supported by a range of reform organizations, including the county attorney, Adam Cornell, who wrote a letter criticizing Fortney's COVID rants. Juan Peralez, president of the local community group Uniting Law Enforcement & Communities (UNIDOS), echoed the sentiment of many who work to elect reform-minded sheriffs: "Things are not going to change unless we have people inside the department who are going to do it."

Dumas in New Orleans had emphasized this to me as well—the people in the community are the ones best situated to decide what reforms are necessary and needed to be involved through official channels. "It is important to listen to people who are directly affected. No one knows more than a person who has lived through it," she told me.

Thinking about the troubles Hutson faced in her campaign and tenure as sheriff thus far, I asked Johnson her views on running as a woman and a reform-minded sheriff. Like Hutson, Johnson did not see herself as a politician and put her campaign as a matter of urgency. "I'm only involved because, honestly, everybody's intimidated by this guy. And nobody would step up," she told me. The community's frustration over Fortney's "constitutional sheriff" ideas enabled Johnson to form a large coalition of support, including former sheriffs and politicians from both political parties. (Johnson is a Democrat.)

In 2023, Susanna Johnson was elected Snohomish County sheriff and was sworn into office in 2024. She was also the first woman to hold the role of sheriff in the county and faced attacks from Fortney that she was "soft on crime" and lacked field experience, even though Johnson had more experience at all levels of law enforcement than Fortney did. "I'm sure there's people out there who won't vote for me because I'm a woman. And I've also encountered people that will vote for me just because I'm a woman, which is weird. But I get that because, like, you know, we're tired of the good old boy system," she told me.

I asked Johnson the question I always do, especially considering Susan Hutson's rocky tenure as sheriff. Her response was refreshingly honest: "It could take a long time to turn a ship like that. But every day, there's an opportunity to do a little bit better. . . . If you're trying to do the right thing, even when you have those setbacks, you're facing the right direction. And it'll be okay."

———————

Levinson pointed out to me that reforming sheriffs county by county is inherently a limited and slow process. "If you go agency by agency, or contract by contract, jurisdiction by jurisdiction," she said, it would take so long that she would "be in a nursing home." So, she argued, "you need to try to go state level whenever you have a window of opportunity."

After the protests against police violence in 2020, many police agencies saw the need for change. But sheriffs remain uniquely hostile to reform. For example, in 2021, when a federal bipartisan commission proposed a series of basic police reforms, mostly limiting use of force and creating accountability structures to track officers who were found guilty of misconduct, the National Sheriffs' Association refused to sign on to the legislation. Many other major law enforcement groups did, even the National Fraternal Order of Police, whose spokesperson expressed frustration with the NSA and said the group "is often upset, and sometimes it is difficult to ascertain the exact reason for it."

Federal regulations, however, cannot bind county sheriffs, who are governed by state law. The Washington Coalition for Police Accountability has worked to create state laws that would require sheriffs and their deputies (including volunteer posse members) to abide by many of the same training and certification requirements as other law enforcement.

Also, in 2021, Washington State passed a number of law enforcement reforms, which include more transparency into misconduct investigations and more rigorous background checks. But sheriffs were excluded from the background check requirements. In early 2024, the state legislature began considering a bill that would require all law enforcement officials—including sheriffs—to submit to a background investigation, which might include membership in violent extremist groups, as well as maintain all training requirements. In essence, sheriffs would be required to adhere to the same standards as all other law enforcement officials. (Levinson called the commonsense proposal "not radical.") At a January 2024 legislative hearing, supporters described the bill as "good governance," and many of the speakers were specifically concerned about far-right sheriffs who were affiliated with groups like the CSPOA and the Oath Keepers.

The Washington State Sheriffs' Association launched into attack mode, writing a letter to call the proposals "undemocratic and politically dangerous" as well as unconstitutional. The association's policy director asked, "Is the sheriff an employee of the county or an elected office?" in describing his group's strong objections to the bill, implying that the legislature could not put additional requirements on sheriffs as an elected office.

Part of the problem is structural. Because sheriffs have their office and duties enshrined in state constitutions, legislatures are often not empowered to change their role directly. Some of this is based on the myth created by sheriffs themselves, not actual case law or legislation. Sheriffs are written into the state constitution in thirty-three states and created by state statute in thirteen states. Every state has statutes that govern the sheriff's office. Dramatic changes, like removing powers, generally require a state constitutional amendment. As a result, the general rule remains that courts, local government, and state government cannot take powers away from the sheriff. But, again, in many states no one has tried, and, as Levinson pointed out to me in our conversation, legislatures have not created coherent and clear procedures.

The truth is that most states are wary of legislating sheriffs. For one thing, every state has a state sheriffs' association, which lobbies the state government on changes to the criminal legal system and policing. In many states, the sheriffs' association holds a lot of weight. Further, in some states, the legislators simply don't know how sheriffs are governed and what their options are. Many legislators prefer to leave them alone, figuring that their impact is limited to rural regions anyway. Finally, legislators rely on the sheriff for local endorsements and are reluctant to fight with their sheriff for fear it will damage their future reelection chances.

Christy Lopez, a Georgetown law professor who worked for the Department of Justice, wrote in the *Washington Post*, "Sheriffs resisting police reform efforts, whether or not they are part of the constitutional sheriff movement, have cited its false tenets. These assertions are often accepted by lawmakers without challenge—thus moving anti-government and racist ideas from the fringe to the policymaking mainstream."

On top of all this, while sheriffs as a group remain hard to reform, removing or reforming the office to prevent right-wing radicalization has been one of the most difficult tasks. Some constitutional sheriffs frame their actions as "reform," by which they mean reform not to increase racial justice but to widen the gap between those favored by the police and those who are not. In many cases, far-right sheriffs are extremely popular with the electorate, making recalls and elections difficult.

Levinson believes that the increased visibility and extreme rhetoric of the constitutional sheriff movement may be partially to blame for the entrenchment of sheriffs everywhere. "The whole rhetoric," she explained, talking about constitutional sheriffs, "is not accidental. They are changing the narrative." As a result of the constitutional sheriff belief that sheriffs have absolute authority, all efforts at reform become an existential battle, rather than an act of compromise. She called the strategy "very Trumpian."

She went on to say that the far-right sheriffs have framed all sorts of issues, from COVID protections to elections to abuse of power, as an issue of "impeding or infringing on the integrity of their independent elected position." The sheriffs, she said, "pound their chests and say, 'We're independently elected. You can't do this.' But that's just not true."

---

Since the beginning of the Black Lives Matter movement in 2012, community advocates, researchers, and lawyers have pressured police departments to establish civilian oversight commissions. These commissions come in many forms. Some are advisory only, which means that their recommendations can be ignored. Others have the power to subpoena documents and conduct investigations, bringing recalcitrant law enforcement officers to court if they refuse to testify.

While many police departments now have oversight and civilian review, few sheriffs do. After 2020, politicians and advocates looked to new policies and legislation to defund or regulate police forces. Sheriffs present an obstacle because their elected positions and independent authority give them broad fiat to manage their jails and personnel as well as directly decide their departments' policies.

On the local level, the county governments are typically entrusted with aspects like managing the sheriffs' budgets. But county officials, who are generally considered on the same level as the sheriff, not superior, cannot tell the sheriff how to hire or fire, nor can they help set policy. In Florida, sheriffs have a statutory right to be "adequately funded" and can actually appeal straight to the governor if they think their funding is inadequate.

Because it is so hard to change laws regarding sheriffs, some counties have implemented civilian oversight boards or civilian review boards. In 2020, California passed a law that permitted each county to create an oversight board for their sheriff's office. As of early 2024, twelve counties have done so or plan to do so. These take a few different forms. Most of them are a group of six to ten people who are appointed by different constituencies. Oversight boards serve a few functions. Some set policies. Others review incidents like use of force or corruption. Some are relatively weak and can only make suggestions to the sheriff's office, which the sheriff does not need to follow.

———

In 2016, a newly elected Los Angeles County Board of Supervisors voted to approve a civilian oversight commission for the sheriff's department, which is the largest sheriff's office in the country with nearly twenty thousand employees, half of them sworn deputies, and a budget of just under $4 billion.

The Los Angeles Sheriff's Department has a long history of misconduct. Deputy gangs, with names like "the Punishers," "the Grim Reapers," "the Wayside Whities," and "the Vikings," with member tattoos to match, have plagued Los Angeles for over fifty years, as detailed in a January 2021 report by LMU Loyola Law School, which delineated eighteen distinct gangs. As one gang framed it in their pamphlet for prospective members, "We are not afraid to get our hands dirty."

Writer Cerise Castle explained in her series "A Tradition of Violence" that these gangs have not only protected their members, they have also risen through the ranks of the department. Those who have defected or snitched on gang activity are outcasts, often harassed with rumors and threats.

In 1998, Sheriff Lee Baca won his first election. Baca promoted many known deputy-gang members, including Paul Tanaka, who would later be convicted of crimes related to his actions in the LASD, and encouraged his deputies to work in "the gray area," which created the perception that he condoned deputy gangs and their occasionally excessive violence. Baca was forced to resign in 2014 after the ACLU released a report revealing rampant abuse inside the jail, largely caused by a powerful deputy gang. In 2017, he was convicted and sent to prison for his role in running a scheme of undercover informants in the jail and attempting to cover it up. After an interim sheriff, voters in 2014 elected a new sheriff, Jim McDonnell, formerly a police chief in Long Beach, who was generally supportive of oversight.

The Civilian Oversight Commission was created in the wake of Baca's criminal conviction with the goal of providing more transparency into the workings of the LASD. The commission has nine members. Four are appointed by the supervisors collectively, and the other five are picked individually by each of the five Los Angeles County supervisors. The oversight commission operates with the relatively new Inspector General's Office, which investigates, collects, and reviews documents and conducts interviews. The reports from the inspector general get used by the COC to make decisions.

In 2018, voters ousted McDonnell and elected Alex Villanueva, a compact Latino man with a swagger from his years as a street cop, a strong contrast to his two predecessors, white men who, despite their decades of law enforcement experience, wore suits and ties. Villanueva was more likely to appear in uniform astride a horse or in a low-rider convertible during a car parade. As a strong supporter of his deputies, he campaigned as scornful of the higher-ups, who didn't understand the brutal realities of police work.

One of Villanueva's first acts was to create a "truth and reconciliation" committee inside the department that would review the cases of deputies who had been fired by the previous administration. He rehired one deputy accused of violently assaulting an ex-girlfriend.

For this, he earned the ire of the Los Angeles County Board of Supervisors, whose members argued Villanueva had violated the law. Villanueva refused to talk to the Civilian Oversight Commission, forcing it to ask a judge for a court order, which meant that the sheriff came to answer questions only because he was facing incarceration in his own jail.

Community members began to complain that under Villanueva there were more incidents of violence and extrajudicial deputy killings. In a 2020 incident, Miguel Vega and Christopher Hernandez, two LASD deputies, shot and killed eighteen-year-old Andres Guardado, a baby-faced teenager who liked to bring groceries to his elderly neighbor. According to a lawsuit filed by the family, who settled for $8 million in 2022, Vega and Hernandez killed Guardado with five shots in his back. The two deputies were not criminally charged for the shooting, but both were terminated from the department and sentenced to federal prison time for unlawfully detaining a twenty-three-year-old skateboarder a few months prior. After the deputies put their victim into the back of their patrol car, Vega crashed the vehicle during a car chase and injured the young man.

This was all just a few weeks after the murder of George Floyd in Minneapolis. For the next few days, the Compton neighborhood was roiled by protests. Jennifer Guardado, Andres's sister, decried the act as murder, plain and simple, to a local news crew: "Even if this is the last day I breathe, I'm not holding this back because I feel it in my soul that my brother was murdered, and this was covered up." Los Angeles Sheriff's Department deputies attacked the protesters—which included the Guardado family and small children from the neighborhood—with rubber bullets and pepper spray. Seven protesters were arrested.

Over the course of Villanueva's tenure, deputy shootings increased, many attributed to deputy gangs. The sheriff also began to harass his critics, assembling a special unit dedicated to the task.

In 2022, a coalition of activists worked hard to vote Villanueva out of office. The new sheriff, the onetime police chief of Long Beach, Robert Luna, has established a more cordial relationship with the Civilian Oversight Commission, which held a series of hearings about the deputy gang problem, seeking to determine the extent of membership.

I asked Castle about the utility of the COC hearings, which did force many high-ranking sworn officers of the sheriff's department to testify under oath about their knowledge of gangs. She pointed out that there is a publicly available list of currently and formerly employed gang members inside the LASD (mostly compiled by Castle). She told me that she thought the COC lacked the power to force the department to change, which would require the firing of deputies accused of misconduct as well as more power for the COC to implement their recommendations. A recent report by the Office of the Inspector General, which has investigatory authority over the sheriff's office, looking at recommendations issued to the sheriff's department from 2019 through 2022, found that 105 out of 136 had not been implemented, including the COC's request that the LASD conduct investigations into the existence of deputy gangs.

———

The years since 2020 have presented a challenge in all areas of criminal system reform. The combined impact of a rise in crime—perceived and actual—and COVID, on top of political instability, has meant that most sheriff's offices, like all law enforcement in the country, have received more funding than they did before. Much of this has come from President Joe Biden, who has taken seriously his promise to "fund the police."

At the same time, the massive momentum for criminal system reform gained during the summer of 2020 has translated into renewed calls for a focus on the sheriff's office, which previously was not a serious target for reform. Groups that focused on immigration came together with groups that were concerned about incarceration to form coalitions that tried to kick "constitutional" sheriffs out of office and pushed for policies that would lead to fewer people in jail and prison. Change has been difficult and slow going.

This leads to how the far-right sheriff movement connects to sheriffs and their office generally. Far-right sheriffs claim discretion and the right to protect communities from an overreaching federal government. But, as Levinson pointed out to me, the propaganda of far-right sheriffs has trickled down to create a narrative that the position of sheriff is a unique elected office that cannot be reformed in the same way other law enforcement departments are. This story goes unchallenged because, for so long, it has been the dominant narrative, promulgated by sheriffs and their organizations, like the National Sheriffs' Association and state associations.

The idea that sheriffs are uniquely above the law cultivates a myth that sheriffs not only do not need reform but that reform is anathema to the historical nature of the office. Particularly taking into consideration the places where sheriffs have the most power—rural counties, the South, and the West—the most powerful constituencies in those regions are those who do not seek criminal justice reform. In fact, they probably want the opposite. Because of these places' histories of racist voter suppression, the pantheon of elected sheriffs do not, in fact, represent the will of the majority. So the sheriffs themselves rely upon a history that is fraught with white supremacy.

Once sheriffs are elected, even if those individuals intend to use their power of discretion to implement reform-minded changes to decrease the impact of mass incarceration, they face a powerful external structure in the form of courts, judges, county leaders, and campaign donors who seek to preserve the office of sheriff as it is. In fact, the National Sheriffs' Association promotes the view that sheriffs themselves are there to protect existing hierarchies, not change them, writing in one document, "The Office of Sheriff protects the Public from undue political influence on a day-to-day basis on local law enforcement and public safety issues." Even state sheriffs' associations will react to blunt the impact of more progressive sheriffs because the system is so designed to tend toward stasis. It is hard to implement criminal system reforms; it is very hard to change an office so imbued with nostalgia.

The efforts—some successful and some not—to elect Black sheriffs in the segregated South show that the resistance to reform exceeds the amount of reform a sheriff can actually accomplish. The same structures that preserve the rights of white men stop working once they are being used to mete out greater justice to those who have been disproportionately impacted. The culture of impunity is so entrenched in the sheriff's office that even with legislation, oversight, and electoral success, change comes only in small steps.

# THIRTEEN

# THE GATHERING STORM

## *Beyond Constitutional Sheriffs*

ON AN EARLY OCTOBER MORNING IN 2022, OVER A DOZEN armed men patrolled the parking lot of a small church that lay between scrub brush and a strip mall offering haircuts and shipping services. They were plainly having a wonderful time. Two documentary crews had come that day to Yavapai County, Arizona, about two hours north of Phoenix, to attend a biweekly meeting of the Yavapai County Preparedness Team (YCPT), which, according to the group, is the largest remaining branch of the Oath Keepers. A journalist from Germany shoved her microphone into the faces of men walking purposefully around the parking lot, securing the perimeter against an invisible enemy.

Inside, inspirational Bible quotes with illustrations lined the walls. Men and women in black-and-yellow Oath Keeper garb ("Guardians of the Republic. Not on Our Watch") set up tables with informational pamphlets along the walls of the gymnasium. There were bumper stickers to support Kari Lake, "Black the Blue," and Oath Keeper T-shirts, and a raffle for an AR-15, as well as one for a "package of survival foods." Chairs sat in neat rows.

The area under the basketball hoop was transformed into a stage. Above the hoop was a gigantic black-and-white rendering of Jesus with the crown of thorns. The YCPT sign unfurled below as a backdrop. The left side of the yellow sign provided a list of nightmare scenarios: "Fires/Floods. Food Shortages. Economic Collapse. EMP Strikes." (EMP stands for "electromagnetic pulse.") The right side read like a scouting wish list: "Communication (HAM radio). Food Preservation and Storage. Medical Skills."

Before the meeting began, two women in their sixties sitting next to me were whispering about the inefficacy of the COVID vaccine. One seemed convinced it was an intentional conspiracy against older Americans. "And then the elderly started dying first," she explained. She saw me, and her lips transformed into a thin line.

The meeting began with a prayer. "Help us to use all the stuff that we learn today in our everyday lives and to influence our friends and neighbors and family that we might influence people to make a better country," intoned a man with a shock of white beard and hair. He wore a long-sleeve Oath Keepers T-shirt and a sidearm like almost everyone there, men and women. The men all removed their baseball caps and looked to the floor, sober and solemn. I stared at the banner, imagining the apocalypse, then bent my head as well.

This group of people were here to listen to Richard Mack speak. They believed in the power of the sheriff to enforce or fail to enforce the laws that they believed would keep their community safe from outsiders, which included the state and federal government. More important, this group was dedicated to localism, the idea that their work in churches and town halls and in their own homes would redeem the country. While they were not violent by nature, they were prepared for violence, judging by the number of firearms, because they believed the end-times were near. The sheriff served as their legitimate government proxy, the only official whose word they would heed.

The YCPT is a 50I(c)(3) led by Jim Arroyo, a compact, loud man of retirement age with a trim white goatee, who says he was an Army Ranger and has a passion for disaster preparedness. Commanding the podium, Arroyo wore a headset, like an aerobics instructor.

In speaking to the media in the room, Arroyo made it abundantly clear that their group split from the national Oath Keepers organization. Arroyo said he was not in D.C. on January 6 and would never go to D.C. under any conditions. He didn't even like Donald Trump that much. Explaining the Oath Keepers split, Arroyo said, "They won the dumbass contest on January the six."

The revelations of the January 6 committee as well as the prosecutions of the leaders of the Proud Boys and Oath Keepers had served to motivate many people affiliated with the militia movement to distance themselves from those who were now going to spend time in jail and prison. Arroyo wanted to be clear that his group had nothing to do with Stewart Rhodes.

"Are we a militia?" he asked the audience, eager to distance his organization from the Oath Keepers in front of reporters from at least three different publications and two film crews who crowded the room with cameras.

Everyone responded with a resounding "No!"

Arroyo instead described the YCPT as an "educational organization that mostly teaches about the Constitution." He resented that the media had described the group as a militia, but his explanation was not all that convincing to me. "To be a militia, you have to have a unit. You also have to have a uniform and a rank structure. And you have to be assigned to some entity within the United States military. I'm gonna give you a quick example. I served in the California State Military Reserve in the state of California that is an unorganized militia. And I served in the 304th Infantry Battalion

[Regiment] assigned to the 40th Infantry Division of the U.S. Army National Guard. That's a real militia. That's how it works."

Is that how it works? I wondered. The California State Military Reserve is an all-volunteer organization. It doesn't have an official website. Its LinkedIn page says the group has "military duties [that] include assisting civil authorities during domestic emergencies and assisting in the mobilization and demobilization process of the National Guard." It is not the California State Guard, which is also a volunteer organization. But Arroyo talked quickly and confidently. I could see how it would be easy to take what he said as true and just move on.

Each meeting consisted of a mix of survivalism and conspiracy theories as well as what Arroyo describes as CPT: community preparedness training. "The whole concept of the CPT was to train the public—you—to be ready for natural and man-made disasters. Fire, flood, earthquake, tornado, hurricane, tsunami, space, aliens, whatever it might be." He then pointed to "man-made" disasters like economic collapse and nuclear war, which featured predominantly in the collective imagination of his audience.

This survivalist component was very important to Arroyo. It was also a vision of disaster that relied on individual competency, not collective survival. He told us, "You're being trained. . . . I'm gonna tell you, you're being trained to get out of the way to survive and stay home. Take care of yourself. Your family, your friends, your neighbors, your community. Whatever happens out there, you have no control over that. You can vote all you want. You have no control of the outcome of the big things. So, you need to be prepared for when it does go sideways."

Before the main meeting, the YCPT held a variety of more specialized group meetings, which, in the military lingo of the group, were called "units." They had different divisions. Some were focused on storing food and water for coming disasters. Others were about teaching people herbal remedies or how to protect their homes against inevitable invaders when the economy collapsed.

I sat through a session on herbal remedies led by a woman who touted the benefits of a variety of dried mushrooms to ameliorate pain and cure disease. Many of the people around me were veterans, mostly from the Gulf War. They wore MAGA hats, varieties of Desert Storm camouflage, T-shirts tucked into Wranglers, work boots, and, of course, sidearms. They passed around sample jars of dried fungus for everyone to examine.

Next to me, a wife poked her husband in the side. They were offering free mason jars for our own homemade herbal remedies. The husband stood to pick one up. "Get a few," the wife said quietly.

Attacks on the power grid and World War III were discussed with the same degree of credulity as inflation and wildfires. One of the YCPT projects was a "time bank," essentially a way for members to lease out their labor to others as a barter system. Arroyo describes the time bank as insurance against economic collapse: "So we set up a time bank, okay. We don't exchange money, gold, silver, rubles, anything else. It's time for labor. If you've never seen one of these, look it up." "Look it up" was one of his favorite phrases.

"Everyone is worried about civil war," Arroyo said. "All we do is threat assessment."

Arroyo spoke in a bullish way about the need to protect oneself from a nuclear attack. An expert introduced himself as an instructor on "nuclear war survival." "I have been trying to get everybody educated on how to survive. Potassium iodide. It floods the thyroid with good iodine," the expert said.

He provided other tips for protecting oneself, like sealing off doors and windows with plastic. A woman in front of me tapped out on her iPhone notes app: "NUCLEAR."

Arroyo added, "Pelosi and Biden are poking the bear. They are bringing in convoys, missile carriers with nuclear missiles on it right outside of Ukraine right now. You don't think this is real? You better start really thinking about it.

"Look it up," he concluded.

———————

Arroyo's other favorite phrase was "Read a history book," which he used as punctuation and chorus, interspersed with military-style commands.

"How about World War III? Anybody think we're there? Yeah, read a history book. World War III is underway, no two ways about it.

"Are we entering the beginning phases of a civil war in this country? Read a history book."

Less than a week before this meeting, the political wing of the YCPT—the Lions of Liberty—had formed an official watch group where members signed up to guard ballot drop boxes in two-hour shifts. In Arizona, early voting for the midterm elections had already begun, and there was a great deal of uncertainty among Democrats and Republicans about the voter turnout as well as worries about outright civil war.

The website said, "Contact us and we'll get in touch with Sheriff Rhodes, who is already aware of what we are doing and will do what he can." ("Rhodes" referred to Yavapai County sheriff David Rhodes, their elected sheriff.)

Brian Mounsey, a large, bearded man who bends his head and shoulders as tall people do and is on the board of the Lions of Liberty, spoke to the crowd. His rhetoric was focused on opposing "leftists," who are "trying to destroy this country." "'Our goal is . . . to win the spiritual battle for the soul of this nation,'" Mounsey read aloud from the group's manifesto. "'And to this end, we on the board mutually pledge to each other our Lives, our Fortunes, and our sacred honor.'"

The Lions' motto was "Servo Vigilante," which translated loosely into "watchful servant" and refers to a passage in the New Testament: "Be dressed ready for service and keep your lamps burning. . . . If the owner of the house had known at what hour the thief was coming, he would not have let his house be broken into."

Mounsey also urged people to sign up for "Operation Drop Box." "We are running Operation Drop Box, trying our best to cover as many hours as we can on these drop boxes. To keep election fraud from happening. So, we need volunteers; please sign up. Help us stop the steal. And I'll leave you with this: we will not go quietly into the night," he implored the room.

In late September, Sheriff Rhodes spoke at the YCPT meeting, shaking the hand of a preteen boy who was being inducted as the youngest known member of the Oath Keepers. Rhodes appeared to give the Lions of Liberty permission to monitor ballot drop boxes as armed militias. While he did not say outright that the 2020 election was stolen, he said that he had referred over a dozen cases of "fraud" to the local district attorney and that he supported efforts to ensure security at ballot boxes.

"We worked together to put cameras on all those ballot drop boxes. . . . [Y]ou provide public safety," he told the group. "I am going to be available and accessible to you." He said, in response to a question, that he would work with the county recorder to resolve all election disputes and promised to "escalate" any complaints about violation of election laws.

In a phone conversation, Kristin Greene, the public affairs and government relations director for the Yavapai County Sheriff's Office, told me the opposite: "The sheriff never said anything about assisting them." I also requested any records of voter fraud investigations and received only one: the county election officials referred to the sheriff's office a case in which a woman filled out her son's absentee ballot, not knowing it was a crime. The officer closed the case without recommending any charges.

The Lions of Liberty also sponsored a weekly protest at the local hospital in opposition to the vaccine mandate. Mounsey described the protests: "They're screaming at us, calling us blankety-blank traitors. Go figure.

We're the ones flying patriotic flags, and they're screaming [that] we're traitors."

After about twenty minutes of introductory speakers, the special guest bounded to the front. Mack was there specifically to address the topic of election security. Wearing a brilliant purple collared shirt and a black cowboy hat, the ex-sheriff looked on the verge of tears.

"There are millions of people in our country who call our Constitution evil," he said, lip quivering. Mack went on, describing this incredible mischaracterization as "part of their scheme to destroy America and replace it with their socialist agenda."

He claimed that Democrats and RINOs had intentionally lied about the security of the 2020 election. "It just goes on. And they keep getting away with"—Mack spread his palms in frustration—"murder."

"This whole thing is the greatest crime ever committed against the American people," he concluded, referring to the Big Lie. "And all we want and all we are asking for is that every county sheriff look at what happened in his county and make sure that we don't fall prey . . ." His voice trailed off. Mack then switched subjects to the conspiracy theory that election machines were hacked.

As for those who might be concerned about violence, Mack added a warning: "If you have your sheriff involved in the process, this will remain peaceful. If you do not have our sheriffs involved in the process, it will not remain peaceful." In support, he loosely quoted Thomas Jefferson about the need for an official to provide "peace and safety and liberty."

"You think this is going to remain peaceful?" Mack asked rhetorically. "They've got to have a place to turn."

———————

In the run-up to the 2022 election, media organizations and nonprofit groups were concerned about the threat of political violence, especially with the memory of January 6 still fresh. There were activated militia-style groups like the YCPT and self-styled voter vigilantes who partnered with sheriffs already primed by groups like the CSPOA to believe in rampant voter fraud. Groups like the Armed Conflict Location & Event Data Project (ACLED) were reporting on an increase in political violence. Everyone I spoke to was on edge.

But it was clear to me that the landscape was changing. It was not the same as January 6. For one thing, Biden was inaugurated as president with no major interruption. The Department of Justice has charged nearly one thousand people with crimes related to January 6. A jury would find Stewart Rhodes guilty of seditious conspiracy just a few weeks after the election and would sentence him in May of 2023 to eighteen years in prison.

As evidenced by my visit to the YCPT, militias were no longer organizing under large national umbrellas. They were, however, continuing to operate on a local level—the same people, the same distrust in government, the same commitment to armed rebellion—just on a smaller scale, such that they were less likely to run afoul of the law. When they did get close to the line of what was legal—a plan for militias to monitor ballot boxes—they backed down. Leaders had seen what happened to those involved in January 6 and did not want to risk prosecution, which would not only bring the threat of incarceration but also would mean the end of their job.

But the militia supporters didn't go away or change their minds. They pursued their policies locally, as Mack himself said, "county by county." What I saw now was the same. County by county, far-right groups were mobilizing and seeking sympathetic local leaders who would give them the leeway to promote their conspiracies. It turned out that the most sympathetic far-right local officials remained the county sheriffs. Mack was not the only person who had figured this out.

In November of 2022, Mack convened a meeting with his most trusted advisers and core supporters. Sam Bushman, who has been involved with the

CSPOA for many years, led the meeting. Bushman was a critical part of the CSPOA infrastructure because he owned an internet radio show that he used to broadcast a variety of far-right conspiracy theories, spout neo-Confederate ideas, and promote the CSPOA.

After a lengthy prayer about the "sacred mission of the CSPOA," Mack explained that he was accepting a new job with an organization called America's Frontline Doctors (AFLDS), a group that distributed ivermectin as a cure for COVID, and that he needed to step back from the CSPOA. AFLDS did not last long; it dissolved when leadership began to fight among themselves and has been mired in litigation.

Mack explained that he and his wife had multiple health problems. In addition to having had two heart attacks over the past decade, he is in his seventies and suffering from arthritis. As a result, the CSPOA would change. Bushman was now the CEO, running day-to-day operations. There would be an advisory board as well as new state chapter leaders. Mack would, of course, still be in charge. But, Bushman explained, he would no longer be in charge of everything.

Bushman cautioned against how the information would be interpreted by the media.

"I'm actually pretty good at shutting down reporters," he bragged, even as he advised people to "be loyal to the CSPOA."

The reorganization of the CSPOA reflects how the far-right sheriff movement has continued to adapt to political circumstances. While the changes to the CSPOA did not impact day-to-day operations—Mack continued to hold trainings—the organization leaders felt as though they were moving toward mainstream GOP politics. Other conservative groups, including groups running far-right candidates for school boards and other local offices, had constitutional sheriffs on their radar as potential partners. The years 2020 and 2021 were big for Mack. In addition to rallies, he had devoted himself to law enforcement training sessions, which a handful of states allowed him to give for continuing education credits. By 2022, both Texas and Arizona—big states for the CSPOA, where they had successfully recruited a lot of sheriffs—had retracted their endorsement of Mack's trainings based on Mack's declining credibility as a messenger and the lack of legal foundation for his principles.

Mack said that this did not deter him, and Bushman has repeated the idea that they will appeal these findings and continue the trainings. However, the trainings have gotten smaller, attracting far-right residents interested in learning how to make their sheriff more "constitutional," as opposed to attracting sheriffs themselves. The publicity Mack generated in 2020 meant more local, state, and even federal officials knew that he posed a threat of increasing recruitment to far-right causes.

Mack and the CSPOA organizers used the opportunity to reorganize and adopt the kinds of changes typical of a nonprofit. For example, they drafted an organizational plan. They engaged in media outreach, attempted to ban unfriendly media and court friendly media. Mack also responded aggressively to his critics, particularly anti-extremist researchers. When students from Arizona State University's journalism school did a series of stories on the CSPOA, Mack published a lengthy retort. I was not exempt from the treatment; he used his weekly calls ("Posse Roundups") to complain about reporters and mocked me in the process.

There was another reason, however. In the course of explaining why he was taking a step back, Mack cited the success of another far-right group successfully "training" sheriffs: the Claremont Institute, a think tank that backed Donald Trump's rise to power and helped plant the seeds for January 6.

———

Located in Southern California, the Claremont Institute sees itself as a bastion of intellectual conservatism. Formed in 1979 by dedicated students of

the conservative political philosopher Harry V. Jaffa, the think tank has remained small but elite, dedicated to reading and interpreting historical and
modern texts to prove that American ideals—individual liberty, Christian
virtue, and universal truth—need protection from encroaching progressive
elements. Claremont is an unusual institution in that it's not strictly "anti-
government," but it has shifted toward something like anti-democracy in its
pursuit of a platonic idea of American values. Journalist Katherine Stewart
wrote of Claremont, "In embodying a kind of nihilistic yearning to destroy
modernity, they have become an indispensable part of right-wing America's
evolution toward authoritarianism." As an institution, Claremont is less concerned with enacting policies or writing laws than it is with spreading conservative ideas through the recruitment and training of willing, upwardly
mobile individuals. Claremont has two publications, the staid *Claremont Review of Books* and the more freewheeling *American Mind*, that it uses as vehicles
to promote its ideas. The real muscle of Claremont, however, are the
fellowships, which bring together up-and-coming conservative thinkers, writers, and politicians, indoctrinate them with the core texts of conservative
philosophy, and, most important, create a community of like-minded
(mostly) men.

Many well-known conservatives have attended Claremont as fellows.
Laura Ingraham, Ben Shapiro, and Jack Posobiec (who in 2024 "called
for the end of democracy and a more explicitly Christian-focused government") all passed through Claremont. Another Claremont fellow was Nate
Hochman, a onetime staffer for Ron DeSantis's presidential campaign who
posted a video with Nazi imagery. Chris Rufo, another fellow, described
Claremont fellowships as a "brotherhood" where "people . . . predominantly
men, could get together, talk about important social and political issues,
look at and investigate philosophical ideas and then chart a practical way
forward."

Since 2016, the institute has dedicated itself to, as one journalist said, "making an intellectual case for Trump." The think tank has long bemoaned what they see as the liberal capture of the country and the unholy remaking of the Constitution as a document of "wokeness." The Claremont Institute was one of the few GOP think tanks willing to make a vigorous defense of Donald Trump as an ideal presidential nominee and a vessel for radically reshaping the country. While most right-leaning groups now support Trumpism, Claremont imbued the 2016 election with unique stakes. Michael Anton, a notable Claremont scholar, wrote an essay before the 2016 election titled "The Flight 93 Election," whose title referred to the airplane on 9/11 that did not crash into its intended target possibly because the passengers attempted to overcome the hijackers. The piece rallied readers by arguing, "You either charge the cockpit or you die. . . . [A] Hillary Clinton presidency is Russian Roulette with a semi-auto." He argued that the state of America had so devolved that drastic measures, like electing Trump, were necessary to save the country.

In 2017, Ryan Williams became president of the Claremont Institute, replacing sixty-three-year-old Michael Pack. Williams was then thirty-five, and he sought a younger crowd, including the so-called New Right, conservative thinkers who see themselves as edgy and less tied to traditional GOP values. His embrace of Trumpism was equally powerful, if not more so. "The mission of the Claremont Institute is to save Western civilization," he said in 2019. Combine his desire for creating a bigger coalition of conservatives with Claremont's California frontier roots and it makes sense that someone ended up with sheriffs as a cause worth adding. (Williams also appears interested in other law enforcement as well as sheriffs, according to emails I have reviewed.)

Claremont's role in perpetuating the Big Lie and in January 6 catapulted the think tank into the mainstream media as a specific and dangerous threat. Immediately after the election, the editors of the *American Mind*, the online, edgier publication, warned that Democrats were claiming to have won the election before all the votes were counted. The piece also argued that Democrats had changed election rules in certain battleground states, setting the stage for what would become one of the dominant conspiracy theories on the right: that the 2020 election was tainted by widespread election fraud.

Nothing really put Claremont in the spotlight more than the role of lawyer John Eastman, who wrote what is informally called the "coup memo," arguing that Trump could wrest power from the other branches of government to declare victory in 2020. Eastman, who is now facing disbarment for his role in January 6, tried to persuade then vice president Mike Pence not to certify the vote results; Pence refused, arguing that Eastman's ideas were not legally sound. You might think that Claremont would have sent him packing. They did not.

The first project that provided a definitive clue to why the Claremont Institute became interested in sheriffs is the result of a war game among conservative think tanks called the "79 Days" report, which envisioned doomsday should Trump lose the 2020 election. The report described a postapocalyptic hellscape that destabilized democracy through riots and other social unrest. Parts of the report portray a role for law enforcement engaging in rebellion against the federal government:

> There are rumors that several sheriffs in conservative counties throughout the country are hinting that they may deputize regular citizens into posses should the lawlessness come to their counties. Social media is ablaze with volunteers from Proud Boys, Three Percenters, and Oath Keepers and other Posse Comitatus groups to form posses.

There are other examples in this report of law enforcement officials defying politicians and unifying an armed citizenry, but the sheriffs are particularly remarkable because they give cover to known militia groups above and beyond the role of police chiefs (who in this scenario also defy the Democratic establishment and lock down urban areas to prevent imaginary unrest).

The 79 Days doomsday scenario felt frighteningly more like reality and not a simulation—a combination of revolutionary-style bloodlust disguised under a badge of law and order—all in the service of a grossly warped vision of America. The report also signaled that far-right intellectuals associated with the Claremont Institute saw sheriffs as an ally against the forces seeking to make America more diverse and equitable. Claremont saw in the constitutional sheriff movement something bigger, grander, and perhaps more antidemocratic than even Mack could imagine.

The sense that local law enforcement was important to the far-right movement appeared to have inspired Claremont's next phase. In the fall of 2021, the institute announced a new program, the Sheriffs Fellowship. An early email describing the intent of the program pointed to the "riots, lockdowns, and electoral disaster of 2020" to explain the need for "uncorrupted law enforcement officials . . . not beholden to bureaucratic masters" whose "jurisdictional latitude . . . places them on the front lines of the defense of civilization."

The same email goes on to cite the need for sheriffs to counter "the perversion of the justice system by which the revolutionary Left seeks to advance its totalitarian agenda." It also gives some practical reasons to focus on sheriffs. They are a "cost-effective" way to "restore the rule of law and America's founding principles." Like the constitutional sheriff movement, Claremont points to sheriffs as "intimately connected with, and answerable to, the people" and argues that their program will "equip sheriffs with strategic knowledge and end their isolation." In other words, it's an "old-fashioned Constitutional revival" translated into the intellectual veneer of the Claremont Institute.

The Claremont Sheriffs Fellowship struck me, at first blush, as an unlikely union of the intellectual right and the populist right. But Claremont and its affiliates have long looked to figures like Barry Goldwater and Donald

Trump to unite right-wing populism with their somewhat obsessive desire to defeat the liberals. (Jaffa was a speechwriter for Goldwater during the Arizonan's presidential campaign.) Considering Claremont's embrace of Trump and the Big Lie, the union feels like an appropriate sign of the times and the signal of the future to come.

In February of 2024, Kyle Shideler, director and senior analyst for homeland security and counterterrorism at the Center for Security Policy and a Claremont instructor for the Sheriffs Fellowship, wrote a paean to the sheriff as the most trusted form of law enforcement. He made two main points. First, he argued, sheriffs do not enforce "nanny state regulations and other intrusive government tedium," which makes them ideal law enforcement for an organization that seeks to dismantle the administrative state, as Claremont does. And second, he pointed to the elected nature of the sheriff, which provides them with "institutional trust." In other words, sheriffs are democratically elected but also useful to Claremont's authoritarian mission.

"Let's make 2024 the year of the American sheriff and see a wave of voters seeking to elect and empower sheriffs to defend their rights and communities," Shideler concluded.

Thus far, Claremont has trained about two dozen sheriffs in three classes of around eight chosen each year. Many of the chosen sheriffs were recommended by previous fellows. Most of the inaugural class were recruited by Claremont leadership personally.

A Claremont program director explained their recruitment strategy: "In our research on who to extend invitations to we took recommendations from friend [sic] of the institute and organizations but one thing that I know stood out to us about your leadership in these times has been how you courageously stood up to unconstitutional covid mandates."

Through public information requests and other reporting, I gained

insight into why the Claremont Institute recruited county sheriffs and what
they wanted those sheriffs to learn. What emerges is a portrait of how the far
right has a deep investment in sheriffs both because the office is already vulnerable to extremism and corruption and because sheriffs also enable and
encourage other extremist actors like vigilantes and militias to wreak havoc
on society. Claremont provides a historical and intellectual cover for sheriffs to continue their march into white Christian nationalism. For Claremont, the sheriffs are elected influencers who can push their message into the
mainstream.

The Sheriffs Fellowship itself is a weeklong, all-expenses-paid trip to the
Waterfront Beach Resort in Huntington Beach. Sheriffs received a stipend of
around $1,500, which some sheriffs turned down because it violated state
rules. Sheriff Eric Flowers, class of 2021, touted this as a positive: "As a
Sheriffs Fellow, my travel, lodging, and expenses are paid by the Claremont
Institute at no cost to our tax payers," he tweeted.

One of the most revelatory parts of the program was the application,
which required sheriffs to write a series of short essays. Some sheriffs, especially in 2021, were recruited for their resistance to COVID orders from
state and federal governments. According to Claremont, they were "selected
for their character, aptitude, accomplishments, zeal, and community reputation." Riverside County, California, sheriff Chad Bianco was specially invited
because he was "highly recommended by many friends of the Institute" and
praised for "the courageous stand [he has] taken over the past year." (Bianco
allied himself early on in the pandemic with anti-vaxxers and expressed
doubts about vaccine efficacy.)

In 2022 and 2023, there was more overlap between the followers of
Richard Mack and the Claremont fellows. Dar Leaf, for example, was a 2022
fellow. Eddy County, New Mexico, sheriff Mark Cage, another fellow, was
named a "top constitutional sheriff in America" by the American Police Officers Alliance, a group linked to the CSPOA founder.

Leaf's responses to the questionnaire illuminate the types of people Claremont recruited. In his essay responses, Leaf wrote that "the Civil Rights Act is racist," elections have been "infiltrated by foreign governments," and Davos and the World Economic Forum are "the central threat to our constitution and limited government." Leaf's paranoid fantasy continued: "This form of government is communism on steroids," he wrote. "The goal . . . ? The New world Order."

Throughout the week, the sheriffs attended a series of discussions, lectures, and fireside chats steeped in Claremont's heady intellectualism as exemplified by Harry Jaffa and his students and followers. The goal? Countering progressive ideals as part of a moral project to ensure the proper path of the country.

Upon acceptance, sheriffs received a box of books, which included Heather Mac Donald's *The War on Cops*, Thomas West's *The Political Theory of the American Founding*, and Charles Kesler's *Crisis of the Two Constitutions*, as well as a nearly three-hundred-page packet of readings, largely by Claremont scholars, and other wordy works in the Claremont canon. "Do not be alarmed by the amount of reading," an email from the organizer warned.

The program has shifted slightly over the three years it has been in place to reflect the Claremont Institute's changing priorities. One consistent emphasis has been on delegitimizing Black Lives Matter and undercutting progressive calls for reform to the criminal legal system. To do this, Claremont called on the Manhattan Institute's Heather Mac Donald, a lawyer who has written dozens of articles arguing that law enforcement in America does not have implicit or explicit racism. She, in fact, blames progressives and criminal system reformers for making people less safe and causing distress to the police. The assigned reading provided a message welcome to many sheriffs: "Are police nevertheless engaging in an epidemic of racist violence, as we hear daily? They are not." In other words, Mac Donald served to comfort law enforcement in their views that their jobs were hard and made harder by Democrats.

Sheriff Brian Hieatt of Tazewell County, Virginia, later echoed Mac Donald when he wrote in a reflection on his time with Claremont scholars, "We are facing movements across our Nation to take away punishments and any disciplinary actions from people committing crimes."

One of the main areas of emphasis included a historical tour through the Founding Fathers and founding documents of the United States as a way to emphasize that the intent behind the founding of America was a Christian nationalist vision of the world, with an emphasis on justifying the power of sheriffs to rectify what Claremont sees as a moral downfall. One of Claremont's tenets is a belief that movements for racial and gender equality are threatening not just the social order but the moral order as well.

Much of the programming was heavy on history, or at least the history according to Claremont. There is a big emphasis on the Founding Fathers, with readings like "The Statesmanship of Washington" and "The Question of Natural Justice: The Declaration of Independence." The Declaration of Independence and texts by George Washington and Thomas Jefferson were featured prominently, including Lincoln's 1857 speech on the *Dred Scott* decision, which was placed in tandem with *New York Times Magazine*'s editor in chief Jake Silverstein's essay about the 1619 Project. Claremont scholars use the Civil War as a key point to justify the concept of a Christian moral law for America; they argue that group movements or other forms of "identity politics" are dividing the nation because they conflict with a Jeffersonian approach to individual rights.

History then took a turn to the classical era, tracing the way in which both Claremont scholars and sheriffs have turned to a pre-America past in order to justify their power. The sheriffs delved into "The American Founding: Natural Law, Natural Rights & the Public Good; Religion & Morality," with readings by Thomas West and C. S. Lewis alongside a plethora of suggested works by Aristotle, Cicero, Justinian, St. Thomas Aquinas, and John Locke. The day ended with a fireside chat on "Antifa's Threat to the Constitution" with Shideler, the expert in national security who praises sheriffs as the ideal law enforcement.

Later learning focused on "Ratification: Natural Rights & the Public Good," which included letters between the Founding Fathers as well as Brutus No. I. The next two sessions—"Morality & Expediency in the Lincoln-Douglas Debates" and "The Statesmanship of Lincoln"—included selections from Jaffa's *Crisis of the House Divided*, a deeply foundational document to the institute. To temper the headiness of such materials, the sheriffs were treated to the requisite "optional group activity" and fireside chats with scholars like Arthur Milikh, who runs Claremont's center in Washington, D.C., and battles "woke" curriculums in higher education.

The reading packet includes "110 Rules of Civility and Decent Behavior," with gems like "When in company, put not your hands to any part of the body, not usually discovered" and "Let your recreations be manful not sinful." Such ideas are both embedded in the masculine history of the sheriff's office as well as an emphasis on the concept of a Christian natural law that justifies even violent protection.

Additional discussions covered various progressive movements and projects, largely, it seems, from the angle of learning about one's enemy—"countering the perversion of the justice system by which the revolutionary Left seeks to advance its totalitarian agenda," in Claremont-speak. This included sessions called "The Federalists vs. The Progressives" (Parts I and II), "Black Power & Identity Politics," and "The Sexual Revolution & Feminism." The last two sessions are notable in what they do include—strangely chopped-up readings from Stokely Carmichael on Black Power and Ibram X. Kendi on the idea of an anti-racist amendment (a bill that Claremont's Ryan Williams admitted to the *New York Times Magazine* would never go through)—as well as what they do not: feminist writers other than Betty Friedan. Race was plainly the focus, as the only reading about LGBTQ+ was a 1971 manifesto from the *Trans Liberation Newsletter,* and all such readings must have been focused on pushing the Claremont myth that modern movements that seek a reorientation of political power away from white men are a threat to the integrity of the nation. The day ended with a screening of the classic John Wayne Western *The Man Who Shot Liberty Valance,* perhaps to appeal to what Claremont thought were sheriff sensibilities and to imbue the weekend with a shared nostalgia.

Before the sheriffs left for the weekend, they covered "Claremont Conservativism"—Michael Anton and Plutarch—as well as "Defeating Critical Race Theory," which focused on higher education. The last session before group picture time was "The American Sheriff," which included James Madison's "On Property": "Government is instituted to protect property of every sort; as well that which lies in the various rights of individuals, as that which the term particularly expresses."

Claremont adjusted its programming in 2022 and 2023 to reflect the far right's changing priorities. For example, they added more material on the Second Amendment, which Claremont casts as a fundamental right sheriffs are uniquely in a position to protect. To that end, the sheriffs read a work by David Raney, a history professor at Hillsdale College, an extremely conservative school in Michigan. Raney's work seeks to find historical precedent for the disputed notion that the individual right to possess firearms is explicitly required by the Constitution. He writes, "[The Founding Fathers] recognized that this right was an extension of the natural rights enshrined in the Declaration of Independence (the rights to life, liberty, and the pursuit of happiness)." Indeed, according to Raney, it is not just that guns are permitted by the Constitution; rather, they are "a vital part of the Western tradition for millennia and . . . our birthright as a free people." Another Hillsdale professor, Kevin Slack, wrote in the *American Mind,* "Given the promise of tyranny, conservative intellectuals must openly ally with the AR-15 crowd."

In a class called "Immigration & National Security," sheriffs read a book by Brian Kennedy called *Communist China's War Inside America*. Kennedy has proposed that the COVID-19 pandemic was part of China's "war" against the United States, further writing that China provided inside intelligence and funding to Black Lives Matter and antifa as part of this master plan. The institute also added more discussion on immigration, specifically promoting the "white replacement" theory. The 2022 and 2023 courses kept the John Wayne movie, which evidently was a big hit with the lawmen.

Most interesting has been Claremont's shift to emphasize the threats of DEI (diversity, equity, and inclusion) initiatives and the so-called deep state, by which Claremont means the regulatory state and agencies like the ATF, EPA, and others. Both of these have been a clear target for the far right and Claremont in the run-up to 2024. The *New York Times* reported in January of 2024 that Claremont-affiliated academics and thinkers guided at least a dozen state leaders in crafting legislation that would eliminate DEI programs from higher education under the guise of protecting free speech. Many of the Claremont individuals most involved were the same ones training sheriffs, including Mac Donald and Scott Yenor (who gave a speech on "the evils that flow from feminism"). In both 2022 and 2023, the weeklong training ended with a celebratory dinner and the American Sheriff Award, presented to one sheriff from the previous year's class. On the last evening of the six-day training session in 2022, Sheriff Mark Lamb received a John Wayne statuette for what Claremont called "his steadfast defense of the Constitution, its blessings of liberty, and the American way of life." In 2023, the honoree was Riverside County sheriff Chad Bianco, who was not just on the leaked list of Oath Keepers that surfaced in 2021; he also has presided over a jail with dozens of deaths in the past few years. On Facebook, Bianco posted pictures of his receipt of the John Wayne statuette and a defiant message to his critics: "Apparently, wanting California to be what it once was, protecting you and your families from emboldened criminals, standing firm behind my oath to the Constitution of the greatest country in the world, being a voice of reason against decriminalization, and supporting the men and women of the Riverside County Sheriff's Office, makes me an extremist. I will wear that badge with honor!"

After I reported on the Claremont Sheriffs Fellows in 2022, Lamb wrote a response published online in the *American Mind*. Titled "A Vow to Serve," it features an image eerily reminiscent of his short-lived television series *American Sheriff*: "It's not simply enough—and here I address my fellow sheriffs— to feel that something is gravely wrong with this picture of our future. We have to understand the why." After accusing the media (and me) of a "gross and purposely obtuse response," he exhorted his fellow sheriffs, "Don't be intimidated. Justice, equality, rule of law, separation of powers, and consent of the governed will erode unless we make it our duty to understand their importance and function."

If sheriffs are slow to move toward a progressive vision, they appear willing to join the far right. While the Claremont program is small—thus far only around two dozen sheriffs have attended the training out of over three thousand sheriffs—the think tank has a history of elevating those with extreme views and placing them near seats of power. In a reflection on the fellowship, Mason County, Michigan, sheriff Kim Cole wrote, "I never saw this day coming to America. A time when Sheriffs are placed in a position to stand in the gap between citizens' rights and a government that seems to reach further and further over that line. Sheriffs must have a knowledge of where that line is and how to address the overreach with confidence." He then credits Claremont with the "Constitutional based knowledge" to make these choices.

One of the most interesting aspects of the Claremont Sheriffs Fellowship program is the union of anti-progressivism with the far right's conception of the unique heritage of America. While Claremont is not a religious movement in the same way some of the constitutional sheriff movements are, the leaders of the think tank are extremely concerned with moral decline, which they link to increased diversity and tolerance. Perhaps this idea of moral decline is best expressed by a poem the sheriffs read, "Annus Mirabilis," by the English poet Philip Larkin, which opens, "Sexual intercourse began / In nineteen sixty-three," and ends, "So life was never better than / In nineteen sixty-three."

The idea that sheriffs are somehow responsible for upholding traditional American values and preventing moral decline intersects with the original intent of founders of the far-right sheriff movements like W. Cleon Skousen. While Skousen and the Claremont founders were from very different backgrounds and cultural roots, they shared a view that linked changes in American culture—acceptance of LGBTQ+ people, increased immigration from non-European countries, the women's movement, racial justice movements—were fundamentally fraying the fabric of what made America unique.

Pulling law enforcement officials into this inherently radical project puts the entire notion of "criminal justice reform" at risk. Sheriffs, already prone to oppose reform both structurally and as individual politicians, now have a spiritual justification for their project. Not only does Claremont give sheriffs permission to ignore their historical complicity in oppression and violence, it also uplifts their role, making the task of policing and managing jails more than just enforcing laws and protecting the public; it allows sheriffs to see themselves as saviors, an alternative government structure that adheres to traditional American values and morals. In preserving the peace, sheriffs are preserving the republic. How, then, can progressives enact change to the office of sheriff without dismantling all of the values, rewriting all of the history, that sheriffs hold dear? Violence becomes righteous when the soul of the nation is at stake.

# CONCLUSION

AS I CONCLUDED WRITING AND REPORTING THIS BOOK IN early 2024, the mainstream GOP has adopted many of the ideas behind the constitutional sheriff movement. Among the Republican hopefuls for president, almost all called for defunding and abolishing at least some of the so-called alphabet agencies, like the IRS, FBI, and ATF. Vivek Ramaswamy, who had never held office before announcing a presidential campaign, said he would abolish the FBI, ATF, Department of Education, and Nuclear Regulatory Commission.

More Republican politicians call for an unlimited right to purchase, own, and carry firearms in public. Almost all of them agree that January 6 was simply a small rally and that there is probably a big problem with voter fraud. Legislators like Marjorie Taylor Greene used doctored footage of January 6 to spread conspiracy theories, and some members of the GOP seem intent on discrediting the January 6 investigation altogether.

Donald Trump is again the Republican nominee for president. He has set forth an agenda that is openly xenophobic and far to the right of the mainstream GOP. He has said, in all seriousness, that he would put immigrants in tent camps and dramatically speed up deportations without due process. Last time he was in office, Trump issued over four hundred executive actions to limit legal immigration and increase enforcement against undocumented immigrants. Campaigning on the Texas-Mexico border with Texas governor Greg Abbott, Trump has promised "a merit-based immigration system that protects American labor and promotes American values" and has threatened mass deportations akin to "Operation Wetback" in 1954.

His speeches since leaving office, even a year before the 2024 election, have focused on domestic threats that call to mind the screeds of William Potter Gale. Historians and political pundits have compared them to the speeches of Hitler and Mussolini. He has argued that the FBI and Department of Justice are unjustly persecuting him as part of a political project. At many of his rallies, he plays a choral rendition of the national anthem sung by individuals currently awaiting trial for crimes they committed on January 6.

We have a more conservative Supreme Court now, one whose far-right majority engages in a textualism that is akin to the way Richard Mack interprets the Constitution. In 2022, the Supreme Court overturned *Roe v. Wade*, returning the issue of abortion legality to the states, many of which have opted for draconian limits on the right of women to terminate pregnancies safely. That same year, the Supreme Court also ruled in favor of Second Amendment advocates in *New York State Rifle & Pistol Association v. Bruen*. The new legal test requires lawmakers to assess whether a gun regulation is in line with what the founders would have wanted. More than 100 million guns have been sold since 2020. More children have been killed by guns. In fact, gunfire is the leading cause of death in children in the United States. Interestingly, as sheriffs have been more supportive of unlimited firearm purchases, they have been unable to deal with the consequences of an armed populace. In 2022, law enforcement in Uvalde, Texas, stood by as a gunman killed nineteen children and two teachers and injured seventeen others at an elementary school. The sheriff who was nominally supposed to assist in coordinating the response (but did very little) had attended a CSPOA training during Mack's Texas Tour. He is still in office.

The summer of 2020 had some of the largest protests against police violence I have seen. Even in my suburban Texas neighborhood, a group of mostly white families marched with "Black Lives Matter" signs to show solidarity with protesters across the country. I genuinely thought there was the opportunity for change, and many politicians, including sheriffs, seemed willing to listen.

But quickly that moment vanished. My neighbors flew a "Let's Go Brandon" flag. In the local public elementary school's parking lot, a group of fathers and sons held a Trump rally complete with barbecue. High school–age boys were shouting for Trump and harassing people walking down the street, including me.

As these far-right forces returned, so did the modest policing reforms fade. A rise in gun violence since COVID led politicians, both Republican and Democrat, to embrace "law and order" politics. President Biden has committed more money to policing than ever—"We will not defund the police," he promised—money that goes to sheriff's departments regardless of the politics of the sheriff.

There is no question we live in dangerous times, times where the rise of racism, anti-immigration sentiment, and misogyny coincides with an increasingly authoritarian state. The 2024 election is starting to feel like a rematch of the 2020 election, now fueled by conspiracy theories that have gone mainstream, increased polarization among Americans, and rising violence, especially political violence.

Sheriffs have been and continue to be at the forefront of these issues at the local level, largely resisting reforms to the office and facing few consequences for their behavior. After January 6, far-right groups began to focus on local-level political campaigns, running for positions like school board member, county commissioner, and, yes, even sheriff. It has become commonplace for sheriffs to announce their position with respect to Richard Mack and the CSPOA.

It should be noted that, in many cases, constitutional sheriffs and their policy proposals have not won on the ballot. In 2023, the Montana legislature, for example, considered but ultimately rejected the "Sheriffs First" bill, a law that would have enshrined the idea that sheriffs had authority over state and local officials in their county. It required that all federal law enforcement agents "check in" with the county sheriff before conducting searches or making an arrest. "It's about returning the power of government back to our people, the citizens," explained one sheriff, Jesse Slaughter of Cascade County, who has been linked to the constitutional sheriff movement. One far-right gun group characterized the legislation thus: "This bill puts teeth into the expectation that federal agents must operate with the approval of the sheriff, or not at all. It also gives the local sheriff tools necessary to protect the people of his county, and their constitutional rights."

During COVID, parents' rights groups called for the intervention of county sheriffs to reopen schools against health guidelines and outlaw masking to prevent the spread of disease. Now those same parent groups, including national ones like Moms for Liberty, call upon sheriffs to support a plethora of causes: removing books about racism and LGBTQ+ youth from school libraries; opposing efforts to support students who may be LGBTQ+; supporting more policing in schools (which is sometimes done by sheriff's offices). These groups have discovered what Mack and FAIR realized: county sheriffs are easier to influence than other law enforcement officials. They are more likely to be conservative. And they believe they are the highest law in the land.

By the time I was finished reporting this book, I came to the conclusion that the county sheriff is an institution that should not exist. For one, there is no shortage of police in America. There are over seventeen thousand policing agencies, many of which consist of just a few sworn officers.

And there are ample reasons to believe that sheriffs, as an institution, committed some of the worst crimes of the criminal legal and policing system. They played a crucial role in systems of convict leasing, which killed one in four Black Americans imprisoned in the years following Reconstruction who were being ostensibly punished for a variety of low-level crimes. Sheriffs run jails, which are incredibly dangerous, and sites of disease, overdoses, and death. And they have played historically important roles in preventing Black Americans from exercising their right to vote, blocking modest civil rights and criminal system reforms, and making a profit from the crimmigration system. In short, the office of sheriff has expanded greatly beyond what sheriffs like to believe were mere "shire reeves" and have become violent institutions.

Beyond the history, sheriffs have not proven themselves to be responsive to the needs for community safety. One of the greatest harms of the constitutional sheriff movement, in my view, is how the politicization of the office causes sheriffs not just to engage in racist and sexist policing but also these elected officials ignore core components of their job as defined by statute. Over and over, I heard about sheriffs who were happy to appear in the media talking about the Constitution, but they ignored missing and murdered Indigenous women in the West and crimes of domestic violence in rural areas, where family violence is endemic. They refuse to serve subpoenas to people because they agree with their political philosophy and, as a result, treat members of militias better than victims of crime. These sheriffs ask for more federal dollars to expand their policing capacity and build better jails, only to turn around and put more people into the criminal legal system, expand pretrial detention, and lobby for harsher laws that penalize migrants.

I spoke with an advocate who works with families in the criminal legal system, and she emphasized to me that every outcome is the result of a specific policy choice. Her point was that the system didn't emerge fully formed but has been made by people making deliberate choices. I interpreted her statement to provide the greatest hope for the future: if the system is the result of policy choices, then these policy choices can be undone.

There are many excellent writers and scholars who have focused on the need to rethink and, yes, abolish the police. Aside from what many others have written, there are additional reasons to eliminate the office of sheriff.

Sheriffs have not only crafted their own history; they have also used it to generate a narrative that places them above the law. It's ubiquitous, regardless of state, political party, or region of the country. I have seen this in action, in legislatures and community meetings and on television. "If you don't like me, vote me out," a sheriff will say, which makes the process seem so simple. And yet, these elections operate in an environment with no accountability and very few checks and balances on the system.

Around one-third of states have no requirements for sheriffs whatsoever. In the majority of the rest, the requirements are fairly minimal and can be fulfilled after the election. Even when sheriffs are required to have certification or experience, there is no required background check that might locate earlier misconduct in another state or lies on a résumé. It is difficult enough to get law enforcement officers decertified when they commit misconduct. It is impossible to remove sheriffs for lying about past misconduct if no one conducts a thorough background check.

Instead, public elections force those with the most to lose to come forward and make accusations against their sheriff in the media, to a government agency, or through the courts. These people put themselves in the public spotlight to their great detriment. Sheriffs and their supporters use social media to discredit these whistleblowers, many of whom have criminal records or histories of drug use. Many a time I have tried to locate someone who had a bad experience with a sheriff's office only to find that the individual died of a drug overdose, moved away, failed to pay their cell phone bill, or was otherwise indisposed to talk. It is a trauma to talk to a journalist, lawyer, or investigator about brutality experienced at the hands of the state that is supposed to protect you. I deeply honor those who do come forward, but I also think this is not their burden to bear.

Investigations into law enforcement should happen through a formal process by a neutral, third-party investigator who can subpoena sheriff records and conduct an investigation while concealing the identities of those who were victims of abuse. Victims should not be forced to identify themselves in the public record, subjecting their lives to vetting in a public forum, through Facebook groups and the media. The sheriff has the upper hand and can easily refute the charges or discredit the witness before an investigation even begins.

In places where state officials eventually find out about sheriff misconduct, generally, no law even requires that these charges be vetted and investigated. The *New York Times* reported that Mississippi state agencies routinely ignored reports of misconduct by sheriffs. Often, state officials are beholden to sheriffs or are elected themselves, making them vulnerable to outside influence and reluctant to make enemies. Sometimes the federal government intervenes, but they cannot always do so, and even when they do, sheriffs still remain in power. They evade convictions because they get the benefit of the doubt.

So, yes, you can vote the sheriff out of office, but at what cost? And how long must residents endure misconduct—often committed in the open—without recourse?

These are all arguments in favor of making sheriffs appointed rather than elected. But there are additional reasons, in my view, to eliminate the institution altogether.

Every policing agency in the United States operates with its own rules and hierarchies. As a result, communities fall through the cracks. Without local news or government oversight, people live in places where their law enforcement operates with near impunity.

Sheriffs have shown themselves to be uniquely harmful, historically and

in the present day. Their involvement in the fraught history of convict leasing, profiting off the labor of people they themselves arrested, is enough to
justify eliminating the position altogether. It is a job shaped by myth, not by
the realities of what communities need and want.

Even further, because sheriffs and their deputies serve as both arresting
officers and jailers, they benefit from a bloated mass incarceration system.
Stemming from the history of sheriffs as independent contractors who are
paid for each arrest and warrant served, sheriffs retain the same sense of ownership over all aspects of the system, from addiction treatment to the arrests
of young people to the houseless population. They engage in jobs that simply
should not be the jobs of law enforcement because they want to retain their
resources and power, which are largely in the form of county jails and the
revenue they provide.

Sheriffs have also shown themselves to be able pawns of presidential
administrations, political parties, lobbyists, and special interest groups that
seek to incarcerate, detain, and deport more people. We have already seen
how Donald Trump courted sheriffs to serve as his personal jailers for the
many immigrants he sought to deport. Groups like the Claremont Institute
have seen how sheriffs can easily implement policies based on their personal
political preferences and seek their support in launching projects ranging
from banning books to ending firearms regulation to eliminating the so-
called deep state. It is hard to see how politicized policing protects anyone
in these circumstances.

I am of the opinion that policing in this country ought to be reevaluated
and, indeed, reduced as much as practical. In essence, I am an abolitionist,
although I see many steps along the route. Eliminating the sheriff's office is
not a difficult call at all.

The sheriff presents unique problems when compared to all other
law enforcement, largely stemming from the fact that they are elected on
the county level. Like the electoral college, county-elected sheriffs

disproportionately provide representation to white, rural Americans, even though most people live in diverse, thriving cities. Certainly, rural Americans are entitled to representation and assistance, but the policies sheriffs support do not engage with the real disinvestment in rural America: the disappearance of hospitals and health care, the rise in houselessness and economic precarity, and the abuse of low-wage workers by industry.

Instead, sheriffs continue to uplift the imagined rural American: the farmer, the rancher, and the yeoman. This plays into the far-right populist narratives and has a mythical ideal rooted in old far-right ideas about producers—those whose work is tied to landownership—and the consumers whose work is viewed as wholly intellectual and elite (writing a book about sheriffs, for instance). You can see it in the ways that people like Ammon Bundy use the image of the hardworking rancher to smuggle in a far-right agenda based on conspiracy theories. And, of course, the sheriff is reluctant to call him out.

Sheriffs, unlike chiefs of police or other appointed law enforcement officials, see their job as fundamentally to remain in office. They are politicians first and foremost. The schism between the parties and the ensuing partisan divide has had a dramatic impact on sheriff elections as well as the ways in which sheriffs institute policies and procedures. Because sheriffs are the primary law enforcement in swaths of rural America, they are mostly aligned with the GOP. And as the GOP takes on issues like the rights of LGBTQ+ citizens, reproductive rights, firearm regulation, and drug treatment and recovery, sheriffs have adopted those same policy positions as their own, regardless of whether or not their job requires it.

The office of sheriff is uniquely able to morph as the sheriff himself requires. It is this very versatility, alongside the freedom to express highly partisan views, that makes the sheriff (and his employees) prone to abuse of office, corruption, and misbehavior.

Many writers, scholars, and activists have engaged with the idea of how

Americans represent history through landmarks, statues, and place-names. Removing statues of slavers, for example, represents a popular change in who we honor as a society. In the same way, we need to engage with law enforcement as another relic of history. While a complete history of law enforcement and policing is beyond the scope of this book, my work has made it clear that the sheriff as an institution represents an imagined history, a lost cause that did not ever exist. We should not have active law enforcement, law enforcement that costs money and extinguishes human lives, who are simply part of a fairy tale that white Americans like to tell themselves.

A real reckoning of the myth of America requires a restructuring of our policing systems. We need to rethink who is policed and why. We need to reconsider the use of prisons and jails. And we need to acknowledge the value of human life and community connections.

Sheriffs, while they claim to be community advocates, do not represent the whole community.

In writing this, I acknowledge that there are many other aspects of local, state, and federal systems that require reform. The change isn't simple. But I think of what a politician told me when I explained the role of the sheriff. "Perhaps," he said, "the sheriff is an office that has outlived its usefulness." To that I might add that the sheriff did serve a purpose, "to keep the county white," as James Baldwin wrote. But that purpose is not one we should valorize or maintain.

# ACKNOWLEDGMENTS

WRITING A BOOK REQUIRES LONG PERIODS OF DEDICATED time as well as funding for writing and research. Much gratitude to the New America Foundation, which provided essential support at a critical juncture. Gratitude to my New America Fellows cohort, who never cease to amaze me, and special thanks to Sarah Baline, Awista Ayub, and Paul Butler. Other parts of this book benefited from funding from the Pulitzer Center on Crisis Reporting and Type Investigations. Sincerely, thank you for helping me with funding to conduct the reporting necessary to make this book happen.

I cannot thank enough my agent, Stephanie Steiker, who believed in this book from the beginning, as well as my talented and coolheaded editor, Cassidy Sachs, who provided invaluable assistance in helping me organize and tame reams of research. Without my tireless and amazing fact-checker, Ethan Corey, this book would not exist. Thank you.

I am grateful to the editors who believed that I had something to say about sheriffs when most people were dubious. Some of the reporting in this book appeared in articles for The Appeal, *Bolts*, *Reveal*, *The Texas Tribune*, and *Politico*. Thank you to my editors Aviva Shen, Ethan Corey, Daniel Nichanian,

Michael Barajas, Margaret Slattery, David Pasztor, Sewell Chan, and Andy Donohue.

The Appeal was my first real writing home, and for that I am forever thankful. Thanks to all of the writers and editors there, past and present. Special thanks to writers who have inspired me and gave me hope that this book would be completed one day: Maurice Chammah, Joshua Vaughn, Josie Duffy Rice, Isaac Simonelli, Cerise Castle, and Keri Blakinger. A note of gratitude to my fellow travelers, especially Jessica Brand and Thomas Jackson. Thank you, friends.

I owe so much to researchers and lawyers who helped me develop the ideas in the book. In addition to everyone I cite, with honor and, I hope, accuracy, special thanks to Aaron Littman, Anne Levinson, Devin Burghart, and Rachel Glasswasser. Thank you for fielding my many queries.

The most important people in the book are all of you who gave me your time, stories, and endless generosity of spirit. This book is for you, for all those who are seeking peace, justice, and a better world. Thank you, Linda Franks, Roberto Reveles, Dr. Phebe Hayes, Amber Walker, Max Rose, Krish Gundu, and innumerable other community organizers and advocates, as well as all those whose loved ones have suffered from the violence of mass incarceration and immigration enforcement. My work was never solely an intellectual activity; it is a sincere gesture of faith that communities can come together and bring about a better world in hope, love, and kindness.

The greatest thanks are owed to my family, those who inevitably bear the brunt of living with a writer. Thank you to my parents for their support even when I made it difficult. Teri Varbel, Jonathan Varbel, and Kelsey Dedoshka contributed their time and love, caring for my daughter at the times when I most needed the help. Thank you.

And finally, thank you to my husband, who manages to put up with me and has always believed I had something to say. Thank you to my daughter, who grew up with the book. You are the future.

# NOTES

## INTRODUCTION

1 *On each chair*: Mark Lamb, Payson Tea Party Gathering, March 16, 2021, https://youtube.com/watch?v=l8bVekAfx60.

1 *group of self-described "constitutional conservatives"*: Payson Tea Party, *Mission Statement* (Payson, AZ: Payson Tea Party, 2021).

1 *ten key principles*: Payson Tea Party, *Mission Statement*.

4 *America's roughly three thousand sheriffs*: "Frequently Asked Questions," National Sheriffs' Association, accessed March 6, 2024, https://www.sheriffs.org/about-nsa/faq.

5 *sheriffs employ 25 percent of sworn law enforcement officers*: Andrea M. Gardner and Kevin M. Scott, *Census of State and Local Law Enforcement Agencies, 2018—Statistical Tables* (Washington, DC: Bureau of Justice Statistics, 2022), 1, https://bjs.ojp.gov/sites/g/files/xyckuh236/files/media/document/csllea18st.pdf.

5 *around 2 million arrests*: Jacob Kaplan, "Uniform Crime Reporting (UCR) Program Data: Arrests by Age, Sex, and Race, 1974–2021," https://doi.org/10.3886/E102263V14. Calculations courtesy of Aaron Littman at the University of California, Los Angeles School of Law.

5 *about 56 million people*: Bureau of Justice Statistics, Census of State and Local Law Enforcement Agencies (CSLLEA), https://www.icpsr.umich.edu/web/NACJD/studies/38771. Calculations by Ethan Corey.

5 *municipalities pay sheriffs' offices for policing services*: Martin J. Schiesl, "The Politics of Contracting: Los Angeles County and the Lakewood Plan, 1954–1962," *Huntington Library Quarterly* 45, no. 3 (Summer 1982): 227–43, https://doi.org/10.2307/3817297. The system of contract cities was called the Lakewood Plan, named for the city of Lakewood in Los Angeles County. For the most part, such arrangements were a way for cities to keep their costs low, attracting more corporations. The City of Industry, for example, is a contract city with almost no residents outside of corporate headquarters.

5 *65 percent of municipalities in America are contract cities*: Brian A. Reaves, *Census of State and Local Law Enforcement Agencies, 2008* (Washington, DC: Bureau of Justice Statistics,

2011), 4, https://bjs.ojp.gov/sites/g/files/xyckuh236/files/media/document/csl
lea08.pdf.

5   *30 percent of all law enforcement killings*: Sam Levin, "'It Never Stops': Killings by US
Police Reach Record High in 2022," *Guardian*, January 6, 2023, https://www
.theguardian.com/us-news/2023/jan/06/us-police-killings-record-number-2022.
Levin cites Mapping Police Violence's Samuel Sinyangwe as the source for this
calculation.

5   *admit 10 million people every year*: Zhen Zeng, *Jail Inmates in 2022—Statistical Tables*
(Washington, DC: Bureau of Justice Statistics, 2023), 2, https://bjs.ojp.gov/doc
ument/ji22st.pdf.

6   *nearly a quarter of the state's counties*: Tony Bartelme and Joseph Cranney, "SC Sheriffs
Fly First Class, Bully Employees and Line Their Pockets with Taxpayer Money,"
*Post and Courier*, March 16, 2019, https://www.postandcourier.com/news/sc-sheriffs
-fly-first-class-bully-employees-and-line-their-pockets-with-taxpayer-money/arti
cle_bed9eb48-2983-11e9-9a4c-9f34f02f8378.html.

6   *no one has the power to arrest or remove a sheriff*: Meagan Flynn, "Sheriff Helped Plot His
Own Deputy's Killing over 'Racially Offensive' Tape, Prosecutors Say," *Washington
Post*, September 17, 2019, https://www.washingtonpost.com/nation/2019/09/17
/granville-county-sheriff-brindell-wilkins-murder-plot/; Connor Sheets, "Etowah
Sheriff Pockets $750K in Jail Food Funds, Buys $740K Beach House," *AL.com*,
March 13, 2018, https://www.al.com/news/birmingham/2018/03/etowah_sher
iff_pocketed_over_7.html.

6   *removed and criminally charged for attempted arson*: Associated Press, "Ousted Sheriff Running for Election," *Fort Worth Star-Telegram*, October 29, 1984, 18A, https://www
.newspapers.com/image/638528992/.

## CHAPTER 1: THE SHERIFF RESURRECTION

13   *"armpit of America"*: Gene Weingarten, "Why Not the Worst?," *Washington Post*, December 2, 2001, https://www.washingtonpost.com/archive/lifestyle/magazine
/2001/12/02/why-not-the-worst/ce6f476e-3125-4e2a-b675-4d8f3415e807/.

13   *"smoothest and most ideal road surfaces"*: "World Human Powered Speed Challenge
2022," International Human Powered Vehicle Association, accessed March 7,
2024, http://www.ihpva.org/whpsc/index.htm.

13   *pay $2,500 for this dubious designation*: Bryan Sparks, Lander County Commission,
March 11, 2021, https://youtube.com/watch?v=4mJxOroRkV8.

14   *hunt down members of Congress*: Donald Trump, "Speech at the Ellipse," transcribed by
CNN, January 6, 2021, https://www.cnn.com/2021/02/08/politics/trump
-january-6-speech-transcript/index.html.

14   *"protecting our freedom"*: Sparks, Lander County Commission, March 11, 2021,
1:04:21, https://youtube.com/watch?v=4mJxOroRkV8.

15 *first history of Battle Mountain*: Dana R. Bennett, "The Origin of Nevada's Battle Mountain Mining District," *Elko Daily Free Press*, March 7, 2024, https://elkodaily .com/news/local/business/mining/the-origin-of-nevada-s-battle-mountain -mining-district/article_634524ce-ce14-11ee-a2f6-fb60ae3f0f5f.html.

16 *made the whole thing up*: Bennett, "Origin of Nevada's Battle Mountain Mining District."

16 *"promise of whiteness"*: Anthea Butler, *White Evangelical Racism: The Politics of Morality in America* (Chapel Hill: University of North Carolina Press, 2021).

16 *About one-fourth of Battle Mountain*: "Battle Mountain CDP, Nevada," U.S. Census Bureau, accessed March 7, 2024, https://data.census.gov/profile/Battle_Moun tain_CCD,_Lander_County,_Nevada?g=060XX00US3201594070.

17 *"a cross between tailgating at a football game and a NASCAR race"*: Doug Richards, "Ex-Sheriff Who Attended DC Trump Rally 'Sick' over Violence at Capitol," 11 Alive News, January 7, 2021, https://www.11alive.com/article/news/politics/conway -on-capitol-violence/85-a22bfe6d-800a-4f93-a019-e68a027996eb.

17 *Sheriffs are elected in every state*: "Frequently Asked Questions," National Sheriffs' Association, accessed April 19, 2024, https://www.sheriffs.org/programs/frequent -questions.

17 *Over three thousand of them*: "FAQ," National Sheriffs' Association, accessed April 19, 2024, https://www.sheriffs.org/about-nsa/faq.

18 *only 4 percent of sheriffs were Black*: Connor Brooks, *Sheriffs' Office Personnel, 2020* (Washington, DC: Bureau of Justice Statistics, 2022), 6, https://bjs.ojp.gov/sites/g/files /xyckuh236/files/media/document/sop20.pdf.

18 *one Texas county elected its first Black sheriff*: Michael Barajas, "Fort Bend County Will Soon Have Its First Black Sheriff Since Reconstruction," *Texas Observer*, December 1, 2020, https://www.texasobserver.org/eric-fagan-fort-bend-county/.

18 *Tenures of forty or fifty years*: Michael Zoorob, "There's (Rarely) a New Sheriff in Town: The Incumbency Advantage for Local Law Enforcement," *Electoral Studies* 80 (2022), 2, https://doi.org/10.1016/j.electstud.2022.102550.

18 *Over half of all sheriff elections*: Zoorob, "There's (Rarely) a New Sheriff," 5.

18 *sheriffs are the least diverse*: Reflective Democracy Campaign, *Confronting the Demographics of Power: America's Sheriffs* (San Francisco: Women Donors Network, 2020), 2, https://wholeads.us/wp-content/uploads/2020/06/reflectivedemocracy -americassheriffs-06.04.2020.pdf.

18 *sheriffs have overall less education*: Maurice Chammah, "We Surveyed U.S. Sheriffs. See Their Views on Power, Race and Immigration," Marshall Project, October 18, 2022, https://www.themarshallproject.org/2022/10/18/we-surveyed-u-s-sheriffs -see-their-views-on-power-race-and-immigration.

18 *open to anyone who wants to run*: John Webb, "Washington State Bill Deemed 'Unconstitutional' by Sheriffs," NonStop Local KHQ, January 16, 2024, https://www .khq.com/news/washington-state-bill-deemed-unconstitutional-by-sheriffs/arti cle_ea056f10-b4d7-11ee-9854-7b4420071002.html.

19  *"consistent with our nation's democratic history"*: "Preserve the Office of Sheriff by Continuing the Election of Our Nation's Sheriffs," National Sheriffs' Association, accessed March 8, 2024, https://www.sheriffs.org/sites/default/files/tb/Preserving_the_Office_of_Sheriff_Through_Election.pdf.

19  *"closest thing there is to being a king"*: John Burnett, "Larger-Than-Life Sheriff Rules Louisiana Parish," NPR, November 28, 2006, https://www.npr.org/2006/11/28/6549329/larger-than-life-sheriff-rules-louisiana-parish.

19  *so-called constitutional sheriff movement*: Cloee Cooper, "How a Right-Wing Network Mobilized Sheriffs' Departments," *Public Eye*, June 10, 2019, https://politicalresearch.org/2019/06/10/how-a-right-wing-network-mobilized-sheriffs-departments.

20  *dissolved in 2021 by the State of Arizona*: *Constitutional Sheriffs and Peace Officers Association*, filed with Arizona Corporations Commission, December 23, 2021, https://ecorp.azcc.gov/BusinessSearch/BusinessInfo?entityNumber=23090337.

20  *"law enforcement powers held by the sheriff"*: "About," Constitutional Sheriffs and Peace Officers Association, accessed March 8, 2024, https://cspoa.org/about/.

21  *estimated the number of CSPOA-aligned sheriffs*: Cooper, "How a Right-Wing Network Mobilized Sheriffs' Departments."

21  *surveyed 500 sheriffs*: Chammah, "We Surveyed U.S. Sheriffs."

21  *around 50 sheriffs*: Jessica Pishko, "The Fringe Ideology of 'Constitutional Sheriffs' Is Attracting Believers Within Texas Law Enforcement," *Texas Tribune*, January 13, 2023, https://www.texastribune.org/2023/01/13/constitutional-sheriffs-texas/.

22  *disavowed Mack's claims*: Larry Amerson and Greg Champagne, "What Is the Legal Meaning of a Sheriff's Oath of Office?," National Sheriffs' Association, accessed March 8, 2024, https://www.sheriffs.org/sites/default/files/uploads/Legal%20Meaning%20of%20Oath%20of%20Office.pdf.

22  *echoes many of the same ideas*: "National Sheriffs' Association Recognizes America's Right to Vote for the Office of Sheriff," National Sheriffs' Association, accessed March 8, 2024, https://www.sheriffs.org/sites/default/files/uploads/Resolution%202014-1%20Americas%20Right%20to%20Vote%20for%20Sheriff.pdf.

24  *"protect her from the government"*: Steve Jordahl, "Sheriff: America Loves Freedom More Than Fears a Virus," One News Now, April 27, 2020, https://onenewsnow.com/legal-courts/2020/04/27/sheriff-america-loves-freedom-more-than-fears-a-virus.

24  *"he protects people who simply want to be left alone"*: Richard Mack, "Oath Keepers Interview," interview by Daniel Hapenny, Real Story, April 19, 2009, https://www.youtube.com/watch?v=tU8M7MHMwgQ.

25  *planned to follow in his footsteps*: Leo W. Banks, "Arizona Sheriff Sticks to His Guns," *Los Angeles Times*, May 2, 1995, https://www.latimes.com/archives/la-xpm-1995-05-02-mn-61363-story.html.

25  *"makes the drug problem worse"*: Richard Mack, *The County Sheriff: America's Last Hope* (self-pub., 2009), 7–8.

25 *He added that Skousen*: Richard Mack, "CSPOA Press Conference in Las Vegas," Las Vegas Freedom Fest, July 12, 2022, https://rumble.com/v1ce6sl-cspoa-press -conference-las-vegas-07-12-2022-full.html.

26 *"this one was converted"*: Tim Steller, "'Sheriff Mack' Wielding New Weapon: A Message," *Arizona Daily Star*, April 5, 2011, https://tucson.com/news/local/govt-and -politics/sheriff-mack-wielding-new-weapon-a-message/article_c0694 e6e-4525-5c5a-92c2-e4c41f3154cd.html.

26 *Skousen was an FBI agent*: "Obituary: W. Cleon Skousen," *Deseret News*, January 13, 2006, https://www.deseret.com/2006/1/13/19748409/obituary-w-cleon -skousen/.

26 *"this people will be the Staff"*: Brigham Young, "Celebration of the Fourth of July," July 4, 1854, *Journal of Discourses*, 26 vols. (Liverpool: Amasa Lyman, 1854), 7:15.

26 *"legendary cranks of the conservative world"*: David Frum, "What Is Going On at Fox News?," *New Majority*, March 16, 2009, archived March 20, 2009, by the Wayback Machine, https://web.archive.org/web/20090320043045/http://www .newmajority.com/ShowScroll.aspx?ID=30edc824-3d2c-40fa-b904-cb1442 e2bcaf.

26 *wrote over twenty books*: Alexander Zaitchik, "Fringe Mormon Group Makes Myths with Glenn Beck's Help," *Intelligence Report*, February 23, 2011, https://www.splcen ter.org/fighting-hate/intelligence-report/2011/fringe-mormon-group-makes -myths-glenn-beck%E2%80%99s-help.

27 *Prominent GOP politicians*: Zaitchik, "Fringe Mormon Group Makes Myths."

27 *Amazon top ten list*: Sharon Haddock, "Beck's Backing Bumps Skousen Book to Top," *Deseret News*, March 21, 2009, https://www.deseret.com/2009/3/21/20308281 /beck-s-backing-bumps-skousen-book-to-top/.

27 *ample evidence suggests that this is not true*: Ernie Lazar, "SKOUSEN, W. Cleon—Report Based upon His FBI Files," Archive.org, March 27, 2021, https://archive.org /details/skousen-w.-cleon.

27 *A 1946 review*: R. B. Hood, annual efficiency report for W. Cleon Skousen, March 31, 1946, https://archive.org/details/foia_Skousen_W._Cleon-1.

27 *"exceptionally interested in the Bureau's work"*: R. B. Hood, annual efficiency report for W. Cleon Skousen, March 31, 1948, https://archive.org/details/foia_Skousen_W ._Cleon-1.

27 *"more promise than any new man"*: C. R. Davidson, memo to Mr. Callahan on W. Cleon Skousen, May 23, 1961, https://archive.org/details/foia_Skousen_W._Cleon-3.

28 *"No longer are communists considered part of the free world"*: "U.S. Resistance to Reds Cited at Officers Meet," *Deseret News Telegram*, June 24, 1955.

28 *"exactly the same manner as the Communists in Russia"*: Dennis L. Lythgoe, "Political Feud in Salt Lake City: J. Bracken Lee and the Firing of W. Cleon Skousen," *Utah Historical Quarterly* 42, no. 4 (1974): 316–43, https://issuu.com/utah10/docs/uhq _volume42_1974_number4.

28  *Lee was just corrupt*: "Cleon Skousen on Getting Fired as SLC Police Chief," 1994, https://www.youtube.com/watch?v=0vzgHkbXRZg.

28  *"unprincipled racketeer"*: W. C. Sullivan, memo on W. Cleon Skousen to A. H. Belmont, January 2, 1963, https://archive.org/details/foia_Skousen_W._Cleon-4.

28  *"Skousen has gone off the deep end"*: W. R. Wannall, memo on "Has Cuba Been Abandoned to Communism?," April 1, 1963, https://archive.org/details/foia_Skousen_W._Cleon-6.

29  *"'wiped clean off the land'"*: W. Cleon Skousen, "Cleon Skousen 10-20-61," Salt Lake Community College Digital Archives, https://www.youtube.com/watch?v=g7 D6JdPiKrg.

29  *"fight communism and big government"*: Matthew L. Harris, *Watchman on the Tower: Ezra Taft Benson and the Making of the Mormon Right* (Salt Lake City: University of Utah Press, 2020), 95.

29  *Skousen's teachings reflect*: Richard Hofstadter, "The Paranoid Style in American Politics," *Harper's*, November 1964, https://harpers.org/archive/1964/11/the -paranoid-style-in-american-politics/.

29  *increasingly critical of Skousen*: Harris, *Watchman on the Tower*, 97.

29  *After his death in 2006*: Zaitchik, "Fringe Mormon Group Makes Myths."

29  *"identical in spelling, capitalization, and punctuation"*: "Pocket Constitution of the United States," National Center for Constitutional Studies, https://nccs.net/collections /pocket-constitution/products/pocket-constitution-of-united-states.

30  *"best job in the world"*: Richard Mack, "CSPOA Press Conference in Las Vegas."

30  *treated them with respect*: Richard Mack, CSPOA Posse Intel Webinar, February 7, 2023, https://cspoa.org/webinar/cspoa-posse-intel-webinar-2-7-2023/.

30  *Montana sheriff named Jay Printz*: *Mack v. United States*, 856 F. Supp. 1372 (D. Ariz. 1994). Mack's case was later combined with Printz's before the Supreme Court.

31  *1995 article in the* Phoenix New Times: John Dougherty, "None Dare Call It Reason: Arizona Is a Hotbed of Constitutionalist Dissent, and Here Are Four Who Fuel the Patriot Flame," *Phoenix New Times*, July 6, 1995, https://www.phoenixnewtimes .com/news/none-dare-call-it-reasonarizona-is-a-hotbed-of-constitutionalist -dissent-and-here-are-four-who-fuel-the-patriot-flame-6424870.

31  *Mack's far-right political statements*: Jennifer Katleman, "Arms for the Whole People," *Tucson Citizen*, May 6, 1995, 1, https://www.newspapers.com/image /579712677.

31  *the "Mack Attack"*: Dougherty, "None Dare Call It Reason"; Associated Press, "Opponent Drops Sheriff's Recall," *Tucson Citizen*, August 3, 1995, 18, https://www .newspapers.com/image/579658583/.

31  *compared him to notorious cult leaders*: Katleman, "Arms for the Whole People."

31  *lost his third campaign for sheriff*: Tess Owen, "How a Small-Town Sheriff Ended Up on a Crusade to Radicalize American Law Enforcement," Vice News, July 28, 2021, https://www.vice.com/en/article/epnkgn/richard-mack-constitutional-sheriff -movement.

31  *Mack moved back to Provo*: Jesse Hyde, "Provo Politician Trying a Reality TV 'Candidacy,'" *Deseret News*, June 10, 2004, https://www.deseret.com/2004/6/10/1983 3842/provo-politician-trying-a-reality-tv-candidacy/.

31  *incarcerated people were being "coddled"*: Bob Bernick Jr., "Candidate Changes Party," *Deseret News*, November 8, 2003, https://www.deseret.com/2003/11/8/1979 4624/candidate-changes-party/.

31  *governor of Utah in 2003*: Bernick, "Candidate Changes Party."

31  *Showtime reality show*: Ann Gerhart, "'American Candidate': A Vote with the Remote," *Washington Post*, July 31, 2004, https://www.washingtonpost.com/archive /lifestyle/2004/07/31/american-candidate-a-vote-with-the-remote/8583b4f7 -6d5f-45d7-a594-2918a2c14994/.

32  *reporter from the* Deseret News: Hyde, "Provo Politician Trying a Reality TV 'Candidacy.'"

32  *campaigned as a Libertarian*: "Why I Am Running," Richard Mack for U.S. Senate (website), archived July 3, 2006, by the Wayback Machine, https://web.archive .org/web/20060703124017/http://www.richardmackforsenate.com/.

32  *"restore personal liberty before it is too late"*: "Why I Am Running," Richard Mack for U.S. Senate (website).

32  *probably a fiction*: Leo W. Banks, "Arizona Sheriff Sticks to His Guns: Lawman Makes a Name for Himself by Attacking Brady Law and Backing Militia Groups. His Words Find Favor at Home," *Los Angeles Times*, May 2, 1995, https://www .latimes.com/archives/la-xpm-1995-05-02-mn-61363-story.html.

32  *"marriage that was made in heaven"*: Mack, "Oath Keepers Interview."

33  *founder of the Three Percenters*: Mike Giglio, "A Pro-Trump Militant Group Has Recruited Thousands of Police, Soldiers, and Veterans," *Atlantic*, November 2020, https://www.theatlantic.com/magazine/archive/2020/11/right-wing-militias -civil-war/616473/.

33  *"cannot tell your sheriff what to do"*: Richard Mack, "Oath Keeper Sheriff Richard Mack," video, recorded April 19, 2009, https://www.youtube.com/watch?v= tU8M7MHMwgQ.

33  *mentalists like Derren Brown*: Adam Green, "How Derren Brown Remade Mind Reading for Skeptics," *New Yorker*, September 30, 2019, https://www.newyorker.com /magazine/2019/10/07/how-derren-brown-remade-mind-reading-for-skeptics.

33  *monthly fee of $11*: "CSPOA Lifetime Posse Membership Package," Constitutional Sheriffs and Peace Officers Association, accessed March 9, 2024, https://cspoa .org/product/lifetime-posse-membership-package/. In the course of reporting, I have paid the monthly fee to access videos and material from the CSPOA.

34  *lost in a landslide to the incumbent*: Ryan Lenz, "Former Arizona Sheriff Richard Mack Seeks 'Army' of Sheriffs to Resist Federal Authority," *Intelligence Report*, November 11, 2012, https://www.splcenter.org/fighting-hate/intelligence-report/2012/for mer-arizona-sheriff-richard-mack-seeks-%E2%80%98army%E2%80 %99-sheriffs-resist-federal-authority.

35 *"if your sheriff started a posse"*: Trish Choate, "Oath Keepers Founder Shares Politics and Preparedness at Wichita Falls Meeting," *Times Record News*, June 25, 2021, https://www.timesrecordnews.com/story/news/2021/06/25/oath-keepers-founder-stewart-rhodes-speaks-wichita-falls-capitol-riot-accusations/5323819001/.

36 *a full slate of far-right speakers*: Gregory Davis, "British Conspiracy Theorists at Heart of Dangerous Anti-Vaxx Movement," *Hope Not Hate*, July 1, 2020, https://hopenothate.org.uk/2020/07/01/british-conspiracy-theorists-key-dangerous-anti-vaccine-movement/; Olivia Little, "A QAnon-Affiliated January 6 Insurrectionist Is Now Organizing US Anti-Vax Trucker Convoys," *Media Matters*, February 17, 2022, https://www.mediamatters.org/qanon-conspiracy-theory/qanon-affiliated-january-6-insurrectionist-now-organizing-us-anti-vax.

36 *helped publish a fifty-four-volume book*: Joachim Hagopian, *Pedophilia & Empire: Satan, Sodomy, and the Deep State* (self-pub., 2021).

36 *drove to the capital and opened fire*: Jason Slotkin, "'Pizzagate' Gunman Pleads Guilty to Charges," NPR, March 24, 2017, https://www.npr.org/sections/thetwo-way/2017/03/24/521377765/pizzagate-gunman-pleads-guilty-to-charges.

37 *"together we represent faith, family, and freedom"*: Chuck Tanner and Devin Burghart, "'Constitutional Sheriffs' Group Teams Up with Antisemitic Conspiracist," Institute for Research & Education on Human Rights, July 2, 2021, https://irehr.org/2021/07/02/constitutional-sheriffs-group-antisemitism/.

38 *forced to pay around $250,000 in sanctions*: Mark Robison, "Nevada Supreme Court Shoots Down Sanctions Appeal in Joey Gilbert Election Fraud Case," *Reno Gazette-Journal*, August 18, 2023, https://www.rgj.com/story/news/politics/elections/2023/08/18/nevada-supreme-court-shoots-down-appeal-in-joey-gilbert-election-case/70624287007/.

41 *drained the funds and stiffed workers*: Justin Rohrlich, "Inside the Disastrous Conspiracy Roadshow That Likely Killed a COVID-Denying Ex-CIA Agent," *Daily Beast*, December 19, 2021, https://www.thedailybeast.com/inside-the-disastrous-arise-usa-election-fraud-roadshow-that-likely-killed-covid-denier-robert-david-steele.

43 *"Anglo-American heritage of law enforcement"*: Jeff Sessions, "Attorney General Sessions Delivers Remarks to the National Sheriffs' Association," Office of the Attorney General (website), February 12, 2018, https://www.justice.gov/opa/speech/attorney-general-sessions-delivers-remarks-national-sheriffs-association.

## CHAPTER 2: POSSE COMITATUS

44 *Daniel Levitas's book*: Daniel Levitas, *The Terrorist Next Door: The Militia Movement and the Radical Right* (New York: Thomas Dunne, 2021).

44 *where he met Wesley Swift*: Levitas, *Terrorist Next Door*, 23; Michael Barkun, *Religion and the Racist Right: The Origins of the Christian Identity Movement* (Chapel Hill: University of North Carolina Press, 1996), 66. Gale has given a few different versions of his

conversion to Christian Identity, although the basic timeline has remained the same. Later on, Gale and Swift had a falling-out.

44 *Swift ordained Gale*: Levitas, *Terrorist Next Door*, 24.

44 *ran for governor of California in 1957*: Levitas, *Terrorist Next Door*, 61.

45 *Christian Identity adherents*: "Christian Identity," SPLC Extremist Files, accessed March 9, 2024, https://www.splcenter.org/fighting-hate/extremist-files/ideology /christian-identity. These adherents included Richard Butler, who helped form Aryan Nations.

45 *"If a Jew comes near you"*: "Aryan Nations," SPLC Extremist Files, accessed March 9, 2024, https://www.splcenter.org/fighting-hate/extremist-files/ideology/aryan -nations. Although the Posse Comitatus movement was not strictly Christian Iden-tarian, there was overlap in the leadership, as seen with Gale.

45 *the posse comitatus was a group of "able-bodied" men*: Joseph Nunn, "The Posse Comitatus Act Explained," October 14, 2021, https://www.brennancenter.org/our-work/re search-reports/posse-comitatus-act-explained.

45 *sheriffs were originally the leaders of local militias*: David B. Kopel, "The *Posse Comitatus* and the Office of Sheriff: Armed Citizens Summoned to the Aid of Law Enforcement," *Journal of Criminal Law and Criminology* 104, no. 4 (2014): 802, https://scholarlycom mons.law.northwestern.edu/jclc/vol104/iss4/3/.

46 *According to the 1941*: William Law Murfree, *A Treatise on the Law of Sheriffs and Other Ministerial Officers* (St. Louis: Gilbert, 1884), 21, https://books.google.com/books ?id=DeY9AAAAIAAJ.

46 *written by an Idaho attorney*: Walter H. Anderson, *A Treatise on the Law of Sheriffs, Coroners and Constables: With Forms*, vol. 1 (Buffalo: Dennis, 1941), 2, https://books.google .com/books?id=GyaIAAAAIAAJ.

46 *"core, essential power of the county sheriff"*: Kopel, "The *Posse Comitatus*," 802.

46 *"filter out sadists and kooks"*: Associated Press, "Chicago Residents Respond to Call," *Jackson Sun*, February 19, 1968, 7, https://www.newspapers.com/image/282086943/.

46 *Law enforcement everywhere was militarizing*: Elizabeth Hinton, *From the War on Poverty to the War on Crime: The Making of Mass Incarceration in America* (Cambridge, MA: Harvard University Press, 2017).

46 *"pre-industrial past of free Aryan yeoman farmers"*: Barkun, *Religion and the Racist Right*, 218.

47 *"repudiate the unlawful acts"*: Colonel Ben Cameron [William Potter Gale], "The Con-stitutional Republic," *Identity* 6, no. 1 (June 1971): 16, quoted in Levitas, *Terrorist Next Door*, 8.

47 *"ONLY LEGAL LAW ENFORCEMENT OFFICER"*: Cameron [Gale], "The Consti-tutional Republic," 16, quoted in Levitas, *Terrorist Next Door*, 8.

47 *a pseudo-magical quality*: Catherine Wessinger, *How the Millennium Comes Violently* (New York: Seven Bridges Press, 2000), 181.

47 *"elaborate, American-sounding ideology"*: Levitas, *Terrorist Next Door*, 3.

47 *interpreted the U.S. Constitution and the Bill of Rights as holy documents*: Barkun, *Religion and the Racist Right*, 169. Barkun describes the relationship between Mormonism and

Christian Identity as "complex" in terms of theology and suggests that Gale picked up some doctrinal teachings and ideology from Mormon populations in Southern California.

47  *One man who took the call seriously*: Levitas, *Terrorist Next Door*, 8; Barkun, *Religion and the Racist Right*, 69.

48  *charged $21 to issue organizational charters*: Eckard Toy, "Posse Comitatus," Oregon Encyclopedia (website), accessed March 9, 2024, https://www.oregonencyclopedia.org/articles/posse_comitatus/#.ZCOFLezMJmp.

48  *pamphlet with a sheriff's star on the front cover*: Henry Lamont Beach, *Sheriff's Posse Comitatus: Official Posse Book* (self-pub., 1973), https://www.scribd.com/document/419422786/Posse-Comitatus-BlueBook.

48  *"It says what it means"*: Beach, *Sheriff's Posse Comitatus*, 3.

49  *they claimed four hundred thousand members*: Larry Stammer, "'God's Law' Posses Fight 'Subversion,'" *Los Angeles Times*, August 28, 1975, 29, https://www.newspapers.com/image/382831603/.

49  *"setting up training facilities on farms and in rural areas"*: Peggy R. Fontenot, "Threat of Terror Real," *Abbeville Meridional*, August 21, 1986, 2, https://www.newspapers.com/image/446243110/.

49  *Nearly one thousand farmers*: Associated Press, "Farmer Suicide Rate Swells in 1980's, Study Says," *New York Times*, October 14, 1991, https://www.nytimes.com/1991/10/14/us/farmer-suicide-rate-swells-in-1980-s-study-says.html.

49  *"tired of seeing our country just given away"*: Bill Norton, "Effort Underway to Establish Area Crime-Fighting 'Posse,'" *Kansas City Star*, June 27, 1975, 4, https://www.newspapers.com/image/676727780/.

49  *"restore constitutional government"*: W. M. Rinehart, letter to the editor, *Odessa American*, September 27, 1974, 10, https://www.newspapers.com/image/301816971/.

50  *"God, guns, and its interpretation of the U.S. Constitution"*: Susan Sward, "Posse Comitatus: God and Guns," *Arizona Daily Star*, November 28, 1975, 67.

50  *"complete disregard and disdain"*: Sward, "Posse Comitatus," 67.

50  *chase away unionizers attempting to organize agricultural workers*: Larry Stammer, "Petitions Filed for Farm Worker Union Elections," *Los Angeles Times*, September 3, 1975, 1, https://www.newspapers.com/image/382815414.

50  *posse members occupied potato sheds*: Levitas, *Terrorist Next Door*, 121.

51  *"we can go over their heads"*: Bill Knutson, "Right-Wing Posse Ready to Hunt Down 'Commies,'" *Post-Crescent*, September 8, 1974, F2, https://www.newspapers.com/image/287965872/.

51  *execute "at high noon" government officials*: Levitas, *Terrorist Next Door*, 109.

51  *Kahl's body was burned beyond recognition*: Levitas, *Terrorist Next Door*, 5.

51  *"only legitimate law enforcement officer"*: Herbert Howard, "Preface to the Second Edition," *A Treatise on the Law of Sheriffs, Coroners and Constables: With Forms*, vol. 1, 2nd ed. (Boise, ID: Publisher in Defense of the Constitution, 1985), v.

53 *Christian dominionists*: Matthew Trewhella, *The Doctrine of Lesser Magistrates* (self-pub., 2013), 92. Dominionism is the idea that Christians should be in charge of all spheres of American life. It comes from a separate line of Christian thought than Skousen and Posse Comitatus, although the concepts are fairly similar. Trewhella similarly preaches a version of interposition, usually in the context of preventing women from receiving abortion care, but also related to COVID mandates. Trewhella roots his theory in 1500s Germany.

54 *"the only law enforcement mentioned in the Bible"*: Daniel 3:2–3 (King James Version). While the word "sheriff" does appear in the King James translation of the book of Daniel, the original Aramaic text uses the word תִּפְתָּיֵ, which more properly means "magistrate" or "lawyer." See "H-8614," *Exhaustive Concordance of the Bible with Hebrew-Aramaic and Greek Dictionaries* (La Habra, CA: Lockman Foundation, 1998), http://lexiconcordance.com/hebrew/8614.html.

54 *"great antiquity, dignity, trust and authority"*: Anderson, *Treatise on the Law of Sheriffs*, 36.

54 *"virtually exercised the powers of a viceroy"*: Bruce Smith, *Rural Crime Control* (New York: Institute of Public Administration, 1933), 38.

54 *"the early English sheriff"*: Smith, *Rural Crime Control*, 31.

54 *"leisurely process of decay"*: Smith, *Rural Crime Control*, 41.

54 *"new vigor and importance"*: Smith, *Rural Crime Control*, 31.

55 *"plenary executive and administrative powers"*: Paul W. Woodward, *County Government and Administration in North Carolina* (Chapel Hill: University of North Carolina Press, 1928), 9–10, quoted in Smith, *Rural Crime Control*, 45.

55 *"most important of all the Executive offices"*: Thomas Jefferson to "Henry Tompkinson" (Samuel Kercheval), July 12, 1816, https://founders.archives.gov/documents/Jefferson/03-10-02-0128-0002.

55 *"the office of sheriff is of venerable antiquity"*: Murfree, *A Treatise on the Law of Sheriffs*, 21.

56 *"he has no superior in the county"*: Anderson, *A Treatise on the Law of Sheriffs*, 5. The treatise goes on to state that sheriffs "must, of course, act according to law," contrary to the Posse Comitatus and other movements.

56 *"principal conservator of the peace"*: Anderson, *A Treatise on the Law of Sheriffs*, 41.

57 *"enthusiasm for local popular election"*: Smith, *Rural Crime Control*, 44.

57 *"beyond their power to circumscribe his common law functions"*: Murfree, *A Treatise on the Law of Sheriffs*, v.

57 *"jurisdiction is co-extensive within the county"*: Anderson, *A Treatise on the Law of Sheriffs*, 42.

59 *against then president Barack Obama*: Brian Chasnoff, "'An Inscrutable Purpose' in Hill Country," *San Antonio Express-News*, April 12, 2012, https://www.mysanantonio.com/news/news_columnists/brian_chasnoff/article/an-inscrutable-purpose-in-hill-country-3442709.php. Weaver said, in full, "I am not a bigot. I am a racist. I think it is wrong, as far as nature is concerned, to mix races. Obama and his wife are bigots."

59 *"My views are not his views"*: Chasnoff, "'An Inscrutable Purpose' in Hill Country."

59  *"the law still would have been enforced and obeyed"*: Mack, "Oath Keepers Interview."

59  *McVeigh was not in a militia*: Amy Cooter, *Nostalgia, Nationalism, and the US Militia Movement* (New York: Routledge, 2024), 85–88; Jeffrey Toobin, *Homegrown: Timothy McVeigh and the Rise of Right-Wing Extremism* (New York: Simon & Schuster, 2023), 57.

60  *the Senate Judiciary Subcommittee on Terrorism held a hearing*: "Hearing on the U.S. Militia Movement, Before the Senate Judiciary Subcomm. on Terrorism," 107th Cong., C-SPAN, June 15, 1995, https://www.c-span.org/video/?65722-1/us-militia-movement.

60  *Jefferson did talk about nullification*: Thomas Jefferson, "Resolutions Relative to the Alien and Sedition Acts," in *Writings of Thomas Jefferson*, ed. Andrew A. Lipscomb and Albert Ellery Bergh (Washington, DC: Thomas Jefferson Memorial Association, 1905), https://press-pubs.uchicago.edu/founders/documents/v1ch8s41.html.

61  *deathblow to nullification*: United States v. Peters, 9 U.S. (5 Cranch) 115 (1809).

61  *Chief Justice John Marshall wrote*: United States v. Peters, 9 U.S. (5 Cranch) 115 (1809).

61  *"depend on Calhoun whether they recognize it or not"*: James H. Read and Neal Allen, "Living, Dead, and Undead: Nullification Past and Present," *American Political Thought* 1, no. 2 (September 2012): 274, https://doi.org/10.1086/667615.

61  *"different interests, orders, classes, or portions"*: John C. Calhoun, "Disquisition on Government," 1851, reprinted in Wikisource, accessed March 9, 2024, https://en.wikisource.org/wiki/Works_of_John_C._Calhoun/Disquisition_on_Government.

61  *if democracy ruled the day*: Read and Allen, "Nullification Past and Present," 281. As additional evidence of Calhoun's pro-slavery stance, he said that it was improper for states to refuse to use local law enforcement to enforce the Fugitive Slave Act of 1850, arguing that this law was affirmed by the Constitution, unlike the tariffs, which he said were not.

62  *"not mere hypocrisy"*: Read and Allen, "Nullification Past and Present," 282.

62  *"affirm and live by civilized standards"*: William F. Buckley, "Why the South Must Prevail," *National Review*, August 24, 1957, https://adamgomez.files.wordpress.com/2012/03/whythesouthmustprevail-1957.pdf.

62  *Nullification came back in 2013*: Robert A. Levy, "Yes, States Can Nullify Some Federal Laws, Not All," Cato Institute (blog), March 18, 2013, https://www.cato.org/commentary/yes-states-can-nullify-some-federal-laws-not-all. In 2013, Oklahoma voted to nullify the ACA and multiple states tried to block its enactment through nullification.

62  *"supersede those of any agent, officer, elected official or employee"*: "About," Constitutional Sheriffs and Peace Officers (website), accessed March 9, 2024, https://cspoa.org/about/.

63  *a booklet by the National Liberty Alliance*: *Sheriff's Handbook* (Hyde Park, NY: National Liberty Alliance, 2021), https://www.nationallibertyalliance.org/sites/default/files/sheriffs_handbook_03-22-21.pdf. A footnote in the booklet provides insight into how some on the far right view lawyers: "Luke 11:52 Woe unto you, lawyers! for ye have taken away the key of knowledge: ye entered not in yourselves,

and them that were entering in ye hindered." According to the Southern Poverty Law Center, the National Liberty Alliance is associated with the sovereign citizen movement. "National Liberty Alliance," SPLC Extremist Files, accessed March 9, 2024, https://www.splcenter.org/fighting-hate/extremist-files/group/national-liberty-alliance.

63 *"a willingness to accept the penalty"*: Martin Luther King Jr., "Letter from Birmingham Jail," African Studies Center—University of Pennsylvania, April 16, 1963, https://www.africa.upenn.edu/Articles_Gen/Letter_Birmingham.html.

64 *sometimes used interchangeably*: Read and Allen, "Nullification Past and Present," 277.

64 *Madison later repudiated nullification*: Read and Allen, "Nullification Past and Present," 269.

64 *epitomized by the "massive resistance" movement*: Jared A. Goldstein, "A Group of Sheriffs Is Refusing to Enforce Gun Laws Based on a 1960s Constitutional Theory from the KKK," *Slate*, March 20, 2019, https://slate.com/news-and-politics/2019/03/washington-constitutional-sheriffs-gun-ban-kkk.html.

64 *"George Floyd would still be alive"*: Maurice Chammah, "Does Your Sheriff Think He's More Powerful Than the President?," Marshall Project, October 18, 2022, https://www.themarshallproject.org/2022/10/18/does-your-sheriff-think-he-s-more-powerful-than-the-president.

64 *multiple states passed resolutions*: Read and Allen, "Nullification Past and Present," 286.

64 *"transcendent national field of State sovereignty"*: James Kilpatrick, "The Right of Interposition," *Richmond News-Leader*, November 22, 1955, https://edu.lva.virginia.gov/dbva/items/show/206.

64 *also called Black people*: Richard Goldstein, "James J. Kilpatrick, Conservative Voice in Print and on TV, Dies at 89," *New York Times*, August 16, 2010, https://www.nytimes.com/2010/08/17/us/17kilpatrick.html.

65 *interposition made sense*: Committee for Courts of Justice, Senate of Virginia, *The Doctrine of Interposition: Its History and Application, a Report on Senate Joint Resolution 3* (Richmond: Commonwealth of Virginia, 1957).

65 *"interpose, intervene, and interfere!"*: Richard Mack, *Are You a David?* (Provo, UT: MC Printing, 2014), 146.

65 *"erect the barriers and keep those at bay"*: Mack, *County Sheriff*, 26.

65 *"any other alphabet soup bureaucracy"*: Mack, *Are You a David?*, 146; Mack, *County Sheriff*, 26.

65 *threats against President Joe Biden*: Sam Bushman, Richard Mack, and Dave Williams, "Radio Show Hour 2," Liberty Roundtable, November 22, 2023, https://www.libertyroundtable.com/2023/11/22/radio-show-hour-2-11-22-2023/. Sheriff Scott Williams of Coryell County claimed he interposed to protect a resident from investigation for Facebook threats. I called the Secret Service and received the file on the matter and could not find any verification that this occurred. Secret Service agents from Waco did investigate a man who made threats on Facebook, but that was the extent.

65 *"they do not want to fight with the sheriffs"*: Richard Mack, "The County Sheriff America's Last Hope Richard Mack Oath Keeper 2 of 72," video, July 5, 2009, uploaded to YouTube January 15, 2011, 2:52, https://www.youtube.com/watch?v=nJwp bUCW6RU.

65 *"nullification performed at the most local level of all"*: Jared A. Goldstein, "To Kill and Die for the Constitution: Nullification and Insurrectionary Violence," in *Nullification and Secession in Modern Constitutional Thought*, ed. Sanford Levinson (Lawrence: University Press of Kansas, 2016), 180.

65 *justifies vigilante violence*: For example, the two white men convicted in the 2020 killing of Ahmaud Arbery, a Black man jogging in Satilla Shores, claimed they were acting as private police under Georgia law, which, under Mack's theory, could be seen as a form of interposition. See Richard Fausset, "What We Know About the Shooting Death of Ahmaud Arbery," *New York Times*, August 8, 2022, https://www.nytimes .com/article/ahmaud-arbery-shooting-georgia.html.

66 *1981 interview with a political scientist*: Lee Atwater, interview with Alexander Lamis, 1981, quoted in Rick Perlstein, "Exclusive: Lee Atwater's Infamous 1981 Interview on the Southern Strategy," *Nation*, November 13, 2012, https://www.thenation .com/article/archive/exclusive-lee-atwaters-infamous-1981-interview-southern -strategy/.

67 *the new militias laundered their old*: Sarah Childress, "The Battle over Bunkerville," *Frontline*, PBS, May 16, 2017, https://www.pbs.org/wgbh/frontline/article/the-battle -over-bunkerville/.

67 *He has complained about the IRS*: Dennis Romboy, "Mack Says He Didn't Know SEC Had Filed Civil Complaint," *Deseret News*, June 20, 1998, https://www.deseret.com /1998/6/20/19387044/mack-says-he-didn-t-know-sec-had-filed-civil-complaint/.

67 *"the scum of law enforcement has risen to the top"*: Jack McLamb, interview with World of Prophecy, quoted in David Booth Denison, "God Is Gone from Government," *Times-Independent*, February 13, 1997, A5, https://www.newspapers.com/image /557135509.

67 *"forming an oligarchy of Imperialism"*: Gerald J. McLamb, *Operation Vampire Killer 2000: American Police Action Plan for Stopping World Government Rule* (Phoenix, AZ: Police Against the New World Order, 1992), 1, https://vault.library.uvic.ca/concern/ge neric_works/79f30599-76ff-4e55-b25f-f012a44d4e4e.

68 *utopian, all-white community*: David Pugliese, "Waiting for Armageddon," *Province*, January 10, 1999, A28, https://www.newspapers.com/image/504590528.

68 *Mack only appeared after the fact*: Richard Mack, "Foreword," in Randy Weaver, *Vicki, Sam, and America: How the Government Killed All Three* (self-pub., 2003). In 1995, Weaver and his daughters received a settlement from the federal government.

68 *"would only talk to Mack"*: Katleman, "Arms for the Whole People," 6.

68 *"increased power for county government"*: William Chaloupka, "The County Supremacy and Militia Movements: Federalism as an Issue on the Radical Right," *Journal of Federalism* 26, no. 3 (Summer 1996): 162.

69	*This usually included supporting ranchers*: Chaloupka, "County Supremacy and Militia Movements," 163.

69	*governor killed it*: Levitas, *Terrorist Next Door*, 307.

69	*"written permission from county sheriffs"*: Associated Press, "Chenoweth Takes Hits from Congressmen Her Federal Agent Permission Bill Called 'Loony Concept,'" *Spokesman-Review*, May 18, 1995, https://www.spokesman.com/stories/1995/may/18/chenoweth-takes-hits-from-congressmen-her-federal/.

69	*National Conference of State Legislatures even published a report in 1995*: Chaloupka, "County Supremacy and Militia Movements," 165.

70	*began speaking at local Tea Party groups*: David Barstow, "Tea Party Lights Fuse for Rebellion on Right," *New York Times*, February 15, 2010, https://www.nytimes.com/2010/02/16/us/politics/16teaparty.html.

70	*audience of believers*: Richard Mack, "The County Sheriff America's Last Hope Richard Mack Oath Keeper 1 of 72," video, July 5, 2009, uploaded to YouTube January 15, 2011, 4:12, https://www.youtube.com/watch?v=kAVhOBxmHYI.

70	*Mack stands in Arizona*: Richard Mack, "Sheriff Richard Mack—CSPOA National Conventions," Van Shaar Productions, November 17, 2011, video, 1:50, https://www.youtube.com/watch?v=leu4FwqIx70.

70	*already had five hundred sheriff followers*: Ryan Lenz and Mark Potok, *War in the West: The Bundy Ranch Standoff and the American Radical Right* (Montgomery, AL: Southern Poverty Law Center, 2014), 26, https://www.splcenter.org/20140709/war-west-bundy-ranch-standoff-and-american-radical-right.

71	*"a high and noble office"*: Mack, *The County Sheriff*, 2.

71	*"one county at a time"*: "Frequently Asked Questions," Constitutional County Project, archived March 31, 2015, https://web.archive.org/web/20150331040014/http://www.constitutionalcountyproject.org/about/faqs.

71	*His first target*: "Frequently Asked Questions," Constitutional County Project.

71	*"run for sheriff"*: Richard Mack, "Richard Mack Announces Plan for 'Constitutional' Takeover of Arizona's Navajo County," Hatewatch, December 13, 2014, video, 0:56, https://www.youtube.com/watch?v=BSxrJxQhLbs.

71	*against far-right candidates*: Adrian Fontes, @Adrian_Fontes, X/Twitter, September 26, 2022, https://twitter.com/Adrian_Fontes/status/1574439758763216899.

71	*"start getting ready for this"*: Mack, "Mack Announces Plan," 2:11.

72	*"they cannot tell us what to do"*: Mack, *The County Sheriff*, 35.

## CHAPTER 3: "THERE'S [NOT OFTEN] A NEW SHERIFF IN TOWN"

73	*On a humid September morning*: David Nakamura, "'There's a New Sheriff in Town': Trump Uses Official Events to Wage Campaign Against Press," *Washington Post*, September 7, 2018, https://www.washingtonpost.com/politics/theres-a-new-sheriff-in-town-trump-uses-official-events-to-wage-campaign-against-press/2018/09/06/8cf4180c-b204-11e8-9a6a-565d92a3585d_story.html.

73  *tax-deductible donations that never made its way to the federal government*: FOX8 Digital Desk, "Rockingham County Sheriff Promotes Crowdfunding Effort to Fund Mexico Border Wall," FOX8, September 19, 2018, https://myfox8.com/news/rocking ham-county-sheriff-promotes-crowdfunding-effort-to-fund-mexico-border-wall/; Julia Harte and Joseph Tanfani, "Border Wall Business: The Non-Profits, Startups and Pacs Seizing on Trump's Dream Wall," Reuters, July 3, 2019, https://www .reuters.com/investigates/special-report/usa-borderwall-business/.

74  *"chain gang" of detainees to help Trump "build the wall"*: Spencer Buell, "Bristol Sheriff Thomas Hodgson Tried to Score Points with Stephen Miller by Snitching on His Own Church," *Boston*, December 5, 2019, https://www.bostonmagazine.com /news/2019/12/05/thomas-hodgson-stephen-miller/.

74  *appreciation from sheriffs nationwide*: Nakamura, "Trump Uses Official Events to Wage Campaign."

74  *anonymous* New York Times *op-ed*: Miles Taylor, "I Am Part of the Resistance Inside the Trump Administration," *New York Times*, September 5, 2018, https://www .nytimes.com/2018/09/05/opinion/trump-white-house-anonymous-resistance .html.

74  *read from a highlighted portion*: Donald Trump, "Presidential Meeting with Sheriffs at White House," C-SPAN, September 5, 2018, video, 7:55, https://www.c-span .org/video/?451125-1/presidential-meeting-sheriffs-white-house.

74  *"the bear pokes back"*: Nakamura, "Trump Uses Official Events to Wage Campaign."

75  *Trump administration actually defunded law enforcement*: Bill Pascrell, "Donald Trump vs. Law Enforcement: All the Ways He's Hurt Policing in America as President," *New York Daily News*, September 3, 2020, https://www.nydailynews.com/2020/09/03 /donald-trump-vs-law-enforcement-all-the-ways-hes-hurt-policing-in-america -as-president/.

75  *an additional $244 million*: David Dayen, "Trump Tries to Defund the Police on His Way Out," *American Prospect*, January 15, 2021, https://prospect.org/politics /trump-tries-to-defund-the-police-on-his-way-out/.

75  *Biden argued that Trump cut around half a billion dollars*: Jon Greenberg, "Fact-Check: Does Trump Want to Cut Law Enforcement Aid?," *Austin American-Statesman*, August 26, 2020, https://www.statesman.com/story/news/politics/elections/2020/08/26 /fact-check-does-trump-want-to-cut-law-enforcement-aid/113872020/.

75  *law enforcement should not "be too nice"*: "Trump Tells Police Officers 'Don't Be Too Nice' When Arresting Gang Members," *CBS Evening News*, July 28, 2017, video, 0:58, https://www.youtube.com/watch?v=noCx808TvZU.

76  *"destroy his career"*: Louis Nelson, "Trump Invites Sheriff to 'Destroy' Texas State Lawmaker Who Opposes Asset Forfeiture," *Politico*, February 7, 2017, https:// www.politico.com/story/2017/02/trump-sheriff-asset-forfeiture-texas-234740.

76  *one of the first modern presidents to talk to sheriffs*: Ronald Reagan, "Remarks at the Annual Conference of the National Sheriff's Association in Hartford, Connecticut," Ronald Reagan Presidential Library & Museum, June 20, 1984, https://www

.reaganlibrary.gov/archives/speech/remarks-annual-conference-national-sheriffs
-association-hartford-connecticut.

77  *90 percent of the time the incumbent wins*: Zoorob, "There's (Rarely) a New Sheriff," 5.

77  *sheriffs ran based on experience*: Lindsey Meeks, "Undercovered, Underinformed: Local
News, Local Elections, and U.S. Sheriffs," *Journalism Studies* 21, no. 12 (2020):
1609–26, https://doi.org/10.1080/1461670X.2020.1781546.

77  *previous experience working in the office they run*: Chammah, "We Surveyed U.S.
Sheriffs."

78  *generally unrelated to presidential voting patterns*: Zoorob, "There's (Rarely) a New Sheriff," 9.

79  *three-hundred-thousand-member-strong Fraternal Order of Police*: Alan Neuhauser, "Nation's
Biggest Police Union Endorses Trump," *U.S. News and World Report*, September 16,
2016, https://www.usnews.com/news/articles/2016-09-16/nations-biggest
-police-union-endorses-trump.

79  *still a member of the CSPOA advisory board*: Walt Bogdanich and Grace Ashford, "An
Alabama Sheriff, a Mystery Check and a Blogger Who Cried Foul," *New York Times*,
December 14, 2017, https://www.nytimes.com/2017/12/14/us/ana-franklin
-alabama-sheriff.html.

79  *"our Nation's democratic traditions and historical political practices"*: "National Sheriffs' Association Recognizes America's Right to Vote for the Office of Sheriff," National
Sheriffs' Association.

80  *crimes of "moral turpitude"*: Ga. Code § 15-16-1; 12 NC Admin. Code § 10B.0305.

80  *experience or training for sheriff candidates*: "Office of Sheriff: State-by-State Elections
Information," National Sheriffs' Association, accessed March 10, 2024, https://
www.sheriffs.org/sites/default/files/tb/Office_of_Sheriff_State-by-State_Elec
tion_Chart.pdf. Requirements to be a law enforcement officer vary widely across
the country. Most sheriffs must obtain some form of certification either before or
after election, but it is generally not the same training required of police chiefs and
officers. As will be discussed later, this makes reforming the office difficult.

80  *eliminate the law enforcement experience requirement*: An act to amend Section 13.5 of the
Elections Code, and to repeal Section 24004.3 of the Government Code, SB-271,
California Senate 2021–2022, https://leginfo.legislature.ca.gov/faces/billVer
sionsCompareClient.xhtml?bill_id=202120220SB271. I agreed to testify on behalf of this measure in front of the state assembly, but it ultimately did not go to
hearing.

80  *"second-chance oasis for cops"*: Abe Streep, "How Violent Cops Stay in Law Enforcement," *New Yorker*, May 21, 2021, https://www.newyorker.com/news/us-journal
/how-violent-cops-stay-in-law-enforcement.

82  *Trump refused to admit that he was wrong*: Jan Ransom, "Trump Will Not Apologize
for Calling for Death Penalty over Central Park Five," *New York Times*, June 18,
2019, https://www.nytimes.com/2019/06/18/nyregion/central-park-five-trump
.html.

82 *"This American carnage stops"*: Donald Trump, "Inaugural Address," January 20, 2017, https://trumpwhitehouse.archives.gov/briefings-statements/the-inaugural-address/.

82 *"just keep doing your job"*: Gregory Korte, "Trump Tells Sheriffs: 'Just Keep Doing Your Job as Well as You're Doing It,'" *USA Today*, February 13, 2018, https://www.usatoday.com/story/news/politics/2018/02/13/trump-tells-sheriffs-just-keep-doing-your-job-well-youre-doing/335057002/.

83 *"made to protect the criminal"*: "Trump to Police: 'Please Don't Be Too Nice' to Suspects," ABC News, July 28, 2017, https://abcnews.go.com/Politics/trump-police-nice-suspects/story?id=48914504.

83 *thirteen people on federal death row*: Asawin Suebsaeng and Patrick Reis: "Trump's Killing Spree: The Inside Story of His Race to Execute Every Prisoner He Could," *Rolling Stone*, January 27, 2023, https://www.rollingstone.com/politics/politics-features/trump-capital-punishment-brandon-bernard-lisa-montgomery-1234664126/.

83 *Trump cheated on his taxes*: Russ Buettner, Susanne Craig, and Mike McIntire, "Trump's Taxes: Red Flags, Big Losses and a Windfall from His Father," *New York Times*, December 21, 2022, https://www.nytimes.com/2022/12/21/us/politics/trump-tax-returns-findings.html.

83 *He faces over eighty felony charges*: Charlie Savage, "The Four Trump Criminal Cases: Strengths and Weaknesses," *New York Times*, August 28, 2023, https://www.nytimes.com/article/trump-cases-counts-charges-strengths.html.

83 *"you can take the hand away"*: "Trump to Police: 'Please Don't Be Too Nice' to Suspects," ABC News.

84 *theft of agricultural equipment*: T. C. Esselstyn, "The Social Role of a County Sheriff," *Journal of Criminal Law and Criminology* 44, no. 2 (1953–1954): 183, https://scholarlycommons.law.northwestern.edu/cgi/viewcontent.cgi?article=4123&context=jclc.

84 *sheriffs in nearly one in four counties*: Bartelme and Cranney, "SC Sheriffs Fly First Class, Bully Employees and Line Their Pockets."

84 *one sheriff was sanctioned for wearing his uniform*: Bob Conrad, "Douglas County Sheriff in Hot Water Again, This Time for Violating State Ethics Law," This Is Reno, September 22, 2022, https://thisisreno.com/2022/09/douglas-county-sheriff-in-hot-water-again-this-time-for-violating-state-ethics-law/.

84 *the nickname of the "Trump of Los Angeles"*: Steve Scauzillo, "Alex Villanueva Challenges Janice Hahn for County Supervisor, Hits on Crime and Homeless," *Los Angeles Daily News*, September 13, 2023, https://www.dailynews.com/2023/09/13/alex-villanueva-challenges-janice-hahn-for-county-supervisor-hits-on-crime-and-homeless/.

84 *Villanueva made a run*: Jas Kang, "Janice Hahn Wins Re-Election, Calls Villanueva 'Two-Time Loser,'" KTLA 5, March 8, 2024, https://ktla.com/news/local-news/janice-hahn-wins-re-election-calls-villanueva-two-time-loser/.

85 *the sheriff has returned to office*: Dan Morse, "Md. Sheriff Charged in Machine Gun Conspiracy Case Returns to Work," *Washington Post*, September 1, 2023, https://

www.washingtonpost.com/dc-md-va/2023/09/01/frederick-county-sheriff
-chuck-jenkins-returns/.

85 *fire deputies if they fail to contribute*: Cameron Austin, "Virginia Supreme Court Upholds
Montgomery County Sheriff's Firing of Former Captain," *Roanoke Times*, February
26, 2015, https://roanoke.com/news/local/virginia-supreme-court-upholds
-montgomery-county-sheriffs-firing-of-former-captain/article_41abe49d-afdf
-5eda-b2b6-5a9cc0d9ad38.html. Although sheriff deputies are very similar to police officers, there is very little research or information about the type of training
deputies receive. Anecdotes suggest it varies widely and is subject to the discretion
of the sheriff beyond state-level certifications.

85 *firing government officials who testified*: Toluse Olorunnipa and Beth Reinhard, "Post-
Impeachment, Trump Declares Himself the 'Chief Law Enforcement Officer' of
America," *Washington Post*, February 19, 2020, https://www.washingtonpost.com
/politics/post-impeachment-trump-declares-himself-the-chief-law-enforcement
-officer-of-america/2020/02/18/b8ff49c0-5290-11ea-b119-4faabac6674f_story
.html.

85 *"ready to get tough in order to protect American jobs and families"*: Maeve Reston, "Arizona's
'Sheriff Joe' Arpaio Endorses Trump," CNN, January 27, 2016, https://edition
.cnn.com/2016/01/26/politics/sheriff-joe-arpaio-donald-trump-iowa/.

86 *CNN called him a "controversial figure"*: Alexander Provan, "The Vigilante," *GQ*, October 13, 2009, https://www.gq.com/story/joe-arpaio-sheriff-phoenix-mexico
-border-immigration; Ashley Hayes, "'America's Toughest Sheriff' No Stranger to
Controversy," CNN, December 15, 2011, https://www.cnn.com/2011/12/15
/justice/arizona-arpaio-profile/index.html.

86 *Obama was not born in the United States*: "Sheriff Arpaio: Obama Birth Certificate May
Be Forgery," NBC News, March 1, 2012, https://www.nbcnews.com/news/world
/sheriff-arpaio-obama-birth-certificate-may-be-forgery-flna285082.

87 *Arpaio gave a press conference*: J. Weston Phippen, "The Last of the Birthers," *Atlantic*,
December 15, 2016, https://www.theatlantic.com/news/archive/2016
/12/sheriff-joe-arpaio-the-birther/510857/.

87 *stop racially profiling Latinos or face contempt of court*: Richard Gonzales, "Feds Will Press
Criminal Contempt Charges Against Ariz. Sheriff Arpaio," NPR, October 11,
2016, https://www.npr.org/sections/thetwo-way/2016/10/11/497577585/feds
-will-press-criminal-contempt-charges-against-ariz-sheriff-arpaio.

87 *fines and fees related to his misconduct*: Colin Dwyer, "Ex-Sheriff Joe Arpaio Convicted of
Criminal Contempt," NPR, July 31, 2017, https://www.npr.org/sections/thetwo
-way/2017/07/31/540629884/ex-sheriff-joe-arpaio-convicted-of-criminal
-contempt.

87 *"we see eye to eye"*: Paul Lewis, "Sheriff Joe Arpaio on Donald Trump: 'My Mission
Is to Get Him Elected,'" *Guardian*, March 22, 2016, https://www.theguardian
.com/us-news/2016/mar/22/sheriff-joe-arpaio-interview-arizona-primary
-donald-trump.

88  *riot gear, tear gas, and batons*: John Wagner, Jenna Johnson, and Danielle Paquette, "Trump Threatens Shutdown, Suggests Controversial Pardon at Arizona Rally," *Washington Post*, August 23, 2017, https://www.washingtonpost.com/politics /trump-holds-campaign-style-rally-amid-large-protests-in-arizona/2017/08/22 /dd7c83c0-8796-11e7-961d-2f373b3977ee_story.html.

89  *Trump rallies in Phoenix in 2018*: Megan Cassidy, "Trump Rally in Phoenix Draws Arpaio, Ward—Plus Cheers and Jeers," *Arizona Republic*, March 10, 2018, https:// www.azcentral.com/story/news/local/phoenix/2018/03/10/trump-unity-rally -phoenix-draws-cheers-jeers-joe-arpaio/413682002/.

90  *"countries we don't even know about"*: Donald Trump, "President Trump Meets with Sheriffs from Across the Country," February 11, 2019, YouTube video, 9:09, https://www.youtube.com/watch?v=Ys04Q5qr7ng.

91  *a sheriff asked Trump to "indemnify sheriffs"*: Donald Trump, "President Trump Remarks on Border Security and Immigration Enforcement," C-SPAN, March 20, 2018, video, 33:06, https://www.c-span.org/video/?442875-1/president-trump-remarks -border-security-immigration-enforcement.

91  *Trump held forth about "stopping bad people"*: Donald Trump, "Remarks by President Trump During Roundtable Discussion with State, Local, and Community Leaders on Border Security and Safe Communities," Trump White House, January 12, 2019, https://trumpwhitehouse.archives.gov/briefings-statements/remarks -president-trump-roundtable-discussion-state-local-community-leaders-border -security-safe-communities/.

91  *surrounded by sheriffs in uniform*: Trump, "President Trump Meets with Sheriffs," 0:44.

92  *forced migrants seeking asylum to wait*: "A Timeline of the Trump Administration's Efforts to End Asylum," National Immigrant Justice Center, accessed March 10, 2020, https://immigrantjustice.org/timeline-trump-administrations-efforts-end -asylum.

92  *he went to El Paso for a rally*: Donald Trump, "President Trump Rally in El Paso, Texas," C-SPAN, February 11, 2019, https://www.c-span.org/video/?457668-1 /president-trump-rally-el-paso-texas.

92  *proposed sending immigrants to sanctuary cities*: Trump, "Rally in El Paso," 1:02:47.

92  *later used by Thomas Homan*: Trump, "Remarks on Border Security and Immigration Enforcement," 3:25.

92  *not every sheriff agreed with Trump's anti-immigration agenda*: Kate Groetzinger, "Texas Border Sheriff: There Is No Crisis and We Don't Want Trump's Wall," *Texas Observer*, January 24, 2019, https://www.texasobserver.org/texas-border-sheriffs-there -is-no-crisis-and-we-dont-want-trumps-wall/.

92  *reduced the federal standards for incarceration*: Eunice Hyunhye Cho, "The Trump Administration Weakens Standards for ICE Detention Facilities," American Civil Liberties Union (blog), January 14, 2020, https://www.aclu.org/news/immigrants -rights/the-trump-administration-weakens-standards-for-ice-detention -facilities.

93  *nearly doubled the number of people in ICE detention*: David J. Bier, "Trump's Detention Surge Failed to Significantly Increase Removals," Cato Institute (blog), January 10, 2024, https://www.cato.org/blog/trumps-detention-surge-failed-significantly -increase-removals.

## CHAPTER 4: "AN OLD-FASHIONED CONSTITUTIONAL REVIVAL"

96  *seeking them out as a source of power and authority*: "Ammon's Army Marches On: People's Rights Network Membership Data, Fall 2021," Institute for Research & Education on Human Rights, accessed March 10, 2024, https://irehr.org/reports/ammons -army-marches-on/. Ammon Bundy's People's Rights Network was 50 percent women, suggesting they were increasingly aligning themselves with the far-right militia-style movements.

97  *homeschooling and food sovereignty*: "What Started as Group of Anti-Vax Moms Led by Stockton Woman Is Now 'Mamalitia,'" CBS News, April 29, 2021, https://www .cbsnews.com/sacramento/news/what-started-as-group-of-anti-vax-moms-is-now -mamalitia/.

97  *"community of constitution loving women"*: "Who We Are," Mamalitia (website), accessed March 10, 2024, https://mamalitia.org/who-we-are.

97  *made far-right sheriff meetings seem less testosterone-filled*: Hannah Wiley, Maria Figueroa, and Lydia Gerike, "Equal Opportunity Extremism: How Women Seized the Moment in California's Far-Right Radical Politics," *Sacramento Bee*, November 29, 2021, https://www.sacbee.com/news/california/article255292486.html.

98  *he said in an interview with the Family Research Council*: "Rex Steninger Overviews His Resolution Declaring Bill of Rights Will Be Upheld in His Jurisdiction," Family Research Council, video, 2:11, https://www.youtube.com/watch?v=qY2NyFofTrI.

98  *a federal fifty-five-miles-per-hour speed limit*: "Mel Steninger," *Elko Daily Free Press*, September 10, 2013, https://elkodaily.com/lifestyles/announcements/obituaries/mel -steninger/article_acf938b0-1a76-11e3-a613-001a4bcf887a.html.

100  *"County by county. State by state"*: "Rex Steninger Overviews His Resolution," 4:42– 6:00.

100  *When COVID first appeared in the United States*: "COVID-19 Timeline," CDC, accessed March 11, 2024, https://www.cdc.gov/museum/timeline/covid19.html.

100  *Coronavirus Aid, Relief, and Economic Security (CARES) Act*: Coronavirus Aid, Relief, and Economic Security Act, S. 3548, 116th Congress (2020), https://www.congress .gov/bill/116th-congress/senate-bill/3548/text.

100  *documents like the Great Barrington Declaration*: Amanda D'Ambrosio, "Who Are the Scientists Behind the Great Barrington Declaration?," MedPage Today, October 19, 2020, https://www.medpagetoday.com/infectiousdisease/covid19/89204.

101  *"siding with American ideals"*: "Maine Sheriff Responds to Gov. Mills' Stay Home Order: 'Will NOT Be Setting Up a Police State,'" *Maine Examiner*, April 1, 2020, archived April 8, 2020 by the Wayback Machine, https://web.archive.org/web

/20230127133631/https://maineexaminer.com/maine-sheriff-responds-to-gov-mills-stay-home-order-will-not-be-setting-up-a-police-state/.

101 *"not Nazi Germany or Soviet Russia"*: Scott Nichols Sr., "A Message from the Sheriff Regarding the Latest Executive Order," Facebook, April 1, 2020, https://www.facebook.com/permalink.php?story_fbid=10158162843827232&id=750637231.

102 *"the good sheriff standing and doing his job"*: Richard Mack, interviewed by Sarah Westall, "Gestapo Alive & Well, Tyranny Rampant: County Sheriff Is America's Last Hope w/ Sheriff Mack," Business Game Changers, May 4, 2020, https://www.transformationtalkradio.com/episode/business-game-changers-radio-with-sarah-westall-gestapo-alive-well-tyranny-rampant-county-sheriff-is-americas-last-hope-w-sheriff-mack,28766.html.

102 *arrested for refusing to leave a playground*: "Protest Starts After Idaho Woman Arrested at Playground Closed Due to Coronavirus," CBS News, April 22, 2020, https://www.cbsnews.com/news/coronavirus-idaho-woman-arrested-closed-playground-protests-meridian-city-hall/; Mack, interviewed by Westall, "Gestapo Alive & Well, Tyranny Rampant." She was part of an organized anti-vax protest and charged with a misdemeanor.

102 *"what we do at the CSPOA"*: Mack, interviewed by Westall, "Gestapo Alive & Well, Tyranny Rampant."

103 *"it might come to that"*: Richard Mack, CSPOA Posse Round-Up Call, August 20, 2020.

103 *arrested Pastor Rodney Howard-Browne*: "Florida Pastor Arrested for Holding Church Services Despite Stay-at-Home Order," CNN, March 30, 2020, https://www.cnn.com/2020/03/30/us/florida-pastor-arrested-river-church/index.html.

103 *memorialized by a 2023 documentary*: "Shop," Caleb Cooper Ministries, accessed March 11, 2024, https://calebcooperministries.com/shop/.

103 *exempted under the state's COVID orders*: Kathleen Sloan, "Sheriff Hamilton Defends Mass Deputization of Religious Sect as 'Symbolic,'" *Sierra County Sun*, May 19, 2020, https://sierracountysun.org/government/county/sheriff-hamilton-defends-mass-deputization-of-religious-sect-as-symbolic/.

103 *Cooper describes himself as a "revivalist"*: "About," Caleb Cooper Ministries, accessed March 11, 2024, https://calebcooperministries.com/about/.

103 *"demonic powers in the unseen realm"*: "Book Release," Caleb Cooper Ministries, accessed March 11, 2024, https://calebcooperministries.com/book-release/.

104 *"we could take back our country tomorrow"*: KrisAnne Hall, *Noncompliant 2: The Sheriff* (Tampa Bay: Sacred Honor Media, 2023), 8:18.

104 *source of sheriff memes online*: @butler.sheriff, "The Constitutional Sheriff #constitutionalsheriff #constitutionalrights #butlercountysheriffsofficeohio #constitutionalelected #sheriffdeputies," TikTok, November 8, 2022, https://www.tiktok.com/@butler.sheriff/video/7163697477219126570.

104 *"go to the local gun shop"*: Richard Mack, CSPOA Posse Round-Up Call, September 26, 2020.

104 *"lie, cheat, steal, and sometimes murder"*: Richard Mack, CSPOA Posse Round-Up Call, November 6, 2020.

105 *"all the voting fraud going on"*: Mack, CSPOA Posse Round-Up Call, September 26, 2020.

105 *deaths of at least 246 people*: Zach Despart, "Did Texas Undercount 2021's Freeze Deaths? COVID and Historical Patterns Cannot Explain Spike," *Houston Chronicle*, February 18, 2022, https://www.houstonchronicle.com/news/houston-texas/houston/article/Did-Texas-undercount-2021-freeze-deaths-COVID-16928281.php. As Despart outlines, many experts believe the state of Texas underestimated the death toll from the freeze.

106 *two "championship" golf courses*: Woodlands Resort (website), accessed March 11, 2024, https://www.woodlandsresort.com/.

107 *An open advocate for Christian nationalism*: Nathalie Baptiste, "GOP's Neo-Confederate Theocrat Wins Council Seat in One of Richest U.S. Counties," *American Prospect*, November 3, 2014, https://prospect.org/power/gop-s-neo-confederate-theocrat-wins-council-seat-one-richest-u.s.-counties/.

107 *leads fellow group members in a rendition of "Dixie"*: Michael Peroutka, "Michael Peroutka Calls 'I Wish I Was in Dixie' the National Anthem," Psychvideos, posted on You-Tube July 27, 2014, https://www.youtube.com/watch?v=EU-yheBdOTI.

107 *Republican nominee for Maryland attorney general*: Joe Heim, "For GOP's Attorney General Nominee, God's Law Comes Before Maryland's," *Washington Post*, October 14, 2022, https://www.washingtonpost.com/dc-md-va/2022/10/14/michael-peroutka-maryland-attorney-constitution/.

107 *refused to concede and alleged voter fraud*: Mia Jankowicz, "A Maryland Republican Who Lost His Race by 300K Votes Says He Won't Concede," *Business Insider*, November 11, 2022, https://www.businessinsider.com/gop-maryland-candidate-refuses-concede-lost-by-300k-votes-2022-11.

108 *Elliott on the cover as David facing Goliath*: Alex Hannaford, "Above the Law," *Texas Observer*, May 2, 2016, https://www.texasobserver.org/above-the-law-pamela-elliott-sheriff/.

108 *used her office to harass and intimidate*: "Alleged Voter Intimidation by Local Sheriff in Edwards County, Texas," Campaign Legal Center, May 5, 2016, https://campaignlegal.org/press-releases/alleged-voter-intimidation-local-sheriff-edwards-county-texas.

108 *potentially a "criminal offense"*: Hannaford, "Above the Law."

108 *botched a murder investigation*: Hannaford, "Above the Law."

108 *former CEO of Curves*: Sandy Engel, "Weighing In with Curves Founder Gary Heavin," CBN, December 10, 2022, https://www2.cbn.com/article/not-selected/weighing-curves-founder-gary-heavin.

109 *Heavin donated $10,000 to the Oath Keepers*: Rebecca Ballhaus, Khadeeja Safdar, and Shalini Ramachandran, "Proud Boys and Oath Keepers, Forceful on Jan. 6, Privately Are in Turmoil," *Wall Street Journal*, June 16, 2021, https://www.wsj.com

/articles/proud-boys-and-oath-keepers-forceful-on-jan-6-privately-are-in
-turmoil-11623859785.

110  *billboards railed against immigrants*: Andrea Grimes, "From 'Friendly' State to Enmity
State," *Texas Observer*, August 5, 2021, https://www.texasobserver.org/opinion
-from-friendly-state-to-enmity-state/.

110  *revolts by ranchers against the Bureau of Land Management*: Jonathan Thompson, "The Rise
of the Sagebrush Sheriffs," *High Country News*, February 2, 2016, https://www.hcn
.org/issues/48-2/the-rise-of-the-sagebrush-sheriffs/.

110  *most of it concentrated in the West*: Phil Edwards, "See How Much of Your State Is
Owned by the Federal Government," Vox, February 16, 2015, https://www.vox
.com/2015/2/16/8046349/federal-government-land-by-state.

111  *the idea of reducing federal regulation of public land*: Paul Dans and Steven Groves, eds.,
*Mandate for Leadership: The Conservative Promise* (Washington, DC: Heritage Founda-
tion, 2023), 308, https://thf_media.s3.amazonaws.com/project2025/2025
_MandateForLeadership_FULL.pdf.

112  *Black people were "better off" during slavery*: John M. Glionna, "Cliven Bundy's 'Better Off
as Slaves' Remark About Blacks Draws Fire," *Los Angeles Times*, April 24, 2014,
https://www.latimes.com/nation/nationnow/la-na-nn-nevada-rancher-bundy
-slaves-20140424-story.html.

112  *two dozen ranchers from Elko*: Grass March Cowboy Express (website), accessed March
11, 2024, https://www.grassmarchcowboyexpress.com/.

112  *died when he fell from his horse*: Hannah Hess, "Grant Gerber, Nevada Activist, Dies
from Fall Sustained on Horseback Ride to Capitol Hill," *Roll Call*, October 28,
2014, https://rollcall.com/2014/10/28/grant-gerber-nevada-activist-dies-from
-fall-sustained-on-horseback-ride-to-capitol-hill/.

112  *helped the Filippinis herd their cattle*: Mary Branscomb, "Filippinis Turn Out Cattle," *Elko
Daily Free Press*, June 4, 2015, https://elkodaily.com/news/filippinis-turn-out-cattle
/article_9ddbc810-960e-571b-a0da-ac5c3bd0ebb2.html.

113  *Elko County held its own Patriotic Social Gathering*: "County Gathering Celebrates Local
Law Enforcement," *Elko Daily Free Press*, June 21, 2021, https://elkodaily.com/news
/local/govt-and-politics/county-gathering-celebrates-local-law-enforcement/arti
cle_d584ce9a-fcc2-5f11-8746-1a5c1b94a748.html.

113  *Steninger played the role of emcee*: Rex Steninger, email to author, February 10, 2023.

113  *"a grassroots uprising from the people"*: Rex Steninger, "Arise USA: Rex Steninger on
Making a Difference One County at a Time," speech in Yankton, South Dakota,
July 9, 2021, https://rumble.com/vjqqfl-arise-usa-rex-steninger-on-making-a
-difference-one-county-at-a-time.html.

114  *switch from Dominion voting machines*: Sam Metz, "Lander County to Replace Dominion
Voting Machines," *Elko Daily Free Press*, December 16, 2021, https://elkodaily.com
/news/local/govt-and-politics/lander-county-to-replace-dominion-voting
-machines/article_7f11691f-8857-56d7-a3be-baffb0c9fb46.html.

114  *resigned after the 2022 midterm*: Sean Golonka, "Nevada's Election Worker Turnover Second Highest Among Western States, Report Finds," *Nevada Independent*, September 26, 2023, https://thenevadaindependent.com/article/nevadas-election -worker-turnover-second-highest-among-western-states-report-finds.

114  *Steninger wrote in an October 2021 email*: Sean Golonka, "How Rural Nevada Became the Next Battleground for the 'Big Lie,'" *Nevada Independent*, October 23, 2022, https://thenevadaindependent.com/article/how-rural-nevada-became-the-next -battleground-for-the-big-lie.

**CHAPTER 5: THE AMERICAN SHERIFF**

116  *Lamb was six foot three and 240 pounds*: Mark Lamb, *American Sheriff: Traditional Values in a Modern World* (self-pub., 2020), 22.

116  *worked at the time for the Lincoln Strategy Group*: "Renowned Digital Innovator Corey Vale Joins Push Digital Group as Vice President," Push Digital Group (website), February 26, 2024, https://pushdigitalgroup.com/corey-vale-joins-push-digital -group/.

116  *leader in the Arizona Christian Coalition*: "Nathan Sproul," Lincoln Strategy Group (website), accessed March 11, 2024, https://lincoln-strategy.org/lincoln-strategy -group/nathan-sproul/.

116  *pled guilty to voter registration fraud*: Associated Press, "Trump Campaign and Republicans Paid $1.8M to Companies Mired in Voter Fraud Claims," *Guardian*, November 5, 2016, https://www.theguardian.com/us-news/2016/nov/06/trump -campaign-and-republicans-paid-18m-to-companies-mired-in-voter-claims.

116  *He also ran Kanye West's*: Sara Murray and Scott Glover, "Kanye West's Campaign Has Hired GOP Operative with History of Controversial Work," CNN, September 22, 2020, https://www.cnn.com/2020/09/22/politics/kanye-west-gop -operative/index.html.

117  *special news segment on "border security"*: *Fox and Friends*, April 22, 2021, https://www .facebook.com/protectamericanowusa/videos/264171445419997.

117  *"those who want more government"*: "Stand Together," Protect America Now (website), archived April 12, 2023, by the Wayback Machine, https://web.archive.org/web /20230412235409/https:/protectamericanow.com/stand-together/.

119  *describes his peripatetic childhood*: Lamb, *American Sheriff*, 4.

119  *descended from an early Mormon convert*: Daniel Webster Jones, *Forty Years Among the Indians* (Salt Lake City: Juvenile Instructor Office, 1890).

120  *"harder to become a flight attendant"*: Janel Lamb, *The Sheriff's Wife: Holding It All Together Behind the Scenes in Politics* (self-pub., 2020), 3.

121  *much more dangerous than police officer*: "Injuries, Illnesses, and Fatalities," U.S. Bureau of Labor Statistics, modified December 19, 2023, https://www.bls.gov/iif/fatal -injuries-tables/fatal-occupational-injuries-table-a-5-2022.htm.

121 *"deep, burning desire to run for sheriff"*: Mark Lamb, CSPOA 2020 Conference, Liberty University, September 30, 2020.

121 *talked about his values*: Mark Lamb, "Vote for Your Values," Mark Lamb for Sheriff, August 12, 2016, https://www.youtube.com/watch?v=ocsuK_X6cBg.

121 *he did not believe in abortion rights*: "Mark Lamb: On the Issues," Mark Lamb for Sheriff (website), archived October 10, 2016, by the Wayback Machine, https://web .archive.org/web/20161010230054/http://lambforsheriff.com/Mark-Lamb -Sheriff-Issues.html.

121 *clips of Hillary Clinton talking about regulating gun sales*: Mark Lamb, "Stop Hillary's Gun Grab," Mark Lamb for Sheriff, August 10, 2016, https://www.youtube.com /watch?v=-ot8SGsBod0.

121 *photos of Lamb and his large Mormon family*: "Vote for Your Values," Mark Lamb for Sheriff.

122 *$40 million budget*: Mariana Dale, "Pinal County Sheriff's Office Reduces Budget Deficit," KJZZ, January 3, 2018, https://kjzz.org/content/587268/pinal-county -sheriffs-office-reduces-budget-deficit.

122 *asking people to send in their early ballots*: Mark Lamb, "Don't Forget to Vote," Mark Lamb for Sheriff, August 18, 2016, https://www.youtube.com/watch?v= 678Bawu85d4.

122 *under the cloud of a $2 million budget deficit*: Jake Kincaid, "Jail Audit Shows Misuse of Millions of Dollars by PCSO," *Casa Grande Dispatch*, October 20, 2017, https:// www.pinalcentral.com/casa_grande_dispatch/area_news/jail-audit-shows -misuse-of-millions-of-dollars-by-pcso/article_bf5196cc-72c6-503e-8773 -d92e73e5b817.html.

123 *"yearly multiplying millions"*: John O'Sullivan, "Annexation," *United States Magazine and Democratic Review* 17, no. 1 (July–August 1845): 5–10, https://web.archive.org /web/20051125043717/http://web.grinnell.edu/courses/HIS/f01/HIS202-01 /Documents/OSullivan.html.

123 *O'Sullivan wrote of the "boundless future" Americans faced*: John O'Sullivan, "The Great Nation of Futurity," *United States Democratic Review* 6, no. 2 (November 1839): 350, https://babel.hathitrust.org/cgi/pt?id=coo.31924085376634&view=1up& seq=350.

123 *"hundreds of happy millions"*: O'Sullivan, "Great Nation of Futurity," 351.

123 *"Arizona became a shelter for desperadoes"*: Richard Josiah Hinton, *The Handbook to Arizona: Its Resources, History, Towns, Mines, Ruins, and Scenery* (San Francisco: Payot, Upham, 1878), 33, https://books.google.com/books?id=ewINAAAAIAAJ.

124 *"golden age of the sheriff"*: Smith, *Rural Crime Control*, 50.

124 *pinnacle of law enforcement and short-lived*: Smith, *Rural Crime Control*, 50.

124 *engaged in "prosaic functions"*: Smith, *Rural Crime Control*, 50.

124 *"deputize men with shadowy backgrounds"*: Larry D. Ball, *Desert Lawmen: The High Sheriffs of New Mexico and Arizona Territories, 1846–1912* (Albuquerque: University of New Mexico Press, 1996), 30.

125  *recruit itinerant workers to register to vote*: Ball, *Desert Lawmen*, 60.

125  *memorialized by neo-Confederates*: Christopher M. Bradley, "Not Set in Stone: Civil War Memorialization at Picacho Pass and the Emergence of a Confederate Fantasy Heritage in Arizona," *Journal of Arizona History* 62, no. 2 (2021): 141–71, https://muse.jhu.edu/article/805150.

125  *literacy tests and other forms of voter suppression*: Grace Oldham, "Arizona Has Suppressed Black, Latino and Native American Voters for More Than a Century," *Arizona Republic*, September 13, 2020, https://www.azcentral.com/story/news/politics/arizona/2020/09/13/arizonas-history-suppressing-black-latino-native-american-voters/5771359002/.

126  *a vigilante gunfighter who became the law*: "The Life of Wyatt Earp," PBS (website), accessed March 11, 2024, https://www.pbs.org/wgbh/americanexperience/features/wyatt-earp-life/.

126  *manifest destiny was "God's will" and not about conquest*: "The Principles of Liberty," National Center for Constitutional Studies (website), accessed March 11, 2024, https://nccs.net/pages/principles-of-liberty.

126  *"the tact and discretion he exercises"*: D. R. Struckhoff, *American Sheriff* (Joliet, IL: Justice Research Institute, 1994), 90.

126  *half of all voters knew their sheriff*: Zoorob, "There's (Rarely) a New Sheriff," 11.

127  *borrowed the image of a kneeling Knight Templar*: Kelly Foreman, "Daviess County Sheriff's Office," *Kentucky Law Enforcement*, March 17, 2020, https://www.klemagazine.com/blog/2020/3/16/daviess-county-sheriffs-office; Valerie Chinn, "New Bullitt County Sheriff Says Changes Are Coming to the Office," WDRB, January 24, 2019, https://www.wdrb.com/news/new-bullitt-county-sheriff-says-changes-are-coming-to-the-office/article_ab5a5484-1fee-11e9-af17-d7a3d20dde85.html. One sheriff went so far as to use the slogan "Inginio Vir Bellator Corde Servi," which translates to "skills of a warrior, heart of a servant." Some people allege that the Knights Templar were the "first police," so it's borrowed as a secret symbol for law enforcement. Christine Mai-Duc, "Fact or Fiction? Rogue Police Force Claims Ties to Ancient Knights Templar," *Los Angeles Times*, May 6, 2015, https://www.latimes.com/local/lanow/la-me-rogue-police-knights-templar-20150506-htmlstory.html.

127  *feature land, air, and sea patrols*: "Riverside County Sheriff—Search & Rescue," Defender (YouTube channel), March 22, 2023, https://www.youtube.com/watch?v=gJIXYnfabhU.

127  *posting the mug shots of people*: Jon Diaz, "Public Records, Like Jail Booking Photos, Can Linger in Iowa After Charges Are Dropped or a Not Guilty Verdict," We Are Iowa, July 1, 2021, https://www.weareiowa.com/article/news/crime/public-records-mugshot-iowa-records-taking-down-mugshot-from-online-internet/524-67c5ef12-d728-49b9-8b56-173ed8723085; Mara Leighton, "A Florida Sheriff Has Been Sued over Weekly 'Wheel of Fugitive' Posts on Social Media in Which He Spun a Wheel of Pictures Like a Game Show," *Business Insider*, January 31, 2023,

https://www.businessinsider.com/florida-sheriff-sued-over-wheel-of-fugitive
-posts-2023-I.

127 *television commercials for Dodge*: Bryan McTaggart, "Classic YouTube: Sheriff J. W.
Higgins and the Dodges of 1970–1971," Bangshift, May 1, 2022, https://bang
shift.com/general-news/car-features/mopar-car-features/classic-youtube
-sheriff-j-w-higgins-and-the-dodges-of-1970-1971/.

127 *"coupled with other evil traits"*: Struckhoff, *American Sheriff*, 93–94.

129 *discrepancies in the foundation's accounting*: Andrew Oxford, "Charity Founded by Pinal
County Sheriff Mark Lamb Has $18,000 in Unaccounted Spending," *Arizona Re-
public*, August 31, 2020, https://www.azcentral.com/story/news/politics/arizona
/2020/08/31/pinal-county-sheriff-mark-lamb-charity-tax-filings/562602
6002/.

129 *the network was sold to TruBlu*: "True Crime Network TruBlu Acquires American Sheriff Network," PR Newswire, June 14, 2023, https://www.prnewswire.com/news
-releases/true-crime-network-trublu-acquires-american-sheriff-network-3018
50812.html/

129 *he caught COVID himself*: "Pinal Co. Sheriff Mark Lamb Tests Positive for
COVID-19," 12 News, June 19, 2020, https://www.youtube.com/watch?v=rm
Ing7XNzyk.

130 *the video, which went viral*: "Pinal County Sheriff Says He Will Never Mandate
COVID-19 Vaccine," FOX 10 Phoenix, August 24, 2021, https://www.youtube
.com/watch?v=h4ZArl-75Fo.

130 *giving people a productive outlet*: Alana Minkler, "Pinal County Sheriff Mark Lamb
Discusses Citizen Posse in Response to Protests," *Arizona Republic*, July 31, 2020,
https://www.azcentral.com/story/news/local/arizona-breaking/2020/07/31/pi
nal-county-sheriff-mark-lamb-new-citizen-posse/5555959002/.

130 *"No longer are Americans going to sit by"*: "Kelly Townsend Discussing Sheriff Mark
Lamb's Citizen Posse," YouTube, November 19, 2022, https://www.youtube.com
/watch?v=Y1JGqnWB0Nk.

131 *harsh and punitive criminal legal system*: Nicole Santa Cruz, "The Invisible Hand of Steve
Twist," *Arizona Republic*, April 5, 2022, https://www.azcentral.com/story/news
/politics/arizona/2022/04/06/how-steve-twist-shaped-arizona-punitive-justice
-system/9474641002/.

131 *"how much blood and guts we have to spill"*: Clifton Abbott, "Prison Rioters Face Guns,"
*Tucson Daily Citizen*, February 7, 1953, A1, https://www.newspapers.com/image
/17398412.

131 *"nearly complete self-contained village"*: Mona Lynch, *Sunbelt Justice: Arizona and the Transformation of American Punishment* (Palo Alto, CA: Stanford University Press, 2009), 43.

131 *one impact of the rise of Arpaio*: Lynch, *Sunbelt Justice*, 163.

134 *violates the NSA's code of ethics*: "Code of Ethics of the Office of Sheriff," National
Sheriffs' Association, accessed April 17, 2024, https://www.sheriffs.org/sites/de
fault/files/NSACodeofEthics.pdf.

135 *"protects the Public from undue political influence"*: "National Sheriffs' Association Recognizes America's Right to Vote for the Office of Sheriff," National Sheriffs' Association.

140 *Lamb may have misused over $200,000*: John Washington, "Pinal Sheriff Mark Lamb's Office Spent $200K on Guns and Ammo from an 'Inmate Welfare' Fund," *Arizona Luminaria*, September 29, 2023, https://azluminaria.org/2023/09/29/pinal -sheriff-mark-lambs-office-spent-200k-on-guns-and-ammo-from-an-inmate -welfare-fund/; "Pinal County Sheriff Lamb Defends Spending of Inmate Welfare Fund on Weapons," *Pinal County News*, SanTanValley.com, October 25, 2023, https://www.santanvalley.com/news/pinal-county-news/pinal-county-sheriff -lamb-defends-spending-of-inmate-welfare-fund-on-weapons; John Washington, "Sheriff Mark Lamb Tells Pinal County Board of Supervisors Guns He Bought Benefit Jail Inmates," *Arizona Luminaria*, October 20, 2023, https://azluminaria .org/2023/10/20/sheriff-mark-lamb-tells-pinal-county-board-of-supervisors -guns-he-bought-benefit-jail-inmates/; Mark Lamb, Pinal County Board of Supervisors Meeting, October 18, 2023, 38:10, https://pinalcountyaz.new.swagit.com /videos/276934.

## CHAPTER 6: "I PAID FOR YOU TO KILL MY SON"

142 *law requires that the sheriff bring them to see a judge*: La. CCRP 230.1, https://legis.la.gov /legis/Law.aspx?d=112388. It's called different things in different states.

142 *cannot afford to pay any amount of bail*: Jessica Brand and Jessica Pishko, "Bail Reform: Explained," The Appeal, June 14, 2018, https://theappeal.org/bail-reform -explained-4abb73dd2e8a/.

143 *85 percent of local jails are controlled by sheriffs*: "Jail Resources," National Sheriffs' Association (website), accessed March 11, 2024, https://www.sheriffs.org/gcps/jail -ops/resources.

144 *people were fascinated by an old house*: Becky Bracken, "Former Sheriff's House Complete with 9 Jail Cells Becomes a Viral Sensation," Realtor.com, August 19, 2020, https://www.realtor.com/news/unique-homes/former-sheriffs-house-with-jail -viral-sensation/.

145 *"bound to have sufficient force to prevent a breach of the prison"*: John G. Crocker, *The Duties of Sheriffs, Coroners and Constables, with Practical Forms* (New York: Banks & Brothers, 1871), 101.

145 *preventing further violence until help arrived*: "Sheriff's Wife a Heroine," *Chicago Tribune*, January 20, 1900, 8, https://www.newspapers.com/image/349282595/.

145 *"abomination in the sight of man"*: Melanie Newport, *This Is My Jail: Local Politics and the Rise of Mass Incarceration* (Philadelphia: University of Pennsylvania Press, 2022), 22.

146 *"profits could be maximized"*: Frank Richard Prassel, *The Western Peace Officer: A Legacy of Law and Order* (Norman: University of Oklahoma Press, 1990), 84.

146  *set long jail sentences for petty theft*: Matthew J. Mancini, "Pig Law," Mississippi Ency-
     clopedia (website), Center for Study of Southern Culture, updated April 14, 2018,
     https://mississippiencyclopedia.org/entries/pig-law/.

147  *"the scale of degradation"*: John N. Henderson, "The Lease System in Texas," in *Proceed-
     ings of the Annual Congress of Correction of the American Correctional Association* (Pittsburgh:
     American Correctional Association, 1898), 298, https://books.google.com/books
     ?id=oHczAQAAMAAJ&pg=PA298.

147  *lose their teeth thanks to scurvy*: Robert Perkinson, *Texas Tough: The Rise of America's Prison
     Empire* (New York: Henry Holt, 2010), 123.

147  *"heterogenous conglomerations of humanity"*: Myrl E. Alexander, *Jail Administration* (Berkeley:
     University of California Press, 1957), 5.

148  *"traditional dumping ground"*: Ronald Goldfarb, *Jails: The Ultimate Ghetto of the Criminal
     Justice System* (New York: Anchor Press, 1975), 4.

148  *"no privacy and no activity"*: Goldfarb, *Jails*, 6.

148  *"cruelest form of punishment in the United States"*: John Irwin, *The Jail: Managing the Underclass
     in American Society* (Berkeley: University of California Press, 1985), xi.

148  *jail admissions in the United States increased*: Newport, *This Is My Jail*, 1.

149  *nearly 9 million admissions*: Zeng, *Jail Inmates in 2022*, 2.

149  *the state pays sheriffs $26.39 per day*: Eyal Press, "A Fight to Expose the Hidden Human
     Costs of Incarceration," *New Yorker*, August 16, 2021, https://www.newyorker
     .com/magazine/2021/08/23/a-fight-to-expose-the-hidden-human-costs-of
     -incarceration.

150  *eleven deaths in one year*: Jason Pohl and Ryan Gabrielson, "California Tried to Fix Its
     Prisons. Now County Jails Are More Deadly," ProPublica, April 24, 2019, https://
     www.propublica.org/article/california-fresno-county-jail-deaths.

150  *one of the sheriffs who met with Donald Trump*: Cresencio Rodriguez-Delgado, "What
     Fresno County's Sheriff Has to Say After Meeting with President Trump at the
     Border," *Sacramento Bee*, April 5, 2019, https://www.sacbee.com/news/california
     /article228901619.html.

150  *"pit bull on your pant leg"*: Abby Steckel, "Three Feet Apart," *New Journal*, September
     27, 2020, https://thenewjournalatyale.com/2020/09/three-feet-apart/.

151  *a chair with straps used to pin the victim down*: "Former Sheriff Victor Hill Sentenced to
     Federal Prison for Civil Rights Violations," United States Attorney's Office, North-
     ern District of Georgia, March 14, 2023, https://www.justice.gov/usao-ndga/pr/for
     mer-sheriff-victor-hill-sentenced-federal-prison-civil-rights-violations; Maurice
     Chammah, "They Went to Jail. Then They Say They Were Strapped to a Chair
     for Days," Marshall Project, February 7, 2020, https://www.themarshallproject
     .org/2020/02/07/they-went-to-jail-then-they-say-they-were-strapped-to-a-chair
     -for-days. The family of Billy Ames, who died in 2019, recently settled with
     St. François County, Missouri, for $1.8 million. Ames had been kept in the chair
     for twenty-four hours, even as he screamed for help and other inmates begged for
     him to be released.

151 *eighteen months in prison for civil rights violations*: "Former Sheriff Victor Hill Sentenced to Federal Prison for Civil Rights Violations," United States Attorney's Office, Northern District of Georgia. Jails can also be sites of sexual abuse. In 2023, the *New York Times* reported on a Mississippi sheriff who groomed and sexually assaulted women in his jail. Ilyssa Daly and Jerry Mitchell, "Where the Sheriff Is King, These Women Say He Coerced Them into Sex," *New York Times*, July 19, 2023, https://www.nytimes.com/2023/07/19/us/mississippi-sheriff-sexual-abuse.html.

151 *At least one thousand jail deaths*: E. Ann Carson, *Mortality in Local Jails, 2000–2019—Statistical Tables* (Washington, DC: Bureau of Justice Statistics, 2021), https://bjs.ojp.gov/content/pub/pdf/mlj0019st.pdf.

152 *a woman gave birth in 2020 on the floor of her solitary jail cell*: Miranda Suarez, "A Woman Gave Birth Alone in a Tarrant County Jail Cell. A Federal Lawsuit Says It's the Jail's Fault," KERA News, January 14, 2022, https://www.keranews.org/news/2022-01-14/a-woman-gave-birth-alone-in-a-tarrant-county-jail-cell-a-federal-lawsuit-says-its-the-jails-fault.

153 *still no official cause of death*: Andrea C. Armstrong, *Dying in East Baton Rouge Parish Prison* (New Orleans: Promise of Justice Initiative, 2018), 6, https://papers.ssrn.com/sol3/papers.cfm?abstract_id=3237620.

153 *"inadequate medical and mental healthcare"*: Armstrong, *Dying in East Baton Rouge Parish Prison*, 6.

154 *changes to health care and staffing*: Graham Ulkins, "Prison Reform Coalition Pushing for Changes Inside EBR Jail," WAFB, June 1, 2018, https://www.wafb.com/story/38323231/prison-reform-coalition-pushing-for-changes-inside-ebr-jail/.

155 *more people had died from homicide per capita*: Jessica Pishko, "Why Do People Keep Dying in Harris County Jail?," The Appeal, March 9, 2023, https://theappeal.org/kim-ogg-fred-harris-jaquaree-simmons-harris-county-jail-deaths/.

155 *killed by a twenty-five-year-old man*: Pishko, "Why Do People Keep Dying in Harris County Jail?"; Alex Stuckey, "Her Son's Killer Was Found Guilty. Now She Wants the Harris County Jail Held Accountable," *Houston Landing*, December 19, 2023, https://houstonlanding.org/her-sons-killer-was-found-guilty-now-she-wants-the-harris-county-jail-held-accountable/; Nicole Hensley, "Man Pleads Guilty in Death of Harris County Inmate Fred Harris Amid Trial," *Houston Chronicle*, November 28, 2023, https://www.houstonchronicle.com/news/houston-texas/crime/article/fred-harris-jail-trial-18519540.php.

157 *an investigation showed*: Pishko, "Why Do People Keep Dying in Harris County Jail?"

157 *"betrayed my trust"*: Matt Harab, "11 Fired, 6 Suspended at Harris County Sheriff's Office Following Death of Inmate in February," Houston Public Media, May 28, 2021, https://www.houstonpublicmedia.org/articles/news/criminal-justice/2021/05/28/399408/11-fired-6-suspended-at-harris-county-sheriffs-office-following-death-of-inmate-in-february/.

159 *jail populations overall dropped*: "The Scale of the COVID-19-Related Jail Population Decline," Vera Institute, August 2020, https://www.vera.org/publications/covid19-jail-population-decline.

159 *Sheriffs were some of the people most in favor*: Chris Gelardi, "In LA County Jails, Coronavirus Chaos Keeps People Locked Up Longer," *Intercept*, March 2, 2021, https://theintercept.com/2021/03/02/covid-jails-los-angeles-court-dates/; Timothy Williams, Benjamin Weiser, and William K. Rashbaum, "'Jails Are Petri Dishes': Inmates Freed as the Virus Spreads Behind Bars," *New York Times*, March 30, 2020, https://www.nytimes.com/2020/03/30/us/coronavirus-prisons-jails.html; Josh McGhee, "Federal Judge Denies Mass Release at Cook County Jail, Named 'Top U.S. Hot Spot' for COVID-19," *Chicago Reporter*, April 9, 2020, https://www.chicagoreporter.com/federal-judge-denies-mass-release-at-cook-county-jail-named-top-u-s-hot-spot-for-covid-19/.

159 *compiled statutes that permitted*: Aaron Littman, *Statutory Release Powers* (Los Angeles: UCLA School of Law COVID Behind Bars Data Project, 2020), https://docs.google.com/spreadsheets/d/e/2PACX-1vTT2_PEwDtlNP39zoCNSllq0IEpuYHRpNu4TqXs75Q5LcjpUI6Qh5Xi6pC3s7FslHvuGYYB_SAR4IKD/pub?output=pdf.

160 *"failed to safeguard the health of the inmates"*: *Barnes v. Ahlman*, 140 S. Ct. 2620 (2020), https://casetext.com/case/barnes-v-ahlman.

160 *engaged in systemic abuses in his jail*: Shannon Dooling, "AG Report: Bristol County Sheriff Violated Civil Rights of Immigrant Detainees; Calls for Transfer of Those in Custody," WBUR, December 15, 2020, https://www.wbur.org/news/2020/12/15/healey-hodgson-bristol-immigration-detainees-report.

161 *"running experiments on us"*: Li Cohen, "'They Used Us as an Experiment': Arkansas Inmates Who Were Given Ivermectin to Treat COVID File Federal Lawsuit Against Jail," CBS News, January 17, 2022, https://www.cbsnews.com/news/covid-19-ivermetin-arkansas-jail-inmates-vitamins/.

161 *passed a resolution praising him*: Maya Yang, "Arkansas Officials Praise Doctor Accused of Giving Inmates Ivermectin Without Consent," *Guardian*, February 8, 2022, https://www.theguardian.com/us-news/2022/feb/08/arkansas-doctor-ivermectin-treated-inmates-lawsuit; Andrew DeMillo, "Arkansas Jail Inmates Settle Lawsuit with Doctor Who Prescribed Them Ivermectin for COVID-19," KATV ABC 7, October 6, 2023, https://katv.com/news/local/arkansas-jail-inmates-settle-lawsuit-doctor-robert-karas-prescribed-ivermectin-covid-washington-county-detention-center-wcdc-us-food-drug-administration-fda-american-civil-liberties-union-aclu-holly-dickson-michael-mosley-medical-board-associated-press; Lara Farrar, "Arkansas Medical Board Takes No Action against Jail Doctor Who Treated Inmates with Ivermectin for COVID," *Arkansas Democrat-Gazette*, June 10, 2022, https://www.arkansasonline.com/news/2022/jun/10/arkansas-medical-board-takes-no-action-against/.

161  *advocates for those who have been abused*: "About Texas Jail Project," Texas Jail Project (website), accessed March 11, 2024, https://www.texasjailproject.org/about-texas -jail-project/.

164  *Gautreaux ran as a Democrat*: Blake Paterson, "Gautreaux Wins Re-Election as East Baton Rouge Sheriff," *Advocate*, October 12, 2019, https://www.theadvocate.com /baton_rouge/news/politics/elections/article_859a1eee-eafc-11e9-9196-9736 39720be1.html.

164  *the effort failed*: Paterson, "Gautreaux Wins Re-Election."

164  *The same thing happened in 2023*: Bonnie Bolden, "Oct. 14 Election: Sid Gautreaux Stays Sheriff in East Baton Rouge Parish, Welborn Still Clerk of Court," BRPROUD, October 14, 2023, https://www.brproud.com/news/local-news/east -baton-rouge-parish/oct-14-election-sid-gautreaux-stays-sheriff-in-east-baton -rouge-parish-welborn-still-clerk-of-court/.

164  *tens of thousands from contractors and construction firms*: Author's calculations, based on Louisiana Ethics Administration Program campaign finance reports filed by Gautreaux's campaign.

165  *which Texas has not adopted*: Kim Krisberg and David Leffler, "Why Texas Republicans Still Oppose Medicaid Expansion," *Texas Tribune*, November 7, 2022, https:// www.texastribune.org/2022/11/07/texas-medicaid-expansion-republicans/.

165  *"should not end their judicially set sentences of incarceration worse off"*: Andrea C. Armstrong, "The Missing Link: Jail and Prison Conditions in Criminal Justice Reform," *Louisiana Law Review* 80, no. 1 (Fall 2019): 32, https://digitalcommons.law.lsu.edu/cgi /viewcontent.cgi?article=6758&context=lalrev.

166  *no oversight or regulatory commission at all*: Michele Deitch, email to Ethan Corey, March 10, 2024. Deitch, director of the Prison and Jail Innovation Lab at the University of Texas's Lyndon B. Johnson School of Public Affairs, explains, "I think it is fair to say that there are 29 states WITH some form of statewide jail oversight, so there would be 21 without any oversight of jails at all. That said, one could certainly take issue with describing some of those 29 states as having oversight, since 4 of them are 'overseen' by the state's Sheriff's Association, which relies on voluntary inspections with no enforcement mechanism if there is non-compliance with standards. . . . No comment on the quality of regulation even in those states that ostensibly have oversight, though."

166  *no mechanism to force them to comply*: Megan Gall, David Janovsky, and Bree Spencer, *A Matter of Life and Death: The Importance of the Death in Custody Reporting Act* (Washington, DC: Leadership Conference Education Fund and Project on Government Oversight, 2023), https://s3.amazonaws.com/docs.pogo.org/report/2023/A-Matter -of-Life-and-Death-the-Importance-of-the-Death-in-Custody-Reporting-Act _2023.pdf; Ethan Corey, "How the Federal Government Lost Track of Deaths in Custody," The Appeal, June 24, 2020, https://theappeal.org/police-prison -deaths-data/.

166 *No comprehensive report ever emerged*: Corey, "How the Federal Government Lost Track of Deaths in Custody"; *Uncounted Deaths in America's Prisons and Jails: How the Department of Justice Failed to Implement the Death in Custody Reporting Act, Hearing Before the Permanent Subcommittee on Investigations*, 117th Cong. 536 (2022) (testimony of Maureen A. Henneberg, Deputy Assistant Attorney General for Operations and Management, Office of Justice Programs, U.S. Department of Justice), https://www.hsgac.senate .gov/wp-content/uploads/CHRG-117shrg50237.pdf. From 2000 until 2019, the Bureau of Justice Statistics reported annual totals for jail deaths in each state, as well as county-level data for the fifty largest jurisdictions until 2006. The Justice Department has not released any official data on jail deaths since 2021.

166 *The last federal report counting jail deaths*: Carson, *Mortality in Local Jails, 2000–2019— Statistical Tables*. According to Armstrong, some jails tried to submit death counts after 2019 but were unable to.

166 *released people just prior to their deaths*: Joshua Vaughn and Brittany Hailer, "Deaths in Pa. Jails Are Undercounted. Our Investigation Found Dozens of Hidden Cases," PennLive, reprinted by Pulitzer Center, November 10, 2023, https://pulitzer center.org/stories/deaths-pa-jails-are-undercounted-our-investigation-found -dozens-hidden-cases.

166 *hearings on jail and prison deaths*: *Uncounted Deaths in America's Prisons and Jails* (testimony of Vanessa Fano, Sister of Jonathan Fano, Brother Died in the East Baton Rouge Parish Prison in Louisiana).

167 *Louisiana does not require that parish jails notify the state*: *Uncounted Deaths in America's Prisons and Jails* (testimony of Andrea C. Armstrong, Professor of Law, Loyola University New Orleans College of Law).

167 *deaths of people serving sentences*: "Death Dashboard," Louisiana Department of Public Safety and Corrections, accessed March 11, 2024, https://doc.louisiana.gov/death -dashboards/. This data is often incorrect. For example, in 2020 the state submitted a total of six deaths in custody for the state of Louisiana. In contrast, Loyola Law students, through public records requests and media searches, identified 180 deaths in Louisiana prisons and jails in 2020. Armstrong told the Senate Permanent Subcommittee on Investigations, "Multiple sheriffs also informed our students that they were no longer required to report deaths in custody for federal data collection." See *Uncounted Deaths in America's Prisons and Jails* (testimony of Andrea C. Armstrong, Professor of Law, Loyola University New Orleans College of Law).

167 *"We trusted the system"*: *Uncounted Deaths in America's Prisons and Jails* (testimony of Vanessa Fano, Sister of Jonathan Fano, Brother Died in the East Baton Rouge Parish Prison in Louisiana).

167 *"Systemic failures and gross deficiencies"*: *Uncounted Deaths in America's Prisons and Jails* (testimony of Vanessa Fano, Sister of Jonathan Fano, Brother Died in the East Baton Rouge Parish Prison in Louisiana), Exhibit A, 3, https://www.hsgac.senate.gov

/wp-content/uploads/imo/media/doc/Fano%20Testimony%20Exhibit%20A %20-%20Homer%20Venters%20Report%20Updated.pdf.

168 *help fund county jails as part of rural infrastructure*: Jack Norton and Jacob Kang-Brown, "Federal Farm Aid for the Big House," Vera Institute, October 22, 2018, https:// www.vera.org/in-our-backyards-stories/federal-farm-aid-for-the-big-house.

## CHAPTER 7: "KEEPING THE PEACE"

169 *spaghetti Western gunslinger*: Jon Jackson, "Jim Lamon Spent Up to $30K on Local Super Bowl Ad, Shoots at Biden, Pelosi," *Newsweek*, February 11, 2022, https:// www.newsweek.com/jim-lamon-spent-30k-local-super-bowl-ad-shoots-biden -pelosi-1678475.

169 *men take aim at Nancy Pelosi, Joe Biden, and Mark Kelly*: Jim Lamon, "Jim Lamon for U.S. Senate: Super Bowl Ad—30 Seconds," YouTube, February 10, 2022, https://www .youtube.com/watch?v=ZObIAXX5hsU.

171 *Twenty-nine states allow qualified individuals*: "State Concealed Carry Permit Require-ments," United States Concealed Carry Association, accessed March 12, 2024, https://www.usconcealedcarry.com/resources/terminology/types-of-concealed -carry-licensurepermitting-policies/unrestricted/.

171 *carry their gun in public*: "Which States Regulate the Open Carry of Firearms?," Ev-erytown Research & Policy, accessed March 12, 2024, https://everytownresearch .org/rankings/law/open-carry-regulated/.

171 *homicide is the leading cause of death for pregnant women*: "Homicide Leading Cause of Death for Pregnant Women in U.S.," Harvard T.H. Chan School of Public Health, Oc-tober 21, 2022, https://www.hsph.harvard.edu/news/hsph-in-the-news/homi cide-leading-cause-of-death-for-pregnant-women-in-u-s/.

172 *child had recently died in a car crash*: Kenneth Wong, "Manslaughter Charges Submitted for Suspect in Crash That Killed Son of Pinal County Sheriff Mark Lamb," FOX 10, February 24, 2023, https://www.fox10phoenix.com/news/police-submits -manslaughter-charges-in-crash-that-killed-son-of-pinal-county-sheriff-mark -lamb.

172 *less militia-minded, more weird fraternity*: "Proud Boys," SPLC Extremist Files, accessed March 12, 2024, https://www.splcenter.org/fighting-hate/extremist-files/group /proud-boys.

173 *2017's Unite the Right rally*: "Proud Boys," SPLC Extremist Files.

173 *sentenced to twenty-two years in prison*: Alan Feuer, "Ex-Leader of Proud Boys Sentenced to 22 Years in Jan. 6 Sedition Case," *New York Times*, September 5, 2023, https:// www.nytimes.com/2023/09/05/us/politics/enrique-tarrio-proud-boys -sentenced.html.

173 *spectacle of thousands of men in military gear*: Chelsea Curtis, "Phoenix 2nd Amendment Rally in Support of Gun Rights Has Largest Turnout Ever, Organizers Say,"

*Arizona Republic*, February 15, 2020, https://www.azcentral.com/story/news/local/phoenix-breaking/2020/02/15/phoenix-2nd-amendment-rally-support-gun-rights-has-largest-turnout-ever-organizers-say/4772304002/.

173 *monument to the Ten Commandments*: Howard Fischer, "ACLU: Thou Shalt Not Use Ten Commandments Monument at State Capitol," *Arizona Daily Sun*, July 16, 2003, https://azdailysun.com/aclu-thou-shalt-not-use-ten-commandments-monument-at-state/article_6f7489f8-b8d7-5222-a289-556161b653d1.html.

174 *a private Christian school in Phoenix*: "Statement of Faith," Tipping Point Academy (website), accessed March 12, 2024, https://tippingpointacademy.com/statement-of-faith/.

174 *"out there getting action"*: "FNDR Cade Lamb Jealous Kyle Rittenhouse," Media Matters, January 12, 2023, https://www.mediamatters.org/media/4004852.

174 *identified as a "responsible gun owner"*: "VD2-22 RidersUSA 2nd Amendment Rally February 18th 2023," Rumble, https://rumble.com/v2a26ny-vd2-22-ridersusa-2nd-amendment-rally-february-18th-2023.html.

174 *about more than guns*: "2nd Amendment Rally February 18th 2023," Rumble.

174 *"we love our family"*: "About Cheryl Todd," Gun Freedom Radio (website), accessed March 12, 2024, https://gunfreedomradio.com/guests/cheryl-todd/.

175 *ruled in favor of gun owners*: *New York State Rifle & Pistol Association, Inc. v. Bruen, Superintendent of New York State Police*, 597 U.S. 1 (2022), https://www.supremecourt.gov/opinions/21pdf/20-843_7j80.pdf.

175 *recent change to ATF regulations on pistol braces*: Bureau of Alcohol, Tobacco, Firearms and Explosives, "Factoring Criteria for Firearms with Attached 'Stabilizing Braces,'" *Federal Register* 88, no. 20 (January 31, 2023): 6478–575, https://www.govinfo.gov/content/pkg/FR-2023-01-31/pdf/2023-01001.pdf.

175 *collapse of the American economic and financial system*: "2nd Amendment Rally February 18th 2023," Rumble.

175 *"Jesus would support the Second Amendment"*: "2nd Amendment Rally February 18th 2023," Rumble.

177 *fired his AK-47 into the darkness of the desert*: Jack Healy, "Death and Justice on the Border: A Migrant Is Killed, a Rancher Is Charged," *New York Times*, April 3, 2023, https://www.nytimes.com/2023/04/03/us/arizona-rancher-migrant-death.html.

177 *free Kelly pending his trial*: J. D. Wallace, "Border Rancher Charged with Murder Rejects Plea Offer," 13 News, January 3, 2024, https://www.kold.com/2024/01/03/border-rancher-charged-with-murder-rejects-plea-offer/.

178 *even if it meant one man died*: "2nd Amendment Rally February 18th 2023," Rumble.

178 *"other side that hates our freedoms"*: "2nd Amendment Rally February 18th 2023," Rumble.

178 *radicalized during the pandemic*: KATU Staff, "Owner of Salem Salon That Re-Opened Despite State Orders Says She Is Moving," KATU, March 3, 2021, https://katu.com/news/local/owner-of-salem-salon-that-re-opened-despite-state-orders-says-she-is-moving.

178 *largely seems to exist online*: Whitney Woodworth and Robert Anglen, "False Claims Prop Up 'Patriot Barbie,'" *Arizona Republic*, March 23, 2021, https://www.pressreader.com/usa/usa-today-us-edition/20210323/281535113763156.

178 *using her platform to dress as a cat*: Yael Halon, "Mom Dons Cat Outfit to Protest Trans School Board Member: 'You Can't Identify as Whatever You Want,'" *New York Post*, December 14, 2022, https://nypost.com/2022/12/14/patriot-barbie-lindsey-graham-dons-cat-outfit-at-school-board-meeting/.

178 *filed a restraining order*: "Gates of Disinformation Hell Opens as AZ School Board Cuts Ties with Anti-LGBTQ Christian University," Arizona Right Watch, March 19, 2023, https://arizonarightwatch.substack.com/p/gates-of-disinformation-hell-opens.

179 *allowing trans women to use women's facilities*: "2nd Amendment Rally February 18th 2023," Rumble.

179 *"speaking or writing words of power"*: Wessinger, *How the Millennium Comes Violently*, 160.

180 *intended for the Second Amendment to be anti-Black*: Carol Anderson, *The Second: Race and Guns in a Fatally Unequal America* (New York: Bloomsbury, 2021).

180 *"undermine the slave system in the South"*: Carl T. Bogus, *Madison's Militia: The Hidden History of the Second Amendment* (New York: Oxford University Press, 2023), 174–75.

181 *did not exist on the federal level until 1934*: National Firearms Act, 73rd Congress, 48 Stat. 1236 (1934).

181 *adopted assault rifles as a sign of Black resistance*: Adam Winkler, "The Secret History of Guns," *Atlantic*, September 2011, https://www.theatlantic.com/magazine/archive/2011/09/the-secret-history-of-guns/308608/.

181 *drafted a statement in support of gun restrictions*: Senate Report No. 90-1097, 90th Cong., 2nd Sess., 1968, http://www.harrislawoffice.com/content/areas_of_practice/federal_firearms/legislative_history/Gun%20Control%20Act%201968%20Senate%20Report%2090-1097.pdf.

181 *courts often reject the same arguments*: Lauren Gill, "Alabama Woman Faces Life Sentence for Killing Man Who Allegedly Raped Her," The Appeal, April 10, 2019, https://theappeal.org/alabama-woman-faces-life-sentence-for-killing-man-who-allegedly-raped-her/. For example, in Alabama, a woman's Stand Your Ground claim was denied even though the man she shot was assaulting her.

182 *"not on the law-abiding citizen"*: Ronald Reagan, "The Gun Owner's Champion," *Guns & Ammo*, September 1975, https://www.defensivecarry.com/forum/attachments/second-amendment-gun-legislation-discussion/5257d1182172805-ronald-regan-gun-owners-champion-ronald_reagan_the_gun_owners_champion.pdf.

182 *"Disarm the thugs"*: Ronald Reagan, "Remarks at a California Republican Party Fundraising Dinner in Long Beach," June 30, 1983, https://www.reaganlibrary.gov/archives/speech/remarks-california-republican-party-fundraising-dinner-long-beach.

182 *"know this from personal experience"*: Ronald Reagan, "Remarks at the Annual Members Banquet of the National Rifle Association in Phoenix, Arizona," May 6, 1963, https://www.reaganfoundation.org/media/128658/nra.pdf.

182  *signed only one gun bill*: Firearm Owners Protection Act of 1986, Pub. L. No. 99-308, 100 Stat. 449, https://www.congress.gov/bill/99th-congress/senate-bill/49.

182  *"most sweeping rollback of gun control laws in history"*: Peter Weber, "How Ronald Reagan Learned to Love Gun Control," *The Week*, December 3, 2015, https://theweek.com /articles/582926/how-ronald-reagan-learned-love-gun-control.

182  *vigorously opposed by ten law enforcement organizations*: David Burnham, "Measure to Relax Gun Rules Denounced by Police Groups," *New York Times*, January 31, 1986, https://www.nytimes.com/1986/01/31/us/measure-to-relax-gun-rules -denounced-by-police-groups.html.

183  *faced vigorous opposition from the National Rifle Association*: "History of Brady," Brady United (website), accessed March 12, 2024, https://www.bradyunited.org/history.

183  *op-ed in favor of the Brady Bill*: Ronald Reagan, "Why I'm for the Brady Bill," *New York Times*, March 29, 1991, https://www.nytimes.com/1991/03/29/opinion/why-i-m -for-the-brady-bill.html.

184  *"violating the Constitution and asking me to help"*: Pierre Thomas, "Sheriffs Challenge the Brady Law," *Washington Post*, September 18, 1994, https://www.washingtonpost .com/archive/politics/1994/09/19/the-brady-law/5d364188-f8ce-4520-a845 -96273e6584f6/.

184  *turned to the courts to challenge the Brady Bill*: Adam Winkler, *Gunfight: The Battle over the Right to Bear Arms in America* (New York: W. W. Norton, 2011), 72. The NRA under LaPierre also helped to spread militia conspiracy theories about Democrats coming to "take your guns."

185  *recognized an individual right to own firearms*: District of Columbia v. Heller, 554 US 570 (2008), https://www.oyez.org/cases/2007/07-290.

185  *became the NRA's Law Enforcement Officer of the Year*: Winkler, *Gunfight*, 87.

186  *"attack law-abiding citizens"*: Associated Press, "NRA Official Defends Terms Used in Letter," *Washington Post*, May 1, 1995, https://www.washingtonpost.com/archive /politics/1995/05/01/nra-official-defends-terms-used-in-letter/eb75fcd2-faa9 -49b9-8f31-04701763b5a1/.

186  *Mormon settlers in 1819 Missouri*: Winkler, *Gunfight*, 106–7.

187  *Americans' stubborn attachment to firearms*: Richard Hofstadter, "America as a Gun Culture," *American Heritage* 21, no. 6 (October 1970), https://www.americanheritage .com/america-gun-culture.

187  *issued a statement blaming gun violence*: "National Sheriffs' Association Releases Statement on Gun Control," WBTV, February 1, 2013, https://www.wbtv.com/story /20936503/national-sheriffs-association-releases-statement-on-gun-control/.

188  *most surveys show general support for red flag laws*: Jeffrey M. Jones, "Majority in U.S. Continues to Favor Stricter Gun Laws," Gallup, October 31, 2023, https://news .gallup.com/poll/513623/majority-continues-favor-stricter-gun-laws.aspx.

188  *"We don't know who the good guy is"*: Molly Hennessy-Fiske, "Dallas Police Chief: Open Carry Makes Things Confusing During Mass Shootings," *Los Angeles Times*, July 11,

2016, https://www.latimes.com/nation/la-na-dallas-chief-20160711-snap-story
.html.

188 *opposed a 2021 law that made open carry permissible*: Christian Flores, "Law Enforcement
Leaders Voice Opposition to Bills Allowing Unlicensed Carry of Handguns," CBS
Austin, April 13, 2021, https://cbsaustin.com/news/local/law-enforcement
-leaders-voice-opposition-to-bills-allowing-unlicensed-carry-of-handguns.

188 *more likely to support individual gun ownership*: Jennifer Carlson, *Policing the Second Amendment: Guns, Law Enforcement, and the Politics of Race* (Princeton, NJ: Princeton University
Press, 2020), 51.

188 *"need to go out there and teach him"*: Caitlin Randle, "Open Carry Texas Plans Rally to
Teach Texas Sheriff 'a Lesson,'" My San Antonio, May 21, 2020, https://www
.mysanantonio.com/news/local/article/Open-Carry-Texas-plans-rally-to-teach
-Ector-15288789.php.

188 *80 percent of Illinois sheriffs said they would not enforce new gun regulations*: Joe Barrett, "Most
Illinois Sheriffs Say They Won't Enforce New Assault-Weapons Ban," *Wall Street
Journal*, January 20, 2023, https://www.wsj.com/articles/most-illinois-sheriffs-say
-they-wont-enforce-new-assault-weapons-ban-11674175079.

189 *recruit sheriffs and other law enforcement officers*: Daniel Trotta, "Emails Show NRA Link
to U.S. Sheriffs Who Promoted Gun 'Sanctuaries,'" Reuters, May 20, 2019,
https://www.reuters.com/article/us-usa-guns-sanctuary/emails-show-nra
-link-to-u-s-sheriffs-who-promoted-gun-sanctuaries-idUSKCN1SQ2H0/. This
was particularly clear in the way the NRA ignored the murder of George Floyd in
2020. See Will Van Sant, "The NRA's Unshakable Support for Police," The
Trace, July 9, 2020, https://www.thetrace.org/2020/07/the-nras-unshakable
-support-for-police/.

189 *letter opposing all gun regulation*: CSPOA, "Growing List of Sheriffs, Associations and
Police Chiefs Saying 'NO' to Obama Gun Control," Constitutional Sheriffs and
Peace Officers Association (blog), February 1, 2014, archived July 6, 2015, by the
Wayback Machine, https://web.archive.org/web/20150706092456/http:/cspoa
.org/sheriffs-gun-rights/.

189 *included groups like Gun Owners of America and the Oath Keepers*: CSPOA, "Growing List
of Sheriffs."

190 *"most critical time in our nation's history"*: Liberty Group Coalition letter to sheriffs,
February 2013, https://web.archive.org/web/20130530224256/http://www
.cspoa.org/sheriffs_say_no/2013%20Liberty%20Coalition%20Intro%20Letter
.pdf.

191 *"protect the killing of unborn children"*: Richard Mack, email to author, August 8,
2022.

192 *the NRA had helped sheriffs*: Trotta, "Emails Show NRA Link to U.S. Sheriffs."

192 *weapons and support for community programs*: Van Sant, "The NRA's Unshakable Support for Police."

192  *become too easy to obtain firearms*: Katherine Schaeffer, "Key Facts About Americans and Guns," Pew Research Center, September 13, 2023, https://www.pewresearch .org/short-reads/2023/09/13/key-facts-about-americans-and-guns/.

192  *"essential to their own sense of freedom"*: Schaeffer, "Key Facts About Americans and Guns."

192  *"a controversial one at best"*: Shawn Fields, "Second Amendment Sanctuaries," *Northwestern University Law Review* 115, no. 2 (2020): 444, https://scholarlycommons.law .northwestern.edu/nulr/vol115/iss2/2/.

193  *twenty-five out of thirty-three sheriffs*: Trotta, "Emails Show NRA Link to U.S. Sheriffs."

193  *most of the counties in Colorado*: David J. Toscano, "The Gun Sanctuary Movement Is Exploding," *Slate*, December 11, 2019, https://slate.com/news-and-politics/2019 /12/second-amendment-gun-sanctuary-movement-constitution.html.

193  *clause in the Virginia Constitution reserving the right to call a militia*: Murry Lee, "Tazewell County Board of Supervisors Passes Resolution to Emphasize Right to Militia," WJHL, December 10, 2019, https://www.wjhl.com/news/local/tazewell-county -board-of-supervisors-passes-resolution-to-emphasize-right-to-militia/.

193  *rather go to jail than enforce a gun law*: Scott McLean and Sara Weisfeldt, "This Colorado Sheriff Is Willing to Go to Jail Rather Than Enforce a Proposed Gun Law," CNN, March 31, 2019, https://www.cnn.com/2019/03/31/us/colorado-red-flag-gun -law/index.html.

193  *over 60 percent of all counties were sanctuary counties*: Noah Davis, "More Than 61% of American Counties Are Now Second Amendment Sanctuaries," Sanctuary Counties (website), June 20, 2021, https://sanctuarycounties.com/2021/06/20/more -than-61-of-american-counties-are-now-second-amendment-sanctuaries/.

193  *fewer than two hundred places designated as immigration sanctuaries*: Jessica M. Vaughan and Bryan Griffith, "Map: Sanctuary Cities, Counties, and States," Center for Immigration Studies, updated March 6, 2024, https://cis.org/Map-Sanctuary-Cities -Counties-and-States.

194  *duped by Sacha Baron Cohen into doing a parodic ad*: Sacha Baron Cohen, "Kinder Guardians," Showtime, July 15, 2018, https://www.youtube.com/watch?v=QkXe MoBPSDk.

195  *FBI arrested some neo-Nazis*: Timothy Williams, Adam Goldman, and Neil MacFarquhar, "Virginia Capital on Edge as F.B.I. Arrests Suspected Neo-Nazis Before Gun Rally," *New York Times*, January 16, 2020, https://www.nytimes.com/2020 /01/16/us/fbi-arrest-virginia-gun-rally.html.

195  *$300,000 Terradyne Gurkha*: Erin Marquis, "Alex Jones Could Lose His $300,000 Armored Truck, Poor Guy," Jalopnik, August 3, 2022, https://jalopnik.com/alex -jones-could-lose-his-300-000-armored-truck-poor-1849367118.

195  *"they will take your guns away"*: @realDonaldTrump, "Your 2nd Amendment is under very serious attack in the Great Commonwealth of Virginia. That's what happens when you vote for Democrats, they will take your guns away. Republicans will win

Virginia in 2020. Thank you Dems!," X/Twitter, January 17, 2020, https://twit
ter.com/realDonaldTrump/status/1218297464941314049.

195 *roundly mocked on Fox News*: Gregg Re, "NBC News' Ben Collins Slammed for Warning of 'White Nationalist Rally in Virginia,'" Fox News, January 19, 2020,
https://www.foxnews.com/media/nbc-ben-collins-virginia-white-nationalist
-rally-guns.

195 *Sheriff Richard Vaughan of Grayson County said*: Allison Brophy Champion, "Va. Sheriff
Will Deputize Residents if Gun Control Laws Pass," *Culpeper Star-Exponent*, reprinted by Police1, December 19, 2019, https://www.police1.com/gun-legislation
-law-enforcement/articles/va-sheriff-will-deputize-residents-if-gun-control-laws
-pass-irWUyrAUsvuEnhiA/.

195 *election funds seized in 2023*: Ted Oberg, Rick Yarborough, Jeff Piper, and Steve Jones,
"FBI Seizes Culpeper Sheriff Campaign Cash," NBC 4 Washington, April 11,
2023, https://www.nbcwashington.com/investigations/fbi-seizes-culpeper
-sheriff-campaign-cash/3327144/.

195 *dozens of civilian deputies*: Allison Brophy Champion and Patrick Wilson, "Culpeper
Sheriff Didn't Properly Train or Keep Records on Reserve Force, Documents
Show," *Culpeper Star-Exponent*, October 16, 2023, https://starexponent.com/news
/local/culpeper-sheriff-didn-t-properly-train-or-keep-records-on-reserve-force
-documents-show/article_5e77d486-6939-11ee-bc1f-a7a06baf57e4.html.

196 *faulty research that links gun ownership to a decrease in crime*: Melinda Wenner-Moyer, "More
Guns Do Not Stop More Crimes, Evidence Shows," *Scientific American*, October 1,
2017, https://www.scientificamerican.com/article/more-guns-do-not-stop-more
-crimes-evidence-shows/. Research around gun ownership and violent crime is
highly politicized, as Melinda Wenner-Moyer shows. For instance, Mark Rosenberg, who led a study on gun violence for the CDC in the 1990s, was fired in response to pressure from the NRA. The pro-gun group published an article in its
official magazine, *American Rifleman*, decrying the CDC's "anti-gun pseudo-scientific
studies disguised as research." In the midst of the furor, Arkansas representative
Jay Dickey introduced an amendment to the CDC's 1996 spending bill that barred
the agency from researching gun violence. Congress has renewed this provision
every year since.

197 *But this does not mean*: Amy Friedenberger, "Attorney General Mark Herring, in
Advisory Opinion, Says Second Amendment Resolutions Have 'No Legal Effect,'"
*Daily Progress*, December 20, 2019, https://dailyprogress.com/article
_02d90207-c486-57ed-826b-b6b94708747a.html; Mark Herring, letter to Jer-
rauld C. Jones, December 20, 2019, https://www.oag.state.va.us/files/Opinions
/2019/19-059-Jones-issued.pdf.

198 *invented for the internet*: Anna Berkes, "Free Men Do Not Ask Permission to Bear
Arms (Spurious Quotation)," Jefferson Monticello (website), modified July 8, 2015,
https://www.monticello.org/research-education/thomas-jefferson-encyclopedia
/free-men-do-not-ask-permission-bear-arms-spurious-quotation/.

198   *In a Sunday video*: Mark Lamb, "It's Sunday. Put your sword down, honor God and sharpen your saw . . . and don't forget to get your signed copy of 'American Sheriff: Rules to Live By' at: www.AmericanSheriff.store #God #Guns #freedom," Facebook, October 23, 2022, https://www.facebook.com/americansheriff/videos/910368199929012.

198   *In a French documentary*: *Un Monde à part*, "Le désert de l'Arizona, le nouveau Far West?," produced by François Mazure and Titouan Marichal, aired July 2, 2023, on RTBF, https://auvio.rtbf.be/media/un-monde-a-part-un-monde-a-part-desert-de-larizona-au-coeur-du-nouveau-far-west-3055371.

199   *tactics sheriffs use to oppose gun regulation*: Carlson, *Policing the Second Amendment*, 176.

199   *"good guys with guns"*: Carlson, *Policing the Second Amendment*, 13.

200   *"a Minuteman protecting his community"*: Erin Ailworth and Talal Ansari, "Kyle Rittenhouse Was Protecting Community During Kenosha Unrest, Lawyer Says," *Wall Street Journal*, August 29, 2020, https://www.wsj.com/articles/kyle-rittenhouse-was-protecting-community-during-kenosha-unrest-lawyer-says-11598738127.

201   *Washington State sheriffs similarly said*: Jason Wilson, "Washington State: At Least 20 County Sheriffs Refuse to Enforce New Gun Laws," *Guardian*, February 22, 2019, https://www.theguardian.com/us-news/2019/feb/22/washington-state-county-sheriffs-refuse-to-enforce-gun-laws.

201   *New York State Sheriffs' Association also opposed the regulations*: Jesse McKinley and Cole Louison, "Another Challenge to New York's Gun Law: Sheriffs Who Won't Enforce It," *New York Times*, October 9, 2022, https://www.nytimes.com/2022/10/09/nyregion/ny-gun-law-sheriffs.html.

201   *Often sheriffs who promise*: Andrew Kenney, "Why the El Paso County Sheriff Says He Couldn't Use Colorado's 'Red Flag' Law to Stop the Club Q Shooting," *CPR News*, December 8, 2011, https://www.cpr.org/2022/12/08/club-q-shooting-el-paso-county-sheriff-red-flag-gun-law/; Chip Brownlee, "In Colorado Springs, Local Officials Resisted the State's Red Flag Law," *The Trace*, November 21, 2022, https://www.thetrace.org/2022/11/colorado-springs-mass-shooting-red-flag/.

201   *refuse preemptively to enact the provision*: Barrett, "Most Illinois Sheriffs Say They Won't Enforce New Assault-Weapons Ban."

202   *majority of people convicted for felony gun possession*: David E. Olson et al., *Sentences Imposed on Those Convicted of Felony Illegal Possession of a Firearm in Illinois* (Chicago: Center for Criminal Justice Research, Policy, and Practice, Loyola University Chicago, 2021), 8, https://idoc.illinois.gov/content/dam/soi/en/web/idoc/reportsandstatistics/documents/firearmpossessionsentencinginillinois.pdf.

## CHAPTER 8: "THIS ISN'T A BADGE, BUT A SHIELD"

203   *alleged plan to kidnap Governor Gretchen Whitmer*: Tom Winter, Michael Kosnar, and David K. Li, "13 Men Charged in Alleged Plot to Kidnap Michigan Gov. Gretchen

Whitmer," NBC News, October 8, 2020, https://www.nbcnews.com/news/us
-news/six-men-charged-alleged-plot-kidnap-michigan-gov-gretchen-whitmer
-n1242622.

203 *"you can make a felony arrest"*: Aaron Parseghian, "Barry County Sheriff Dar Leaf Asks
If Alleged Kidnappers Were 'Trying to Arrest' Gov. Whitmer," FOX 17, October
9, 2020, https://www.fox17online.com/news/local-news/michigan/man-charged
-in-plot-to-kidnap-whitmer-shared-stage-with-west-michigan-sheriff-at
-rally.

203 *began to report on the constitutional sheriffs in earnest*: Sara Sidner, "Sheriff Spoke in Defense
of Accused Domestic Terrorists," CNN, October 14, 2020, https://www.cnn
.com/2020/10/14/us/michigan-sheriff-militias/index.html.

204 *gave militias legitimacy*: Mark Pitcavage, "Camouflage and Conspiracy: The Militia
Movement from Ruby Ridge to Y2K," *American Behavioral Scientist* 44, no. 6 (2001):
957–81, https://doi.org/10.1177/00027640121956610.

204 *a patina of legitimacy and claims to lawfulness*: Levitas, *Terrorist Next Door*, 301.

204 *"sanctioned by law but uncontrolled by government"*: Pitcavage, "Camouflage and Conspiracy," 958.

205 *violence of war as well as tactical training*: "The Militia Movement (2020)," Anti-
Defamation League, October 19, 2020, https://www.adl.org/resources/back
grounder/militia-movement-2020.

205 *the most ideal militia man of the era*: "Bo Gritz," SPLC Extremist Files, accessed March
12, 2024, https://www.splcenter.org/fighting-hate/extremist-files/individual/bo
-gritz.

205 *Sylvester Stallone's Rambo character*: "Bo Gritz," SPLC Extremist Files.

205 *part of the broader white power movement*: Kathleen Belew, *Bring the War Home: The White
Power Movement and Paramilitary America* (Cambridge, MA: Harvard University Press,
2018).

205 *more subtle form of white supremacy*: Cooter, *Nostalgia, Nationalism, and the US Militia Movement*, 103–5.

206 *Aitor Narvaiza, who immigrated from Spain*: Protect America Now USA, "Hear from
Protect America Now member Elko County, Nevada Sheriff Aitor Narvaiza, who
was born in Ermua, Biscay. When he was eight, his family moved to the U.S. in
search of a better life, and settled in Elko, Nevada," Facebook, June 1, 2021,
https://www.facebook.com/ElkoNevadaGOP/posts/1062708590802535/.

206 *"more subtle forms of racism"*: Cooter, *Nostalgia, Nationalism, and the US Militia Movement*, 104.

207 *"form the militia to defend the people"*: *Hearing on the U.S. Militia Movement Before the Senate
Judiciary Subcomm. on Terrorism*, 107th Cong. (1995) (testimony of Norman Olson),
https://www.c-span.org/video/?65722-1/us-militia-movement.

208 *presidential runs of Ron Paul*: "Elmer Stewart Rhodes," SPLC Extremist Files, accessed
March 12, 2024, https://www.splcenter.org/fighting-hate/extremist-files/individ
ual/elmer-stewart-rhodes; Tess Owen, "How a Small-Town Sheriff Ended Up on

a Crusade to Radicalize American Law Enforcement," Vice News, July 28, 2021, https://www.vice.com/en/article/epnkgn/richard-mack-constitutional-sheriff -movement. Paul ran in both 2008 and 2012. Rhodes volunteered for the 2008 campaign, as did Mack. The same libertarian ideas Paul espoused in his campaigns became the foundation for both men's work.

208 *brief report on right-wing extremism*: Extremism and Radicalism Branch, Homeland Environment Threat Analysis Division, *Rightwing Extremism: Current Economic and Political Climate Fueling Resurgence in Radicalization and Recruitment* (Washington, DC: Department of Homeland Security Office of Intelligence and Analysis, 2009), https://irp.fas.org/eprint/rightwing.pdf.

208 *"unique drivers for rightwing radicalization and recruitment"*: Extremism and Radicalism Branch, Homeland Environment Threat Analysis Division, *Rightwing Extremism*, 2.

208 *posted on the Oath Keepers' website*: Janet Reitman, "U.S. Law Enforcement Failed to See the Threat of White Nationalism. Now They Don't Know How to Stop It," *New York Times*, November 3, 2018, https://www.nytimes.com/2018/11/03/magazine /FBI-charlottesville-white-nationalism-far-right.html.

209 *she apologized and erased the mention*: Eric Marrapodi, "Napolitano Apologizes to Veterans over 'Extremist' Flap," CNN, April 24, 2009, https://www.cnn.com/2009 /POLITICS/04/24/napolitano.am.legion/.

209 *one such ex–national security official*: James Kitfield, "How Mike Flynn Became America's Angriest General," *Politico*, October 16, 2016, https://www.politico.com /magazine/story/2016/10/how-mike-flynn-became-americas-angriest-general -214362/.

209 *train their deputies on how to spot Muslim "terrorists"*: Lindsay Schubiner, "How Anti-Muslim Operatives Are Indoctrinating Local Police," Imagine 2050, February 14, 2017, https://www.newcomm.org/islamophobia-academy-anti-muslim-operatives -indoctrinating-local-police/; Stephen Piggott, "Disgraced Former FBI Agent John Guandolo to Travel to Phoenix Next Week," SPLC Hatewatch, June 2, 2016, https://www.splcenter.org/hatewatch/2016/06/02/disgraced-former-fbi-agent -john-guandolo-travel-phoenix-next-week.

209 *"it's at the local level"*: "Understanding the Threat," SPLC Extremist Files, accessed March 12, 2024, https://www.splcenter.org/fighting-hate/extremist-files/group /understanding-threat.

209 *demonstration outside a mosque in Phoenix*: Evan Wyloge, "Hundreds Gather in Arizona for Armed Anti-Muslim Protest," *Washington Post*, May 30, 2015, https://www .washingtonpost.com/news/post-nation/wp/2015/05/30/hundreds -gather-in-arizona-for-armed-anti-muslim-protest/.

210 *blocked immigrants from Muslim-majority countries*: "A Licence to Discriminate: Trump's Muslim & Refugee Ban," Amnesty International UK, October 6, 2020, https:// www.amnesty.org.uk/licence-discriminate-trumps-muslim-refugee-ban.

210 *"not violating any Michigan or federal law"*: Rogers Worthington, "Militia Movement

Fears Government," *Oklahoman*, April 23, 1995, https://www.oklahoman.com /story/news/1995/04/23/militia-movement-fears-government/62393427007/.

210 *sheriffs even called upon militias to assist*: Lee Higgins, "Bridgewater Township Official Turns to Militia for Help; Watchdog Groups Question Decision," *Ann Arbor News*, March 25, 2010, https://www.annarbor.com/news/bridgewater-township-turns -to-militia-for-help/.

210 *defines "unorganized militias" as*: "Fact Sheets on Unlawful Militias for All 50 States Now Available from Georgetown Law's Institute for Constitutional Advocacy and Protection," Institute for Constitutional Advocacy and Protection (press release), September 22, 2020, https://www.law.georgetown.edu/icap/our-press-releases /fact-sheets-on-unlawful-militias-for-all-50-states-now-available-from -georgetown-laws-institute-for-constitutional-advocacy-and-protection/.

211 *no prosecutions of militias*: Malachi Barrett, "They Call Themselves 'Militias,' but Actual Militias Report to the Governor in Michigan," MLive, February 24, 2021, https://www.mlive.com/politics/2021/02/they-call-themselves-militias-but -actual-militias-report-to-the-governor-in-michigan.html.

211 *militias saw themselves as "super citizens"*: Cooter, *Nostalgia, Nationalism, and the US Militia Movement*, 19–20.

212 *Owosso barber reopen his shop*: Kara Berg, "Owosso Barber Reopens Despite State Orders: 'I Was in Despair, I Had to Go Back to Work,'" *Lansing State Journal*, May 6, 2020, https://www.lansingstatejournal.com/story/news/2020/05/06/owosso -barber-orders-whitmer-michigan-haircut-hair-covid-coronavirus/5174541002/.

212 *gray beard in two large braids*: Luke Mogelson, "The Militias Against Masks," *New Yorker*, August 24, 2020, https://www.newyorker.com/magazine/2020/08/24 /the-militias-against-masks.

213 *"That's what that represents"*: Maija Cutler Hahn, "American Patriot Rally, Grand Rapids, MI. Listen to These patriots! Sheriff Dar Leaf, Senate Majority Leader Mike Shirkey, Constitional attorney Katherine Henry, Jason Howland, Ryan Kelley, and others spoke tonight at this amazing rally! It was great to see many of my patriotic friends there! I appreciate everything you do to educate, support, and inspire us to Rise Up and get active in our state! Theresa BE, Mary Klukowski, Allie RS, Karen Allen, Rachel Bosscher-Atwood, Ruth VanHoven, Lisa Ellison, Parker Ostrander, Jason Howland, Ryan D. Kelley, Jennifer Hendricks, Tim Walenga, Erica Marie Alfaro, and Katherine Henry," Facebook, May 18, 2020, https://www.facebook .com/maijahahn/videos/10158323872683895.

213 *It was a demonstration*: Maija Cutler Hahn, Facebook, May 18, 2020.

214 *"His comments were dangerous"*: Tracy Samilton, "Michigan Sheriffs' Association Condemns Sheriff Who Defended Alleged Plotters Against Governor," Michigan Public Radio, October 15, 2020, https://www.michiganpublic.org/law/2020-10-15 /michigan-sheriffs-association-condemns-sheriff-who-defended-alleged-plotters -against-governor.

214 *the rest pled guilty*: Arpan Lobo, "3 Years After Plot to Kidnap Gov. Gretchen Whitmer, Here Are the Trial Outcomes, Verdicts," *Detroit Free Press*, September 18, 2023, https://www.freep.com/story/news/local/michigan/2023/09/18/whitmer-kidnapping-trial-verdict-guilty-acquitted/70889492007/.

215 *mass consumer culture was not around yet*: Andrew C. McKevitt, *Gun Country: Gun Capitalism, Culture, and Control in Cold War America* (Chapel Hill: University of North Carolina Press, 2023), 13.

215 *George Washington famously complained*: "From George Washington to Lund Washington, 30 September 1776," Founders Online, National Archives, https://founders.archives.gov/documents/Washington/03-06-02-0341. [Original source: *The Papers of George Washington, Revolutionary War Series*, Vol. 6: *13 August 1776–20 October 1776*, ed. Philander D. Chase and Frank E. Grizzard Jr. (Charlottesville: University Press of Virginia, 1994), 440–43.]

216 *early America had a strong tradition of militias*: Robert Churchill, *To Shake Their Guns in the Tyrant's Face: Libertarian Political Violence and the Origins of the Militia Movement* (Ann Arbor: University of Michigan Press, 2011), 36–40.

216 *"transgress the will of God"*: Churchill, *To Shake Their Guns*, 32; Jonathan Mayhew, "A discourse concerning unlimited submission and non-resistance to the higher powers: with some reflections on the resistance made to King Charles I. and on the anniversary of his death: in which the mysterious doctrine of that prince's saintship and martyrdom is unriddled: the substance of which was delivered in a sermon preached in the West Meeting-House in Boston the Lord's-Day after the 30th of January, 1749," *Evans Early American Imprint Collection*, University of Michigan, https://quod.lib.umich.edu/cgi/t/text/pageviewer-idx?cc=evans;c=evans;idno=n05197.0001.001;node=N05197.0001.001:6;seq=45;page=root;view=text.

216 *militia clause refers to state militias*: "Addressing Political Violence, Unlawful Paramilitaries, Threats to Democracy, and Gun Violence," Institute for Constitutional Advocacy and Protection, accessed March 12, 2024, https://www.law.georgetown.edu/icap/our-work/addressing-political-violence-unlawful-paramilitaries-and-threats-to-democracy/.

216 *systemic violence against Indigenous tribes*: Roxanne Dunbar-Ortiz, *Loaded: A Disarming History of the Second Amendment* (San Francisco: City Lights, 2018), 53; Patrick Blanchfield, "The Brutal Origins of Gun Rights," *New Republic*, December 11, 2017, https://newrepublic.com/article/146190/brutal-origins-gun-rights.

216 *vilified by Southern Democrats*: Gregory Mixon, "African Americans and the State Militia," Black Perspective, September 22, 2023, https://www.aaihs.org/african-americans-and-the-state-militia/.

217 *far-right movement that emerged in the 2000s*: Churchill, *To Shake Their Guns*, 168–69.

217 *firearm owners to act as church defense*: Kyle Olson, "Michigan Sheriff Dar Leaf Offers 'Militia Course,'" *Midwesterner*, December 23, 2023, https://www.themidwesterner.news/2023/12/michigan-sheriff-dar-leaf-offers-militia-course/.

218 *what ideology motivated Rudolph*: Mark Potok, "Eric Rudolph, at Last," *Intelligence Report*, August 15, 2003, https://www.splcenter.org/fighting-hate/intelligence-report /2003/eric-rudolph-last.

222 *"count according to their divisions"*: Numbers 1:2–3 (New International Version).

222 *heard arguments in* United States v. Rahimi: *United States v. Rahimi*, Oyez, accessed March 12, 2024, https://www.oyez.org/cases/2023/22-915.

223 *written by a man named Brent Allen Winters*: "About the Common Lawyer," Common Lawyer (website), accessed March 12, 2024, https://commonlawyer.com/?page=about.

223 *an array of courses*: "Course: Drafting a Common-Law Asset Protection Trust," Common Lawyer (website), accessed March 12, 2024, https://commonlawyer.com /?page=courses_drafting_a_common_law.

224 *the right to form "citizen juries"*: "Sovereign Citizens Movement," SPLC Extremist Files, accessed March 12, 2024, https://www.splcenter.org/fighting-hate/extremist -files/ideology/sovereign-citizens-movement; "ADL: Sovereign Citizens Create Vigilante 'Grand Juries' in Latest Attempt to Flout the Law," Anti-Defamation League, February 20, 2014, https://www.adl.org/resources/press-release/adl -sovereign-citizens-create-vigilante-grand-juries-latest-attempt-flout.

224 *clashed with right-wing militias*: Erica Chenoweth and Jeremy Pressman, "Black Lives Matter Protesters Were Overwhelmingly Peaceful, Our Research Finds," *Spokesman-Review*, October 20, 2020, https://www.spokesman.com/stories/2020/oct/20 /erica-chenoweth-and-jeremy-pressman-black-lives-ma/; Roudabeh Kishi and Sam Jones, "Demonstrations and Political Violence in America: New Data for Summer 2020," Armed Conflict Location & Event Data Project, September 3, 2020, https://acleddata.com/2020/09/03/demonstrations-political-violence -in-america-new-data-for-summer-2020/.

225 *most became disillusioned*: Kim Strong, "Pennsylvania Militia Say They Protect BLM Protesters, Experts Disagree," *York Daily Record*, August 19, 2020, https://www.ydr .com/story/news/2020/08/19/pennsylvania-militia-say-protect-black-lives -matter-protesters-experts-disagree/3343192001/.

225 *"When the looting starts"*: Barbara Sprunt, "The History Behind 'When the Looting Starts, the Shooting Starts,'" NPR, May 29, 2020, https://www.npr.org/2020/05 /29/864818368/the-history-behind-when-the-looting-starts-the-shooting-starts.

225 *sheriffs alike amplified the GOP messaging*: "Incoming NSA President Sheriff David Mahoney Makes Statement on George Floyd Death," National Sheriffs' Association, accessed March 12, 2024, https://www.sheriffs.org/Incoming-NSA-President -Sheriff-David-Mahoney-Makes-Statement-George-Floyd-Death. The NSA did issue a message sympathetic to BLM.

225 *"turn us into a communist country"*: Jacob Bertram, "Songer Speaks at 'We the People' Rally," *Columbia Gorge News*, July 29, 2020, https://www.columbiagorgenews.com /greater_gorge/songer-speaks-at-we-the-people-rally/article_98075852-d12f -11ea-8b28-972b4032d1fe.html.

225 *tacitly endorsed by their local sheriff*: Sidner, "Sheriff Spoke in Defense of Accused Domestic Terrorists."

225 *warn Black and Native people to leave town*: Carly Sauvageau, "As Minden Siren Persists, Lawmakers Hope to Close Loopholes in 'Sundown Siren' Law," *Nevada Independent*, April 7, 2023, https://thenevadaindependent.com/article/as-minden-siren -persists-lawmakers-hope-to-close-loopholes-in-sundown-siren-law.

226 *covering the cops' bodies with swastikas*: "Two Cops, Three Others Killed in Las Vegas Shooting Spree," NBC News, June 8, 2014, https://www.nbcnews.com/storyline /vegas-cop-killers/two-cops-three-others-killed-las-vegas-shooting-spree -n125766.

226 *Jerad Miller had appeared in a photograph with Mack*: Mark Potok, "Alleged Las Vegas Cop-Killers in 'Patriot' Movement, Warned of 'Sacrifices,'" SPLC Hatewatch, June 9, 2014, https://www.splcenter.org/hatewatch/2014/06/09/alleged-las-vegas-cop -killers-%E2%80%98patriot%E2%80%99-movement-warned-%E2%80%98 sacrifices%E2%80%99.

226 *"center the voices and experiences of Black library workers"*: "Mission & Priorities," American Library Association (website), accessed March 12, 2024, https://www.ala.org /aboutala/node/229/; "PLA Statement and Call to Action for Public Library Workers to Address Racism," American Library Association (website), accessed March 12, 2024, https://www.ala.org/pla/initiatives/edi/calltoaction.

226 *called her and inquired about the statement*: Anjeanette Damon, "Library Chairwoman Distances Herself from Diversity Statement That Enraged Douglas Sheriff," *Reno Gazette Journal*, July 30, 2020, https://www.rgj.com/story/news/2020/07 /30/douglas-sherriff-dan-coverley-black-lives-matter-library-statement /5551762002/.

227 *"good luck with disturbances and lewd behavior"*: Jenny Kane, "Douglas County Librarian Who Drafted BLM Letter of Support Resigns," *Reno Gazette Journal*, July 14, 2021, https://www.rgj.com/story/news/2021/07/14/nevada-librarian-who-drafted-blm -letter-support-resigns-minden-douglas/7973186002/. The posts have since been deleted from the sheriff's account.

227 *language echoed a letter*: Steven Marshall et al., Republican State Attorneys General Letter to Congressional Leaders, June 22, 2020, https://www.alabamaag .gov/wp-content/uploads/2023/05/AG-Marshall-Leads-Letter-to-Congress -Supporting-Law-Enforcement.pdf; Tim Elfrink, "A Nevada Library Wanted to Back Black Lives Matter. The Sheriff Said He Wouldn't Respond to 911 Calls There," *Washington Post*, July 29, 2020, https://www.washingtonpost.com/nation /2020/07/29/nevada-sheriff-911-blm/.

227 *walked back some of his comments*: Elfrink, "Nevada Library Wanted to Back Black Lives Matter."

229 *brace themselves for an assault*: "August 8, 2020 Protest," Douglas County, Nevada (website), accessed March 12, 2024, https://www.douglascountynv.gov/govern ment/departments/emergency_management/august_8__2020_protest; Lucia

Starbuck, "Black Lives Matter Protest in Carson City Ends in Yelling Match," *This Is Reno*, June 21, 2020, https://thisisreno.com/2020/06/black-lives-matter -protest-in-carson-city-ends-in-yelling-match-photos/. The sheriff's office was aware of the protest and posted information. There were at the time weekly protests in Carson City at the capitol. According to Kelsey Penrose, the BLM group from Carson City decided not to go to Minden, which left the kids on their own.

229 *"will not tolerate violence or the destruction of property"*: "Official Statement from the Doug- las County Board of County Commissioners," Douglas County, Nevada, August 6, 2020, https://www.facebook.com/Douglascountynv/posts/pfbid03KsLNN bKWr8cvSfhnAvGjq16XXy3Hih5rErgrwJUpVNLkSwquCLj7rInTavH4NKol.

230 *the sheriff addressed the counterprotesters*: "Douglas County Sheriff Dan Coverley Media Briefing August 8, 2020," Douglas County Nevada (YouTube channel), August 8, 2020, https://www.youtube.com/watch?v=FqIWQZ_INSI.

231 *positioned as in opposition to the BLM marchers*: Brian Bahouth, "A Conversation with a Nevada 'Patriot,'" *Sierra Nevada Ally*, August 17, 2020, https://sierranevadaally .org/2020/08/17/a-conversation-with-a-nevada-patriot/.

231 *video shot by local journalist Kelsey Penrose*: "Assault during Black Lives Matter Protest in Gardnerville, NV 8/8/2020 FULL VIDEO," Kelsey with Carson Now (YouTube channel), August 9, 2020, https://www.youtube.com/watch?v=flXGIKLzE8E.

233 *Coverley's job under state law*: Steve Timko, "AG Ford Says Douglas County Sheriff Should Not Threaten to Withhold Protection for BLM Support," KOLO 8, July 30, 2020, https://www.kolotv.com/2020/07/30/ag-ford-says-douglas-county -sheriff-should-not-threaten-to-withhold-protection-for-blm-support/.

233 *"no government official should issue a threat"*: Douglas County Public Library Board of Trustees, August 25, 2020, meeting minutes, approved September 30, 2020, 2, https://douglascountynv.iqm2.com/Citizens/FileOpen.aspx?Type=12&ID= 2129&Inline=True.

233 *no real consequence for Coverley*: Kurt Hildebrand, "Grand Jury Clears Sheriff in Aug. 8 Protests," *Record-Courier*, September 2, 2021, https://www.recordcourier.com/news /2021/sep/02/grand-jury-clears-sheriff-aug-8-protests/.

234 *Trumpian candidate for the U.S. Senate*: Matthew Rosenberg, "The Heir: In Nevada, a G.O.P. Candidate Sheds His Political Inheritance," *New York Times*, November 1, 2022, https://www.nytimes.com/2022/11/01/us/politics/nevada-senate-adam -laxalt-republican.html; Bob Conrad, "Douglas County Sheriff in Hot Water Again, This Time for Violating State Ethics Law," *This Is Reno*, September 22, 2022, https://thisisreno.com/2022/09/douglas-county-sheriff-in-hot-water -again-this-time-for-violating-state-ethics-law/.

234 *"fundamentally opposed to the American Way of Life"*: "We Won't Back Down: BLM Fund- ing Database Stabilized," Claremont Institute (press release), March 18, 2023, https://www.claremont.org/we-wont-back-down-blm-funding-database -stabilized/.

234 *"join posses, not militias"*: "CSPOA Posse Intel Webinar 10-03-23," Constitutional
     Sheriffs & Peace Officers Association (website), October 3, 2023, https://cspoa
     .org/webinar/cspoa-posse-intel-webinar-10-03-23/.

235 *"the same types of firearms"*: Kopel, "The *Posse Comitatus*," 806.

235 *"answerable only to the U.S. Constitution as they interpret it"*: *Confronting White Supremacy (Part
     VII): The Evolution of Anti-Democratic Extremist Groups and the Ongoing Threat to Democracy,
     Hearing Before the House Committee on Oversight and Reform Subcommittee on Civil Rights and
     Civil Liberties*, 117th Cong. (December 13, 2022) (statement of Mary B. McCord,
     Executive Director, Institute for Constitutional Advocacy and Protection, Visiting
     Professor of Law, Georgetown University Law Center), 2, https://www.congress
     .gov/117/meeting/house/115236/witnesses/HHRG-117-GO02-Wstate
     -McCordM-20221213.pdf.

235 *given more attention and political support*: Hassan Kanu, "Prevalence of White Suprema-
     cists in Law Enforcement Demands Drastic Change," Reuters, May 12, 2022,
     https://www.reuters.com/legal/government/prevalence-white-supremacists-law
     -enforcement-demands-drastic-change-2022-05-12/.

## CHAPTER 9: KEEPING THE COUNTY WHITE

238 *"keep the Republic white"*: James Baldwin, "To Crush a Serpent," in *James Baldwin: The
     Cross of Redemption, Uncollected Writings*, ed. Randall Kenan (New York: Pantheon
     Books, 2010), 195.

239 *one of the earliest Southern police forces*: Neal Shirley and Saralee Stafford, "Where Do the
     Police Come From?," *Scalawag*, September 7, 2016, https://scalawagmagazine.org
     /2016/09/where-do-police-come-from/.

239 *compares them to the posse commitatus*: Jill Lepore, "The Invention of the Police," *New
     Yorker*, July 13, 2020, https://www.newyorker.com/magazine/2020/07/20/the
     -invention-of-the-police.

239 *fears of Black rebellion*: Jonathan Hope Franklin, *The Free Negro in North Carolina, 1790–
     1860* (Chapel Hill: University of North Carolina Press, 1943), 70, https://archive
     .org/details/freenegroinnorth00fran_0/page/n5/mode/2up.

240 *period of 1865 to about 1877*: Eric Foner, *Reconstruction Updated Edition: America's Unfinished
     Revolution, 1863–1877* (New York: HarperCollins, 2014), 163.

240 *"atop the pyramid of local power"*: Foner, *Reconstruction*, 504.

241 *three out of four lynchings in Louisiana*: Adam Fairclough, *Race & Democracy: The Civil Rights
     Struggle in Louisiana, 1915–1972* (Athens: University of Georgia Press, 2008), 26.

241 *"best paying office in the state"*: Foner, *Reconstruction*, 504.

241 *refused to register Black men*: Fairclough, *Race & Democracy*, 25–26.

241 *"threatened, beaten, jailed, 'run out of the parish,' or slain"*: Fairclough, *Race & Democracy*, 26.

241 *loss of local control was even more distressing to Southern Democrats*: Foner, *Reconstruction*, 79.

241 *the role of sheriff required a bond*: N.C. General Statutes, § 162-8, https://www.ncleg
     .gov/EnactedLegislation/Statutes/PDF/ByArticle/Chapter_162/Article_2.pdf.

242 *pay this fee up front*: Foner, *Reconstruction*, 504.

242 *at least two thousand Black people were killed*: Equal Justice Initiative, *Reconstruction in America: Racial Violence After the Civil War, 1865–1876* (Montgomery, AL: Equal Justice Initiative, 2020), 44, https://eji.org/wp-content/uploads/2020/07/reconstruction-in-america-report.pdf.

242 *around one thousand of those deaths*: Equal Justice Initiative, *Reconstruction in America*, 53.

242 *more per year during that brief period*: Equal Justice Initiative, *Reconstruction in America*, 44–45; *Lynching in America: Confronting the Legacy of Racial Terror*, 3rd ed. (Montgomery, AL: Equal Justice Initiative, 2017), 4. The Equal Justice Initiative has documented roughly four thousand racial terror lynchings in twelve Southern states between the end of Reconstruction in 1877 and 1950, an average of roughly fifty-five per year. During the twelve years of Reconstruction, lynchings killed more than 166 Black people each year.

242 *a small handful in the South*: Foner, *Reconstruction*, 504.

242 *white mob killed fifty Black people*: Equal Justice Initiative, *Reconstruction in America*, 54.

242 *One such insurrection happened in Iberia Parish*: Gilles Vandal, "Politics and Violence in Bourbon Louisiana: The Loreauville Riot of 1884 as a Case Study," *Louisiana History* 30, no. 1 (Winter 1989): 23–42, https://www.jstor.org/stable/4232706.

243 *physically retook the courthouse*: Vandal, "The Loreauville Riot," 35.

243 *"fled in all directions"*: "The Solid South," *Leavenworth Times*, November 4, 1884, 1, https://www.newspapers.com/article/the-leavenworth-times-loreauville-riot/9436737/.

243 *"the day of doom had come"*: *Times-Picayune*, November 3, 1884, 3, https://www.newspapers.com/article/the-times-picayune/96992457/.

243 *still finding the bodies*: Vandal, "The Loreauville Riot," 38.

243 *"most deplorable and bloody affray"*: "Riot at Fausse Point," *Shreveport Times*, November 3, 1884, reprinted by *Bossier Banner-Progress*, November 6, 1884, https://www.newspapers.com/image/348624599/.

244 *myth of the grand plantations*: Khalil Gibran Muhammad, "The Sugar That Saturates the American Diet Has a Barbaric History as the 'White Gold' That Fueled Slavery," *New York Times*, August 14, 2019, https://www.nytimes.com/interactive/2019/08/14/magazine/sugar-slave-trade-slavery.html.

245 *faculty member at the University of Louisiana at Lafayette*: "Phebe Hayes," University of Louisiana at Lafayette Center for Louisiana Studies (website), accessed March 12, 2024, https://louisianastudies.louisiana.edu/node/29863.

245 *first Black female physician*: Shanna P. Dickens, "A Legacy Remembered," *Daily Iberian*, December 10, 2018, https://www.thedailyiberian.com/acadiana-lifestyle/a-legacy-remembered/article_52ebdade-f410-11e8-b8d0-e3dd9776eb9c.html.

246 *"lived and labored at the site"*: Shadows-on-the-Teche (website), accessed March 12, 2024, https://www.shadowsontheteche.org/.

248 *agreement he struck with the newly freed workers*: "Slavery," Shadows-on-the-Teche (website), archived by the Wayback Machine, August 5, 2018, https://web.archive.org/web/20180805160535/http://www.shadowsontheteche.org/slavery.

248 *"labor productivity was higher under slavery"*: Mark D. Schmitz, "Postbellum Developments in the Louisiana Cane Sugar Industry," *Business and Economic History* 5 (1976): 91, https://www.jstor.org/stable/23702782.

249 *"any person pursuing immoral activities"*: Gilles Vandal, "Regulating Louisiana's Rural Areas: The Functions of Parish Jails, 1840–1885," *Louisiana History* 42, no. 1 (Winter 2001): 82, https://www.jstor.org/stable/4233719.

249 *punish people accused of vagrancy*: Vandal, "Regulating Louisiana's Rural Areas," 80.

250 *labor riots rocked southern Louisiana*: Vandal, "Regulating Louisiana's Rural Areas," 81.

250 *white militias, lawmen, and vigilantes murdered one hundred Black men*: Foner, *Reconstruction*, 810.

250 *leased everyone in its prisons*: Foner, *Reconstruction*, 809.

250 *tens of millions of dollars for state governments*: Ethelbert Stewart, *Federal and State Laws Relating to Convict Labor* (Washington, DC: Bureau of Labor Statistics, 1914), 12, https://books.google.com/books?id=xIMzAQAAMAAJ&pg=PA12. The report notes that many states reported incomplete data, so this figure should be taken as a minimum value.

250 *"religious, moral and philanthropic forces"*: Ida B. Wells, "The Convict Lease System," in *The Reason Why the Colored American Is Not in the World's Columbian Exposition: The Afro-American's Contribution to Columbian Literature*, ed. Ida B. Wells (self-pub., 1893), https://digital.library.upenn.edu/women/wells/exposition/exposition.html#III.

251 *"sentenced in large numbers to long terms"*: Wells, "The Convict Lease System."

251 *still white and held (and still hold) the reins of power*: Matthew J. Mancini, "Convict Leasing," 64 Parishes (website), accessed March 12, 2024, https://64parishes.org/entry/convict-leasing.

251 *"irrelevant or something to be repressed"*: Roger B. Handberg and Charles M. Unkovic, "Southern County Sheriffs: A Changing Political Institution," *Free Inquiry in Creative Sociology* 8, no. 1 (May 1980): 45.

252 *"tried to keep any civil rights movement out"*: Edran Auguster, interview with Michelle Mitchell, July 19, 1994, in *Behind the Veil: Documenting African American Life in the Jim Crow South*, John Hope Franklin Research Center, Duke University, https://repository.duke.edu/dc/behindtheveil/btvct06050.

252 *stockpiling ammunition for a race war*: Adam Fairclough, "Racial Repression in World War Two: The New Iberia Incident," *Louisiana History* 32, no. 2 (Spring 1991): 195, https://www.jstor.org/stable/4232879.

252 *fired a pistol to make sure he did not turn around*: Fairclough, "Racial Repression," 192.

253 *"armed to the teeth"*: Fairclough, "Racial Repression," 195.

253 *one lyncher and three police brutality cases*: Fairclough, *Race & Democracy*, 93.

254 *"A Neanderthal image"*: Handberg and Unkovic, "Southern County Sheriffs," 44.

254 *"independence and a sovereign nature"*: "LSA—Role of the Sheriff—Half Hour," Louisiana Hometown (YouTube channel), June 3, 2016, video, 5:57, https://www.youtube.com/watch?v=Y7Hzc32UoSk.

255 *Business owners praise the system*: Adam Nossiter, "With Jobs to Do, Louisiana Parish Turns to Inmates," *New York Times*, July 5, 2006, https://www.nytimes.com/2006/07/05/us/with-jobs-to-do-louisiana-parish-turns-to-inmates.html.

255 *"they're going to let them out"*: Jonah E. Bromwich, "Louisiana Sheriff's Remarks Evoke Slavery, Critics Say," *New York Times*, October 12, 2017, https://www.nytimes.com/2017/10/12/us/prison-reform-steve-prator.html.

256 *documented over four thousand lynchings*: Equal Justice Initiative, *Lynching in America*.

256 *In 1873, a white mob*: Michael J. Pfeifer, "The Origins of Postbellum Lynching: Collective Violence in Reconstruction Louisiana," *Louisiana History: The Journal of the Louisiana Historical Association* 50, no. 2 (Spring 2009): 200.

257 *"unwilling to shoot into the crowd"*: Arthur Raper, *The Tragedy of Lynching* (Chapel Hill: University of North Carolina Press, 1933), 13, https://babel.hathitrust.org/cgi/pt?id=mdp.39015047438612&seq=7.

258 *"protect white supremacy without the help of the rabble"*: James L. Baggett, "'A Law Abiding People': Alabama's 1901 Constitution and the Attempted Lynching of Jim Brown," *Alabama Review* 71, no. 3 (July 2018): 211, https://doi.org/10.1353/ala.2018.0025.

258 *the new 1901 constitution*: Baggett, "'A Law Abiding People,'" 230.

258 *"an agreeable surprise"*: "Discouraging Lynch Law in Alabama," *New York Times*, July 11, 1901, https://www.nytimes.com/1901/07/11/archives/discouraging-lynch-law-in-alabama.html.

259 *a three-day festival*: Laura Rutherford, "The Louisiana Sugar Cane Festival: Celebrating All Things Sugar for 80 Years," Sugar Association (blog), September 2023, https://www.sugar.org/blog/the-louisiana-sugar-cane-festival/.

264 *shot in a car on her way home*: Dan Fenster, "Across the Bayou, It's Different," Hey Brother Media, June 2018, http://www.bryanfenster.com/bayou.

264 *"not stats that we keep"*: Fenster, "Across the Bayou, It's Different."

264 *warn their friends to take care*: John Simerman, "Lack of Trust in New Iberia: Grappling with a Community That's Lost Faith in Law Enforcement," *Acadiana Advocate*, November 25, 2018, https://www.theadvocate.com/acadiana/news/crime_police/lack-of-trust-in-new-iberia-grappling-with-a-community-thats-lost-faith-in-law/article_efd2c25e-ed3a-11e8-a65f-dbc482d9fdd4.html.

265 *a deep well of humiliation*: Hannah Rappleye, "Iberia Parish Sheriff's Office Under Scrutiny for Treatment of Inmates, Others in Custody," *Acadiana Advocate*, February 8, 2016, https://www.theadvocate.com/acadiana/news/iberia-parish-sheriff-s-office-under-scrutiny-for-treatment-of-inmates-others-in-custody/article_a71574d5-c321-5fbd-88f9-7e0b049678d3.html.

266 *"gets the job done"*: "2016 Best of the Teche," Issuu, July 28, 2016, https://issuu.com/wickcommunications/docs/2016_best_of_the_teche#google_vignette.

266 *ten others pled guilty*: "Judge Sentences Three Law Enforcement Officer Defendants in Iberia Parish, Louisiana, Civil Rights Case," U.S. Department of Justice, May 3, 2017, https://www.justice.gov/opa/pr/judge-sentences-three-law-enforcement -officer-defendants-iberia-parish-louisiana-civil-rights; Sabrina Canfield, "Louisiana Sheriff Cleared of Racist Acts in Jail," Courthouse News Service, November 9, 2016, https://www.courthousenews.com/louisiana-sheriff-cleared-of-racist -acts-in-jail/.

## CHAPTER 10: BORDER WARS

271 *deeply resented being forced to consult with the federal government*: Lyda Longa, "His Life and Love: Rancher John Ladd Prevails Despite Dealings with Government, Migrants," *Herald/Review*, November 28, 2021, https://www.myheraldreview.com/news/bis bee/his-life-and-love-rancher-john-ladd-prevails-despite-dealings-with -government-migrants/article_cf485552-17f9-11ec-8646-27d74736ca19.html.

271 *migrants not only trespassed on his property*: Longa, "His Life and Love."

271 *a man named Robert Krentz*: Randal C. Archibold, "Ranchers Alarmed by Killing Near Border," *New York Times*, April 4, 2010, https://www.nytimes.com/2010/04/05 /us/05arizona.html.

271 *"hands of the Border Patrol are tied"*: Lyda Longa, "Rancher Says Migrants Running Through His Land Is a 24-7 Way of Life, but He Refuses to Give Up His Home," *Herald/Review*, October 29, 2022, https://www.myheraldreview.com/news/bisbee /rancher-says-migrants-running-through-his-land-is-a-24-7-way-of-life-but/arti cle_e6895e0c-5581-11ed-939b-5b302cbbb4aa.html.

272 *about one hundred migrants crossing his property each day*: Elizabeth Heckman, "Arizona Rancher Makes Desperate Plea to Biden After Finding Total of 16 Dead Migrants on Property," Fox News, October 27, 2022, https://www.foxnews.com/media /arizona-rancher-makes-desperate-plea-biden-finding-total-16-dead-migrants -property.

272 *affidavit for a lawsuit against the Department of Homeland Security*: John Ladd, Affidavit, October 3, 2016, in Amended Complaint at Exhibit 16, *Whitewater Draw v. DHS*, No. 3:16-cv-02583, https://cis.org/sites/cis.org/files/Litigation/NEPA/White water-Draw-v-DHS/Amended-Complaint/Exhibit16_Affidavit-John-Ladd .pdf.

272 *immigrants commit fewer crimes than citizens*: Krysten Crawford, "The Mythical Tie Between Immigration and Crime," Stanford Institute for Economic Policy Research, July 21, 2023, https://siepr.stanford.edu/news/mythical-tie-between-immigration -and-crime.

274 *NumbersUSA is a grassroots organization*: Caleb Kieffer, "The Social Contract Publishes Its Last Tract," SPLC Hatewatch, April 23, 2020, https://www.splcenter.org /hatewatch/2020/04/23/social-contract-publishes-its-last-tract.

275  *"social and political San Andreas Fault?"*: John Tanton, "'Witan Memo' III," October 10, 1986, reprinted by *Intelligence Report*, https://www.splcenter.org/fighting-hate/intel ligence-report/2015/witan-memo-iii.

276  *"a key FAIR goal for many years"*: *Crossing the Line: U.S. Sheriffs Colluding with the Anti-Immigrant Movement* (Chicago: Center for New Community, 2017), 3.

276  *translates to We Are America*: Sonya Geis and Michael Powell, "Hundreds of Thousands Rally in Cities Large and Small," *Washington Post*, April 11, 2006, https://www.washingtonpost.com/archive/politics/2006/04/11/hundreds-of-thousands-rally-in-cities-large-and-small/6a94e7bf-5f05-4949-9ee5-4c60b577ba66/.

276  *most infamous anti-immigrant bill, SB 1070*: Randal C. Archibold, "Arizona Enacts Stringent Law on Immigration," *New York Times*, April 23, 2010, https://www.nytimes.com/2010/04/24/us/politics/24immig.html.

277  *invalidated many of the provisions of the bill*: "Supreme Court Issues Ruling on Arizona Anti-Immigrant Law," National Immigrant Law Center, June 25, 2012, https://www.nilc.org/2012/06/25/supreme-court-decision-on-sb-1070/.

277  *filed a civil rights lawsuit against Arpaio*: "Department of Justice Files Lawsuit in Arizona Against Maricopa County, Maricopa County Sheriff's Office, and Sheriff Joseph Arpaio," U.S. Department of Justice, May 10, 2012, https://www.justice.gov/opa/pr/department-justice-files-lawsuit-arizona-against-maricopa-county-maricopa-county-sheriff-s.

277  *allocate funds and land*: "Kris Kobach: Lawyer for America's Nativist Movement," SPLC Hatewatch, November 18, 2016, https://www.splcenter.org/20161118/kris-kobach-lawyer-americas-nativist-movement. Kobach himself attended Harvard and Yale and worked in the DOJ for a time after 9/11, when he gained a deep distrust of immigrants and linked them to terrorism and crime. A virulent anti-immigration activist, he shaped John Kerry's immigration policies in 2012, served on Donald Trump's transition team, had a failed run for the Senate, served as Kansas attorney general, and now represents a group of Texas sheriffs who are suing the federal government for what they argue is ineffective immigration policy.

278  *"meet with FAIR's senior staff"*: *Crossing the Line*, 3.

278  *send incarcerated people to help build Trump's border wall*: Buell, "Bristol Sheriff Thomas Hodgson Tried to Score Points with Stephen Miller."

278  *implied that the border school was sanctioned*: *Crossing the Line*, 4.

278  *"value the sheriffs we meet"*: *Crossing the Line*, 5.

279  *Illegal Immigration Reform and Immigrant Responsibility Act*: Kica Matos, "25 Years of IIRIRA Shows Immigration Law Gone Wrong," Vera Institute, June 28, 2022, https://www.vera.org/news/25-years-of-iirira-shows-immigration-law-gone-wrong.

279  *became automatically deportable overnight*: Dara Lind, "The Disastrous, Forgotten 1996 Law That Created Today's Immigration Problem," Vox, April 28, 2016, https://www.vox.com/2016/4/28/11515132/iirira-clinton-immigration.

280 *"hard to explain where the criminal justice system ends"*: César Cuauhtémoc García Hernández, "What Is Crimmigration Law?," *Insights on Law and Society* 17, no. 3 (Spring 2017), http://www.antoniocasella.eu/nume/Crimmigration.law_spring 17.pdf.

281 *politicize their anti-immigrant bona fides*: Jessica Pishko, "When Sheriffs Choose to Help ICE," The Appeal, June 9, 2020, https://theappeal.org/politicalreport/the-badge -sheriffs-ice-in-jails/.

281 *kicked the sheriff out of the program*: Ray Stern, "Feds Pull 287(g) Authority from Maricopa County Jails Because of Civil Rights Violations," *Phoenix New Times*, December 15, 2011, https://www.phoenixnewtimes.com/news/feds-pull-287-g-authority -from-maricopa-county-jails-because-of-civil-rights-violations-6631025.

281 *"we can make him disappear"*: Josie Duffy Rice, "'We Can Make Him Disappear': The Power of County Sheriffs," The Appeal, May 7, 2018, https://theappeal.org/we -can-make-him-disappear-the-power-of-county-sheriffs-b27de57061e4/.

282 *In 2006, after he joined*: Oliver Hinds and Jack Norton, "No Chance Alamance: Immigration Detention and Jail Expansion in the North Carolina Piedmont," Vera, In Our Backyards Stories, July 28, 2020, https://www.vera.org/in-our-backyards -stories/no-chance-alamance.

283 *fear of deportation proceedings*: "Sheriff David Mahoney: ICE Entanglement Reduces Public Safety," *Wisconsin State Journal*, April 11, 2021, https://madison.com/opin ion/column/sheriff-david-mahoney-ice-entanglement-reduces-public-safety/arti cle_450701e4-1822-59c4-a832-d3a05027d3d1.html.

285 *Lamb filmed a political ad*: Melissa Del Bosque, "Sheriff Hollywood: The Far Right's New Darling Kicks Off His Campaign at the Border," Border Chronicle, May 2, 2023, https://www.theborderchronicle.com/p/sheriff-hollywood-the-far-rights; @janel.lamb, "Social media is shadow banning this video put out by Pinal County Sheriffs Office, I wonder why? 😵 This is not pretend, these are real problems that we as a country must fix! Because of federal laws such as SB1070 and case law, Arizona is very limited in what we can do on the state and local level, which is incredibly frustrating!! I guess if you want something done right, you gotta do it yourself as they say. . . . Which is a huge part of the reason Sheriff Mark is running for the US Senate for the people of Arizona. He's been sounding the alarm for years, now it's time to go to DC and get things done!!! #pcso #bordercrisis #thisisreality #sherifflambforsenate," Instagram, April 27, 2023, https://www .instagram.com/p/CrjQL7bP2hQ/; "Fact Sheet: Operation Stonegarden," National Immigration Forum (website), April 27, 2020, https://immigrationforum .org/article/fact-sheet-operation-stonegarden/.

285 *a 2017 report by the Office of Inspector General*: John E. McCoy II, *FEMA and CBP Oversight of Operation Stonegarden Program Needs Improvement*, OPIG-18-13 (November 2017), 2, https://www.oig.dhs.gov/sites/default/files/assets/2017-11/OIG-18-13-Nov17 .pdf.

285 *flying over his county without permission*: Del Bosque, "Sheriff Hollywood."

286 *allegations of sex trafficking a minor*: Elias Weiss, "Amid Sex Trafficking Probe, Matt Gaetz Shows Up in Arizona for a Border Diatribe," *Phoenix New Times*, March 25, 2022, https://www.phoenixnewtimes.com/news/republican-matt-gaetz-joins-andy-biggs-sheriff-mark-lamb-at-arizonas-border-with-mexico-13292471; Ryan Nobles et al., "DOJ Tells Matt Gaetz That He Won't Be Charged in Sex Trafficking Probe, His Lawyers Say," NBC News, February 15, 2023, https://www.nbcnews.com/politics/congress/doj-decides-not-charge-rep-matt-gaetz-sex-trafficking-investigation-rcna70839; Robert Draper and Michael S. Schmidt, "Chief Witness Against Gaetz Is Cooperating with House Ethics Investigation," *New York Times*, February 9, 2024, https://www.nytimes.com/2024/02/09/us/politics/gaetz-sex-trafficking.html. The U.S. Department of Justice announced it would not pursue charges against Gaetz in 2023, but the House Ethics Committee has opened an inquiry into the allegations.

286 *received at least $16 million*: Department of Homeland Security, Response to FOIA Request, September 29, 2023, Operation Stonegarden grants to Pinal County, 2023-FEFO-00600.

286 *so many sheriffs joined the 287(g) program*: Claudia Flores, "Rapidly Expanding 287(g) Program Suffers from Lack of Transparency," Center for American Progress, October 9, 2018, https://www.americanprogress.org/article/rapidly-expanding-287g-program-suffers-lack-transparency/.

287 *lists of "noncooperative" sheriffs*: Caitlin Dickerson, "Trump Administration Moves to Expand Deportation Dragnet to Jails," *New York Times*, August 21, 2017, https://www.nytimes.com/2017/08/21/us/sheriffs-immigration-jails.html; Caitlin Dickson, "'Sanctuary' Battle Heats Up as Trump Kicks New Yorkers from Program for Expedited Entry," Yahoo! News, February 10, 2020, https://www.yahoo.com/entertainment/sanctuary-battle-heats-up-as-trump-kicks-new-yorkers-from-program-for-expedited-entry-013326660.html.

287 *poured more money into immigration enforcement*: Todd Miller, "The Real Border Surge: The End of Title 42 and the Triumph of the Border-Industrial Complex," Border Chronicle, June 8, 2023, https://www.theborderchronicle.com/p/the-real-border-surge-the-end-of.

287 *"send them to hell!"*: "Sheriff: 'We'll Send Them to Hell,'" CNN, September 6, 2014, https://www.cnn.com/videos/bestoftv/2014/09/06/ctn-isis-sheriff.cnn.

288 *through ports of entry, hidden in cargo*: Christian Penichet-Paul, "Illicit Fentanyl and Drug Smuggling at the U.S.-Mexico Border: An Overview," National Immigration Forum, October 25, 2023, https://immigrationforum.org/article/illicit-fentanyl-and-drug-smuggling-at-the-u-s-mexico-border-an-overview/.

288 *Advocates for Victims of Illegal Alien Crime (AVIAC)*: "About Us," Advocates for Victims of Illegal Alien Crime (website), accessed March 12, 2024, https://www.aviac.us/about-us.

288 *Donald Trump to bolster his policies*: Kenneth P. Vogel and Katie Rogers, "For Trump and 'Angel Families,' a Mutually Beneficial Bond," *New York Times*, July 4, 2018, https://www.nytimes.com/2018/07/04/us/politics/trump-angel-families-bond-backlash.html.

289 *argues for something close to net-zero migration*: "Statement of Positions," Constitutional Sheriffs & Peace Officers Association (website), accessed March 12, 2024, https://cspoa.org/statement-of-positions/.

290 *Carlson said on his show*: Steve Rose, "A Deadly Ideology: How the 'Great Replacement Theory' Went Mainstream," *Guardian*, June 8, 2022, https://www.theguardian.com/world/2022/jun/08/a-deadly-ideology-how-the-great-replacement-theory-went-mainstream.

290 *"violation of their rights by the invasion of illegal aliens"*: "Statement of Positions," CSPOA (website), https://cspoa.org/statement-of-positions/.

291 *Almost all of the Texas sheriffs*: Jessica Pishko, "The Fringe Ideology of 'Constitutional Sheriffs' Is Attracting Believers Within Texas Law Enforcement," *Texas Tribune*, January 13, 2023, https://www.texastribune.org/2023/01/13/constitutional-sheriffs-texas/.

291 *increase sheriff enrollment in 287(g)*: Debbie Cenziper, "Under Trump, ICE Aggressively Recruited Sheriffs as Partners to Question and Detain Undocumented Immigrants," *Washington Post*, November 23, 2021, https://www.washingtonpost.com/investigations/interactive/2021/trump-ice-sheriffs-immigrants-287g/.

291 *helps to connect sheriffs with FAIR*: Caleb Kieffer, "Cadre of Nativist Groups, Figures Have Long Pushed Replacement-by-Immigration Ideas into Mainstream," SPLC Hatewatch, July 14, 2022, https://www.splcenter.org/hatewatch/2022/07/14/cadre-nativist-groups-figures-have-long-pushed-replacement-immigration-ideas-mainstream.

291 *FAIR border school in 2015*: Crossing the Line, 5.

291 *"agreeing to stop illegal immigration"*: Crossing the Line, 11.

292 *Howard Buffett, a son of Warren Buffett*: Beau Hodai, "Howard Buffett's Border War: A Billionaire's Son Is Spending Millions in Cochise County," *Phoenix New Times*, January 13, 2019, https://www.phoenixnewtimes.com/news/howard-buffetts-warren-buffet-son-border-war-cochise-county-11103225.

292 *an undocumented person in a drunk-driving crash*: "Nephew of Idaho Sheriff Killed by Illegal Immigrant," Fox News, June 3, 2021, https://www.foxnews.com/video/6257275386001.

## CHAPTER 11: A MAN ON A MISSION

294 *announced a partnership with True the Vote*: "CSPOA Strongly Encourages Sheriffs and Local Law Enforcement to Investigate Alleged Election Fraud in Their Jurisdictions," Constitutional Sheriffs & Peace Officers Association (website), accessed

March 12, 2024, https://cspoa.org/press-release-urgent-cspoa-2022-calling-all
-americans-and-law-enforcement/; Cassandra Jaramillo, "She Helped Create the
Big Lie. Records Suggest She Turned It into a Big Grift," Reveal, June 8, 2022,
https://revealnews.org/article/true-the-vote-big-lie-election-fraud/.

294 *"get more sheriffs to investigate the evidence"*: Richard Mack, email to author, August 8,
2022.

294 *"peaceful future as a free people"*: "CSPOA Strongly Encourages Sheriffs and Local Law
Enforcement to Investigate Alleged Election Fraud."

295 *allegedly historical incidences of voter fraud*: S. J. Ackerman, "The Vote That Failed,"
*Smithsonian*, November 1998, https://www.smithsonianmag.com/history/the-vote
-that-failed-159427766/; Lones Seiber, "The Battle of Athens," *American Heritage*
36, no. 2 (February/March 1985), https://www.americanheritage.com/battle
-athens.

295 *"Election Fraud HAS HAPPENED"*: Alexandra Berzon and Nick Corasaniti, "2020
Election Deniers Seek Out Powerful Allies: County Sheriffs," *New York Times*, July
25, 2022, https://www.nytimes.com/2022/07/25/us/politics/election-sheriffs
-voting-trump.html.

296 *substantiate these initial complaints of voter fraud*: Judy L. Thomas and Jonathan Shorman,
"Johnson County Sheriff Tells Las Vegas Crowd His Election Fraud Investigation
Continues," *Kansas City Star*, July 16, 2022, https://www.kansascity.com
/news/politics-government/article263436243.html.

297 *looked for the two hundred complaints but only found one*: Steve Vockrodt, "Johnson County
Sheriff Claimed He Got 200 Tips of Election Fraud. A Records Request Yielded
Only One," KCUR, July 28, 2022, https://www.kcur.org/news/2022-07-28
/johnson-county-sheriff-claimed-he-got-200-tips-of-election-fraud-a-sunshine
-request-yielded-only-one.

297 *"attempting to interfere with an election"*: Jonathan Shorman and Judy Thomas, "'Attempting to Interfere': Johnson County Sheriff Suggested His Staff Transport Ballots,"
*Kansas City Star*, July 18, 2022, https://www.kansascity.com/news/politics
-government/article263574188.html.

297 *ballot box tampering*: Jamelle Bouie, "Trump Is Playing with Fire," *New York Times*, January 12, 2024, https://www.nytimes.com/2024/01/12/opinion/trump-political
-violence.html.

298 *"He was mean"*: "The Right to Vote (Transcript)," SPLC Learning for Justice (website), accessed March 12, 2024, https://www.learningforjustice.org/professional
-development/the-right-to-vote-transcript.

298 *Clark's openly racist hostility*: Associated Press, "Wilson Baker, 60. Sheriff in Selma,"
*New York Times*, September 12, 1975, https://www.nytimes.com/1975/09/12/ar
chives/wilson-baker-60-sheriff-in-selma-safety-director-during-civil.html.

298 *case called* Shelby County v. Holder: *Shelby County v. Holder*, 570 US 529 (2013),
https://www.oyez.org/cases/2012/12-96.

299 *passed around one hundred laws to restrict voting*: "Effects of *Shelby County v. Holder* on the Voting Rights Act," Brennan Center for Justice, June 21, 2023, https://www.brennancenter.org/our-work/research-reports/effects-shelby-county-v-holder-voting-rights-act.

299 *definition is fairly slippery*: "Fact Sheet: Protecting Against Voter Intimidation," Institute for Constitutional Advocacy and Protection, accessed March 12, 2024, https://www.law.georgetown.edu/icap/wp-content/uploads/sites/32/2020/10/Voter-Intimidation-Fact-Sheet.pdf.

299 *Mack spoke at a "Stop the Steal" rally*: "Sheriff Richard Mack—Voter Fraud Rally," Sheriff Mack (YouTube channel), December 4, 2020, https://www.youtube.com/watch?v=8uzEUpFGqh0&t=1s.

300 *voted two to one for Trump over Biden*: "Election Summary Report," Barry County (website), accessed March 12, 2024, https://www.barrycounty.org/Departments%20&%20Officials/Officials/County%20Clerk/Elections/ElectionSummaryReportRPT.pdf.

301 *one of the most segregated places in the country*: Mike Wilkinson, "Michigan's Segregated Past—and Present (Told in 9 Interactive Maps)," Bridge Michigan, August 8, 2017, https://www.bridgemi.com/michigan-government/michigans-segregated-past-and-present-told-9-interactive-maps.

302 *judge promptly dismissed the lawsuit*: Craig Mauger, "Barry County Sheriff's Suit Must Be Dismissed Because He Didn't Sign It, State Police Says," *Detroit News*, August 10, 2022, https://www.detroitnews.com/story/news/local/michigan/2022/08/10/barry-county-sheriff-suit-must-dismissed-because-he-didnt-sign-it-state-police-says/10286621002.

302 *They were all dismissed*: Peter Eisler and Nathan Layne, "Inside One Far-Right Sheriff's Crusade to Prove Trump's Bogus Voter-Fraud Claims," Reuters, July 29, 2022, https://www.reuters.com/investigates/special-report/usa-elections-michigan-investigation/.

302 *returned with the seal broken*: Eisler and Layne, "Inside One Far-Right Sheriff's Crusade."

303 *"not something your department needs"*: Jonathan Oosting, "Sheriff Dar Leaf: Michigan Is Trying to Thwart My Probe into 2020 Election," Bridge Michigan, June 6, 2022, https://www.bridgemi.com/michigan-government/sheriff-dar-leaf-michigan-trying-thwart-my-probe-2020-election.

303 *"became a little contentious"*: Barry County, Michigan, Board of Commissioners meeting, October 25, 2022, video, 32:50, https://www.youtube.com/watch?v=LMLXbGYYHEY.

304 *"job is to seek justice"*: Barry County, Michigan, Board of Commissioners meeting, October 25, 2022, 13:13.

304 *"deals with actual violent crime"*: Barry County, Michigan, Board of Commissioners meeting, October 25, 2022, 27:38.

304 *"We got victims suffering"*: Barry County, Michigan, Board of Commissioners meeting, October 25, 2022, 38:38.

305 *"whistleblowers from all around the country"*: Barry County, Michigan, Board of Commissioners meeting, October 25, 2022, 55:41.

305 *prove that they had been hacked in some way*: Eisler and Layne, "Inside One Far-Right Sheriff's Crusade."

306 *"disillusioned with the whole process related to elections"*: Catherine Engelbrecht, interviewed by Cade Lamb, "Podcast #1: True the Vote," *Fear Not Do Right Podcast*, June 2022, https://open.spotify.com/episode/1DIfYEY6L8BT3QjLIfnnpW.

307 *"dumping into these ballot boxes"*: Mark Lamb, interviewed by Cade Lamb, "Podcast #8: The American Sheriff," *Fear Not Do Right Podcast*, August 2022, https://www.youtube.com/watch?v=UFiutFJ0YpM.

307 *spent at least $40 million*: Peter Stone, "MyPillow Chief Spends Tens of Millions in Fresh Crusade to Push Trump's Big Lie," *Guardian*, August 4, 2020, https://www.theguardian.com/us-news/2022/aug/04/mypillow-mike-lindell-trump-big-lie-election-fraud.

307 *announced his new partnership with True the Vote*: "Former President Trump Holds Rally in Prescott, Arizona, Introductory Speakers," C-SPAN, July 22, 2022, video, 42:46, https://www.c-span.org/video/?521718-101/president-trump-holds-rally-prescott-arizona-introductory-speakers.

307 *he asked for donations*: Protect America Now (website), archived August 1, 2022, by the Wayback Machine, https://web.archive.org/web/20220801190831/https://protectamerica.vote/. The Protect America Website is no longer online, and the video is not playable through the Wayback Machine.

308 *"protect their constituents"*: Protect America Now (website).

308 *button to "contribute" cash donations*: Protect America Now (website).

309 *"discourage law breakers from any organized effort"*: "Sheriff's Toolkit," True the Vote (website), archived January 5, 2024, by the Wayback Machine, https://web.archive.org/web/20240105192309/https://truethevote.org/sheriffs-toolkit.

309 *complain about the election process*: Pinal County Board of Supervisors meeting, August 3, 2022, https://pinalcountyaz.new.swagit.com/videos/178240.

310 *"make sure that nobody is breaking the laws"*: Mark Lamb, "A message from Sheriff Lamb regarding recent election issues . . . ," Facebook, August 4, 2022, https://www.facebook.com/watch/?v=405735614871719.

312 *Lamb's political rhetoric outside official meetings*: Jessica Pishko, "The 'Big Lie' Messengers Who Carry a Badge and Gun," *Arizona Mirror*, August 26, 2022, https://azmirror.com/2022/08/26/the-big-lie-messengers-who-carry-a-badge-and-gun/.

312 *"What a giant turd I was"*: "Live Special Report: 'The Pit' Presented by True the Vote," *Pete Santilli Show*, Rumble, August 13, 2024, https://rumble.com/v1ftj3f-live-special-report-the-pit-presented-by-true-the-vote.html.

313 *story about Lamb and True the Vote*: Jessica Pishko, "The Big Lie Messengers Who Carry a Badge and Gun," Bolts, August 24, 2022, https://boltsmag.org/true-the-vote-sheriffs/.

313 *Engelbrecht and Phillips were arrested*: Jessica Huseman, "Two Leaders of True the Vote Jailed by Federal Judge for Contempt of Court," *Texas Tribune*, October 31, 2022, https://www.texastribune.org/2022/10/31/true-the-vote-leaders-jailed/.

313 *Fox settled the case*: Intelligencer Staff, "All the Texts Fox News Didn't Want You to Read," *New York*, May 9, 2023, https://nymag.com/intelligencer/2023/05/all-the-texts-fox-news-didnt-want-you-to-read.html.

314 *"Americans who have questions about election integrity"*: "Rep. Dan Goldman Grills Sheriff Mark Lamb on 2020 Election Results," *Politico*, February 28, 2023, https://www.politico.com/video/2023/02/28/rep-dan-goldman-grills-sheriff-mark-lamb-on-2020-election-results-847142.

314 *didn't agree with the election denial partnership*: Evan Goodenow, "Chapman Says He's Not in Election-Denying Sheriff's Group After Appearing on Group's Site," *Loudoun Times-Mirror*, August 1, 2022, https://www.loudountimes.com/news/chapman-says-he-s-not-in-election-denying-sheriff-s-group-after-appearing-on-groups/article_abc67b76-11b4-11ed-92e8-133e3d0f448c.html.

314 *believed that Biden had not properly won*: Jennifer Aglesta and Ariel Edwards-Levy, "CNN Poll: Percentage of Republicans Who Think Biden's 2020 Win Was Illegitimate Ticks Back Up Near 70%," CNN, August 3, 2023, https://www.cnn.com/2023/08/03/politics/cnn-poll-republicans-think-2020-election-illegitimate/index.html.

314 *confusing for most people to understand*: Ese Olumhense, "Big Lie Proponents Are Creating Harsh Criminal Penalties for Elections Activity," Reveal, October 27, 2022, https://revealnews.org/article/election-crime-legislation-voter-suppression/.

315 *"16 voting/registration open cases"*: "Yuma County Voting Fraud," Yuma County Sheriff's Office (press release), May 11, 2022, archived by the Wayback Machine, February 19, 2024, https://web.archive.org/web/20240219034417/https://www.yumacountysheriff.org/pr-2022/PR-2022-30-Yuma-County-Voting-Fraud.pdf.

316 *took surreptitious video of Fuentes*: Kira Lerner, "'A Witch-Hunt': How Arizona Jailed a Grandmother for Ballot Collecting," *Guardian*, February 11, 2023, https://www.theguardian.com/us-news/2023/feb/11/arizona-ballot-collecting-law-guillermina-fuentes.

316 *Arizona lawmakers made it illegal*: Ariz. Rev. Stat. § 16-1005 (2016), as amended by H.B. 2023, 52d Leg., 2d Reg. Sess. (Ariz. 2016), https://www.azleg.gov/legtext/52leg/2r/laws/0005.PDF. The bill made it a felony to "knowingly collect voted or unvoted early ballots from another person," unless that voter is a household member, family member, or caregiver.

316 *voted in 2021 to uphold the law*: Brnovich, Attorney General of Arizona v. Democratic National Committee, 594 U.S. 647 (2021), https://www.supremecourt.gov/opinions/20pdf/19-1257_g204.pdf.

316 *appears to make a mark*: Lerner, "How Arizona Jailed a Grandmother for Ballot Collecting." The video, which is no longer online, is included in Dinesh D'Souza's film *2000 Mules*.

317 *went to Yuma to meet with local law enforcement*: William Knuth, Prosecution Report SIS-2020-0323, October 27, 2020, obtained under Arizona Public Records Law from the Arizona Office of Attorney General.

317 *told the investigators that there was a "ring"*: Lerner, "How Arizona Jailed a Grandmother for Ballot Collecting."

317 *come to collect their ballots*: Lerner, "How Arizona Jailed a Grandmother for Ballot Collecting."

318 *Mark Brnovich indicted Guillermina Fuentes and Alma Juarez*: "Two Individuals Accused of Ballot Harvesting in Yuma County," Arizona Attorney General (press release), December 23, 2020, https://www.azag.gov/press-release/two-individuals -accused-ballot-harvesting-yuma-county.

318 *two years of probation*: Lerner, "How Arizona Jailed a Grandmother for Ballot Collecting."

## CHAPTER 12: REFORMING THE OFFICE OF SHERIFF

321 *if you don't like it*: Celeste Fremon, "'Don't Elect Me!' Two LA Newspapers Call for Candidates to Answer Lee Baca's Challenge . . . and More," Witness LA, March 4, 2013, https://witnessla.com/dont-elect-me-two-la-newspapers-call-for-candidates -to-answer-lee-bacas-challenge-and-more/.

321 *"better hit the ditch"*: Hasan Kwame Jeffries, *Bloody Lowndes: Civil Rights and Black Power in Alabama's Black Belt* (New York: New York University Press, 2009), 35.

321 *"great experiment in democracy"*: Hasan Kwame Jeffries, "Lowndes County and the Voting Rights Act," Zinn Education Project, accessed March 12, 2024, https://www .zinnedproject.org/materials/lowndes-county-and-the-voting-rights-act/.

322 *booklet about the sheriff*: "Political Education," SNCC Digital, accessed March 12, 2024, https://snccdigital.org/our-voices/black-panther/part-4/.

322 *chairperson for the LCFO*: "John Hulett," SNCC Digital, accessed March 12, 2024, https://snccdigital.org/people/john-hulett/.

322 *Two thousand Black people came to watch*: Jeffries, *Bloody Lowndes*, 207.

322 *Hulett himself faced later opposition*: Jeffries, *Bloody Lowndes*, 234.

323 *a margin of around 10 percent*: "Joe Arpaio Outspent Paul Penzone by over $11M in Maricopa County Sheriff's Race," KTAR News, January 19, 2017, https://ktar .com/story/1429709/joe-arpaio-outspent-paul-penzone-11m-maricopa-county -sheriffs-race/. Penzone's victory was fueled in part by a large infusion of cash.

323 *seven largest counties elected Black men as sheriff*: Joe Killian, "Black Sheriffs Make History in Sweep of Seven Largest NC Counties," NC Newsline, November 8, 2018, https://ncnewsline.com/2018/11/08/black-sheriffs-make-history-in-sweep-of -seven-largest-nc-counties/.

323 *deportation of nearly 1,500 people*: Thomasi McDonald, "Wake County Sheriff Faces Plenty of Criticism from Challenger Ahead of Election," *News & Observer*, October 24, 2018, https://www.newsobserver.com/news/local/article220486565.html.

323 *Willie Rowe, who worked under Baker*: Jeffrey Billman, "The Winding Road to Ending ICE Collaboration in Raleigh," Bolts, August 26, 2022, https://boltsmag.org /north-carolina-sheriffs-ice-collaboration/.

324 *a bathroom stall with a large sign*: "Meet Charmaine McGuffey for Sheriff," Charmaine McGuffey (YouTube channel), November 3, 2020, https://www.youtube.com /watch?v=RZcVVW6Mb0E.

325 *floodwater threatened to drown some of the people*: ACLU National Prison Project et al., *Abandoned & Abused: Prison Conditions and Prisoner Abuse After Katrina* (Washington, DC: ACLU, 2006), https://www.aclu.org/wp-content/uploads/publications/oppre port20060809.pdf.

325 *jail population ballooned to 6,500*: Paige M. Harrison and Allen J. Beck, *Prison and Jail Inmates at Midyear 2004* (Washington, DC: Bureau of Justice Statistics, 2005), 10, https://static.prisonpolicy.org/scans/bjs/pjim04.pdf.

325 *one of the deadliest in the nation*: Laura Maggi, "Death Rate at Orleans Parish Prison Ranks Near Top," NOLA.com, February 8, 2009, https://www.nola.com/news /article_cf3a1b49-9e6f-5494-b8a2-26a219e23a90.html.

325 *endemic violence committed by guards*: Jones v. Gusman, 2:12-cv-00859, https://clearing house.net/case/12097/.

325 *documented eighteen deaths at the jail*: Andrea C. Armstrong et al., *Louisiana Deaths Behind Bars, 2015–2021* (New Orleans: Incarceration Transparency, 2023), https://www .incarcerationtransparency.org/wp-content/uploads/2023/06/Death-Behind -Bars-Report-2023-Final-06.05.23.pdf.

327 *quoting ex-mayor Mitch Landrieu*: *Times-Picayune* Editorial Board, "'Most Incarcerated City' Is Not What New Orleans Should Be: Editorial," NOLA.com, August 14, 2016, https://www.nola.com/news/politics/most-incarcerated-city-is-not-what -new-orleans-should-be-editorial/article_dcd79b80-559b-5f56-b938-2cecf a6ee637.html.

327 *incarcerated population is capped below 1,300*: Nick Chrastil, "In Final Vote, Council Approves Use of Temporary Detention Center for Inmates with Acute Mental Health Needs," The Lens, January 16, 2020, https://thelensnola.org/2020/01/16/in -final-vote-council-approves-use-of-temporary-detention-center-for-inmates-with -acute-mental-health-needs/.

327 *"we will help our neighbors"*: Nick Chrastil, "New Sheriff in Town," The Lens, December 11, 2021, https://thelensnola.org/2021/12/11/new-sheriff-in-town/.

328 *she called for the city to replace Wellpath*: Matt Sledge, "Huge, Controversial Contract for New Orleans Jail Health Care Undecided," NOLA.com, March 15, 2022, https:// www.nola.com/news/politics/huge-controversial-contract-for-new-orleans-jail -health-care-undecided/article_8768e672-a4b5-11ec-b35e-c797069ca608.html.

328 *stop the construction of a new $109 million jail*: Nick Chrastil, "How Phase III Came to Be," The Lens, January 2, 2024, https://thelensnola.org/2024/01/02/how-phase -iii-came-to-be/.

328 *not be seen as a failure of organizers*: Chrastil, "How Phase III Came to Be."

328 *another died in a fight*: Jillian Kramer, "New Details Emerge in New Orleans Jail Deaths, as Safety, Staffing Concerns Grow," NOLA.com, June 13, 2022, https://www.nola.com/news/courts/new-details-emerge-in-new-orleans-jail-deaths-as-safety-staffing-concerns-grow/article_513f2f0e-eb6c-11ec-969c-471b543c1509.html.

329 *working on law enforcement reform for decades*: Kate Shefte, "Early Title IX Complaint Sparked Career in Public Service for Seattleite Anne Levinson," *Seattle Times*, June 23, 2022, https://www.seattletimes.com/sports/early-title-ix-complaint-sparked-career-in-public-service-for-seattleite-anne-levinson/.

329 *women's professional basketball team*: Reign FC, "Seattle Reign FC Legend: Anne Levinson," Medium, July 4, 2016, https://medium.com/@ReignFC/seattle-reign-fc-legend-anne-levinson-2da550f08e79.

330 *happened to be Fortney supporters*: Brian Platt, "Sheriffs Gone Wild," Mechanical Freak, May 4, 2020, https://mechanicalfreak.website/sheriffs-gone-wild.

330 *declared via his Facebook page on April 21*: Michelle Mark, "Washington State Residents Are Trying to Recall a Sheriff After He Called the Stay-at-Home Order Unconstitutional and Said He Wouldn't Enforce It," *Business Insider*, May 5, 2020, https://www.insider.com/washington-sheriff-refuse-enforce-stay-at-home-order-recall-petition-2020-5.

330 *barber said he was inspired to open his shop*: Nicole Brodeur, "A Snohomish Barbershop Defies Orders to Remain Closed During Coronavirus—and Customers Line Up," *Seattle Times*, May 19, 2020, https://www.seattletimes.com/seattle-news/a-snohomish-barbershop-defies-orders-to-remain-closed-during-coronavirus-and-customers-line-up/.

331 *hired a contract killer to murder a deputy*: Flynn, "Sheriff Helped Plot His Own Deputy's Killing."

331 *removal statute was ambiguous*: N.C. General Statutes § 128-16, https://www.ncleg.net/EnactedLegislation/Statutes/PDF/ByArticle/Chapter_128/Article_2.pdf.

331 *sheriff agreed to a suspension*: Spectrum News Staff, "Granville County Sheriff Suspended," Spectrum News I, September 23, 2019, https://spectrumlocalnews.com/nc/charlotte/news/2019/09/23/granville-county-sheriff-suspended.

331 *"acts of malfeasance, misfeasance, or violation of oath of office"*: Wash. Rev. Code § 29A.56.110, https://app.leg.wa.gov/rcw/default.aspx?cite=29A.56.110.

331 *Snohomish County advocates attempted a recall*: "Snohomish County Sheriff Faces Recall Campaign After Judge Says That Signature Gathering Can Begin," My Edmond News, May 18, 2020, https://myedmondsnews.com/2020/05/snohomish-county-sheriff-faces-recall-campaign-after-judge-says-that-signature-gathering-can-begin/.

332 *an incredibly rare legal moment*: In re Recall of Adam Fortney, No. 98683-5, https://law.justia.com/cases/washington/supreme-court/2021/98683-5.html.

332  *"unless we have people inside the department"*: Jessica Pishko, "Controversial Sheriff with Right-Wing Ties Faces Voters in Washington State," Bolts, November 2, 2023, https://boltsmag.org/snohomish-sheriff-election-2023/.

334  *maintain all training requirements*: HB 2027, Washington State Legislature (2023–24), https://app.leg.wa.gov/billsummary?BillNumber=2027&Year=2023&Initiative=false.

334  *concerned about far-right sheriffs*: House Community Safety, Justice & Reentry Public Hearing, Washington House of Representatives, January 8, 2024, video, 45:00, https://tvw.org/video/house-community-safety-justice-reentry-2024011158/?eventID=2024011158.

334  *launched into attack mode*: John Webb, "Washington State Bill Deemed 'Unconstitutional' by Sheriffs," NonStop Local KHQ, January 16, 2024, https://www.khq.com/news/washington-state-bill-deemed-unconstitutional-by-sheriffs/article_ea056f10-b4d7-11ee-9854-7b4420071002.html.

335  *thirty-three states and created by state statute in thirteen states*: "Legal Meaning of Sheriff's Oath of Office," National Sheriffs' Association.

335  *"from the fringe to the policymaking mainstream"*: Christy Lopez, "'Beware the Extremist Dangerous and Unconstitutional 'Constitutional' Sheriffs," *Washington Post*, December 17, 2021, https://www.washingtonpost.com/opinions/2021/12/17/constitutional-sheriffs-extremist-dangerous-unconstitutional/.

337  *budget of just under $4 billion*: Rebecca Ellis, "Sheriff's Department Gets $4 Billion amid 'Unconscionable' Conditions in L.A. Jails," *Los Angeles Times*, June 26, 2023, https://www.latimes.com/california/story/2023-06-26/la-county-budget-sheriffs-department-4-billion-pleas-for-cuts.

337  *delineated eighteen distinct gangs*: Sean K. Kennedy et al., *50 Years of Deputy Gangs in the Los Angeles County Sheriff's Department* (Los Angeles: LMU Loyola Law School, 2021), https://lmu.app.box.com/s/ho3rp9qdbmn9aip8fy8dmmukjjgw5yyc.

338  *risen through the ranks*: Cerise Castle, "A Tradition of Violence: The History of Deputy Gangs in the Los Angeles County Sheriff's Department," Knock LA, March 22, 2021, https://knock-la.com/tradition-of-violence-lasd-gang-history/.

338  *later be convicted of crimes*: Celeste Fremon, "The Downfall of Sheriff Baca," *Los Angeles*, May 14, 2015, https://lamag.com/news/downfall.

338  *rampant abuse inside the jail*: Sarah Liebowitz, Peter Eliasberg, Margaret Winter, and Esther Lim, *Cruel and Usual Punishment: How a Savage Gang of Deputies Controls LA County Jails* (Los Angeles: ACLU National Prison Project and ACLU of Southern California, 2011).

339  *more incidents of violence and extrajudicial deputy killings*: Keri Blakinger and Brittny Mejia, "2nd Former L.A. Deputy Sentenced to Federal Prison for Abducting Compton Skateboarder," *Los Angeles Times*, April 14, 2023, https://www.latimes.com/california/story/2024-01-23/former-la-deputy-sentenced-to-federal-prison-for-abducting-compton-skateboarder; Spectrum News Staff, "Whistleblower:

California Deputy Killed Teen to Join Department's 'Gang,' Spectrum Bay News 9, August 31, 2020, https://baynews9.com/fl/tampa/news/2020/08/31/whistleblower--deputy-killed-teen-to-join-department-s--gang--; "Two Former LASD Deputies Charged with Violating the Civil Rights of 23-Year-Old Skateboarder Who Was Falsely Imprisoned," Justice Department (press release), April 13, 2023, https://www.justice.gov/usao-cdca/pr/two-former-lasd-deputies-charged-violating-civil-rights-23-year-old-skateboarder-who.

339 *five shots in his back*: Cerise Castle, "The Compton Executioners," Knock LA, April 6, 2021, https://knock-la.com/the-compton-executioners-andres-guardado/.

339 *"the last day I breathe"*: "LA County Sheriff's Deputy Shoots, Kills 18-Year-Old Man in Gardena," NBC 4 Los Angeles, June 18, 2020, https://www.nbclosangeles.com/news/local/la-county-sheriffs-deputy-kills-man-in-gardena/2382640/.

340 *special unit dedicated to the task*: Alene Tchekmedyian, "L.A. County Sheriff's Unit Accused of Targeting Political Enemies, Vocal Critics," *Los Angeles Times*, September 23, 2021, https://www.latimes.com/california/story/2021-09-23/sheriff-alex-villanueva-secret-police.

340 *currently and formerly employed gang members*: "Databases of Known Associates of Deputy Gangs in the Los Angeles County Sheriff's Department and Deputy Shootings 1984—Current," Knock LA, accessed March 12, 2024, https://lasd.knock-la.com/#gangs.

340 *105 out of 136 had not been implemented*: Report Card on Sheriff's Department's Reforms 2019 to 2023 (Los Angeles: County of Los Angeles Office of Inspector General, 2024), https://assets-us-01.kc-usercontent.com/0234f496-d2b7-00b6-17a4-b43e949b70a2/7d15d121-0ec1-49e3-83ac-0faaeb44daac/Report%20Card%20On%20Sheriff%27s%20Department%27s%20Reforms%202019%20to%202023.pdf.

## CHAPTER 13: THE GATHERING STORM

344 *a sidearm like almost everyone there*: "General Meeting 10 8 22," Yavapai County Preparedness Team, accessed March 12, 2024, https://ycpt.org/aiovg_videos/general-meeting-10-8-22/.

345 *says he was an Army Ranger*: militaryphonies, "James Arroyo—US Army Ranger, Part of Operation Eagle Claw, Blog of Shame," Military Phonies, December 27, 2018, https://militaryphony.com/2018/12/27/james-arroyo-us-army-ranger-part-of-operation-eagle-claw-blog-of-shame/.

346 *"That's how it works"*: "General Meeting 10 8 22," Yavapai County Preparedness Team.

346 *Its LinkedIn page*: "California State Military Reserve," LinkedIn, accessed March 12, 2024, https://www.linkedin.com/company/california-state-military-reserve/about/.

351 *charged nearly one thousand people with crimes*: "18 Months Since the Jan. 6 Attack on the Capitol," United States Attorney's Office, District of Columbia, August 10, 2022, https://www.justice.gov/usao-dc/18-month-jan-6-attack-capitol.

353 *bastion of intellectual conservatism*: Laura K. Field, "What the Hell Happened to the Claremont Institute?," Bulwark, July 13, 2021, https://www.thebulwark.com/what-the-hell-happened-to-the-claremont-institute/.

354 *"nihilistic yearning to destroy modernity"*: Katherine Stewart, "The Claremont Institute: The Anti-Democracy Think Tank," *New Republic*, August 10, 2023, https://newrepublic.com/article/174656/claremont-institute-think-tank-trump.

354 *"called for the end of democracy"*: Ben Goggin, "Nazis Mingle Openly at CPAC, Spreading Antisemitic Conspiracy Theories and Finding Allies," NBC News, February 26, 2024, https://www.nbcnews.com/news/us-news/nazis-mingle-openly-cpac-spreading-antisemitic-conspiracy-theories-fin-rcna140335.

354 *Another Claremont fellow was Nate Hochman*: Stewart, "The Claremont Institute."

354 *described Claremont fellowships as a "brotherhood"*: Elisabeth Zerofsky, "How the Claremont Institute Became a Nerve Center of the American Right," *New York Times*, August 3, 2022, https://www.nytimes.com/2022/08/03/magazine/claremont-institute-conservative.html.

355 *"intellectual case for Trump"*: Zerofsky, "How the Claremont Institute Became a Nerve Center of the American Right."

355 *airplane on 9/11 that did not crash into its intended target*: Publius Decius Mus [Michael Anton], "The Flight 93 Election," *Claremont Review of Books*, September 5, 2016, https://claremontreviewofbooks.com/digital/the-flight-93-election/.

355 *the so-called New Right, conservative thinkers*: James Pogue, "Inside the New Right, Where Peter Thiel Is Placing His Biggest Bets," *Vanity Fair*, April 20, 2022, https://www.vanityfair.com/news/2022/04/inside-the-new-right-where-peter-thiel-is-placing-his-biggest-bets.

355 *"save Western civilization"*: "Welcome to the Claremont Institute," Claremont Institute (YouTube channel), October 25, 2019, https://www.youtube.com/watch?v=s967BBddruI.

356 *Claremont would have sent him packing*: Field, "What the Hell Happened to the Claremont Institute?"

356 *envisioned the doomsday should Trump lose*: "79 Days to Inauguration Taskforce Report," Claremont Institute and Texas Public Policy Foundation, October 20, 2020, https://www.justsecurity.org/wp-content/uploads/2022/01/january-6-clearinghouse-claremont-institute-79daysreport.pdf.

357 *early email describing the intent of the program*: Ryan Williams, Letter to Claremont Institute Supporters, October 8, 2021, https://www.thebulwark.com/wp-content/uploads/2021/10/Claremont-fundraising-letter.pdf.

358 *wrote a paean to the sheriff*: Kyle Shideler, "Return of the Sheriff," *American Mind*, February 26, 2024, https://americanmind.org/salvo/return-of-the-sheriff/.

359 *"no cost to our tax payers"*: @Flowers4Sheriff, "I am proud to announce that I was chosen as one of the eight Sheriffs selected from around the country to be in the inaugural class of Sheriffs Fellows at the Claremont Institute! As a Sheriffs Fellow, my travel, lodging, and expenses are paid by the Claremont Institute 1/2," X /Twitter, November 12, 2021, https://x.com/Flowers4Sheriff/status/145929011 5297986970?s=20.

361 *"movements across our Nation to take away punishments"*: "Brian Hieatt," Claremont Institute (website), accessed March 12, 2024, https://www.claremont.org/alumni /brian-hieatt/.

362 *Ryan Williams admitted to the* New York Times Magazine: Zerofsky, "How the Claremont Institute Became a Nerve Center of the American Right."

363 *"this right was an extension of the natural rights"*: "McDonald v. Chicago (2010)—Guest Essayist: David Raney," Constituting America, accessed March 12, 2024, https:// constitutingamerica.org/mcdonald-v-chicago-2010-guest-essayist-david -raney/.

364 *"openly ally with the AR-15 crowd"*: Kevin Slack, "The Constitution, Citizenship, and the New Right," *American Mind*, June 15, 2023, https://americanmind.org/fea tures/the-constitution-citizenship-and-the-new-right/.

364 *specifically promoting the "white replacement" theory*: Jeremy Carl, "End Mass Immigration and White Stigmatization to Boost Assimilation," *American Mind*, February 17, 2022, https://americanmind.org/features/replace-the-ruling-class/end-mass -immigration-and-white-stigamatization-to-boost-assimilation/.

364 *guided at least a dozen state leaders*: "'America Is Under Attack': Inside the Anti-D.E.I. Crusade," *New York Times*, January 20, 2024, https://www.nytimes.com/interac tive/2024/01/20/us/dei-woke-claremont-institute.html.

364 *"the evils that flow from feminism"*: "Boise State Political Science Professor Scott Yenor Grabs Headlines with Speech on 'Evils That Flow from Feminism,'" *The Arbiter*, November 29, 2021, https://arbiteronline.com/2021/11/29/boise-state-political -science-professor-scott-yenor-grabs-headlines-with-speech-on-evils-that-flow -from-feminism/.

364 *"his steadfast defense of the Constitution"*: "Mark Lamb," Claremont Institute (website), accessed March 12, 2024, https://www.claremont.org/alumni/mark-lamb/.

365 *"wear that badge with honor!"*: @sheriffbianco, "Last night I was presented with the American Sheriff Award by the Claremont Institute . . . ," Instagram, November 10, 2023, https://www.instagram.com/sheriffbianco/p/CzeH0typhKR/?img _index=4.

365 *wrote a response published online*: Mark Lamb, "A Vow to Serve," *American Mind*, October 24, 2022, https://americanmind.org/salvo/a-vow-to-serve/.

CONCLUSION

367 *said he would abolish the FBI*: Kathryn Williams, "Presidential Candidate Vivek Ramaswamy Details Plan to Abolish 3 Government Agencies at Town Hall in Manchester," WMUR, updated July 20, 2023, https://www.wmur.com/article/ramaswamy-government-agencies-nh-town-hall/44605624.

367 *big problem with voter fraud*: Robert Draper, "Far Right Pushes a Through-the-Looking-Glass Narrative on Jan. 6," *New York Times*, June 23, 2023, https://www.nytimes.com/2023/06/23/us/politics/jan-6-trump.html.

367 *discrediting the January 6 investigation altogether*: Luke Broadwater, Alan Feuer, and Angelo Fichera, "Johnson's Release of Jan. 6 Video Feeds Right-Wing Conspiracy Theories," *New York Times*, November 23, 2023, https://www.nytimes.com/2023/11/23/us/politics/mike-johnson-jan-6-video.html.

368 *Trump issued over four hundred executive actions*: "Trump Completed 472 Executive Actions on Immigration During His Presidency, Many That Could Have Lasting Effects on the U.S. Immigration System," Migration Policy Institute, February 1, 2022, https://www.migrationpolicy.org/news/trump-472-executive-actions-immigration-during-presidency.

368 *has threatened mass deportations*: Chris Tomlinson, "Abbott Auditioning for VP, Trump Promising Massive Labor Shortage," *Houston Chronicle*, November 22, 2023, https://www.houstonchronicle.com/business/columnists/tomlinson/article/abbott-trump-texas-border-promise-barbed-wire-18504412.php.

368 *compared them to the speeches of Hitler and Mussolini*: Michael Gold, "After Calling Foes 'Vermin,' Trump Campaign Warns Its Critics Will Be 'Crushed,'" *New York Times*, November 13, 2023, https://www.nytimes.com/2023/11/13/us/politics/trump-vermin-rhetoric-fascists.html.

368 *More than 100 million guns have been sold*: Federal Bureau of Investigation, "NICS Firearm Background Checks: Month/Year, November 30, 1998—February 29, 2024," accessed March 12, 2024, https://www.fbi.gov/file-repository/nics_firearm_checks_-_month_year.pdf.

369 *"We will not defund the police"*: "Biden Backs Funding More Police to Fight Crime Wave," BBC, June 23, 2021, https://www.bbc.com/news/world-us-canada-57589416.

370 *enshrined the idea that sheriffs had authority of state and local officials*: Joshua Margolis, "House Judiciary Hears Sheriffs First Bill," NBC Montana, February 24, 2023, https://nbcmontana.com/news/local/house-judiciary-hears-sheriffs-first-bill.

370 *"federal agents must operate with the approval of the sheriff"*: "'Sheriffs First' Model Legislation," Pro Gun Leaders (website), accessed March 12, 2024, https://progunleaders.org/SheriffsFirst/; Mike Maharrey, "Montana House Committee Passes 'Sheriffs First' Bill," Tenth Amendment Center (blog), March 1, 2023, https://blog.tenthamendmentcenter.com/2023/03/montana-house-committee-passes-sheriffs-first-bill/.

370  *are over seventeen thousand policing agencies*: Gardner and Scott, *Census of State and Local Law Enforcement Agencies*, 1.

372  *Even when sheriffs are required*: Even states that require background checks for deputies exclude sheriffs from these requirements.

373  *Mississippi state agencies routinely ignored reports of misconduct*: Ilyssa Daly, Jerry Mitchell, and Rachel Axon, "Who Investigates the Sheriff? In Mississippi, Often No One," *New York Times*, December 28, 2023, https://www.nytimes.com/2023/12/28/us /mississippi-sheriff-lawsuits-abuse.html.

# INDEX

and "law and order" politics, 369
and lockdown protests, 100–104
and parents' rights groups, 370
and politics of the West, 110–13
and *Printz v. United States*, 185
relief funds, 168
and religious liberty, 104–5
reporting during, 8
restrictions as right-wing rallying point, 100–110
and scope of ideological divisions, 16
and Steninger, 98–100
vaccinations and antivax sentiment, 36, 38, 95–96, 104, 344
and Woodlands conference, 105–6
crime rates, 264
criminal justice reform, 3, 366
*Crimmigration Law* (García Hernández), 280
*Crisis of the House Divided* (Jaffa), 362
*Crisis of the Two Constitutions* (Kesler), 360
Cuen-Buitimea, Gabriel, 177
Curry, Hilda, 263

*Daily Advertiser*, 262
*Daily Iberian*, 266, 267
Daly, Ilyssa, 409n151
Dannels, Mark, 292
Davis, Kim, 193
Daye, Anthony, 266
*D.C. v. Heller*, 185, 196
Death in Custody Reporting Act, 166
death penalty, 82–83
Declaration of Independence, 363
defamation, 313
Deitch, Michele, 411n166
Democratic National Convention, 46
Department of Public Safety, 317
DePerno, Matthew, 302, 305
DeSantis, Ron, 100–101, 354
desegregation, 47, 64, 66
Dickey, Jay, 419n196
Diggs, Danny, 196–97
discretionary power of sheriffs, 84, 319–20, 341–42, 344, 371
*District of Columbia v. Heller*, 185
diversity, equity, and inclusion initiatives, 364
*The Doctrine of Lesser Magistrates* (Trewhella), 53
Dodson, Amy, 226–28, 233–34

domestic terrorism, 7, 59, 66, 68, 185, 209
domestic violence, 18, 171, 222–23, 371
Dominion Voting Systems, 114, 302, 305, 313
Dominionism, 53, 389n53
Donahue, Kieran, 292
Dorsey, Eddie L., 237
Douglas County Board of Supervisors, 229
Douglas County Public Library, 226–30
Douglas County Sheriff's Office, 227
Doves of the Valley, 68
*Dred Scott v. Sandford*, 361
drug trafficking, 288–89
Drugs, Death, Destruction and the U.S. Border (panel), 292
D'Souza, Dinesh, 294
Ducey, Doug, 299–300
due process, 49
Duke University, 252
*Dukes of Hazzard* (TV series), 127, 254
Dumas, Sade, 326–27, 332
Dunbar-Ortiz, Roxanne, 216
Dundas, Leigh, 36
Dye, Shirley, 1

Earp, Wyatt, 126
Earth First!, 30
East Baton Rouge Parish Prison, 141–42, 154
East Baton Rouge Parish Prison Reform Coalition, 154, 164
East Baton Rouge Sheriff's Office, 142, 153
Eastman, John, 356
educational requirements for sheriffs, 18, 80, 372
Edwards Plateau Rangers, 108
Eisenhower, Dwight D., 28, 45
El Salvador, 275
election fraud. *See* voting and election fraud
election of sheriffs
and anti-immigrant sentiment, 93
Black sheriffs, 325–29
and case for eliminating office of sheriff, 374–75
and efforts to reform sheriff's office, 321–24, 329–38, 341–42
and Posse Comitatus movement, 56
states that elect sheriffs, 17–18

United Nations, 29, 70, 206, 218
*United States v. Peters,* 61
*United States v. Rahimi,* 222–23
Uniting Law Enforcement &
 Communities, 332
University of Arizona, 30
University of Kansas, 329
University of Louisiana at Lafayette, 245
U.S. Border Patrol, 272, 284–85, 293
U.S. Congress, 38–39, 81, 92
U.S. Constitution
 and the Claremont Institute, 365
 Constitutional Studies for Peace Officers,
  25–26
 and efforts to reform sheriff's office, 330
 and election fraud claims, 300, 306, 308
 and far-right militia movement, 203,
  214–15, 219, 222–23, 230, 235
 and growth of constitutional sheriff
  movement, 19–20
 and gun rights issue, 184, 190–91,
  198–99
 as holy document, 47
 and immigration policing, 272
 and militias, 345
 and nullification, 390n61
 and oaths of office, 331
 and origins of Oath Keepers, 32
 and political status of sheriffs, 81,
  168, 371
 and Posse Comitatus movement, 48, 50,
  51, 52, 60–62
 and role of constitutional sheriffs, 39–40
 and Skousen's background, 28–29
 and Tea Party activism, 1
 and White Horse Prophecy, 26,
  111–12, 131
 *See also* Bill of Rights; *specific amendments*
U.S. Customs and Border Protection, 284
U.S. Department of Agriculture, 168
U.S. Department of Education, 367
U.S. Department of Homeland Security, 10,
 74, 208, 272, 280, 358
U.S. Department of Justice
 and Capitol insurrection arrests, 351
 and charges against Trump, 83
 and deaths in custody, 166
 and efforts to reform sheriff's
  office, 335
 and far-right militia movement, 235

and fears of right-wing violence, 194
and immigration policing, 277
and racial conflict in America, 253, 255,
 262, 266
reversal of policing reforms under
 Trump, 75
and "Texas Tour" event, 108
and Trump's political agenda, 368
U.S. Drug Enforcement
 Administration, 278
U.S. Food and Drug Administration, 65, 67
U.S. Grazing Service, 111
U.S. House of Representatives, 277
U.S. Immigration and Customs
 Enforcement, 5, 74, 92–93, 149,
 280–82, 286–87, 322–23, 328
U.S. Marshals, 5, 58, 149
U.S. Nuclear Regulatory Commission, 367
U.S. Secret Service, 65, 391n65
U.S. Senate, 38–39, 61, 66, 139–40
U.S. Supreme Court
 and COVID restrictions in churches, 38
 and election fraud claims, 298, 316
 and far-right militia movement, 219, 222
 and growth of constitutional sheriff
  movement, 19
 and gun rights issue, 30, 175, 179,
  183–85, 196, 200
 and immigration policing, 277
 and incarceration role of sheriffs, 160
 and Mack's training course, 105
 and media presence of sheriffs, 132
 and nullification/interposition
  principles, 61, 64
 and Posse Comitatus movement, 49
 and prison overcrowding, 149
 and racial conflict in America, 253
 and right-wing conspiracy
  theories, 218
 and "Texas Tour" event, 107
 and Trump's political agenda, 368
Uvalde, Texas, school shooting, 200,
 368–70

vaccinations and antivax sentiment, 36, 38,
 95–96, 104, 344
vagrancy laws, 249–50
Vale, Corey, 116–18, 132–33

# ABOUT THE AUTHOR

**Jessica Pishko** is a journalist and lawyer who graduated from Harvard Law School and Columbia University's MFA program. Her writings about criminal justice have been featured in *The New York Times, Rolling Stone,* The Appeal, *The New Republic, The Nation, Slate,* and *The Guardian,* and have been anthologized in *Dismantling Mass Incarceration: A Handbook for Change.* She has been awarded journalism fellowships from the Pulitzer Center and Type Investigations and was a 2023 New America fellow. After turning her attention to sheriffs in 2016, she served as a fellow in the Sheriff Accountability Project at the University of South Carolina School of Law, where she examined state laws related to sheriff elections and sheriff removal procedures. Her work was the first to put many of the issues related to sheriffs on the political map.